A LIFETIME OF LABOR

The Cross-Cultural Memoir Series introduces original, significant memoirs from women whose compelling histories map the sources of our differences: generations, national boundaries, race, ethnicity, class, and sexual orientation. The series features stories of contemporary women's lives, providing a record of social transformation, growth in consciousness, and the passionate commitment of individuals who make far-reaching change possible.

A LIFETIME OF LABOR

THE AUTOBIOGRAPHY OF ALICE H. COOK

Foreword by Arlene Kaplan Daniels

The Feminist Press
at The City University of New York

Published by
The Feminist Press at The City University of New York
Wingate Hall/City College
Convent Avenue at 138th Street
New York, NY 10031

First edition, 1998

Library of Congress Cataloging-in-Publication Data

Cook, Alice Hanson.
    A lifetime of labor : the autobiography of Alice H. Cook :
foreword by Arlene Kaplan Daniels.—1st ed.
    p. cm. — (The cross-cultural memoir series)
ISBN 1-55861-189-4 (hardcover : alk. paper)
1. Cook, Alice Hanson. 2. Women labor leaders—United States—Biography. 3. Women college teachers—United States—Biography. 4. Feminists—United States—Biography. I. Daniels, Arlene Kaplan, 1930–   . II. Title. III. Series.
HD9073.C66A3 1998
331'.092—dc21   98-18433
[B]   CIP

Publication of this book was made possible, in part, by a grant from the Ford Foundation. The Feminist Press gratefully acknowledges the Ford Foundation for its support.

The Feminist Press would also like to thank Janet E. Brown, Mariam K. Chamberlain, Helene D. Goldfarb, Jane S. Gould, Florence Howe, Joanne Markell, Caroline Urvater, and Genevieve Vaughan for their generosity in supporting the publication of this book.

Text design and typesetting by Dayna Navaro.
Printed on acid-free paper.
Manufactured in the United States of America.

CONTENTS

FOREWORD

I first met Alice Cook one day about twenty-five years ago when I was on a research trip to Washington, D.C. She was in the company of a dear friend of mine, Val Lorwin, and they had come to town to settle some of the business connected with the receipt of a German Marshall Fund grant to do a comparative study of women in European trade unions, which Alice had instigated. I remember that we met in some foundation building near DuPont Circle where Val and Alice were completing their arrangements. I also remember that from the first moment, the three of us got on like a house afire. In the euphoria of that first meeting, I extravagantly promised to help them in any way I could and thought nothing further about it. But in the ensuing years, as the research got underway and the first drafts of reports began to develop, Val and I spent more time, during sociable visits and by mail, reviewing the material together while I made editorial suggestions. At the same time I was becoming a friend of Alice's and a tacit admirer of her friendship with and loyalty to Val, who was a dearly beloved friend and colleague, but not necessarily the easiest person with whom to collaborate. It was becoming clear that it might not be possible for anyone to fulfill Val's expectations of what a polished manuscript would look like.

This problem took a particularly poignant turn as Val became seriously and then fatally ill. On my last visit with him, he was clearly weakened by his illness and saddened by the bleakness of his future. To cheer him up, I announced that I would help Alice finish the joint part of their collaboration—the book of research articles on women and trade unions in eleven industrialized countries, generated by the grant and now awaiting the final touches by Val and Alice. They were writing their own contributions—Val on Great Britain and Alice on what was then West Germany—but the major job of editing all the contributions and writing the framing materials had yet to be done. Since my offer to help conclude this work-in-progress did not seem sufficiently cheering, I also offered to help Alice finish Val's own work, scheduled as a more comprehensive analysis of the problems of women in the trade union movements of various industrialized countries and the overarching issues that beset them, whatever the specifics of particular countries.

When I called Alice to say, rather sheepishly, what I had promised for the two of us to undertake, she wasted no time in exasperated recrimination but dryly remarked, "I see you have made us the literary executors." I was greatly relieved to see that she was prepared to make good on my impulsive act, which also required a considerable commitment on her part. In fact, it required commitments that I could not have fulfilled on my own. In effect, then, I had pledged Alice to tasks that would take up a large part of her working life for the next four or five years. That we became and remained close friends despite such an exercise of chutzpah on my part is just another example of her generosity and magnanimity to her friends.

One aspect of Alice Cook's appeal to her many friends and admirers was her great zest for life. That general characteristic included curiosity about the world, willingness to reflect upon the experiences of others as well as her own, and an enormous capacity to enjoy whatever came her way. Wherever Alice went, in the United States or abroad, she forged strong and lasting relationships. Of course, age narrowed the venues in which she could operate, but as a person of great energy and ability, she retained the capacity to transcend the physical vicissitudes of the moment. She could always beat the socks off me in her favorite game of Scrabble, and even during her bouts of ill health, it was difficult for me to secure more than one or two wins out of several rounds. When she was in her late eighties she had more staying power than I, an energetic person more than thirty years her junior. I can remember various trips to Ithaca, when we were working together on drafts of her work. After an early morning start and a heavy bout of writing, discussing, and plotting chapters, I would find myself flagging in midafternoon. "Don't you want to take a little nap, dear Alice?" I would ask, in some desperation. "You go right ahead, my dear," she would say, giving me a shrewd look. "No, no," I would say competitively. "If you wish to continue working, I'm game for it."

Of course, each friend and colleague of Alice's had a unique experience, but I am sure one of the common denominators was basking in the warmth of her understated but clear acceptance and love. Make no mistake, Alice was always as unsentimental, matter-of-fact, and—certainly on issues of principle—uncompromising a person as one is likely ever to encounter. But she showed her friends an unwavering affection that was built on an underlying assumption that she and they shared a strong bond.

Alice's sensitivity to what she could do to accommodate the wishes of others showed in her desire to help her friends in any ways she could. I can remember visiting Alice when her dearest friend, colleague, and neighbor, Rose Goldsen, was dying. Alice was deeply distressed; but as a practical, no-nonsense person, she was not inclined to repine on the waning of her friend and companion of so many years. Instead, she sat at her desk for a few hours each day, attending to Rose's accounts and keeping her affairs in order. She said to me, "This is how I do my grieving." This is just one example of the countless, daily acts of generosity and thoughtfulness in which Alice was always engaged. Another was her suggestion that we dedicate the book we had undertaken to complete together to Madge, the widow of Val Lorwin, and also that we allocate the royalties to her.

In turning to a discussion of the importance of Alice Cook's long career, I think it is important to show how the characteristics of warmth, generosity, and concern for others that colored her friendships and her living style also colored her work. Long before she came to Cornell, where she spent the largest part of her professional career, Alice was focused on the ways in which working conditions could be improved for women and men. Her early forays into union organizing and worker education, her efforts to help working women through the YWCA, and her earliest experience in the settlement work of Jane Addams show how much of her interest and focus centered upon the most needy and defenseless members of the working class. Without sentimentalism or dewy-eyed romanticism, Alice set about to consider practical ways to better the lives and working conditions of young women. In this regard her determination to be independent herself spread to a concern for how other women might achieve an independent life. Such experience served her well at the end of her marriage, when she undertook to raise her two sons as a single parent.

In addition, one cannot fail to acknowledge the fact that Alice was a remarkably prodigious worker. Her great curiosity, her appetite for collecting data, her ability to move easily in many worlds and to befriend and be befriended by key informants who could help her, and her important archival skills all contributed to making her a significant chronicler of some of the key stages in the growing movements for women's equality in the workplace. She was the key figure in keeping track of the growth of comparable worth in the United States and was always a tireless documenter and analyzer of the place of the working woman in scholarly society. In this regard, she was a one-woman antidote to the tendency, among scholars who study the place of women in the workforce, to focus primarily on professional, academic, and generally middle-class women.

In pursuit of her own academic career, however, Alice had many occasions to help academic as well as other working women. She was always a leader at Cornell in the struggle to integrate women into the academy and to equalize their salaries and working conditions. Her appointment as the first ombudsman at Cornell toward the end of her formal career there was a great honor for her, but it was equally a bounty for Cornell. As her colleague Jennie Farley said, "They couldn't have picked a better person, for she was not afraid to accept a complaint from anyone." In referring to the management of her own complaint, Jennie said, "She resolved it in a way that let me think I had resolved it." As the first ombudsman, she set the tone for the conduct of the office: the ombudsman was to be an independent fact finder, free from interference by Cornell administration. Alice's only power in that job was one of persuasion, but she was (or became) an expert at arm-twisting. On the very fractious Cornell campus of the late sixties and early seventies, Alice's toughness, credibility, and persistence helped mightily to keep the peace. Beyond her specific work in the complaint area and her work for women protesting discrimination in the case of the "Cornell Eleven," Alice left a lasting impression on the curriculum at Cornell. She taught the first course on working women and was the guiding genius for the installation of women's studies—the first such program in the country.

The experiences of these years led one of her admirers to say—reflecting my own experience, certainly—that Alice was the best friend a person could possibly have. And so many people of all ages, races, and genders have had occasion to support this view, perhaps because Alice was always so accepting and respectful of them, so interested in them, as they expressed their views.

Alice's contributions at Cornell, both to individuals and to the welfare of the community at large, are certainly matched by her pioneering efforts to understand the relationship of working women to both workplace and family. Her early work for the Ford Foundation, after her formal retirement, stands as a landmark achievement in our understanding of what working mothers face, around the world, in caring for children while holding down jobs. She not only looked at nations and their social policies on issues of child care but also went into the field—and onto the shop floor—to ask women: What would help you in the morning?

As a result of her investigations into the problems of working women, Alice's interest came to focus on the plight of single working women, including single mothers. She never fell into the trap of thinking about what a single woman could do by herself. She always saw the social forces—and social obligations—that created the dilemmas and conflicts under which women operated in the workforce.

Alice's groundbreaking work influenced much social thinking on what employers could do for their women workers. It took the field of management more than two decades to act on Alice's findings, but we are now beginning to see some of her ideas come to fruition. This is one of her many legacies, which will long outlast her lifetime.

The way Alice has lived, worked, and made friends made her a model for women of all ages, but certainly for the younger women who came into her circle. In her personal and professional life, she came to represent an intellectual and a personal model that showed the way for women to be independent and connected, whether they were single or had partners. Alice created a sense of possibility for women—the possibility that we could do scholarly work but also remain committed to activist ideals, that we could devote ourselves to work but also lead a full life, a rich life with family, friends, and colleagues. This is another legacy, which will endure through the lives of the women she knew and inspired.

Underlying this picture of a career and a life is a feminist bent that was observable long before Alice would have used that term to describe herself. Of course, as she herself said, her strong and independent mother, one of the early suffragists, was a great guide and model for her, as was her grandmother. But Alice was sui generis, a woman who used the background and experiences of her life to create something unique. She developed a sense of the incredible scope and wealth of detail that had to be understood in order to encompass the larger issues facing women at work. And she combined this encyclopedic capacity with a wide range of close friendships sustained over a wonderfully long lifetime of scholarly and practical attainments.

Reading this memoir is in some ways reading the history of a century. It provides portraits of union organizing and worker education in many parts of the world, as well as a picture of our developing understanding of the place of working women in the world. It is also the history of the course of intricate and intimate friendships discovered and nurtured in this endeavor. I invite you to join me in reading about this life and marveling at its accomplishments—and at the great spirit who lived it.

Arlene Kaplan Daniels
Belmont, California
April 1998

A NOTE FROM THE PUBLISHER

I met Alice Cook in the fall of 1979, when we both held Mellon Fellowships at Wellesley College. Our offices were side by side, and our apartments in the same building. From seminars, we learned about each other's work, and in the evenings we sometimes dined together. I was especially curious about Alice's work habits, for no matter how early I arrived at my office, she was already in hers, typing away. One night in November after we had had dinner together in my apartment, I ventured a personal question. I was fifty that year, and I assumed that Alice was twenty-five years older. "How is your life different at seventy-five," I asked, "from the way it was when you were fifty?" Her reply was swift: "I can't work after dinner anymore the way I used to," she said. I followed up with another question: "But what time do you get up in the morning?" "Around five," she said, and volunteered, "I used to run two miles, but I can't do that now, and so I swim two miles, then walk a mile or so before breakfast." "Well," I remarked, "were I to get up at five in the morning, I couldn't even work before dinner!" I knew then that no one could match Alice's energy. When I went to Cornell thirteen years later, in 1992, to discuss the first draft of her autobiography, she was in the throes of Bell's palsy, and yet, through the long day, she continued to ask me whether I needed to rest.

Through the 1980s, Alice and I continued to correspond, mainly through the fund-raising letters I wrote to The Feminist Press's constituency. Alice would always send a check, and I would, in my thank-you note, ask how the autobiography she said she would never write was coming along. Late in the decade, she wrote back, saying, "As a matter of fact, I'm in chapter four." Delighted, I wrote at once to say that, while I was certain she had a publishing contract, I'd be honored to be named one of her readers. She wrote at once to say that she had no publisher and that she would be "honored" to be published by The Feminist Press. By then we had established the Cross-Cultural Memoir Series, and I sent Alice a contract. *A Lifetime of Labor* amply fulfills the requirements of the series, for it illuminates the developing consciousness of an activist working for social change. Indeed, since Alice Hanson Cook lived ninety-four years, and was the daughter and granddaughter of women who also worked for social change, her story illuminates a century of change.

When Alice was growing up during the first years of this century (she once wrote in a series of brief responses to her grandchildren's questions), school desks were nailed to the floor, ice was delivered daily, washing and ironing clothes were daylong chores, and after sixth grade an allowance of twenty-five cents a week made her feel "rich." When her grandmother needed to be nursed by her mother, Alice was given "all the cooking and dishwashing to do. . . . No cake mixes or bread mixes, no frozen foods." She cooked for a large family, when even breakfast demanded "pork chops and eggs as well as hot cereal and coffee and toast." Entertainment was family-made. There were no radios, no motion pictures. There were also no world wars. One could say that her childhood ended with World War I. When Alice graduated from college in 1924, "kind friends" asked whether she was "going to marry or have a career." Indeed, in 1950, I heard the same question. Fortunately for all of us, her life's work helped to change that question for all women. She learned early on from her mother and grandmother that people working together could make change. The desks nailed to the floor could be freed for movement.

At the end of her autobiography, Alice Cook describes the way in which, as she wrote and rewrote the manuscript over many of the last years of her life, she came to understand fully its pattern and meaning. In 1980, as she was award- ed an honorary degree from the Grand Valley State Colleges, she wrote an account of what she called her "patchwork career," which "included adult educa- tion, social work, labor organizing, a tour with the foreign service, and, for the last twenty years before my retirement," teaching. She described the study of working mothers in nine countries she undertook for the Ford Foundation "immediately upon leaving Cornell" and then two equally ambi- tious studies of working women, trade unions, and labor education that fol- lowed. At that point, she wrote, "Lo, the meaning of the great variety of early work came clear: it was preparation—through practice and teaching in labor relations—for a focus on working women." She credits her childhood most of all, and sees herself following in the footsteps of her mother and grandmother, who "helped achieve the Nineteenth Amendment to the Constitution and gave me that matter-of-fact acceptance of women as people having equal rights."

For more than five years, Alice Cook and I worked on chapters in this book through three and sometimes four revisions, often interrupted by Alice's need to write a chapter for another book or a paper for a conference she was going to attend. Even as she finished the fourth revision of chapter 15—in 1996, when she was ninety-three—she reminded me that she would be busy for the next several months revising a chapter for another book and reading proofs for still another. Long before she began to work on the autobiography, she had mas- tered the computer, and so she could do her own revisions, even including the production of footnotes at the bottoms of pages.

From the first, as her publisher, I was delighted that Alice Cook was the kind of activist who combined street smarts with serious scholarship. Her politics, moreover, were not left in her briefcase or on the streets where she marched. She carried them home into the communal living arrangements she preferred all her life. If she could not get adequate child care for her son, she would take in other people's children and share child care with their parents or do it herself. As Alice Cook's publisher, I was also heartened by her prodigious memory and the vast accumulation of diaries and letters available to her as she wrote, including the letters she had written home to her mother during her graduate school years in Germany, from 1929 to 1931. As publisher, I thought I had to solve two "problems": First, how to control the enormous quantity of information Alice poured forth, not only about labor education and trade unions the world over, but about the people she met whose histories she could always narrate, since she never seemed to "lose" a friend, except to death. Second, how to modify Alice's reticence about her personal life, not uncommon among members of her generation. I asked Alice to move into endnotes the history of friends she was reluctant to omit, as well as additional bibliography and commentary. And especially in the final chapters, Alice generously shared the details of both her family pride and the pain of aging.

I had not, of course, expected to publish Alice Cook's autobiography without her active presence throughout the necessary six months of fact checking, copyediting, and proofreading. Alice's eyes had failed by the time she received the first three copyedited chapters, with queries that needed checking. Even then, she tried valiantly to deal with these through Beatrice MacLeod, a friend who read them to her. But the process was short-lived.

After Alice's death, Fran Herman stepped in to help me complete the preparation of the manuscript for publication, reading it herself, working with Cornell librarians, faculty, and family members, as well as with Alice's address book, to check the facts. Without her help, and her friendly moral support, I could not have done the work of the past six months. We have been on the phone daily. She flew to New York for three days of decision making on details in the manuscript as well as to complete the work of producing a new version of chapter 12 that combined Alice's first, second, and third drafts. The first and second versions of chapter 12 recounted, in one hundred pages of narrative, the visits to nine countries during the years 1971 to 1973, in which Alice was doing the research for her study of working mothers. The third version omitted all narrative and summarized the study's findings. Fran worked for more than a week choosing and reworking salient narrative sections of Alice's larger version, and then, together, we cut and pasted elements of the two drafts to produce the chapter as it now appears in this volume.

Three chapters in this volume are partly or wholly focused on Germany. For weeks of fact checking and general scholarly advice about these chapters, I want to thank Hanna Beate Schöpp-Schilling, who consulted on occasion with Adelheid (Adi) Tröscher and her assistant, Richard Kortmann. For fact checking on labor history in the United States, I want to thank Alice Kessler-Harris. Many people helped Fran Herman check facts. Among them, I want to offer special thanks to Professor Jennie Farley of the School of Industrial and Labor Relations at Cornell University, as well as to Susan La Cette, information assistant on the staff of the Martin P. Catherwood Library at the School of Industrial and Labor Relations, in addition to reference librarians Constance Finlay and Stuart Basefsky, as well as Philip Cook.

As a gift to Alice Cook's memory, her colleagues at the Industrial Relations Center (IRC) of the University of Hawaii at Manoa offered to prepare the index to this volume. The work was done by Joyce M. Najita, director of the IRC, and Helene Tanimoto. I want also to thank three people for their assistance in collecting photographs for this book and in writing captions: Philip Cook, Hope Hoetzer-Cook, and Fran Herman. Several people assisted in the final preparation of the manuscript for publication: I wish to thank Jean Casella, Sara Clough, Helene D. Goldfarb, Susan Heath, Marna Miller, and Nancy Riddiough. For design of the volume and its cover, I wish to thank Dayna Navaro.

I'm certain that Alice Cook would have thanked many more people on this occasion, other friends with whom she may have discussed early drafts of her book. I trust that they will forgive me for mentioning them here only as a group. They will understand, as I do, how glad Alice would have been to know that so many hands contributed to the making of a book that will, in the manner of all fine literature, both teach and entertain us. While I grieve still that I cannot place this book into Alice's hands, I am comforted by the fact that hundreds of her friends will have it to hold and read and, further, that thousands of others will be able to read the life story of a remarkable woman who helped to change the world of labor for all of us.

Florence Howe
New York
April 1998

THE TWIG IS BENT: 1903–1920

THE VERY EARLY YEARS

I have no recollection of my birthplace in Alexandria, Virginia, though the stories about it filled a large place in family lore. The location of our home was—as were many homes that followed—an artifact of my father's work as a railroad accountant. He had come home from three years' service as a foot soldier in the Spanish-American War in Cuba and the Philippines to marry his fiancée, Flora Alice Kays. They moved straightaway to Alexandria, Virginia, where he worked for the Southern Railroad in its bookkeeping department. My parents shared a remarkable house, Colross, with my father's superior and his family. Colross was a genuine colonial structure that had originally been the center of an early Virginia plantation. It had no gaslights, and running water only in the kitchen. Progress had doomed the house, for it stood in the midst of railroad tracks. I remember seeing it only once, when I was about ten years old and Mother took my two brothers and me for a visit. The stable still had horses; the elegant plaster ceilings were still intact; the great oak doors still stood behind the massive white columns that supported the veranda roof. Shortly thereafter the house was sold, carefully taken down, and reconstructed in a more suitable setting.

MY FAMILY BACKGROUND

Though housed in grandeur, my parents were quite modest, lower-middle-class folk. As the second of seven sons of Swedish immigrants, Father had had only an elementary school education. His family had settled on the northwest side of Chicago soon after the Civil War and were burned out in the Great Chicago Fire. At that time, when Father was perhaps three years old, they moved to Colfax Street in Evanston, Illinois.

Father's father had been a sailor and his mother a peasant, the youngest girl of a large family from the same village, Kalmar,[1] a day's walk (as Grandma Hanson later explained), from Stockholm. Grandfather had traveled the world and been injured in a mine accident in Australia before coming to the United States. He had decided to come here when he heard that immigrant volunteers for the Northern Army in the Civil War would receive immediate citizenship. He arrived, however, soon after Appomatox, too late to test the validity of that promise. He experienced a change of name at immigration when the official who dealt with his case decided that Hanson was an easier name for a Swede than Haakinson, the surname with which he was born.

Grandma Hanson was brought to the United States by her next older brother when she was in her teens. Uncle Peterson was expected to find a husband for her before he found a wife for himself. In the Chicago Swedish community, he heard of an unmarried older man who had come from their own village. That fact alone may have been enough to persuade Uncle Peterson that he had found the right man.

Grandfather Hanson died when I was three or four. He and my grandmother were living in Washington, D.C., near four of their seven sons. After his death, Grandma Hanson lived in a kind of rotation among several of her married sons, including my father. Father told us that before he went to school he spoke only Swedish, but once in school he and his brothers quickly adapted to English. As adults they all spoke only English and without a trace of accent. Grandma Hanson had had to learn English to communicate with her sons, and until her death, she spoke it with a heavy accent. At one time we talked about her teaching me Swedish, but the plan never came off. My one cultural inheritance from this side of the family is a nursery rhyme that counts my five fingers.

My father worked all his life for various employers connected with the railroad industry, as did five of his brothers. The family traveled a good deal on railroad passes, as we moved from one city to another in the East and Midwest every two years or so, depending on his assignments. I count that until I was married at twenty-three, I had lived in at least twenty different houses in Washington, Virginia, Maryland, North Carolina, Illinois, Wisconsin, Indiana, Missouri, and Arkansas.

In contrast to Father's immigrant origins, Mother's background was pure Yankee over several hundred years. In order to join the Daughters of the American Revolution, she traced her family not quite to the Pilgrims but to Anglo-Scots immigrants who arrived in Massachusetts in about 1640 and settled in Ashland. After the Revolutionary War various branches of the family moved westward and by the mid-1800s had settled in Kansas, Missouri, and Iowa. My maternal grandmother, Ora Amelia Graves Kays, told me that when she was four, in 1849, she had seen covered wagons pass her sod house in Missouri on their way to the California Gold Rush. Her father, about whom she told many stories, mainly of discipline, stubbornness, and commitment to the progressive thinkers of his period, was a free-thinking pioneer in the Midwest.

Ora Graves became a teacher almost as soon as she finished elementary school and was only a few years older than her pupils. In her teens she attended a church revival service and became strongly committed to a pietistic Christianity. In doing so, she broke openly with her free-thinking father. When she was about twenty, she married a Civil War captain, William Kays. He had practiced homeopathic medicine for a time but then read law and practiced in Memphis, Missouri, where Mother grew up as the seventh of nine children, three of whom died in infancy. Grandfather Kays died when Mother was six. His early death left Grandma Kays a widow with a Civil War pension of thirty dollars a month to support her still-young family. She took in sewing and taught my mother to be a seamstress. Church life was central to the community for my grandmother and her children. Perhaps it was through this tie that she and her daughters also became committed members of the Women's Christian Temperance Union (WCTU), the largest organization of women that has ever existed in the United States. Their ideals of womanhood were Frances Willard, a founder of the WCTU, and her secretary and successor as national president, Anna Gordon.

Almost certainly this organization and its leaders were instrumental in Grandma Kays's decision to move to Evanston in 1887 with her two unmarried daughters and her unmarried son, Will. Here the girls could prepare to enroll in Northwestern University, in whose founding in the 1860s Frances Willard had played a part. Will, already a skilled housepainter, could help support the family. Grandma Kays opened a dressmaking business, in which my mother assisted her, as they established themselves for the first time in a new location. My grandmother's only hesitation about this move was that in coming to Illinois she lost the right to vote in local and state elections, which women had gained some years earlier in Missouri.

Grandma Kays's plan was carried out, and both young women were accepted at the university. My mother applied to the Cumnock School of Oratory, later renamed the School of Speech, which then offered a two-year diploma in dramatic reading, or elocution, what today would be called theater arts. Mother graduated in 1900, in the class of "naughty-naught," and received not only her diploma but a letter of strong support from the school's director, Dr. Cumnock, who found her "rarely talented" and predicted for her a "brilliant future." Her younger sister, Lucretia, known as "Crete," graduated in biology four years later with a Phi Beta Kappa key.[2]

Mother spent the two years after graduation on tour doing dramatic readings under various auspices. At least one summer she was at Chautauqua Lake in New York State, where she did "readings" in a spiritualist encampment. Her major activity, however, was touring Canadian towns in southern Ontario with a full evening's program of dramatic readings. Travel at that time was of course by train, and in the Canadian winter weather one adventure followed another. Living in the discomforts of Canadian small-town hotels was grim and exhausting, but the memories of it all, as she recounted these travels, were mainly of her artistic triumphs, verified in yellowed clippings from Stratford papers.[3] We children were awash all our young lives with the events and readings that had made up her Canadian programs. She was proud of her rendering of Scots, Irish, and various Southern whites' dialects and often continued to entertain friends at home with poems and stories.

I do not know how my mother and father met or how long they knew each other before he enlisted to fight under Teddy Roosevelt in the Spanish-American War. They were certainly engaged by the time he left for Cuba. In our home, as we grew up, we still had copies of their letters, which took months to reach their destinations, particularly after he was sent to the Philippines. His were written in two colors of ink: he would first cover the length of his paper in black, then turn it around 180 degrees and write across the same page in red. During the three years of his enlistment he had no home leave. Somewhere he had a serious bout of yellow fever, which must have cut off the letter writing for several weeks. My mother insisted that she had a mystic knowledge of his illness and prayed him well. In any case, he did fully recover. He came home with a soldier's souvenirs, which included some daggers left behind by "rebels" and perhaps a hundred mounted pictures of scenes in the Philippines. My mother later reported that he came home with a dislike of war so great that she remembered him saying, "Anybody who wants to can tear up the flag in my backyard and I won't stir out of the house." He preferred to forget this, becoming in later years a loyal member of the Spanish War Veterans and turning visibly patriotic as Americans joined the Allied forces against Germany in World War I.

My Life Begins

My parents' wedding took place in Evanston on June 27, 1902, and the newlyweds moved almost immediately to Father's first civilian job in Alexandria. There, I and my brother, Theodore ("Tedo"), were born, I on November 28, 1903, and Tedo eighteen months after me. Frederick ("Fritz" or "Fred") came two years and three months later, by which time we had moved to S Street in Washington, where Father had his office in the splendid new Union Station. Crete and Grandma Kays lived with us from time to time, undoubtedly making it possible for Mother to keep up with the demands of three very young children. Crete soon married Father's younger brother, Herman Karl, on his return from the Klondike where he had gone in the great 1898–1901 Gold Rush, and from which he came back with a few gold nuggets that were distributed throughout the family as tie pins and brooches.

While Fred was still an infant we moved to Charlotte, North Carolina. I remember a loosely built house on stilts high enough so that we could play under it. Grandma Kays lived with us and must have been a necessary help not only with the children but with the chores that had to be performed in primitive conditions: drawing water from a pump in the garden, doing the laundry over an outdoor fire, preparing food, and heating the windy house.

Then, before I was ready for kindergarten, we were back in Washington to live in a duplex flat on V Street. My first sustained memories come from here. Aunt Crete—known to us by the baby name we gave her, "Ongie"—and Uncle Herman lived on the first floor with their first baby, also a Lucretia, while we occupied the second floor. Not only Grandma Kays but Grandma Hanson as well lived from time to time with each family.

Grandma Kays was, from my first recollection onward, ardently interested in politics. Despite the fact that her only cash income over the many years of her widowhood continued to be her pension of thirty dollars per month, she nevertheless subscribed to her own newspaper in order "to have the news straight." However, she remained at home with us on March 4, 1908, a stormy day, while our parents watched the inaugural parade for William Howard Taft. By the next presidential election she had become a "Bull Mooser"—a supporter of the dissident Republicans who ran Teddy Roosevelt as a third-party candidate against Taft and unwittingly secured the election for Democrat Woodrow Wilson.

As Ongie's family increased in size, Ongie and Uncle Herman moved to another part of the city with little Lucretia and their two boys, Harry and Karl. I learned early to master the Washington trolley cars and could visit them in Eckington— first with Mother or Grandma Kays, and then, by the time I was seven, quite by myself.

Ongie was always conscious of being the intellectual in the family. It was her way of somehow getting even with her beautiful sister, my mother, who had had such a colorful career as an actress. This rivalry was a source of stress (and distress) in their relationship all their long lives. Part of Ongie's pretentiousness was to use a few French phrases she had learned in college. For instance, one did not go to the bathroom at Ongie's—rather, one asked to *"faire de l'eau."* I was, however, heavily impressed with this daily use of a foreign language and particularly with the fact that one could use it to disguise those common needs that ought not to be voiced above a whisper and then only to parents. I considered Ongie by far my favorite aunt; in turn, she cherished me, I sometimes thought and hoped, even more than she did her own children.

On V Street I experienced my first friendship outside the family. Elizabeth Farnham lived in a big house across the street. Her father was a photographer and her mother colored his glass slides. I spent time looking through her parents' projector, a simple instrument with a handle and two eyeholes through which one could see the picture or slide considerably enlarged. Elizabeth's father had the first privately owned automobile I ever rode in, a topless carriage that had to be cranked to start and went perhaps twenty miles an hour.

It was here, while I was still not more than five or six, that I also had my first personal experience of class divisions. To my parents, Elizabeth's family was something better than ours—my father's tone in referring to it told me that much. But when a guest of Elizabeth's mother inspected me one day, noted my dark bloomers under my dotted-Swiss pink dress, and spelled out, "Is she p-o-o-r?"— a word I had long since learned to read—I realized there were gradations in society that put me and mine below the level of our neighbors. In fact, Mother, a great admirer of the early suffragists, had decided that bloomers were more suitable for little girls than panties and had put me into them. At this point it never occurred to me that I might be a victim of my mother's unusual taste and judgment, as it would surely have done a few years later. Instead, while I recognized an intended put-down for what it was, I felt superior to my critic, for although I was not yet in school I had penetrated the lady's secret code! I perceived that her intent was not kindly meant, and I felt myself her better.

I was already beginning to read to my brothers before I was sent to kindergarten. I knew that I had "special eyes" and for that reason would be delayed in being sent to school. In fact my right eye saw very little, and in its effort to focus with the good left eye, it had become crossed. I wore glasses from the time I was three, presumably to strengthen my weak eye, though they also served to focus my natural farsightedness on the reading page. In addition I had problems with a tear duct in my right eye and had several operations to widen it or clear it. These ended with its removal a few years later, but the crossed eye remained through my college years until a Swedish osteopath, "Dr. Gussie," to whom my mother and her close friends in Chicago were devoted, gave me exercises that provided the needed muscle strengthening. In terms of vision, however, my right eye remains to this day quite useless.

Because of the recurrent eye problems, I did not start school at six. Tedo and I were placed together in a kindergarten that was part of a Washington training school for kindergarten and primary teachers, and we went daily on our own by trolley. We churned milk to butter, made bread, caught bugs and identified them, and greatly widened our horizons. My reading all the while also widened, and I tried to teach my brothers, but Tedo was a slow learner in this regard and Fred much too young to begin.

Our next move was to Hyattsville, Maryland, then an early suburb of Washington. Our house on Baltimore Street, a narrow two-story, five-room, gaslit copy of others on the block, had a big backyard with a sandbox and a hammock. But the yard was grassless, hard clay—a mire in rainy weather, cold in winter, and breathlessly hot in the Maryland summer. I began to do special household chores, brushing down the steps, setting the table for dinner, remembering that a well-set table had on it "salt and pepper, bread and butter, sugar and cream" at every meal. Since we were on the same trolley line that ran by V Street, our trips to kindergarten continued from Hyattsville.

Baltimore Street, however, was only a stepping-stone to the greatest family achievement of my childhood. We built a house! Largely designed by Mother, it was farther north in Hyattsville in a new development on Maple Street, on what had been the long, sloping lawn of a now crumbling and uninhabited mansion. Our new house was bigger and had its own yard. It had seven rooms and a bathroom, a special room for Grandma Kays, and another for me. The boys shared a room, and Mother and Father had their own. But what was most remarkable, Mother had succeeded in introducing, despite the builder's resistance, many innovations of her own: an outside icebox that opened into the kitchen but was serviced by the iceman from outside; a kitchen sink built to Mother's height and not at the plumber's prescribed elevation, which would have made her bend over to do dishes; a window seat in the living room with cupboards underneath that could be used to store games, piano music, books, flower vases, and other things; a wide veranda that could serve as a sleeping porch for us children; cupboards upstairs under the eaves with drawers or shelves as best fitted in; and walk-in closets. It was our dream house.

The room the boys shared was our playroom, and a big assortment of building blocks was the basis of our favorite joint enterprises. We built forts and whole towns in which we acted out scenarios that took days or weeks to live through.

STARTING SCHOOL

I started school in Hyattsville when I was eight years old, entering first grade with Tedo, who was six. Within a few weeks I was in third grade. From that time forward, my hitherto close relationship with Tedo became more and more distant as interests and companions separated us and for me, at least, new friendships with girls became more important in many ways than family.

The school had only seven grades with an ill-prepared staff of teachers. In sixth grade, for example, I was aware that the teacher opened the exam questions furnished by some outside agency only a few days before the date prescribed and saw, as I am sure she feared, that she must hurriedly teach us several as-yet-untested grammatical and mathematical constructions. An exception to this generalization was Mrs. Sturgis, the principal's wife, who became a warm friend and adviser to me in the seventh grade. I remained in touch with her for several years after we left Hyattsville for the Midwest.

Family fun in these early days consisted mainly of playing card games together; of singing with neighbors and visitors around the piano, where Mother presided at the keys; of walks with Father in parks and along nearby roads (cars were very few and not very fast); of a few trips to the movies, where admission cost five cents—though we hesitated to ask Mother for even this amount. My chief recollections, however, are of travel, since railroad passes were always available.

One summer when we were quite small, we went to a summer resort in the West Virginia mountains to which we had to be driven from the station into the hills in a flatbed wagon. My happiest memory is from when I was ten or eleven, when Father was granted the great boon of a two-week vacation. My parents used the time to take each of us children on a trip alone. I was taken to New York City and to a show at the old Hippodrome, where I sat entranced and amazed as animals came on the stage and troops of singers and dancers performed. I had my first experience of living in a hotel, eating in restaurants, taking a ride on a ferry, and going to an art museum. But most enjoyable of all was the experience of being an only child.

RELIGION, COMMITMENT, AND ACTIVISM

Church life was a dominant part of our existence, both on Sunday and during the week at home. Mother here as elsewhere was the determining factor. As we moved to a new location, she would visit a short list of Protestant churches and decide where we were to enroll. The choices were usually between Congregational and Presbyterian. Methodist was acceptable, but Episcopalians were too high-class for the modest Hansons and Baptists, somehow, too low. The Catholic Church was unthinkable: "idol-worshipping," "gaudy," "priest-driven," according to Mother. Jews were unknown to us children, but my father, who was a committed Mason, made clear that while the Order was opposed to Catholics, it welcomed Jews.

Mother repeatedly tried, with Grandma Kays's help, to introduce Bible reading each morning at breakfast, but the demands of getting three children off to school and a husband off to work seem to have defeated the establishment of such a routine. No meal, however, began without "a blessing," always uttered by Father—if he were present, for his frequent business trips for the railroad took him off sometimes for several weeks. My grandmother sought always to deepen our interest in and knowledge of the Bible. At one time she paid me a dollar, which for both of us was an enormous amount of money, to learn the books of the Bible in their order in the King James text. Thus our childhood was clearly imprinted with a rather simplistic Protestantism that was unfanatical and conservative. On our knees before going to bed, we prayed directly to a listening God, thanked him regularly for the gift of his son, Jesus, reported our daily shortcomings and achievements, and asked for strength to do the right thing in the twenty-four hours ahead.

My mother found another center of activity in the WCTU. Both there and in the church, she made or found a place for us children. She enrolled me, for example, in the Loyal Temperance Legion (LTL), the children's branch of the WCTU. The goal of the WCTU was to purge the world, and particularly Western society, of alcohol addiction. Its early members, including Grandma Kays in her Missouri days, did this through direct action, holding prayer meetings in or in front of saloons. In the nineteenth century, when programs of social welfare for women and children were no more than a distant dream, these women saw alcohol abuse as the major cause of poverty and specifically of the widespread abuse and victimization of women and children.

The organization founded the Florence Crittenden homes for unmarried mothers. In labor's founding days, WCTU women attended labor conventions as fraternal delegates to show their sense of identification with the men and women of the working class; they also hoped to perform as behavior models for working-class families, whose men were seen as driven to alcohol by the terrible toil demanded of them, which deprived their wives and children of a decent livelihood and of loving fathers. The WCTU attacked the problems of alcoholism both within the family and by seeking a constitutional amendment that would make alcohol manufacture and use illegal. No doubt convinced, as the suffragists were, that women's higher morality could and would influence political decisions for the better, the WCTU strongly advocated women's suffrage and became an important element of support for that movement. Historians of the WCTU have pointed out that it was the largest women's organization ever to have existed in the United States. Its seedbed was the Protestant churches of various denominations.

Initiation into the LTL included a pledge never to use alcohol or tobacco, a form of "lips that touch liquor will never touch mine." Taking the pledge was a bit like joining the church, a life-determining commitment, to be placed as compellingly as possible before the twelve-year-old at a point when he or she purportedly had reached an age of reason. It became part of the WCTU's missionary activity not only with children but with their parents as well. Various more or less enticing activities were offered these newly committed converts. The activity into which I was at once enrolled was a declamatory contest, for which one memorized stories and essays for recital, to compete for a bronze, and then for silver, gold, and even diamond medals. I was tutored by my talented and professionally experienced mother. I became a consistent winner, gaining confidence and stage presence before an audience, a sense of self-improvement demonstrated in accomplishment, and the experience of personal dedication to a cause to which others might be won both by reason and example.

My mother's and grandmother's sense of mission to others, and their dedication to a cause, were primarily expressed through the many aspects of their WCTU activity. These principles continued to guide my mother's life to the end, long after her children had established quite other ways of living. When she was over seventy, she became a national officer of the organization, in charge of exhibits, plays, and pageants. These pageants were often the high point of the national conventions of the organization. My father supported her in this as in all her life decisions. On the other hand, her relationships with her adult children were often somewhat strained by the fact that we no longer felt bound by these childhood commitments, by which she believed we had promised to be governed forever.

Although Father was much less politically and socially active than Mother, he joined her, even happily submitted to her, as his mentor in these matters. They both voted "the Prohibition ticket," though I am sure they were both aware that no candidate of theirs would ever be elected.[4] I grew up accepting that these votes, unsuccessful as they invariably were, were not by any means "thrown away." On the contrary, they represented one's genuine choice and were cast as a token of faith in a better future. My persistence in my later years in supporting Socialist Party candidates throughout the whole Roosevelt era was surely sustained by this early example.

During this period we all shared the excitement of Mother's appearance as an actress in Washington in the winter of 1915 in a pageant, written and directed by Percy MacKaye, which was performed as part of a national women's suffrage campaign. A well-known actress was to play the lead role of Susan B. Anthony, and Mother was selected to be her understudy. At some early point in rehearsals, the leading lady withdrew and Mother was chosen to play the role herself. I was to play a small part as a child who, at one of Ms. Anthony's public appearances, steps forward with a curtsy to present flowers to the great lady. As the pageant neared its opening night, I practiced that curtsy tirelessly. All the characters of the nineteenth-century women's movement became living people for me: Amelia Bloomer, the doctor who dressed in pantaloons as appropriate for a woman constantly on her rounds by day or night and whose name became attached to my early undergarments; Elizabeth Cady Stanton, close friend of Anthony's; Lucretia Mott, the cofounder of the 1848 Seneca Falls convention that adopted "The Women's Declaration of Independence"—these were all people who knew me by name and with whom I exchanged greetings at rehearsals. Certainly I have always seen Susan B. Anthony with my mother's face. This experience peaked on the evening President Wilson came to see the pageant. Whether he did in fact come backstage to congratulate Mother I am no longer sure, but some presidential salute to her filtered into our family legend of the evening.

Grandma Kays, Mother, and I shared in quite another aspect of the movement when we joined a suffragists' march that originated in Boston, passed through Hyattsville, and ended at the gates of the White House, where we helped make up a picket line meant to catch the attention of President Wilson.

Early Civics Lessons

Mother repeatedly made clear to us that we were very fortunate people to live so near the national capital. She had a Midwesterner's awe of all that was governmental and monumental in Washington. Relatives who visited us from the Midwest always wanted to see the Washington sights, and Mother was always willing to oblige. Indeed, she became an experienced as well as an enthusiastic guide. If we were not in school, we children went along. We climbed the Washington Monument, stood in awe before the Supreme Court, the White House, and the Capitol building, visited the Pan-American building and the newly built DAR hall, strolled down the Mall, took a boat trip down the Potomac to Mt. Vernon, and participated in ceremonies at the National Cemetery in Arlington.

Very early we understood something of the separation of powers, the privilege and consequence of building a majority and tolerating a minority, if for no other reason than that it might some day be the majority. We believed firmly in the values identified with standard American teaching, including the separation as well as the cooperation of church and state, so long as the church was reliably Protestant. We believed in America's destiny as a model for other, less privileged countries, such as Cuba and the Philippines where Father had fought for their liberation. We thought it possible that someday we would be as great and beneficent an imperial power as the mother country, Great Britain. Later I would come to question some of the particular assumptions upon which these values were based, yet my family provided a model of civic concern that would remain with me all my life.

My family also believed in the possibility of every American becoming rich and influential, and we believed that a sure route to such a position ran through a college education. It was never in doubt, even when I was in grade school, that, like my mother and my aunt, I would go to college; this was assumed no less for me than for my brothers. Such attitudes on the part of my family—along with the model of Mother's and Grandma Kays's strength and activism—shaped me to believe implicitly in the complete equality of men and women.

OUR MOVE TO THE MIDWEST

At breakfast one morning in the spring of 1915, Mother, in a tone of deep regret said, "I feel in my bones we are going to move again." Not long after, we moved to Chicago, a move that for both my parents could only mean Evanston. But before we left, we visited a session of Congress, where we heard a bit of a debate and saw a vote taken. Mother wanted our last impressions of Washington to be active and vivid ones of its role as capital of the republic.

The move must in fact have been fairly sudden, for we had no house to move into but stayed for a few weeks in a boardinghouse on Garfield Street kept by an English family, the Broads, who were trying to make their start in the United States. When we found a flat, it was in a three-apartment building on Simpson Street owned by William Knapp, a professor of voice and organ in the School of Music at Northwestern. His wife, Nina, a teacher of piano there, became my mother's closest friend, while their daughter Virginia, whom we all knew as "Bunny," became mine.

Mother had entered us in Noyes Street School, though it was late April with only two months left before the end of term. In tests, except for grammar and penmanship, I seemed ready for the eighth-grade graduating class. The eighth-grade teacher offered to tutor me in both subjects, and, depending on a test at the end of the school year, I might actually be judged ready for high school in the fall. At term's end my grades were high except for grammar, so I agreed to study in summer school to get the grounding I needed. I enjoyed the game of parsing sentences, diagramming subject and verb, and then hanging on to each part of the sentence all its dependent adjectives, adverbs, and subordinate phrases and clauses. If understanding the sentence structure of English were a necessary qualification for high school, I grasped that knowledge with delight. The puzzle was solved; I could play the game and win.

I got some early experience of the high school building that same summer, when I decided under Father's urging to take a course in typing. He brought home an ancient machine from his office, which he promised could become mine if and when I learned "the touch system." This typewriter must have been one of the first models ever sold, for one had to lift the platen from below to see what had been written on the paper, which was quite out of sight. Once it was home, Father brought brief reports and tables from his office for me to type. He paid me twenty-five cents an hour for my work on them. Thus began my career as a self-supporting secretary.

My brothers and I quickly found our way around Evanston—to the stores and the movies on Davis Street; to the city library, which began to supply all my wishes for books; to church, the First Presbyterian and its Christian Endeavor Society, where a Welshman, Dr. David Jones, preached to my mother's satisfaction.

As I made friends at Noyes Street School, it was satisfactory to know that we would keep each other company as we walked to high school, then at Dempster Street, about a mile south of my home and an endurance test in Evanston's freezing winters. I think it was the PTA that decided we needed some instruction of another kind, for we girls were called together for a meeting as graduation neared to hear a talk by one of the famous Evanston women, Catherine McCulloch, who in that early day was a lawyer practicing with her husband, Hugh, in a prestigious Chicago firm. (Her youngest son, Frank, was a member of our high school class and, much later, chair of the National Labor Relations Board.) The burden of her talk was to warn us of male strangers whom we might encounter as we walked to and from school. Yet even this outspoken lady, used to expressing herself in the clearest language, failed to make clear to me and to at least some of my comrades what exactly it was we had to fear. The matter became the subject of speculation among us as we took this walk day after day. It was the unwritten law of the time that one did not discuss matters of sexual import explicitly with the young. Most of what I learned in that department was not learned from my mother, who often presented herself after the fact, somewhat teary and apologetic, to provide the instruction I had already won from friends.

THE SIMPSON STREET LEAGUE

The Simpson Street house with its three flats shortly became something of an extended family. Certainly the warm ties we developed with the Knapps lasted our lifetimes. On the third floor lived the Greers, a family made up of a widowed mother and four children, with whom our association was less close. The three oldest Greer children were years beyond us, one already at Northwestern University. But the youngest, Barbara, became one of the "828 Simpson Street Children's League."

We were engulfed with music from the Knapp's first floor. Students came there for their lessons; both Mr. and Mrs. Knapp practiced for their own recitals; and the family owned an early phonograph—one that had to be wound up as each new thick record was put on the machine—and we loved its music. I saw my first opera, *Aida*, as a guest of the Knapps and from time to time was invited to join them for symphony concerts. Bunny was musically gifted and already a good pianist, even a composer of simple songs. We created plays and musicals, and I became her writer of lyrics of every kind from romantic to martial. The adults were our audience, often convulsed with laughter but always supportive of our efforts. We had only to announce that we were ready to raise a curtain on our latest production to have them assemble in the Knapp living room, from which they had a full view of the stage in the dining room.

Living in the Knapp household as a ward rather than a relative was Bernard Malmstrom, a young Swede whom Mr. Knapp had brought home from a church group he led in Chicago. Bernard, who was perhaps eighteen, lived in the basement and acted as janitor of the apartment house. He was also king of the movie projector that Mr. Knapp had acquired somehow, somewhere, and with which we privileged children had our home movies. Although Mr. Knapp never acquired more than a few reels, we were shown them again and again, never wearying of the magic of the black-and-white pictures we came to know very well. Our acquaintance with other movies and the lure of the movie theater really began in Evanston, where at the Star Theater we saw Mary Pickford and her generation of stars in films whose titles, plots, and actors have long since been forgotten. Mother had never willingly given us the nickel that a trip to the movies cost, but in Evanston we were old enough to be allowed to go by ourselves, and about this time we had begun receiving weekly allowances to cover our school lunches and a bit of entertainment.

Our life in Evanston was quickly shaped by the lake. Father was a great hiker, and we had many walks in the forest preserve to the west of Evanston, along the lake, and to North Evanston. My first appreciation of natural beauty came in those many walks along the lake, in all seasons, at all hours of the day and early evening, and my diary was in part a series of exercises in expressing in writing what I saw and felt there. We spent hours on and in the water all during the summer. We learned to swim, and each of us somehow acquired a second hand canoe in which we could paddle the length of the Evanston beach. Our family outings were mostly beach parties with dinners cooked over an open fire or served out of a picnic basket. Indeed, I felt pity for people who could reach the lake only after a long trip by trolley.

We came to love the northside Chicago city parks as well. To reach them we had to go on the "El," the elevated train that brought commuters from the suburbs into the downtown "Loop." My ability to get about on public transportation, learned from kindergarten days in Washington, transferred readily to the Evanston trolley and the Chicago El. Trips to the city's museums and theaters became part of the joy of living.

Father organized a softball team of the boys on our street, and as a matter of course I played with them. This all took place on a vacant lot next door, which in winter was flooded for a skating rink. Family visits and afternoons and evenings with friends and neighbors were cherished occasions where we played checkers and card games, listened to the grown-ups' conversations, and ate richly of food prepared by other mothers. We had few dull moments.

HIGH SCHOOL

I entered Evanston Township High School (ETHS) in the fall of 1915, when I was not yet thirteen. So far as I know, no teacher, and certainly not my mother, raised a question as to whether a twelve-year-old was mature enough to go to high school.

All that seemed to matter was book learning. Of course I felt I was ready for it and would overcome whatever difficulties might present themselves.

ETHS was, by comparison with anything I had known, a large school, directed by a classicist principal. Latin was a required subject in the freshman year, and Greek was offered to sophomores, along with a choice of French or German. As a freshman I signed up for English, algebra, civics, and science. Not only were these subjects completely different from anything I had studied in grade school, they were also dealt with differently; the scope of discussion, the assignments, and the measures of achievement were new to me. High school routines were decidedly different from those shaped by the maternal care of the grade school teacher: a new teacher took charge of each succeeding class, and lunch was in a school cafeteria. Although high grades were not so easily achieved, I made the honor roll the first time around, having achieved an average of 83 or above. By the end of my freshman year my best subjects were Latin, 98 for the year, and algebra, almost as high.

My sophomore year I decided on Greek as my second language, for no better reason than that I liked Latin so much. I signed up also for French and chemistry, while plain and solid geometry were requirements. I am sure English was also on the roster, and I went into my second year of Latin.

The predictable routines of school were interrupted in the spring of 1917, as the Americans entered World War I and we all became ultrapatriotic. In the summer I was active in the Patriotic League, making face protectors. I was also learning to knit under Red Cross tutelage, making washcloths for "the boys in the service."

At home, too, Bunny and I were caught up in the patriotic spirit. We composed a song closely modeled on one that had swept the nation, "Over There." Our song began with a verse addressed apparently to our whole army in France:

> Over the top with the flag, boys,
> Over the top with a cheer!
> Who's there who dares to lag, boys,
> Who's there who does not fear?

In the show of which this was a part, I harnessed my two brothers to a leash and led them onstage as "the dogs of war."

We moved in 1917 to a flat on Wesley Avenue, west and south a bit from Simpson Street, where again a next-door vacant lot supplied the place for our active play. My brothers dug trenches and together we created our war games. Obviously, I was still child enough at thirteen and fourteen to let my imagination run full in play. In the fall, I alone in the family fell victim to the great influenza epidemic that swept the country, and I was desperately ill. My recovery was long and slow, and my concerned parents gave me a great deal of attention.

Late that same year, Father was assigned a new job and left for Green Bay, Wisconsin. When he had found a house for us, we followed. He was assigned to a cluster of four small railroads out of Green Bay, a consequence of the government's decision to take over the railroads for the duration of the war and thus to consolidate the country's many railroad companies, schedules, and equipment for their most efficient use in transporting men and matériel.

East Green Bay High School (EGBHS), which I entered in the spring of 1917, was small in comparison with Evanston, but I found teachers whom I appreciated and became attached to, particularly in Latin, French, and English. Greek was not available. Altogether I liked the school and thrived there. In Evanston, I remember no athletic program; here, it was an important part of high school life. Some of our school athletes were later, after college at Wisconsin or Notre Dame, famous as members of the Green Bay Packers. I made many friends at EGBHS, including Jennie Cohen, my first Jewish friend, whose brother, Mike, became my first beau.

Winters were bitter, but winter sports were new and fascinating: hockey, ice-boating on the bay, even a little skiing. The local public library became a kind of second home for me. Mother found her WCTU and in the spring was elected its president. As usual, she visited several churches before deciding on the one with which we would affiliate, and we accepted her decision as practically heaven-sent. I took an active part in the young people's activities at our Green Bay church and attended a conference, at which I was elected chair of a continuing committee to plan the next year's meeting. Without experience in leadership across local boundaries, I suffered a severe attack of guilt as time went by and I did nothing to hold our own church group together or to build a regional association, which I certainly had not the slightest idea how to do.

During the first Green Bay summer I learned to play tennis with Fred Call, who had his own court, and also with John Minehan, whose family belonged to the country club and hence to another world I could not enter. Nevertheless, John joined us from time to time on the court next to Fred's house. Both Fred and John, excellent and experienced players, became my tutors and tolerated my attempts to be worthy of them.

Clubs were an important part of EGBHS life. In Mask and Wig we read literary papers to each other that were designed as reviews of books and plays. We had a French Club under the maternal eye of our French teacher, "Madame," where we actually tried to speak French and, oh joy and privilege, often met in her apartment for tea. I tried to join the debating society but was declared ineligible, since it was designed only for boys. Quickly, however, I learned of declamatory contests for both boys and girls and, with Mother's tutoring, chose a story to memorize and practice with such good effect that I won the statewide contest, held in its last stages at the University of Wisconsin at Madison. EGBHS enjoyed for the first time the glory of winning first place in both the boys' and the girls' contests; John Minehan was my partner in victory.

I wrote my first research paper in science, for which I undertook to investigate the optimum form of household heating, and to my happy amazement I won the approbation of my teacher for concluding, "based on sound research and reasoning," that it must be hot-water heat.

At the end of my junior year I was the guest of honor at the boys' Lincoln Club banquet, the only girl who had enjoyed such an honor. And I was elected president of Mask and Wig for my senior year, which began the fall before I turned sixteen. In my senior year Mother became the coach of the senior play. We selected *Pride and Prejudice*, and I had a secondary role. During the two summers in Green Bay I went with other YWCA girls to camps at Sturgeon Bay, where in various orchards we picked cherries, a big local crop. We reveled in the evening beach parties. We swam and hiked and shared discussions of our interests, our problems, our families and friends. In addition, we had the happy experience of bringing home at the end of the summer what for us was a pleasantly substantial sum of money, perhaps twenty-five or thirty dollars.

During our time in Green Bay, Grandma Hanson came to live with us. We knew she was ill; indeed, my recollection is that she was coming to us because no other daughter-in-law except Mother would or could care for her. Mother made it clear to me that Grandma's care would be so time consuming that I must now take over some of Mother's duties. I would become the household cook and kitchen manager. Mother taught me to roast meat, to make cakes from scratch; no semi-prepared foods for the household would be available at the grocer's for several years to come. Moreover, these were still the days when one ate food as it ripened in one's countryside. Vegetables in winter were carrots, cabbages, sweet and white potatoes, turnips, dried corn, and whatever one had "put up" as fresh vegetables during the summer.[5] This training stayed with me, and I learned to plan ahead so as to use what was on hand.

The "Green Bay boys" who came back from World War I marched through town on May 20, 1919. Reflecting the popular illusion that this had been "the war to end all wars," Mr. Ream, the high school principal, told us in a special assembly that this would be the first, last, and only time we would see soldiers coming home from war.

With war's end and the return of the railroads to private owners, we moved back to Evanston in the summer of 1920, after my high school graduation. Although after my first visit to Madison, I wanted very much to go to the university there, my parents said they could not afford to have me live away from home. In fact, another and decisive factor was the reputation of a leading professor of philosophy at Madison: should I fall under his influence, I would most surely "lose my religion." That was above all to be avoided. Our move back to Evanston was thus, from my parents' point of view, conveniently timed.

It was during this summer of 1920 that Grandma Kays died while visiting my Uncle Warbasse at his farm in Kansas. Mother went by train to her funeral, leaving me in full charge of the household. In addition to my household duties, I spent my time preparing to go to college in the fall. Dresses had to be made, books read, and old acquaintances—chiefly Bunny Knapp—to be sought out and readjusted to at a more mature level, even though Bunny herself was not yet ready for college. Still, the summer dragged. It was now clear that I would go to Northwestern, my mother's university. One important era was over; another, the college experience, waited just over the horizon, and I was eager to get on with it.

2

COLLEGE YEARS: 1920–1924

When we returned to Evanston from Green Bay in the summer of 1920, we moved into a flat at 1934 Sherman Avenue, between Foster and Emerson. It was a short walk to Northwestern University and the lake shore, not far from our earlier apartment on Simpson Street and within easy walking distance of the business center on Davis Street—altogether familiar territory. It was a roomy ground-floor apartment with a big screened-in sleeping porch, where children— and we were all still looked on as children—were expected to sleep for their good health in all but the most inclement weather. However distant in interests I then felt from my brothers, we bedded down together on our separate cots until deep into the autumn.

My acceptance at Northwestern University consisted of a visit to the School of Speech with my mother in the course of the summer of 1920, a chat with the registrar, and some business about opening day, available courses, and tuition payments. At least one of the courses, Interpretation, was taught by a classmate of my mother who had graduated with her in 1900—Professor James L. Lardner, who followed my career through the four years to graduation. He was my severest critic and on the whole a wise adviser, although as a teacher and interpreter of literary texts, he was rarely inspired or inspiring.

I spent the summer, in part, renewing my friendship with Bunny Knapp, mainly by playing tennis with her, but she, too, was destined to be henceforth out of my circle, not only because she was a year and a half younger than I and still several years behind me in high school but because her interests and her future lay in quite another area from mine. I also discovered that my inability to use my right eye resulted in little depth perception with which to locate tennis balls; I had to decide to give up tennis as a sport.

During the summer Mother was called back to Green Bay because Grandma Hanson was failing. She had been left quite alone in the hospital there, too fragile to move, when we left Green Bay. Once again I was designated household manager until Mother could return. Grandma Hanson died soon thereafter, and it was Father who went to Green Bay "to wind up her affairs."

My parents agreed that I could have a roommate at home, so as to give me something like the experience of dormitory living that most of my classmates would have. My choice fell on Harriet Cross, a two-year student in the School of Speech, who brought new experiences into my narrow range of family life: she had a divorced mother, with whom she strongly identified, and when her mother reverted after the divorce to her maiden name, Harriet too changed hers and became Harriett Lovell. She had a sister, as well—an experience I lacked—who was a graduate student in nutrition at the University of Chicago. Harriet was a person of profound feelings on which she could draw for the dramatic work in her "readings," as well as in her interpretation and drama courses.

By contrast, I felt then, and for many years afterward, that I could not experience deep emotions. Even where my parents were concerned and much as I depended on my mother and used her as my role model, I felt no special love either for her or Father; we were not a family in which love was openly stated or expressed. Nor did I have a sense of home as the center of life. No matter how distantly or strangely I have traveled, I have never experienced homesickness. This ability to adjust almost immediately to new environments I have come to attribute to our frequent moves in these early years. While I had and continued to develop strong attachments to many friends who helped me find my place and role in each new environment, these feelings arose, I think, more out of my personal need for ongoing attachment than out of love. Similarly, my religious feelings never ran deep but were rather a product of my need to belong to a group and the expectation that I would conform to its Christian norms. In general, I took what came without upsets. Changes of place and circumstances belonged in my life and caused me neither pain nor joy.

College Opens

Harriet and I were innocents as we started college. We were innocents about the ways of a university. We knew nothing of faculty hierarchies or of academic politics, of deans and provosts and presidents, of funding and endowments. We were also innocents intellectually. We knew nothing of theories and hypotheses and schools of thought, of the contributions of economics or history or sociology or science to common knowledge. We were prepared neither politically nor scholastically for participation in a university. We had to find our own way into its life as best we could, yet always within the limits of prescribed but unwritten guidelines, as we came to know them through implicit circumstance or, occasionally, explicit admonition.

We were innocents as well in the larger political and social life of our time. We had no friends or acquaintances who were foreigners; none who were African Americans, except for occasional household help our mothers might have employed; no Asians, no Latinos. Indeed, to us South America was a blot of undifferentiated countries populated by brown, primitive people. We knew nothing of their governments, their universities, their origins and histories, their struggles for independence, the variety of their peoples, their languages.

Closer to home, we were innocents about our own country and its political life and social problems. To be sure, we were aware in the fall of 1920 that our president, Woodrow Wilson, had failed to gain congressional consent to his dream of a League of Nations and that he now lay very ill with a mysterious disease never identified or described in the public press. We knew vaguely, but with no sense of significance, that his attorney general, A. Mitchell Palmer (known, when he entered office, as the "Fighting Quaker," and when he left, as the "Quaking Fighter," had become a freewheeling power of his own, determined to eradicate the Industrial Workers of the World (IWW), destroy Communists, and deport anarchists. To be sure, certain names had filtered down to us—Emma Goldman, Jane Addams, Big Bill Haywood, Eugene Debs, William Jennings Bryan—but we had no sense of them as persons living personal lives, no realization of their motivations and goals, their own tragedies, or the tragedies or blessings or purposes they had created for and in the lives of others. Our own attachments—or dislikes—were to people we saw every day, in settings that included, however invisibly, ourselves. Our issues were still all local and personal.

In our limited student sphere, we were vaguely aware that sororities and fraternities were in control of student social life, that athletics were important (almost as important as courses themselves), that grades were the measurement of achievement in courses, and that two or four years later we would emerge from this potpourri of study, activities, work, and play, presumably matured and fully ready for the adult world of work and marriage. Like all freshmen, I received several invitations from sororities to their "rushing" parties. But after all the parties I did attend, I was not invited to become a "sister." Once again I had learned that I was not up to standard in some way—dress, manners, or social skills. Once again I took it as a reaffirmation of what I really knew. The Hansons, for some reason not altogether clear to me, were below accepted social standards, and properly so. I was hurt but not seriously wounded. In a foggy way I knew my place and I accepted it, at the same time feeling reasonably sure that I could well beat them all out, or certainly equal them, in grades and academic achievements.

THE SCHOOL OF SPEECH

The School of Speech was a small college in the university, and its students had all the benefits of intimacy with faculty, together with the sense that most of the professors knew most of the students personally and took an interest in their developing maturation and professional growth.

The four-year course at the School combined a liberal arts program in social studies and literature, elementary requirements in math and science, and a strong emphasis on all aspects of the speech program. As a freshman, I found that I enjoyed math and was a quick student in advanced algebra. At the end of the first semester I was excused from taking the final exam and came through with an A. Had there been any kind of vocational guidance or career planning in those days, I might have been directed to a math/science career, but all my advisers saw me as fixed in speech arts, and there I remained.

In decided contrast to the math experience, a freshman class with my mother's old classmate, Professor Lardner, should have told me and my mother that

I was in the wrong school. His comment after my first class presentation was, "You are dead from the neck down, Miss Hanson."

In many other ways, both in class and out, but mainly in a required course in economics in my sophomore year, I repeatedly felt I was hopelessly misplaced and unprepared. Many of my classmates were veterans of World War I, men who seemed much older than I, as some were by six or seven years. Unlike anything I had studied up to that point, economics was sheer theory. Yet to these veterans, it described or challenged life as they had experienced it. They asked questions that stretched my understanding; they debated with the professor, whom I could not think of opposing. Indeed, I barely comprehended him. At home, I begged mother to let me leave school, just to give me time to grow up enough to behave in some kind of adult way. She felt I had not given the class and indeed the whole college experience a fair trial. She said I must not be a quitter. I stayed on.

One course in my sophomore year was all positive. To fulfill my science requirement, I had chosen astronomy. My professor, Mr. Fox, to whose person and subject matter I was very attracted, invited me, along with a few other students, to get some hands-on experience with the telescope. Northwestern was part of a consortium of universities in this field, and as such was carrying through a program of photographing double stars. Our night sessions were followed by a social hour in the astronomy library, where Mr. Fox had set up one of the very first new radios. These informal sessions became the center of my interest for the entire academic year, and in fact continued during the summer following the course. I came to know the graduate assistants and spent evening after evening, sometimes whole nights, at the telescope with one or another of them. But it was the social hours, centering on the new invention of the radio, and particularly its offerings of the opera, which provided me a continuing expansion of my information and sensibilities. By modern standards, the radio reception would seem pitiful, but nevertheless, the world of opera opened up as an intensely emotional experience, in which the vocal and instrumental arts combined. I had had no tutelage in understanding music; to this day, I only vaguely apprehend it as beautiful, even magnificent, but sharing it with the group of students, assistants, and the professor made these evenings memorable.

By my junior year I had overcome the sophomoric sense of inadequacy. My sociology professor, Mr. Bailey, whose class I repeatedly praised in my diary, gave me a C on my first paper, a daunting start. Yet by the midpoint of the semester, my diary records, "Today's class was a constant alarm, set to wake the blissfully unconscious to a vitally interesting world!"

By the final semester of my senior year, I applied to Bernard DeVoto for admission to his class, Creative Writing, which friends had highly recommended. Despite the fact that I had not fulfilled his requirements for admission, he responded positively to my written inquiry. As I worked through that semester, I spent many evenings with Benny and his wife, Avis, and Wesley Cook, a student of theology, to whom I was by now deeply attached. Avis, who was not much older than I, and her husband seemed to me the most sophisticated people I had yet met. They were of course widely read and widely acquainted. Benny was actually on the verge of publishing his first book, a novel; indeed, he let me read it in manuscript.

The four years in the School of Speech were designed to give the students a taste of its whole curriculum, including theater arts, interpretation of literature, and speech making to achieve various ends: presentation of facts, argumentation, and persuasion. Interpretation was a one-on-one coaching tutorial, which we took each of the four years, with a different professor. Argumentation might culminate in membership on the debating team, which entailed rigorous exercise to prepare for competition with other university teams. Making the team meant receiving credit and implied a good deal more work than the typical course. I wanted nothing so much as to make the team. I tried out again and again without success and finally made it the second semester of my junior year. By my senior year I was captain of the team, which won a series of victories in the Big Ten universities.

Another competitive experience was in an intramural oratorical contest. Contestants wrote their own oratorical submissions. I won round after round, thoroughly enjoying trips to other universities in the Big Ten, and in my senior year came home with the winner's cup.

The professor whom I most appreciated was Lew Sarett, who in my junior and senior years taught advanced courses in public speaking. A Native American, he was an outdoorsman and naturalist, a poet, and a performer of all these arts and crafts on the public stage. In my eyes he was the epitome of what the School of Speech could offer in a teacher. He took time to see me for discussions of my shortcomings, which he did frankly and kindly. I feared these critiques, but at the same time, I had some sense that they were the stuff I needed and must use. The crowning of this relationship came in the fall of my senior year, when he asked me to teach his freshman class once while he was away. His praise as we evaluated the experience was almost too much to endure. He summed it up by saying, "You have the finest brain of any woman I know."

Miss Lovedale, my senior coach in interpretation, was a lady in dress and manner. After months of criticizing my dress, my posture, and my not infrequent lack of sufficient preparation for our weekly sessions, she finally decided that my appearance in my senior recital was "promising." All the women students who planned to go on the stage or into elocution wanted to work with her. For my part, I was never really comfortable with her, but I certainly recognized that her approval was its own cachet. It contributed to the growing sense of competency with which I left the school, expecting to find a job as a teacher of public speaking and a debate coach in some high school.

Extracurricular Activities

At least three organizations came to play an important part in my college life. The first was the student YWCA under the directorship of Miss Hill (the "secretary," as the Y called its program staff members). The second was the Epworth League of the local Methodist Church. The third group developed later, perhaps as late as my junior year. It was the Liberal League, which I may have even helped found, and in which, in any case, I developed a strong proprietary interest.

Each put me into a close circle of like-minded and congenial people who became friends and coworkers and who reinforced my rapidly developing interest in social and political questions. Each contributed to my education, giving a permanent slant to what became my lifelong way of dealing actively, as well as intellectually, with social issues. Each even gave shape to my early career choices.

As I later came to know, the Y was then in an important phase of its own development, one strongly influenced by the Social Gospel movement in the Protestant churches, a movement guided by the principles of Christian living in the modern world: "If Christ walked the streets of Chicago today, what would he do and say?" Responses were framed to deal with social problems of poverty, race, war, the rights of women—indeed, of all God's children in their struggles to deal with unemployment, child labor, urban tenement housing, long hours and low wages at work, the struggles of unions to exist and to improve the conditions of their members, the prevalence of work-induced disease (tuberculosis above all, but we also read of radium and lead poisoning), the prevalence of industrial accidents, the need for factory inspection.

Before long I was a member not only of the student Y but of its executive body, the cabinet, where programs were planned and strategies for action or further education worked out. The Y taught us through the "discussion method." A leader, perhaps Miss Hill but very often a senior woman, led off with questions about campus or off-campus issues. We were encouraged to ask questions, make comments, discuss the topic's relevance to us and our acquaintances, study its content, and then move step by step to a consideration of remedies and a program for achieving them. The process was action-oriented, and that approach spoke to my impatience with abstract discussion of these questions.

I was deeply challenged by new issues and new views. I felt concern for people less fortunate than I and wanted desperately to do something to correct their misfortunes and what I came to see as the systemic evils that caused them. Y conferences and weekend retreats offered the opportunity for concentration on such issues. We came in touch with people outside the Y—local leaders in the social gospel movement, theologians, educators, social workers, professors, a labor man or two, some socialists. I was seventeen, and a new world was opening up to me.

23

New friends and challenging ideas were also part of my attraction to the young people's group, the Epworth League at the Methodist Church. Several circumstances probably combined to pull me there. Northwestern was historically a Methodist foundation, and the First Methodist Church was sometimes called the university church. The pastor there was Dr. Ernest Tittle, a veteran of World War I and an outspoken pacifist. His sermons inspired both heated opposition and warm espousal. Supported by Dr. Tittle, the Epworth League turned more and more to the issues that he raised of nonviolence, antiwar activity, and advocacy of pacifism. In addition, my family by this time was no longer a unit in its attachment to the Presbyterian Church favored by my mother. Fred was singing in the Episcopal choir; Tedo was attracted to a girl attending the Congregational Church, and Father had become interested in Christian Science. This made it easy for me to move over to Methodism and become involved in the Epworth League, although I did not join the Methodist Church till almost the end of my time in college.

The Liberal League had a connection with the national Student League for Industrial Democracy (SLID), whose speakers' bureau supplied us with a rich offering of nationally known liberals as speakers at our meetings, people who had shaped the Progressive movement from the beginning of the century onward. Some were student leaders, mainly from such Eastern campuses as Harvard, Columbia, and Johns Hopkins, who seemed to us very sophisticated veterans of civil liberties battles and labor strikes. More memorable still, however, were the famous—among them, social economist and editor of *Labor Age*, Harry Laidler, controversial author Paul Blanshard, future Socialist presidential candidate Norman Thomas, Rabbi Stephen Wise, educator John Dewey, American Civil Liberties Union cofounder Roger Baldwin, theologian Reinhold Niebuhr, *Nation* editor Oswald Garrison Villard, IWW poet Ralph Chaplin, and Alexander Meikeljohn of the University of Wisconsin. Occasionally a labor leader was a speaker. Our attempt, however, to invite the notorious Socialist educator, Scott Nearing, was blocked by the university president himself.

There came as well, student leaders of the *"Nie wieder Krieg"* ("No More War") movement that was founded in Germany, Holland, and Belgium following World War I. These young men were all pacifists. Their charisma as well as their commitment to nonviolence captured us entirely. Their visit sparked my interest in postwar Germany, its young people, and their Youth Movement facing the overwhelming problems of building a democracy on the ashes of the old empire. It was an interest that, as it developed, would weave a significant thread throughout the fabric of my entire life.

By my junior year, as a result of these exposures, I began with other friends to explore life outside the university. Six of us visited the Dill Pickle Club in Chicago, a well-known haunt for hoboes and radicals. My diary observation, after an evening there with several couples, was that the radicals "seemed to try too hard to be radical . . . while we, the visiting bourgeoisie, arrived in such numbers that we saw almost only ourselves." I think it was at the Dill Pickle Club that I met Dr. Ben Reitman, one of Emma Goldman's lovers, who had shared with Goldman the horror of the Colorado Coal and Iron strike, when the company transported the strikers to the desert and left them there to find their way out of the extreme heat and cold, if they could. Reitman had later come to Chicago and established a medical practice whose chief clients were prostitutes, but much of his time went into his radical activities, which were loosely related to the IWW. He founded an institution called the Hobo College, where radicals made up the faculty. I attended some of these "classes" out of fascination with the students, who for the most part participated heatedly in ideological discussions. One student at the Hobo College, Nels ("Andy") Anderson, was an older student at the University of Chicago, studying the new science of sociology in the new field of occupational sociology. He later turned his Ph.D. dissertation on the hobo into a book. Andy became a lifetime friend with whom I worked years later in Germany in the days immediately after World War II. Ben Reitman's daughter, Helen, studied at Northwestern for a year or so, and we became friends. She was the first lesbian whom I had met.

Some of us also visited Hull House, perhaps through connections established during the visit of the European pacifist students. Acquaintances formed through these visits included Jane Addams herself and her assistant, Bill Byron, later a sociology professor at Northwestern. There were also members of the Women's International League for Peace and Freedom (WILPF), of which Addams was a founding member. I became acquainted, too, with men who had spent the war in federal prisons as conscientious objectors, a fraternity who now were welcomed at Hull House, where they could meet each other in freedom.

One consequence of these Hull House contacts was that I was invited to speak to groups all over Chicago. Pacifism was an answer to the doctrinaire patriotism of the pervasive American Legion. On a soapbox, long before the days of electronic voice magnification, my School of Speech training served me, as it did often throughout the next decade, by providing me with lung power sufficient for my hastily gathered and curious audiences. Among the people I met in this period, under varying circumstances, were Paul Douglas, professor of economics at the University of Chicago and later senator from Illinois; Robert Morse Lovett, a famous professor at the University of Chicago; and Alice Henry, an Australian, who wrote many books on American women workers and their unions.

A MIXED BAG OF LOYALTIES

I soon counted myself a convinced pacifist. In part, it was the ongoing influence of Dr. Tittle; in part, the model of the European visitors and of the women in the WILPF. In a memorable meeting with the Liberal League, one of these women presented the pacifist movement as a countermeasure to the evil conspiracies of international munitions makers, who, in selling arms for profit, had allied themselves with the military class of our own country and had grown powerful in their administration of the recent world war.

One of the many Liberal League strategies for disseminating the pacifist doctrine and increasing our membership and influence on campus was to attend student conferences as delegates and attempt to convince these student organizations to join our rolls. We appealed to a fund that Jane Addams and Robert Morse Lovett administered to support our travel expenses. They gave us one thousand dollars, a good deal of money at this time. One organization that we hoped to persuade to endorse pacifism was the Student Volunteers, a national organization of students who had answered the call to be Christian missionaries in countries abroad. I was one of five persons named to go to their convention in Indianapolis. In preparation, we gathered material, rehearsed tactics, divided responsibilities, and, once there, worked like beavers to cover all the workshops and to raise the antiwar issue. In my own case, I tended to overdo my welcome and was booed for attempting to take the floor too often. Nevertheless, we won a clear victory with the Volunteers' endorsement of our antiwar pledge.

At the same time that I identified myself with these liberal or even radical issues of the time, I remained to a considerable degree a woman student of the times, subject to peer group tradition and romantic student customs. By my junior year I was a leading student on campus, despite the fact that I had no sorority affiliation. I had, in fact, rejected an invitation to join a sorority in my junior year that had come, I felt, too late. I no longer needed that kind of help in establishing a circle of friends. I recognized that I could make it on my own and that on the whole I was leading a more interesting life than most sorority sisters.

Perhaps it was an event in that year that made clear to me for the first time that my chief handicap was that of being a woman. As the academic year began, the top item on the campus agenda, as laid out by the student paper, the *Daily Northwestern,* was the upcoming football season. A request, probably from the athletic department, came to the junior class for us to give up our traditional right to put forward a woman as class president and instead allow a man, preferably a member of the football team, to take over that office in the interest of establishing a super male presence, in support of Northwestern as the putative champion of the Big Ten in 1922. I allowed myself to be impressed with the fact that this proposal came labeled as a one-time sacrifice that would testify to university alumni and off-campus supporters that every element of the student body stood solidly behind the team, joining in its determination to win the championship. The persuasive element was the old, presumably flattering request to the ladies to stand behind their men. No administrative fiat or post facto announcement would have had the same effect. I, no less than my sisters, felt that we had done the right thing, and even the heroic thing.

It is hard now, so many years later, to understand myself as I was in the early 1920s. I saw and accepted the fact that men dominated the world on both a personal and a global scale. I clearly enjoyed the position of campus prominence I had achieved from representing a somewhat unpopular political view. But I must have taken for granted that women on their own could not achieve leadership. They could influence outcomes, but victory would depend on men. I think that during these college years and for a long time afterward I wanted to be accepted by men, but to achieve that meant using men as models, learning how to live with them, speak their language, think the way they thought, and aim for a career like theirs. I am sure I had already heard women say that to achieve this kind of goal, one needed to work twice as hard and be twice as good as the men, since one would always be measured by their "objective standards." But I accepted that price, mainly because it did not occur to me that one might set up other standards and goals.

An Unwitting Radical

At the same time I was a visible and identifiable "leader" in the Epworth League. We continued to discuss antiwar issues and counted ourselves very largely pacifist. One Sunday evening we planned a meeting at which one of the conscientious objectors, Brent Dow Allison, would speak. On that occasion we were visited unannounced by the local American Legion group, bearing an American flag, and with some members in uniform. Dr. Tittle was as usual present. He called for an orderly meeting, a request that was on the whole fulfilled. In the course of a tense but not particularly tumultuous session, one of our self-invited guests asked for a raised-hand vote of those willing to take a pledge that under no circumstances would we support our country in carrying on a war. He did not ask for, nor did we take, a list of names of those who raised their hands. But someone else did. A reporter from the *Chicago Tribune* shortly published a detailed report of the episode, in which he identified me as the group leader and presumably the president of the Northwestern student pacifists, "the 38." (The number indicated the accepted number of those who had raised their hands.)

Thereafter I was pursued for weeks by reporters from several newspapers, all hungry for stories, and not just of pacifists and pacifism. Above all, they wanted to name me as an IWW member, or better yet, a Communist. I could only reply that I knew such people but was not one of them. The *Tribune* carried some version of this story about Northwestern student radicals on its front page longer than it had ever carried any other story. I received mail both laudatory and accusatory. I got to know several Northwestern alumni who were proud of their alma mater and of her present students. The most important for me was Lillian Herstein, a graduate of the class of 1916 and a founder of the Teachers Union in Chicago, where she was a teacher at Crane Junior College. She remained a lifelong activist and civil libertarian, and our paths would cross again several times.[1]

On the campus itself, the *Daily Northwestern* carried a tirade against "the 38." A petition began to circulate, urging the administration to bar us from the university. The Reserve Officer Training Corps (ROTC) issued a statement calling for our expulsion from the university. A patriotic demonstration was planned for Patten Gymnasium. Rumors of a bomb plot by the pacifists against Northwestern's president, Walter Dill Scott, began to circulate. Alan Monroe, my close friend, was expelled from his fraternity, and all of us who had been named in the press reports were to some degree ostracized.

Halfway through my final semester, the president called me to his office. Against this background, I feared the worst. His problem, he said, was that because of the continuing "bad publicity for the university" he faced poor public relations. To deal with it, he needed to know who "the 38" were. Would I tell him? I tried to explain that we had no pacifist organization as such; that we were for the most part members of the Epworth League with no official connection with the university; that indeed the count of thirty-eight in support of an anti-war pledge was a highly informal count, requested by the American Legion. I had the clear impression that my explanation did not satisfy his need. Indeed, I thought I heard him hint that he might interfere, either by delay or by fiat, with my graduation.

I pointed out that it was not I who had publicized this matter but the press in its hunger for news. The president then raised the matter of his earlier decision against allowing the Liberal League to bring Scott Nearing to the campus. He insisted he had never forbidden Nearing's appearance; indeed, it was contrary to his principles to do so. His intent, he maintained, had been to avoid the damaging publicity that followed Nearing's appearance wherever he went! A few weeks later, when the League submitted the name of Bertrand Russell as a speaker, he too was prohibited from appearing on the campus. The reason given this time was that Russell led an immoral personal life. It was my first exposure to the ongoing practice at many universities at the time of making the victim the culprit.

HOME AND SOCIAL LIFE

My parents were sharply divided over the whole affair. As a result of many years of indoctrination by the Spanish War Veterans' Association, Father had become a patriot. He deplored my activities, and family discussion became pretty hostile from time to time. Mother, on the other hand, chose to go to meetings with me. I felt then that she chose this way more to support me than to support the causes I espoused. I thought of her as tolerant and curious but not punitive. We never discussed her role or her reason for choosing thus to share part of my life. These experiences marked the beginning of my ongoing separation from the family's accepted values and the substitution of my own values and loyalties, however confused and inconsistent, for theirs. But the independence I was acquiring was entirely intellectual. It was only after graduation that I began to think realistically of living entirely on my own, for then it was understood that the child had become an adult and would of course take full responsibility for herself.

In the meantime I continued perforce to live at home. Aside from a few odd jobs on and off campus, I was totally dependent economically on my parents, a fact of which my father frequently reminded me, particularly when tuition was due. But living at home, and having two younger brothers there, heightened the assumption that I was still a child, with my mother the guardian of our good behavior. In the spring of my sophomore year she took me to task for staying out late at night and being with friends in public places, even on Sundays. "It doesn't look right for a girl who has a home to spend Sunday evening at an eat shop with her friends," she pointed out. I wondered in my diary whether this was a way the older generation had of holding back their young as long as possible. And yet, in her defense, I supposed that "If one has only one daughter, one naturally wanted her to do the right and conventional thing, i.e., bring her friends home to meet the family."

My dependence on the family never went so far as to make me feel repressed. Rather, I felt their admonitions were well meant but no longer the way to deal with grown children. They were doing their best, but it did not fit my needs. I was constantly reevaluating what I thought Mother and Father stood for. With Father, I began to hear and want to correct his ungrammatical sentences and to differ sharply and occasionally openly with what I saw as his misguided patriotism when he said, for instance, "This country first and above all others"; "This country right or wrong"; or "This country, on the model of Great Britain, a benevolent imperialism—see our benign imperialism in Cuba and the Philippines." Closer to home, I found his almost abject devotion to Mother and total deference to her ideas as evidence of his dependence on, even subordination to, her. At the same time I was critical of his leaving all the household work to her, when they had taken over a large house on Sherman Avenue as a rooming house that would produce income to make ends meet.

I brought this complaint to Mother, asking if she weren't working beyond her strength and therefore why she didn't call on him for help. She hoped I would never raise these questions within his hearing. Her answer was an apology for him: "He has enough to handle." I became more and more annoyed at what I saw only as his exploitation of her and her protection of him. I began to feel embarrassed for them both for not dealing with their relationship more openly and rationally. In short, I began to feel superior to them. I felt I knew better than they how to organize their lives.

As for Mother, I became less tolerant of her devotion to church and WCTU as the sources of her spiritual and worldly faiths. I was finding my own beliefs in both those areas to be quite other than hers. I began to share the growing public opposition to the proposed Eighteenth Amendment to the Constitution, which would prohibit the use and marketing of all alcoholic beverages, and I disagreed with her belief that cigarette smoking in any form or quantity was taboo. My differences developed slowly and hesitantly. They hardened into assertive statements of my changing views, which I knew hurt them both but which I nevertheless felt compelled to express.

At the same time I remained, on the whole, the good daughter. I took walks along the lake shore or sat on the beach with my dates. Whether our time together consisted of serious talk or of flirtatious banter, we always ended our evenings with a sundae at our favorite ice cream parlor. The Epworth League was a good place to meet companionable men, interested in pursuing the questions raised over pacifist issues and the university's reaction to "the 38." Although we were not a formal organization, many of us were intimates, who worked hard on pacifist projects, saw each other on or off campus, and enjoyed these personal evenings. I took pleasure in dancing, though my talents in this field were barely passable.

My interest in boys developed late. My first experience was with Mike Cohen in the Green Bay High School and was almost casual. He sent me some gifts of flowers and candy. I was flattered by his attention, but I have no recollection of having had a "date." I assume we went to some school events together. In any case we parted forever when I left Green Bay.

At Northwestern I had many male friends with whom I walked and worked and played. Howard Becker, later the head of sociology at Wisconsin, was one of these. Howard came to the university several years later than most of us did, very wise in the ways of the world and very widely read, having grown up with his father in the West, where schools were rare and lives were very mobile. He was the first person who talked to me about homosexuals, both male and female, and always in unpleasant, rough terms, which he had learned from his father's companions. He was completely independent, attracted the attention of professors as a candidate for exchanges with foreign students, and took such a position, as a return engagement with our German pacifist friends for a year in Germany when I was a junior or senior. His first book on the German Youth Movement was a product of this experience. When I, considerably later, had my opportunity to go to a German university, I relied strongly on Howard for contacts and information.

Alan Monroe, a speech major, was another good friend, and I thought seriously about him as a partner. He was a constant companion and coworker in both the Epworth League and the Liberal League, where we joined forces in all their social and programmatic activities. Yet when the junior prom came along, I had no invitation from a male friend. I invited one to be my partner, an apolitical man I knew as a classmate, rather than one of my more intimate friends.

But that year I met Wesley Cook and things began to change. He and I became a couple. Wesley was working his way through college with the help of a scholarship granted him as the son of a Methodist minister. Among various jobs he was assigned was that of janitor in the School of Speech in the late afternoons and early evenings. Our first and frequent meeting place was in one of the practice rooms on the third floor of Annie May Swift Hall, where I would go to practice my interpretive readings. From the first we were drawn to each other, but it was perhaps months before we said anything about it or enjoyed our first kiss. I was for some time, even after graduation from college, not fully persuaded that Wesley was in every respect to be preferred over Alan. Meanwhile, Alan continued to visit me at home, joining in the family card games, walking me home from meetings, working closely with me on conferences and programs.

HORIZON HOUSE

One project that several of us took on in the late spring followed from the continuing friendships and acquaintances at Hull House. It was to assist over the summer in the management of a new undertaking called Horizon House. Several of the Hull House pacifists conceived of renting for the summer a big house on the North Shore that could be used as a conference center. We students would staff the house as "worker bees" to serve weekend conferences and even weeklong seminars on peace issues. Evelyn Byron, wife of Jane Addams's assistant, Bill Byron, and a social worker in a Chicago agency, would be in charge of programs and invitations to participants. The house Evelyn decided on was both attractive and suitable, near the lake beaches and not far from the summer opera at Ravinia.

Visitors came to Horizon House in a steady stream, including many from Europe. Among them were women who had shared the experience of the 1917 Ford peace ship that had carried American delegates to Switzerland for a women's world conference in a last-ditch attempt to end World War I before the United States was drawn into it. I vividly remember Rosa Schwimmer, a Hungarian who came to Horizon House with an entourage of Central European women and their American hostesses. Madame Schwimmer was a brilliant pianist whose daily concerts were a special joy. Hopes were high that summer that the recently established League of Nations had the means to establish world peace. An immediate issue was whether the United States could be brought into the League despite President Wilson's failure to achieve this earlier.

Wesley and I volunteered as two of the worker bees, along with other students both from Northwestern and Chicago. We found many hours to be together for long talks on the nearby beach. It was these hours that led to close friendship and even love. The fact that at the same time we were working on a project to which we were both dedicated intensified our personal relationship. We ended the summer, with its elevating experiences and acquaintances, with our hopes for world peace fortified.

TO MARRY OR NOT TO MARRY

Wesley and I began to discuss the possibility of marriage even in the Horizon House summer, but I held back. While I had no clear-cut picture of my future career or personal life, I wanted to shape each of them for myself, however they might develop. Wesley was studying to be a Methodist minister, and I saw marriage to a minister as marriage to his profession as well—a marriage for which the wife's job description was completely prescribed and full time. Wesley was, I am sure, completely genuine in believing that we could draw our own pattern and that neither of us need adopt either traditional or imposed functions or ways of living. Yet, despite his confidence that he could shape his own life and allow me to shape mine, I was still not fully reassured by his view of our marital future.

My agonizing about being a minister's wife was based on the example of my poor, dear mother-in-law-to-be, measured against the current stereotypes of what a minister's helpmeet might or ought to be. With her image before me, I saw myself as a Sunday school teacher, leader of youth groups, visitor to the elderly and the sick, mediator of disagreements in the congregation, organizer of bake sales, guest at Sunday dinner with one after another of the families in the congregation, attendant at weddings, funerals, and baptisms, hostess for my husband's dinner visitors, substitute teacher in the public schools to bring in supplementary money to the impoverished household, and activist in the women's societies. Such an image left no minute for myself and little time for a personal life with my husband. It was not a life I wanted, and if it were thrust upon me, I did not believe I could long endure it. At no time did it occur to me that I had never met Ernest Tittle's wife, nor any other ministers' wives, and that I had no idea how they shaped their lives.

My picture was drawn entirely from what I had observed on visits to the senior Cooks, when Wesley's father was still actively ministering to congregations in one small Michigan town after another. During these years he was mainly engaged in preparing rather single-mindedly for his retirement. To do so he carried out a very secular plan. He would become a fruit farmer on land near Traverse City, where he shortly bought an established but somewhat neglected orchard. Its demands fully occupied him, and he had very little time for his parish and his parishioners. His wife was drawn into both sides of his overactive life. She helped out by running a fruit and baked goods stand in front of the house. She was an excellent cook and winter and summer baked the goods she sold. She picked cherries and peaches in season and oversaw the "girls" from the mental hospital whom she hired as pickers in the orchard; in addition, she managed the bills and the payroll, while he negotiated mortgages and loans, trucked fruit to market in Detroit, sprayed the trees, planted new acreage, and each morning at breakfast laid out the tasks for his wife to accomplish during the day. It was an authoritarian household that embraced but neglected the churches he served while serving, almost slavishly, the demands of the new undertaking that was to sustain him in old age and his approaching retirement.

In addition to my doubts about what would become of me if I married Wesley, I saw him as living in a philosophical dimension that I had never experienced nor really wanted to enter. In my junior year I had become a regular attendant at the Methodist Church and looked to Dr. Tittle as guide in both religious and secular matters. I was, however, hesitant about joining the church; I continued to attend it, but with decreasing regularity. I noted in my diary that on one Sunday I found Dr. Tittle "inspiring, but not convincing." A few months later I must have raised with him the question of my joining the church, as much to explain and excuse myself for not having done so earlier as for any conviction that I ought to take the step. My reason for hesitation was that I often found the church and its members self-satisfied and even hypocritical. Dr. Tittle was patient. In an effort to be helpful, he suggested that I not join until I felt fully ready. "The church, you must know," he pointed out, "is not the Kingdom of God, but is only a means to that end." When one of my friends, Jim, an older student and war veteran who described himself as a "humanist" rather than a Christian, spoke in the Epworth League on the topic "How Can We Know God?" he substantiated many of my doubts. That evening, for the first time, I openly debated Dr. Tittle when he responded to the questions Jim raised. And yet shortly thereafter I told Dr. Tittle I was ready to join the church, "since I have come to see its reality." Nevertheless, my church attendance became even less frequent, and by the time I graduated I could only describe my religious state as being a "booming, buzzing confusion, in which I am unable to come to terms with its questions."

Having rejected any positive position, I had no notion of whether I now held a negative view of religion and its institutions. Did I owe someone a statement such as Jim had made in his presentation to the Epworth League? Could I put it all together coherently? Was it more a feeling than a belief—or nonbelief? I was in fact not ready to say either yes or no. I was not sure this was an appropriate worldview for a minister's wife, and I feared it might be a barrier between Wes and me.

Yet more and more I was in love with Wes. I don't believe that it occurred to me to try to dissuade him from continuing to prepare for the career he had chosen. Nor did he spend much time contemplating its eventual accomplishment; it would come in its own due course. We would spend these years together and, knowing each other well and having both become established with work we enjoyed, would continue to incorporate our separate lives in a single and acceptable whole. The immediate future needed no live-or-die decisions or debate. We would go on living in the present, which would serve as a training ground for a future that we could manage.

THE JOB SEARCH BEGINS

So ended our college years. Throughout the summer I had been sending out applications for a job as a high school teacher of public speaking. I received only discouraging replies, which I put down largely to my age. I was indeed only twenty, and a protected, immature, middle-class daughter with a record—

thanks to the *Tribune*—that might brand me as a young woman possessed of dangerous thoughts and radical companions. Wesley was going on to graduate school in theology at Garrett Institute, bordering the Northwestern campus. I contemplated finding part-time work in that school and enrolling for a master's degree.

It was late in August when a happy, but accidental, circumstance came my way. It was the beginning of a pattern that was repeated many times in my later job searches and was one that I saw for many years as descriptive of my working life. Quite suddenly and unexpectedly, I was offered a job.

3

JOBS AND JOBS—AND A MODERN MARRIAGE:
1924-1928

At a Hull House meeting in the late summer of 1924, I sat next to a pleasant man who introduced himself as Paul Benjamin, the head of a family service agency, the Family Society, in Indianapolis. He asked what I did or was planning to do, and when I told him that I had no job, indeed was in a desperate search for one, he offered me a position as a junior social worker in his agency. I accepted on the spot.

JOB 1: INDIANAPOLIS

When I got back home and told my parents I had a job, my father's first question was, "What are you going to earn?" I didn't know. If I had even thought to raise such a question in that odd and spontaneous interview, I would have been too embarrassed to ask my newfound benefactor. His was the largesse; my response was simply gratitude. In any case, a job was a job and would surely pay enough to live in a modest way. As it turned out, it paid ninety dollars a month, but there were no deductions in the twenties. My father furnished a railroad pass to Indianapolis, and with a few dollars in my purse, which Mother thought wise to advance me, I reported for work, where I was assigned to a friendly and helpful supervisor to begin to learn how to be a social worker.

When my professor of sociology, T. D. Eliot, heard that I was now a social worker, he wrote Benjamin an indignant letter, assuring him that I had no training for such a job (hardly a profession in those days)—as indeed I had not—and implying that I must have presented myself for it under false pretenses. Benjamin showed me the letter and assured me he had not been misled.

As a junior in the agency, I was introduced slowly to the responsibilities of a family visitor. I was given a caseload of five families who had applied for assistance and was tutored a bit in doing initial interviews, before being sent out into the poorer streets of Indianapolis. I was quickly overwhelmed by the reality of the problems of people I had up till now only heard about under such generalizations as "the poor." This was years before the United States knew anything of public welfare and social security. Unemployment was widespread, and Indianapolis was filled with people who in desperation had moved out of Appalachia—from Kentucky, West Virginia, Tennessee—in a futile search for work in the city.

The Family Society had limited funds, mainly thought of as "emergency help" to "tide people over" until "they could get on their feet." We were expected to go to the grocery store with our clients to "help them shop" in the most economical way. While I thought I had been doing this—either with or at the behest of my mother—I had done it always with her carefully organized shopping lists in hand. I felt a kind of helplessness born of absolute ignorance of how a family could best "make out" against a background of total need. Clients lived in flats using their broken-down car seats as furniture, babies were everywhere, and often another was on the way. We were given no tutoring in dealing with the possibility of birth control, about which I had heard, but only in the abstract— that it was a good, even necessary thing, espoused by a remarkable woman named Margaret Sanger, a heroine for all women. But about what she offered, how it might be used, how women might learn about it—even get it—I knew nothing. On a trip home that fall I visited Benny DeVoto, my senior English professor, and told him I was learning a whole new vocabulary. "Being in a family way," I said, meant being pregnant. I was genuinely surprised that he was already acquainted with the phrase.

Another expression that now became reality for me was "Ku Klux Klan." Indianapolis was then the Klan's national headquarters. In many of my clients' homes, KKK regalia were hanging on a hook on the door; pictures of demonstrations, even lynchings, might be on the mantel. Conversation rarely centered on these displays, but I realized I now knew people for whom the Klan's word was close to law. I do not remember having any African-American clients, and in thinking back, I have no explanation for this. To be sure, the African-American influx to the North had not reached the proportions that came somewhat later, but it had begun during World War I. Did our agency not serve them? There were certainly no African-American social workers on the staff. Was I by accident or design assigned only to the white poor? I do not know.

I made new friends with some of my colleagues but was more interested in the people I met at the Unitarian Church. The friendship that lasted a lifetime was with Mary Chase. We were soon hiking together in the country on Sundays, during which I heard stories of her fascinating family, so unlike my own.[1] I found other friends in the church—a group of men and women, deeply involved in Robert La Follette Sr.'s campaign for the presidency. I threw myself into this first and consuming political campaign for the fall of 1924. The campaign committee included some progressive ministers, local railroad union leaders, liberal teachers, leaders in women's organizations, and a lawyer or two. Although the campaign of the Progressive Party was probably hopeless from the beginning, as third party efforts have generally been in the United States, I was too inexperienced to have any doubts. The candidate was an outstanding man with a program and platform that spoke to all the public issues of concern to me. Moreover, Wisconsin, La Follette's home state, represented the very essence and model of progressivism, and his chief backers were the powerful allied railroad unions—a combination that seemed to me must be unbeatable. Our night of disappointment fell, however, with the national election in November, a few weeks before my twenty-first birthday, when I could have voted. Nevertheless, my first political experience had introduced me to a satisfying activity.

Another episode of political interest was the opportunity to hear Eugene V. Debs soon after my arrival in Indianapolis. On Labor Day I joined the small crowd that had come to hear the old man, recently released from many years in Leavenworth Prison as a political objector to World War I, and now once again the presidential nominee of the Socialist Party. I remember his slight figure, still able to make himself heard in an outdoor setting without amplification.

Both Wesley and Alan visited me in Indianapolis. Wesley came from Evanston, where he was now taking a graduate degree at Garrett Biblical Institute. Alan was not far away at Purdue University as a young professor. My landlady strongly advised me to choose Alan for a husband. But my heart, never more than warmed by Alan, belonged more and more to Wesley, although I still had serious doubts about becoming the wife of a Methodist minister. Wesley continued to assure me everything would and could be worked out to our own wishes. More and more I wanted to believe he was right.

My Indianapolis life ended, however, almost before it had begun. As Paul Benjamin told us a few weeks later, the Klan demanded, and apparently the agency's board of directors agreed, that Benjamin and those of his staff who were not natives of Indianapolis should leave, in the interests of contributing to solving the unemployment of local people who could take our places. Thanks to Benjamin, through his network of professional friends we were all placed in better-paying jobs elsewhere. For me it was to be a junior family visitor for the Provident Society in St. Louis, at a hundred and ten dollars a month— comparative riches and a totally new environment. I said a regretful good-bye to Mary, who gave me the names of old family friends who were living in Carondelet, the St. Louis district where I found myself assigned.

Job 2: St. Louis

The Provident Society was a much larger and more bureaucratically organized institution than its Indianapolis counterpart, as I learned in my first-day interview with the director.[2] It operated through a number of branches in various parts of the city, each under a district supervisor. Mine was a young and ambitious woman, Julie Altman, who took me immediately in hand.

Through some friendly advice, I found a boarding house occupied mainly by women social workers. For about six dollars a week I had a room and two meals a day. Although I found some of the women there interesting and even hospitable, and though I had a reasonably good working relationship with my coworkers in the district, I never became comfortable in my work in St. Louis. I was not prepared for it, and while I learned a good deal about how families in need could be helped, I never felt that I had within myself the resources for the understanding and sympathy they needed. I was too young, had been too sheltered, and was too inexperienced to do other than put all the blame for this on myself. That the system of social work might itself be an inadequate answer to improving on the way poor people lived was a matter quite beyond my understanding at the time.

I would never have been at all comfortable in St. Louis had it not been for Mary's friends, the Tuckermans, with whom I shortly made contact. Their faces and figures are still clear to me, as they sat around their dinner table, where I was a weekly guest, or as they strolled through their extensive, untended grounds, enjoying the long views from their rise above the Mississippi River. They were the parents of grown children, one boy still intermittently at home. Mr. Tuckerman was a member of an old St. Louis family and for years the full-time secretary of the City Club, a men's organization that was in the vanguard on many civic issues. His wife, very much in charge of house and family, was a Christian Science practitioner. Wesley stayed there when he came to visit me in the early spring.

Another St. Louis family, the Browns, was unique in my experience. When I met them, the family was headed by a widowed mother, called "Sweetie" by her grown children, Harold and Frances. Harold, known as "Brownie," and Frances were both unusually thin and tall with long bones and prominent, dark eyes. Neither Brownie nor Frances had ever had any formal schooling. Yet both of them were widely read in philosophy, history, and literature.[3] The Brown family led me to a change in career direction that influenced the rest of my life.

Brownie was an avid motorcyclist and used to travel widely on his machine. Although he was barely older than I, he had already worked closely with Roger Baldwin in his early undertakings in civil liberties cases and counted Baldwin as a friend and mentor. At Llano, one of many radical, presumably self-supporting enterprises at the time, through which the participants aimed to demonstrate a possible way of life outside the system of exploitation that capitalism represented to them, Brownie had fallen in love with and married Ruth Sutherland.[4] They had allied themselves with the group that assembled around William Zeuch to establish a labor-centered college, Commonwealth, which was now located at Mena, Arkansas.[5] In the course of our many conversations, I told them of my experiences and my interest in labor education, and soon they urged me to come to Commonwealth whenever I felt I could leave the St. Louis job. I was very tempted by all they told me of the building of the school and its opening in 1925. Everything there seemed possible, and I decided that at the end of 1925, after a year in St. Louis, I could decently leave.

With friendly but not regretful farewells I left St. Louis at Christmas, never to return. I went first to Evanston for the holidays. The fact that work at Commonwealth would pay nothing was no cause for me to hesitate about going. The school guaranteed the essentials—housing and food—and that seemed quite sufficient. My parents made no protest about my decision.[6] Neither did my new job raise any problems between Wesley and me; it was part of my search for meaningful employment. In January, with no apprehension and with keen anticipation I took the train to Mena, Arkansas.

JOB 3: COMMONWEALTH COLLEGE

At Commonwealth I met the odd and picturesque dissident group who had left Llano under William Zeuch's leadership to seek out land and put up the first buildings of a school, a few miles outside Mena. Though they were mainly faculty, a few had come as staff or even as students.[7] Zeuch was founder, president, and chair of the executive board. He lacked a sense of humor and was quite rigidly set in his own views, both on educational theory and the scientific method; he was a rationalist of the first order. While Zeuch was tolerant enough about allowing others to differ from him, he had no skill or talent for handling opposition that became direct and personal. Kate Richards O'Hare, a symbol of an earlier radicalism and of a recent martyrdom, lived intermittently at the school and was a member of its executive board.[8]

The faculty was soon to become sharply divided between its older and younger members, with Zeuch in early middle age caught between the generations. I, of course, was personally drawn to the younger group, composed of Brownie and Ruth and close friends of theirs, including Harold Coy and his mother.[9] Brownie and Coy had formed a fast friendship, expressed in their joint pen name, Harold Bronco, they used in their coeditorship of the Commonwealth paper, the *Fortnightly,* which became both a news sheet and a money raiser for the college. I was soon invited to work with Coy and Brownie on the newspaper. Coy knew and enforced the finest niceties of style, grammar, and punctuation. While I had not been a slouch in these matters in my schools, I learned from him and came to practice a pretty sound set of editors' rules under his tutelage. What I had particularly to learn was that composing the most didactic of speeches and the most straightforward reports are two quite different skills, each of which commands its own rule book and thesaurus.[10]

Zeuch was indeed the school's founder. But Brownie, both in his travels for the school and in his capacity as Bronco, was responsible for much of its growth and liveliness, its far-flung acquaintances, and its support throughout the progressive and radical communities. Brownie was unquestionably the leader of the younger group. He and his circle would become more and more critical of Zeuch and many of his decisions. They mocked Zeuch's favorite phrases— for example, his "you only amuse me" response to Brownie and his group, whose views he frequently refused to discuss at all, on the grounds that they were belief, not fact, something stated but not proved, not scientific.

SCHOOL LIFE

Daily life at Commonwealth was primitive. The school was meant to be self-supporting. We ate basically what we grew; we burned wood that was harvested from our nearby woodlands; afternoons were devoted to work, further building, and maintenance. Most of the women were kept busy in the kitchen or the laundry, working over a coal stove or an open fire. Gaslight and fuel existed only in cities, and electric light still waited on the rural electrification policies of the New Deal for wide introduction. Our menus were built around sweet potatoes; sweetening came mainly from molasses. We had meat when a pig was slaughtered.

I had a dormitory room in a rough-built, one-story structure, where each inhabitant had a bunk bed, a tin stove for heat in the short but cold winter, a rough table-desk, and a few bookshelves. I could now enter the career for which I had been trained; I would teach public speaking. I was urged by some of my new colleagues to also teach a course on the English novel. Depending on some of them to supply at least as much critical wit as I could possibly show, I undertook that job as well.

Entertainment for us as for many, many families at the time consisted of evenings of reading aloud to a group whose members busied themselves with tasks of repairing tools or clothing. From time to time and with a little rehearsal, we would read a play. Visitors came through Mena to see the new school and would lecture or report on their travels in return for lodging. We invited neighbors in for evenings of folk dancing. A. A. Milne was my discovery. As a new genre of adult entertainment, I read his poems and *Winnie the Pooh* with extraordinary pleasure for myself and my listeners. When shopping was necessary, a few of us would be selected to go off to town and were granted the reward of eating dinner for twenty-five cents at the one boardinghouse in Mena. There we could eat our fill of a home-cooked meal of mashed white potatoes, gravy and meat, four or five vegetables, and homemade pie for dessert. We took long hikes up and down the hills to the Oklahoma border about eight miles away, and we organized hayrides in our own wagons, to picnic with singing and talk under the stars.

When the semester ended in late spring, I was to travel as far as St. Louis with Brownie on his motorbike. So, on a May morning in 1926 I settled myself, not uncomfortably, on the pillion seat, took a grip on a handle in front of me, and we were off, over Arkansas and then Missouri roads, many of them ungraded and unpaved. At first I was stiff and cramped in my confined space, but after a few miles I began to relax and could dare to grip with only one hand, to turn to observe and admire the hilly scenery and to feel that this adventure had great possibilities for pleasure and new experience. Our route led eventually to the Mississippi River and then north along the river into Missouri. Although during the course of that first day's ride I must have climbed on and off the bike several times, as we prepared to dismount for the night, I could not lift a leg to get off the machine. With some help, Brownie lifted me straight up, stiff as a ramrod, and helped me up some stairs and into our host's house. I despaired of being able to start again, but in the morning I was somewhat better, though still in pain with every movement. By the second night, however, which we spent in Hannibal, Missouri, the birthplace of Mark Twain, I was free of both pain and stiffness and was quite adapted to pillion riding over Missouri roads. As a Mark Twain fan, I insisted on our playing the tourist in Hannibal for an hour or so, before moving on to St. Louis.

There our trip was over. We unpacked and bathed at Sweetie's, and soon I took the train back to Evanston to live with my parents for the summer. I spent much of the summer typing and mimeographing scenes from plays for the drama department at the School of Speech, and I quickly found some evening baby-sitting.

THE WEDDING

After this long absence, Wesley and I indulged in a more and more passionate courtship. We decided we must marry. Persuaded by Wesley, I joined him in designing our marriage as a free and open relationship in which each of us would accept the other as we were and as we would become. We would be independent of one another in our occupations, accepting that this meant that from time to time we would be living apart. I think that it did not occur to us that, for example, I would not return to Commonwealth in the fall. We would of course incorporate our various friendships into our joint lives. I would keep my own name.

On July 2 we announced to my parents that we would marry the next day. We had overlooked the need for a license. My father leapt into that breach and offered to get it for us on his lunch hour in Chicago the next day. He was clearly very relieved that we had finally come to this decision and half admitted that he had feared we would enter into a marital relationship without the proper ceremony.[11] We were agreed that Dr. Tittle, under whose auspices we had met at the Epworth League and whose church we had attended during the last year or two of college, would perform the ceremony and that it would be in the Simpson Street apartment. But a wedding on July 3 was not possible. Father could not substitute for Wesley in getting a license. Dr. Tittle was unavailable for a few days. Nor could Wes get a license on July 4. The wedding finally took place on the evening of July 6, 1926. Mother had insisted on a new dress for me—green silk with tan piping, quite the most elegant I had ever had. Dr. Tittle agreed to changes we wanted in the ceremony, changes that included omitting any promise on my part to obey my husband.

We found an apartment for the summer in a building at the corner of Emerson Street and Sherman Avenue, within easy walking distance of Wesley's work and of the campus where we were both spending much of our days. Wesley was working that summer as a night kitchen cleaner and dishwasher at the Orrington Hotel. He would come home very late at night, bearing leftovers or ice cream from the kitchen, wake me up, and we would have a feast of delicacies. The summer in Evanston was a long delight.

We visited Wesley's parents in a small Michigan town where his father had been assigned to the local Methodist church. Once more I saw in sharp focus the conventional life of the minister's wife, a weight that had caused me so much anxiety, lest it fall on me. But now I felt quite free of that possibility. Wesley had been right; we could shape our own lives.

When the time came to return to Commonwealth, we arranged that I would hitchhike there with Harold Coy. Blurred pictures of dusty countryside and endless farms are all that come back to me. We stuck to the roads through several days of mediocre luck with rides. Traffic was light and roads were narrow, hot, and dusty.

COMMONWEALTH AGAIN

Once back at the school, I had a series of visitors, including one of the old pacifist campaigners from Northwestern, Elizabeth Laws, and my brother Tedo, who considered for a time coming to Commonwealth, rather than returning to the Business School at Illinois. Wes joined me for his fall break.

Commonwealth's internal life, however, once again became the center of my existence. The differences between the ideas and wishes of young and old that had merely caused bad jokes and scornful laughter in the spring now intensified and centered mainly around Zeuch, the school's director.[12] Although he was, among many things, a strong believer in academic freedom—at least he was willing to surround himself with a faculty of rather widely differing views— Zeuch was at bottom what somewhat later came to be called a technocrat. He put his "reliance on the talented tenth and his mistrust of people [was decisive]," write the school's historians, Ray and Charlotte Koch.[13] The cutting issue this time was what we in the younger group saw as the need to democratize both the school's legal structure and its administration. The critical discussion centered on adding faculty and student representatives to the three-person board of directors.[14]

The final break occurred as the result of an editorial Brownie wrote in the *Fortnightly*. He had read a news article about the general strike of 1926 in England, which reported that the conservative government had offered scholarships to American students at British universities if they would take the jobs of strikers. As Brownie saw it, if American students were educationally qualified they could scab on British workers. His editorial asserted that there must be a limit to accepting all labor theory as equally valid. "[T]o take pains to accept all of them" so as to turn out well-grounded students is all very well as a point of departure, but at some point along the line of complete open-mindedness, there must be a halt if one was in danger of producing strikebreakers.

Although Brownie's editorial made no reference to Commonwealth and its leaders and faculty, Zeuch saw Brownie's ideas about a limitation on total freedom of advocacy in labor matters as criticism of Zeuch's views on free speech at the school. In short, the editorial was read to say that a labor school that would accept strikebreakers went so directly against the solidarity necessary to build a labor movement that it should be outlawed; that a board that would tolerate such a view badly needed the representation of outright labor interests, among others.

The local debate turned into an attack on Zeuch's so-called elitism and academic approach. The precipitating event occurred when Zeuch dismissed Brownie by letter while Brownie was on a fund-raising trip to New York. Immediately six of us resigned and prepared to leave the school at Christmas. The Koches's comment on the passing of this era sums up Commonwealth history at the end of its second year:

> Our teachers fell into two general categories: the old and the young. . . . In the early days some of the under-thirty instructors specialized in skepticism and indulged in boundless irreverence. They lived on mountain tops of intellectual, poetic, and artistic interest, from whose heights they hurled bolts of derision against dullards, money grubbers, exploiters and hypocrites. Mencken was their model. . . . They engaged in the eternal battle against the established, and frequently challenged notions of morality. . . . When Zeuch fired Harold Brown, and other faculty members left in protest, many students felt orphaned. Students who came later and had never been exposed to the extraordinary stimulation of their presence had no way of knowing what richness and variety they had missed.

Zeuch stayed on in full command for a few years, but in the end he had to bow to renewed opposition from our replacements.

RETURN TO EVANSTON

When I left Commonwealth at Christmas 1926, I was just past my twenty-third birthday. In making still another move, I felt that my life, in its continual job changes, was responding to little more than the luck of the draw. As I endeavor now to understand what each of these experiences gave me, I am sure that the year at Commonwealth presaged a sketch of my future in strong outline, even if at the time I did not plan or understand that. The fact is, however, that I came away with strong attachments to the Parnassians, a tie that has lasted all our lifetimes. I had also gained satisfactory experience in adult education. Although many of the students at Commonwealth were my seniors, in all respects they were engaged with me in a joint enterprise, a give-and-take approach out of which I learned as much as they. I had come to see how the adult education of working people fitted a pattern that might shape my own life. I had begun as well to understand how individual life experiences at work were the stuff of which economics was made; how to read literature so that it had personal meaning; and that if life were to be improved, individuals had to combine in organizations to acquire enough power to produce change. I had been part of building a functioning, powerful movement, and I had Brownie and Coy to thank for their rigorous criticism of my writing. Moreover, I had matured to the degree that I had more self-confidence; I was ready to take steps on my own in meeting people and undertaking projects.

JOB 4: THE CHICAGO YWCA

I started at once to look for a job. Wes was still working on his M.A. at Garrett and somewhat unsure of what was to come next. The issue of my place in his professional life was still a point of some doubt and discussion between us. It is possible that I went straight into the job market to make sure I was not to be taken as his dependent; certainly his earnings from manual work of various kinds were no guarantee at this point of even his self-support. Rather, we assumed that my income would secure us both until he could enter his professional career.

I thought of course of teaching, but it was a bad time of year to find a teaching job. I had always been grateful that my father had made me learn touch typing when I was about eleven, for I have often said that every academic should, as well as earning a degree, have learned a trade on which he or she could rely when professional employment was not available. I advertised myself as a secretary and rather quickly was promised a job by an architectural firm in Evanston; before that arrangement could be consummated, however, an acquaintance from the Hull House circle told me that Anne Guthrie, executive secretary of the Chicago YWCA, whom I had met casually while I was still in college, was looking for a private secretary. A long interview with her secured me the job, and I quickly made my choice to go to the Y.

Although the Y then and later played an important part in my life, I had only a vague idea of what a city Y, in contrast to the one on campus, might do and what aims and principles underlay its program. My previous Y activity on campus had of course been a stimulating and satisfactory experience and had certainly informed me that the urban Y, like the campus branch, was a center of social commitment and activism. I took the job with great anticipation, for implicitly it promised considerably more than clerical duties.

The Central Branch of the Chicago YWCA was the home of its executive offices as well as offering recreational, physical, educational, and social activities to its members. Other branches with similar programs but drawing different ethnic and social groups were situated on the West Side in the garment district, and on the South Side in the black district, with programs designated for African-American women. A board of directors governed the institution, with branch boards watching over local developments and programs. Central Branch, where I was to work, was located in the Loop on East Randolph Street between Wabash Avenue and Michigan Boulevard, and occupied two floors or so of a midtown office building. As I took over in Anne's office, her open door gave me a view of the big, chintz-decorated lounge that invited women to drop in for rest and relaxation.

Anne described the organization's structure and its activities programs. Departments, each under its own professional director, known as a "secretary," existed to serve business and professional women, industrial women, and "girl reserves" or teenagers. Girls and women could join the Y simply to enjoy its physical education facilities as individuals using the swimming pool or gym; department members could also use those facilities. The "secretaries" were often trained as group social workers in contrast to social casework. In addition, the Y was a worldwide organization and two of our staff at Central had worked in the Y in China. The professionals were all Christian women who were strongly allied with the advocates of the Social Gospel, an interpretation of the ministry of Jesus that had been particularly espoused by Walter Rauschenbush at the Rochester Theological Seminary and Reinhold Niebuhr at Union Theological. In the twenties both men influenced many other theological seminaries and their graduates, though not Garrett, where Wesley was enrolled. I viewed the professors at Garrett as too doctrinaire and evangelical for the Social Gospel model that guided many YWCA leaders.

I was not a perfect private secretary. I did not know how to make myself invisible and useful at the same time. I was less than a perfect typist, and at best a beginning stenographer. After a short time Anne told me she thought I would be happier in the Industrial Department, where a new secretary for Central Branch was needed. I could have the job and she would find another more experienced person for her office.

I was delighted; she was probably relieved. For me it was a step up from the clerical to the professional. It meant more money, perhaps $150 a month. The city industrial secretary, Clara Kaiser, whose office was on the same floor as Anne's, was close at hand to train me for my new functions. Clara was a large and dynamic woman, enthusiastic about her program and sure of her skills. She was a degree-holding social worker in the new field of "group work." I met the industrial secretaries from the other branches, of whom I especially remember Frankie Adams of the South Side Branch, a lively young woman with whom I quickly bonded. She was a Tuskegee graduate, who sang gospel hymns with a full, true voice and entertained her friends with a skit of a black gospel preacher that might have instructed a Jesse Jackson of the twenties. The West Side secretary, located in the garment district, near the headquarters of the new union of Amalgamated Clothing Workers, had her constituency of union women garment workers all around her. She introduced me to Agnes Nestor and Elizabeth Christman, who ran the national headquarters of the Women's Trade Union League (WTUL). We all became a team, with Clara as our captain.

As for my own possible clientele, Clara helped me locate them among the women working in the Loop. Not the office workers, for they belonged to the Business Girls Department, but among what today would be designated the blue-collar and pink-collar occupations. I got in touch with the Waiters and Waitresses Union, with the people doing office cleaning, and with food workers. Anne's mother, Mrs. Guthrie, our housekeeper/hostess in Central Branch, called my attention to the fact that the busy bustle on Thursday afternoons was a celebration of maids' day off. Before long, it was these women, many well past middle age, who were my special clients. We formed clubs made up of groups that knew each other or had come to know each other from casual Thursday meetings. We had a club, for example, of newly arrived German girls; one of English and Irish women who had been ladies' maids or worked in the homes of the rich and noble in England; and a club of young Native-American women, fresh from the schools on the reservations in Wisconsin and Minnesota.

I learned about the upcoming summer Y conferences, lasting a week or longer in southwestern Michigan; about finding candidates for election to Y office on boards and committees at Central Branch; about lobbying for protective laws at Springfield; and about meetings or visits among club members from all the branches to prepare for these events and select representatives and delegates. I became familiar with the Y's public affairs agenda on women's work and women's health issues. I came to know at least the names of national leaders on Y staff and committees as these people spoke at conferences or visited Chicago. I got to know personally a number of national leaders in the Industrial Department, including Lucy Carner, Grace Coyle, and Blossom Perry. Altogether it was a woman's world, in which I felt comfortable, stimulated, proud, and satisfied.

I also found personal friends among the young women in the clubs. One of those was Lydia Schaeffer, then a young German woman, who had come to this country out of the poverty of post–World War I German inflation. Lydia's aim was to earn enough to assure her younger bother, Fritz, an education and to accumulate her own dowry. After her arrival in the United States she had a disastrous experience in working for the people who had paid her way over on condition she repay them with her services over several years. Once she had paid them back, however, she left that peonage and found her way to Chicago where in two Quaker families she made lifelong friends that one of her daughters was still honoring thirty-five years later. She also met Tassilo Tröscher, a young agronomist exchange student at the University of Illinois. She broke her engagement with her Schwäbisch fiancé in Germany and married Tassilo. My life, as will become apparent, has been closely intertwined with this family ever since. No other friendship has endured so long—it is now nearly seventy years old and has included four generations.

The Native-American women's problems at first seemed to me to be mainly those of country girls unused to city life. But I began to realize that their difficulties arose from more than migration from rural to urban life. Most of these young women were products of reservation boarding schools, where they had been programmed to move only when a bell rang: they had risen by a bell, eaten meals by a bell, gone on to the next task by a bell. They had gone to bed by a bell and turned the lights out at the day's final bell. If no bell rang, they idled the time away and were not prepared to move on their own. The clocks they knew hung on walls but had nothing to do with daily living. Many of them could not tell time, or, if they could, time on the clock bore no relation to task performance, the keeping of appointments, or the regularity of a program. I first noticed this syndrome when scheduled meetings could take place only after hours of delay, or not at all.

These women had mainly found jobs as domestic servants in Chicago homes. I often wondered how they and their Chicago employers managed at all. Of course some did not; and these were often the unemployed. After a while some of the young women with whom I had made friends took me to meetings of the Tribal Councils and introduced me to other Native Americans. I saw how many of them were trying to live and make a living in different locations and occupations. I learned about reservation life and about the desire of these young women to put that all behind them.

In many respects, the reservation schools were doing their job of indoctrinating Native Americans in exactly the same way as evening schools were teaching immigrants and other diverse groups in the changing American community to become middle-class Protestant Yankees. In part, the young women who had come to Chicago and were now enrolled in my programs at the Y saw their exodus from the reservation as the first step to establishing themselves in that community. As in Indianapolis and St. Louis, I had neither the experience nor the training that would help me to understand their immediate problems. I could empathize with their struggles because I, too, was emerging from a patterned past. But I was also attempting to change the America they had been taught to want. To this degree my leadership role was confusing.

Job 5: The Y Summer Camp

The experience we had attending the Y summer camp at Paw-Paw, Michigan, was important to me that first summer in the Y and to many of the young women from the clubs I sponsored. National Y staff assigned to our Midwestern region were responsible for setting up the program as a learning situation, modeled in fact on the American labor summer schools I first came to know the following summer. Outstanding economists, sociologists, and social theologians lectured in the mornings. These lectures were followed by discussion groups in which leaders dealt with the relationship of the members' work and life experiences to the teachers' analytical generalizations about social problems. In both teaching modes Y staff and Y members were participating students. Women's problems as gender problems in all their variety were not yet the focus of our concerns. Rather, the Industrial Department was concerned with wage-earning women, who were understood to be self-directing beings, i.e., persons who could become competent to deal with the injustices they constantly encountered. If they were going to become effective in changing their circumstances, they must start by getting acquainted with people and situations that otherwise they—and we—could only speculate about: African Americans, immigrants, people of other religions.[15]

YWCA summer camps were interracial. Black and white women shared tents. It was evident here, as well as later at the longer sessions of the summer schools, that intense friendships often formed across a racial barrier that was elsewhere insurmountable. Women, both black and white, seemed released in this atmosphere to reach out to one another in a way that normal American life did not encourage, indeed prohibited, in written or unwritten law.

The memorable event of this camp session came as an extra on the program. Two Y secretaries who until recently had worked in one of the northern Indiana towns—it may well have been the steel capital of Gary—reported on an open attack that the dominant companies of the town had launched against "the radicalism of the YWCA." Ethlyn Christensen and Pattie Ellis told their story of standing up to these massive corporations and to the smaller businessmen allied with them. The result was of course predictable—an overwhelming victory for the corporate coalition. Both Ethlyn and Pattie were fired. For the first time I faced the possibility that standing for unpopular ideas in groups labeled "dangerous" could indeed leave one out in the cold, unsupported and unprotected by one's helpless, because isolated, organization.[16]

Ethlyn became and remained a role model for me. She was sure of herself but never imposed her view on others; she was committed to working with people as equals by encouraging their participation in shaping programs she could further. In this view, people came to adult classes not simply to gain know-how but to find ways out of difficulties through organized action and through taking charge of solutions. I see, as I look back, that I became aware of these skills and learned to exercise them in the Y. My teachers were a whole coterie of women who were its staff. The atmosphere there was positive and active, despite the depressing outlook that was emerging from the dominant analyses of social problems.

Among these influential women I count first my supervisor, Clara, who resigned to take another job a few months after I had joined the staff.[17] Her replacement was another of the "greats" among these Y women, Annetta Dieckmann. Whereas many of the senior Y staff were graduates of the women's colleges, Annetta was a Cornell graduate in the class of 1917. She seemed, when measured against my inexperience, years older than I, but probably she was my senior by fewer than ten years. Her critique of my work and programs was invariably helpful and positive, but it never spared my shortcomings. I felt no hostility in our evaluation sessions but emerged from them quite clear about the areas for improvement. Her approach was perhaps closer to that of a mother—admonitory, pedagogical, concerned, and loving all at once. Her job, we both understood, was to make a good leader out of me, and I never doubted her intentions.

The approaches that both she and Ethlyn incorporated were those widely evident throughout the Y, producing a methodology inherent in the organization's ideology. In broad terms this ideology involved an acquaintance with and concern for the life problems of our members, together with a commitment to helping them help themselves by viewing their problems in a social setting and finding their solutions in social action. Our own training was continuous. Once a year or so, we would participate in more formal staff training sessions. These typically included an eminent theologian—a Reinhold Niebuhr,[18] or later a Paul Tillich; perhaps a woman scholar such as Elizabeth Brandeis, Gladys Palmer, or Josephine Goldmark; and outstanding organizational leaders, of whom I especially remember Florence Thorne, who had been Samuel Gompers's and was later William Green's assistant in the president's office at the AFL.

Annetta's central concern was with racial problems; mine was with the labor movement, a movement still very exclusive to the skilled trades, small in numbers, and unconcerned with the mass of semi- and unskilled blue-collar workers. I belonged to no union nor ever had. My knowledge of the labor movement came mainly from my Commonwealth contacts and, much less precisely, from some of my old Hull House acquaintances. Among the industrial secretaries at this time there was some interest in building a union within the Y. Annetta and I by no means saw eye to eye on this matter; indeed, she opposed it. What changes would it bring about that we were not already capable of putting into motion? she asked. I stressed the potential in an alliance with the labor movement and access to it. She wanted to know what union we could join. On this issue I was less certain—perhaps the teachers'? She was not sure they would be able or even interested in giving us much attention; nor, in her opinion, were we likely, once within the organization, to have much influence over its priorities and program. This discussion took place, it should be remembered, in the last half of the twenties, at the very nadir of American labor's organization and soon after Gompers's death.

I was selected to go to the national convention of the Y in Boulder, Colorado, and took my first trip—of course by train—to the Rocky Mountain West. The effort a group of us industrial secretaries made to place unionism on the agenda was defeated, and I suffered my first sense of disappointment with the organization. For me, the undertaking was something of a test of the Y's bona fides, and I left the convention with doubts as to whether even this group of dedicated and intelligent women could be relied upon to live their—or was it my?—faith in the doctrine they advocated.

JOB 5: THE BRYN MAWR SUMMER SCHOOL FOR WOMEN WORKERS

One of my many activities as Central Branch industrial secretary was to host the committee of Chicago women who were supporting the Bryn Mawr Summer School for Women Workers. Chair of the group was Helen Hohman, wife of a Northwestern University professor of economics, and herself a Ph.D. in the same field.[19] The committee included alumnae from Bryn Mawr and other women's colleges, along with representatives from a variety of organizations.

Among these of course was the WTUL, and it was in the summer school meetings that I came to know Agnes Nestor and Elizabeth Christman. Two other women on the committee were personnel officers at two large industrial firms, who also impressed me greatly with their knowledge of industrial workers and their problems. This committee was responsible for recruiting women students to the school and for raising enough money to support them there for its eight-week session.[20] A former Bryn Mawr dean, Hilda Worthington Smith (widely known as Jane), was the school's director for almost a decade.[21]

Founders and Students

The idea of the Bryn Mawr school was a new one for this country. Its founders were among the women most often exemplified in the settlement movement, who were concerned with the wide gap between themselves as college-educated, middle-class women and the immigrant women who filled the factories and lived in tenements. Unable to speak the language and largely cut off from the educational and cultural life of the cities where they lived, these immigrant women had no sense that they would be welcomed as participants in any of the organizations that might in turn help them. Some had never gone to school in the new country, or, if they had gone for a few years as children, were then pulled out of school to go to work or to care for a growing family of younger children while their mothers worked.

In addition, the many young U.S.-born girls who had poured into the factories during World War I to escape from the isolation and backbreaking labor of American farm life had also been deprived of further education and of social life in the industrial towns to which they had been drawn. The eight-week program at Bryn Mawr could fill some of the gaps in the education of all these women and relate science, literature, and economics to their everyday lives, thus equipping them for aspects of community life.

Since, with the exception of the garment workers, the unions of this period had relatively few women members, it was unrealistic to think of this as a trade union school. By the time I joined the group, the plan was to have half the hundred students who could attend each summer come from unions, and half from community organizations. The WTUL was almost the sole key to reaching other union women; Y Industrial Department members represented probably the largest pool of nonunion women; and a few candidates came from settlements and church-affiliated groups. Local committees existed in many industrial communities. Our Chicago committee interviewed all applicants from the vicinity and raised the money, mainly from the alumnae of the women's colleges, to support the selected students.[22]

Faculty and Students

After a season of my doing the staff work for the Chicago committee, Helen Hohman asked me in the spring of 1928 whether I would be interested in teaching at the school. Faculty for the most part taught one of three courses—English, economics, or science. Of these, English was clearly my choice. The Y granted me leave for the summer, and in June I drove from Chicago to Bryn Mawr.

I had ended my year at Commonwealth with a clear determination to find work in labor education, but without much idea of developing a teaching method geared to adults with little formal education. At the Bryn Mawr Summer School I found a faculty that, at the instigation of its directors, was consciously linking work experience to learning. Much of the school's teaching was concerned with self-expression, and we endeavored to create situations in the classroom that encouraged students to bring their work and life experience to bear on what they read and heard there. Teachers aimed to help students generalize from their everyday experience to the full range of an economic concept, or to identify the emotional presentation of a novel or poem with their own lives. Few textbooks existed that could serve this kind of student, and faculty were encouraged to write their own.[23] I decided that my sections in English would mainly read poetry. I think that at the time I felt the novel, the short story, and the drama had been taken by other English teachers. The circumstances suggested to me that it would be well for me to choose another field of writing.[24]

The faculty included many famous names in their fields, who returned summer after summer.[25] Among them were Gladys Palmer, research economist at the Wharton School, a woman far ahead of her time in her studies of women in various occupations. Another was Louise Brown of Wellesley who worked with a staff of graduate students to introduce women to the telescope and what it revealed of the universe. Esther Peterson was in charge of physical education, music, and dancing and chose plays and other entertainments that included material from many other countries, as well as folk music from our own.

Classes were small, and faculty were expected to share leisure as well as instruction with their students. The school aimed each year to have a few students from abroad, and those who came were mainly from Scandinavia, Germany, or Britain. Hilda Smith made a point of including them in the school program, so that our curiosity about these women, their schools, and their labor organizations was both stimulated and satisfied. Everyone participated in the "sings" and entertainment. Students who came from nearby towns entertained their families on the weekends. Trips were organized to visit nearby factories and historic monuments.[26] Faculty and students lived close together in two dormitories at the entrance to the Bryn Mawr campus and were encouraged to drop in on each other. Our accommodations were still sparse, those a Quaker institution had provided for its students at its founding in the 1890s.[27]

The experience was altogether an intensive one. For me, it was a rich summer, and one that set my feet more firmly on the path of labor education than had been the case when I arrived. Without having at all planned at this point to devote my own career specifically to women workers, one thing had so conspired with another that my role models were nearly all women, and the institutions in which I worked, dedicated as they were to women's needs, gave me great satisfaction. Many of my colleagues came from a strong tradition of Christian service, conveyed through the women's colleges the majority of them had attended.[28] They placed high value on the work open to women—teaching, health service, and social work. As I remember my work with the Y and Bryn Mawr and reflect on their concerns with working women, I do not so much see a feminist movement in the modern sense; rather, I discern a profile of those women reformists and innovators that fitted my sense of a satisfactory lifestyle and career.

My experience at Bryn Mawr left me more focused on labor education and much the wiser. I had come to know about the wave of establishment and growth of labor education in the decade of the twenties, both in this country and in Europe.[29] I knew at this point that I should like to go to Europe and get to know their institutions.

Alice at sixteen, in 1919.

Alice and the debate team,
Northwestern University, circa 1923.

Alice in knickers holding the banner, the Executive Board of the Northwestern
University YWCA, 1924, at Lake Geneva.

Alice Hanson and Wesley Cook, circa 1928.

Alice in Wales on a bicycle trip, summer 1930.

Alice in Europe, circa 1939–1931. From left to right, [in Alice's handwriting on back of photo]: "Blount (English), me, Heller (Polish), Zosea (American), Richard (German). At the Brunhilde Felsen where Brunhilde slept till Siegfried wakened her."

Alice Hanson and Wesley Cook,
Frankfurt, Germany, January 11, 1931.

Alice, February 26, 1936.

Alice H. Cook and son Philip Cook
(at eighteen months), circa 1940.
Photo: Helen W. Post.

Flora and August Hanson, Alice's parents, in 1941. Inscribed "With love/Mother 1949."

Alice singing at Hudson Shore Labor School, summer 1941.

Alice speaking to an enthralled audience, Hudson Shore Labor School, summer 1941.

Alice in Germany, summer 1947.

Alice and Wesley on the *Queen Mary*, 1948, on their way to Austria.

4

STUDENT DAYS IN GERMANY: 1929–1931

When I returned to Chicago from that fruitful summer at Bryn Mawr, I had the sense that I had found the career I wanted to follow. In the field of workers' education, however, there were very few full-time positions, and all of them were hazardous, dependent on the unions' commitment to this field of labor activity. The alternative—to work for an institution, such as Bryn Mawr or Brookwood, supported mainly by liberals sympathetic to the labor movement and to the education and training of its rank-and-file members—was almost equally risky.

In the course of his graduate studies Wes had made a new acquaintance, Dr. Ludwig Müller, a visiting professor in modern languages from Germany. Dr. Müller was the beneficiary of an exchange program, Deutscher Akademischer Austauschdienst (DAAD), which arranged exchanges for students and professors between Germany and a number of countries, including the United States. He suggested that in view of our interests in Germany we apply to DAAD for scholarships. Wesley could advance his theological studies, and I would have an opportunity to make firsthand observations and contacts as I wished.

Since we thought it unlikely that DAAD would take us both, we decided to make two applications and let the Germans decide which of us would be acceptable. However, with Dr. Müller's strong support, we were both accepted. Wes chose to attend the theological faculty of Humboldt University in Berlin, and I applied to the Johann Wolfgang von Goethe Universität at Frankfurt am Main,[1] because I knew that a top trade union school, the Academy of Labor, was located there.

Before we left for Germany, we decided to visit people and places important to us in the United States.[2] The year abroad stretched a great distance ahead, and the trip was a celebratory way of saying good-bye.

THE SUMMER IN EUROPE

In order to learn German, we decided to go to Europe in June, although the fall semester would not begin until November.[3] We were bound for Hamburg for the summer, where I had letters of introduction to trade unionists and adult educators, people I hoped would help me in understanding the German trade union educational system.

We sailed on the *America*, where, thanks to father's youngest brother, then with U.S. Lines, we were assigned to a first-class cabin for our economy-class payment. Mother and Father came to see us off on the ship. We sailed to

Bremerhaven, and from there we took the train first to Bremen for a weekend of walking in that city and then on to Hamburg, where Etta Pfluger, a friend of mine from St. Louis, met us and took us to her home to meet her mother.[4]

That first afternoon we took a trip down the Elbe for afternoon coffee in Blankenese, where we, with half of Hamburg, watched the ships go out to sea from Hamburg's great harbor. On the second day, we began our search for a pension, in the course of which we traveled Hamburg's River Alster, including its two inner-city lakes—and from them through its endless canals bordered with spacious homes. We also acquainted ourselves with the local transport system. The place we found was expensive for us but oh, so satisfactory. It was in what had been a splendid house, where we were offered a spacious room at the rear, overlooking a big garden. The June days were warm and sunny; and our first breakfast was served before an open door to the garden in early full bloom. Our new home was not far from the university, and we soon learned of the summer program for foreign students that would start in a few weeks.

I, however, had come with auxiliary plans in mind. Through my friends in labor education in the United States I had an invitation from a young Dane to visit the international Folkehöjskole (evening school for adults) that he had founded near Elsinore in Denmark. I knew far too little about what European adult education schools were doing or how they fitted in to the whole educational system in Scandinavia, Germany, or England. I did know that they were developed out of a real local need, were recognized in some way by the total educational system in their respective countries, and that they might be structured either as evening or residential schools. I was also aware that my colleagues in the Bryn Mawr Summer School saw our efforts at residential education there as related work. In particular, the European programs were useful in showing how to serve the needs of workers whose educational backgrounds were inadequate in preparing them for citizenship in countries entering their first experiences with democracy. The invitation to the Folkehöjskole near Elsinore would be my first opportunity to learn what was going on. I planned to go for a few weeks before settling in Germany, while Wesley would pursue our other contacts in Hamburg and begin work on his German.

I met a very international body of both teachers and students at Elsinore. An early acquaintance was Winifred Braithwaite, a New Zealander, with whom I saw the Kronborg—the castle where Shakespeare set Hamlet. I began exchanging German/English lessons with a German student and became friends with a young Swede, Lars Jonsson. One group of students, made up of Welsh miners, tended to dominate the student body by their sheer numbers and unanimity. They were very critical of the school's director, impervious to his attempts at discipline, and rejecting of his efforts to set up some kind of self-government that would carry out his ideas of democracy. They maintained their identity as a group mainly by insisting on speaking Welsh in loud voices in every public place and succeeded in preventing the installation of any order within the school. As a result, we non-Welsh formed our own little cliques, became friends, and were likewise rather turned off by the faculty, who seemed unable to provide the leadership that the situation demanded. The experience made me see, even more clearly than I had at Commonwealth and at Bryn Mawr, how important the special function of the school's leader was in creating a useful learning environment for adults who came from various cultures and with their own experiences, needs, and outspoken demands.

It appeared to me that this particular problem lay with a director so enclosed in his own rigid world that he could not share leadership with either his faculty or his students. Indeed, his view of the workers whom he wished to bring to the school from many nations was: "Workers cannot control themselves." A young American couple on the faculty added, "There can be too much democracy."

My disappointment with this first of many school visits was lessened by the friendships I made with other students there, chiefly Winifred Braithwaite, then living in England, and Lars Jonsson, with whom I corresponded for years.

Shortly after I left for my trip to Denmark, Wesley learned that a woman professor of botany was about to visit the United States for the first time and wanted to have an opportunity to meet Americans. She offered to share her apartment in the suburb of Ahrensburg with us and to leave us there while she was in the United States.

Ahrensburg, as I came to know the town in 1929, had a life and history of its own. Although it was only a half-hour by commuter train from Hamburg, it was still surrounded by a forest and had its own castle, as well as picturesque houses with thatched roofs. Dr. Stöppel left for the United States in early August.[5]

Once we had said good-bye to our host, we redoubled our efforts to find tutors in German, in addition to enrolling in the university's summer school for foreign students. Indeed, largely because Wesley had also been invited to audit courses in the university's summer semester in philosophy, we found ourselves in a somewhat hectic round of meeting people. Among them were Dr. Wendt, librarian of the Warburg Art History Library, and Dr. Noack and two of his students, rather sophisticated young men, eager to go to England and take part in its academic culture. I had contacts with a union in the building trades, where two young people welcomed our invitation to exchange English and German. The days were full.

At the end of August I was alone in London to attend the World Conference on Adult Education, where I hoped to meet many Germans in the field of workers' education. I had some contact with a domestic workers' organization and exchanged experiences with a leader of the group, based on my work with the domestic workers' clubs in the Chicago Y. I met up with Winifred Braithwaite, and we fulfilled the plans we had made in Denmark to walk in the Rupert Brooke country around Grantchester. I found the conference sessions unpardonably dull, but I did meet adult educators from all over the world; those from Germany I planned to meet again, in the course of study and school visits.

On my return to Ahrensburg, Wes and I began to think of getting to our respective universities. With the news of my acceptance at Frankfurt came specific information about life and financing. I learned that my stipend would be two hundred Reichsmark (RM),[6] (the equivalent at the time to fifty dollars) a month. This amount would allow me to pay for a room, my meals at the student Mensa, and my university tuition. I would have to pay extra for light, heat, and baths, but I could go for half price on trolleys and at the movies, opera, and theater. Wesley would live in a Lutheran student home in Berlin.

During the final days in Hamburg, I visited Dr. Hauert in the Volkshochschule (adult evening school). He took me to some classes and gave me an introduction to the director. I also visited apprentice schools in Altona and found them segregated for boys and girls since, except for watchmakers, the two sexes never entered the same trades. I gathered from my reading on German vocational education for girls that, despite the fact that many married women worked in shops and factories, they were almost invariably assigned to unskilled work and apparently had no possibility of training in the skilled trades. Moreover, a law prescribed that no woman could remain a state employee after marriage. When the phrase *"Die Tochter einer Lehrerin"* (the daughter of a female teacher) appeared in a book I was reading on the German apprentice system, my tutor remarked, "That is an impossible expression. No female teacher can be married."[7] The system directed the girls to courses in household arts; the kitchens and laundries at Altona seemed to me old-fashioned indeed—no sinks, laundry done on a scrub-board, no hot running water.

And then, on the spur of a moment, we were invited by a Youth Movement group to bike with them to Holland. We bought secondhand bikes in a hurry for fifty RM and set off for Amsterdam, after enjoying a farewell tea with Etta and her family.

The group was a replica of the original Youth Movement—its members were extreme vegetarians, who wore no leather products. It was, in addition, devoted to the practice of folk dancing and singing and insisted upon discussion of all its programs and plans by everyone in the group. Our preference for overnighting was to seek out a peasant barn. We avoided cities, except for a day in Amsterdam, where we stayed in a youth hostel. Our departures every morning were typically delayed in favor of singing and evaluations of our communal living behavior on the previous day. The trip gave Wesley and me an intimate view of the Netherlands, both because of our leisurely means of travel and our contact with Dutch peasants.

It took us eight days to reach Amsterdam, against a strong west wind off the ocean. Wes and I left the group soon after Amsterdam, for a visit to the Müllers, and bicycled to the German border in two days with the wind at our backs. In

Wuppertal-Barmen we were received with familial warmth and began to cherish not only the Herr Doktor but his warm and hospitable wife and their three children. Many years later, when Frau Müller visited me in Ithaca after World War II, I learned that her husband was one of the tens of thousands of unidentified men who died at Leningrad, as the Russians heroically and successfully defended their city.

UNIVERSITY

Since I arrived only a few days before the term began, I was too late to find a room easily. Everything I found would have absorbed most of my stipend. I landed at the Quaker headquarters, where an English Friend who had been in Germany since World War I put me in touch with a student, August Lorey, who helped me find a room in the Kuhwaldsiedlung. This area was mainly occupied by minor civil servants in the post office and was only a fifteen-minute walk from the university. My rent, plus coal to heat the room, was thirty-five RM per month; my landlady would do my laundry for one RM. The coal bill at the end of the semester was five RM, and the laundry turned out to include ironing (which had to be done on everything before the advent of wash-and-wear garments) and mending—important too in the days before nylon stockings. I felt I could allow myself a subscription to the *Frankfurter Zeitung*, which I read as carefully as I could in pursuit of achieving an acceptable command of German.[8]

At the university's office for foreign students, I met the ten other Americans in the DAAD program, who were working in many fields from physics to literature. I studied the rich curricular offerings for courses in economics, law, politics, and sociology, and signed up for far too many.[9] The office for foreign students (Auslandsstelle) put me in touch with the local adult evening school director, Frau Epstein, and with the codirectors of the Academy of Labor (Akademie der Arbeit), Drs. Sturmfels and Michel. In early visits with them all, I was cordially received and given permission to visit courses as I wished. I audited lectures at the academy for two hours a day, which introduced me to German labor relations, the structure of German unions and the laws governing them, and the unions' collective bargaining with management. Others of my professors included Hendrik De Man, a Belgian, who could be said to have founded the field of human relations in employment with his book that had just been translated into English as *The Joy of Work*. De Man had a considerable history as head of the Youth Division of the Socialist International. He had been sent by the Belgian government to the United States during World War I to acquaint people here with the German Army's oppression of Belgium as it over-ran that country as part of its plan to reach the Atlantic Coast.

Out of my social work experience, minimal as it was, I saw an opportunity to do further comparisons between social systems in Germany and the United States and was put in touch with Frau Dr. Hellinger, the head of the welfare program for the city of Frankfurt.[10] She invited me to visit clients with her on Saturday mornings. Unemployment was growing fast, and even middle-class people, who had previously been quite independent, were now seeking aid from her agency. These visits, together with trips arranged by the Auslandsstelle to inspect "social" housing around Frankfurt, gave me a sense of the growing misery of the German working class. Meanwhile, the Hitler period was approaching, with the promises of employment it would hold out to these desperate people.

All the somewhat various and disconnected activities that I undertook in the first semester arose out of sheer eagerness to immerse myself in this new experience of living in another country. It was aimed, too, at helping me to settle on further study in a distinct career. Should I be headed for the uncertainty of making a living in labor education? Had I decided too early that social work was not after all the better route? I had not yet thought of being able to stay in Germany longer than the summer of 1930 on the resources at our command, which consisted entirely of the remains of some savings and the DAAD stipend. Consequently, I saw this year solely in terms of my own possible future employment in the United States, somehow serving working people.

One of my few disappointments in this learning experience was with the university's library facilities. I had learned to appreciate and use libraries freely in my undergraduate years, but in Frankfurt I found them shockingly badly organized. There was no central catalog, and the library under each of the five university faculties operated under its own system. In one, books were listed only by authors; in others, by subject and title. Moreover, since the libraries were open only for limited hours, and in general books could not be taken out (or in any case took days to obtain), study was greatly hampered.

In my end-of-semester report to the DAAD office, I wrote that I wanted to spend the remaining six months of my time visiting evening and residential schools for workers to observe teaching methods and curricula, as well as the influence of sponsorship by trade unions and the Sozialdemokratische Partei Deutschlands (SPD). In our time and afterward, we always referred to the SPD as the Socialist Party, rather than the Social Democratic Party, its proper translation. The SPD then was much to the left of today's Social Democratic Party, for it was indeed Socialist.[11]

CHRISTMAS HOLIDAYS IN BERLIN

During the whole of the first semester, Wes and I carried on a correspondence in which he reported his general unhappiness with his position at the seminary and both of us agreed that we were lonely in being separated. We decided that I should go to Berlin to see something of the city, a visit that would give us the opportunity to resolve these problems. I had three weeks in Berlin, two and a half of which I spent as one should spend Christmas vacation—theater and opera, heaps of sleeping, eating, and talking, a little hiking, and sightseeing. Among the events I still remember was my introduction to Brecht, in *Aufstieg und Fall der Stadt Mahagonny,* and to political cabaret, then a very popular entertainment that cut close to the nerve with its devastatingly witty comments on the events of the day. I also met two of Wesley's friends, who over the years remained my good friends as well.[12]

Wes's dissatisfaction with courses at the seminary was fairly easily resolved. My reports on life at Frankfurt with American and German friends were persuasive, but his information that the famous liberal theologian, Paul Tillich, was moving to Frankfurt determined Wes's decision to move there too. Although I would be traveling in and out looking at labor education institutions, we would have much more time together and would work things out as we lived intermittently with each other.

For my part, I had begun to take a look at what was going on in Berlin to see if I might be interested in returning for a longer period. I talked with the head of the schools of the SPD, and when I learned that they had, in addition to a clearly structured program for evening classes in the major cities, two residential schools at Tinz and Harrisleefeld, I added those schools to my already too ambitious list of future visits. I learned that members of the SPD were developing the use of a new medium, the radio; that they had also established contacts with film centers; and that the Party had a national coverage through its own press in 172 locations. It conducted a workers' travel bureau and encouraged the establishment of workers' libraries. I visited one such in Neukölln, a working-class section of the city, where an attempt was being made to make books easily available. The Party also supported the celebration of workers' festivals commemorating events in labor history, and Die Naturfreunde (Friends of Nature), an organization of outdoors people. All these activities included children, organized as Die Kinderfreunde (Children's Friends) and Die Falken (The Hawks) for teenagers. Through this connection, I got an insight into what was meant by labor culture as well as by labor education.

The training school for trade union functionaries, supported by the Prussian state and located near Berlin, was housed in an old castle. It had been founded in 1926 and had about forty students who, despite the building's spaciousness and shabby grandeur, had to exist with stove heat, no electric lights, and in rooms so enormous that eight or nine students lived in one together. In contrast, its extensive park was beautiful. Students selected by the school faculty had to have taken a year of extension courses and written nine papers on specified subjects. Those admitted were then supported with stipends by their unions for courses lasting ten months. It was the only state-supported school that I found, although several others had substantial support from cities.

BETWEEN SEMESTERS

In the long interval of almost three months between winter and summer semesters, I traveled, living for one to six weeks at each stop at a labor school. Thanks to arrangements with a fellow student at the Academy, I was able to live with his wife in Leipzig and thus to see its great variety of educational programs from evening schools to the "apartment schools."[13] Leipzig was also the home of what might be called the national library, which received a copy of every book published within the country. Workers' libraries were under the direction of Hans Hofmann, whose innovations interested me. He had abolished cumbersome catalogs in favor of subject matter guides, hoping to relate readers' interests to the books available. Librarians aimed to interview every would-be reader and to advise a program of reading based on one of these guides.

To complete the wide range of my concern with adult education, I visited the Universität in Leipzig, which offered the only seminar in this field under the tutelage of Dr. Hans Pflug. The university contained what was probably the most complete library in Germany on adult education. Although the university was not in session, Dr. Pflug gave me a description of the seminar and the extra privilege of being able to take books out of the seminar's library to read at home.

After Leipzig I went to Habertshof for a week, to visit one of the "free" residential schools. Students of all political persuasions were accepted; the director, Eduard Weitsch, had once been a minister. Classes were mainly devoted to current political problems. The director also emphasized personal questions and had an assistant who led discussions on sex relations, the education of children, and parental roles. It was at this school that I met Paul Bernstein, whose son I took into my family years later after Paul had met his fate in a gas chamber at Auschwitz. Paul had entered the German army late in World War I, as he turned seventeen. He had joined the revolt of the army in November 1918, wearing a red cockade in his army helmet, thus becoming a part of the Socialist revolution that forced the Kaiser's abdication and led to the formation of the Weimar Republic, in the last days of which we were living. He was a Democratic Socialist at a time when Rosa Luxemburg represented the revolutionary wing of the Party.

THE SUMMER SEMESTER

The summer semester at this time lasted only ten weeks. Again I registered for more courses than I could possibly follow and in selecting topics that interested me, I decided to seek out professors with whose views I wanted to acquaint myself.[14]

In going back over my notes of these days, I am impressed with how unaware I was during this period of the impending Nazi scourge. That awareness came much more sharply in the second year with my fall semester at the Hochschule für Politik in Berlin. I explain this lack in part by the fact that I was so immersed in labor affairs that I paid all too little attention to general political events outside that immediate circle. Furthermore, those professors who dealt with politics were still assuming that Nazi propaganda could not penetrate the working class and its powerful SPD—the party in which they placed their faith even when they themselves were enrolled in one of the center parties.

The intensity with which I was pursuing my labor education goals also precluded serious attention to social work activity. Nevertheless, I was still very much in touch with the man directing the social work seminar at the university. He invited me to attend a week's conference in June in a village in north Hesse for social workers seeking exposure to new theoretical concepts in the field. We visited a variety of institutions including a penitentiary, a home for the feebleminded, a peasant adult school, and a one-room village school. The village where we lived was in the Schwalm, an area that at that time still retained old folk customs and costumes. On May Day eve the boys and girls of the village gathered at the bridge and cracked long whips to frighten away the evil spirits. Then they joined a long parade, which marched by torchlight from village to village to welcome in the summer.

During the spring vacation in May, five of us Americans went to the Black Forest for a hike down to the Bodensee (Lake Constance), where we spent several days swimming and visiting villages. In those spring days I learned from Ruth Sutherland that her husband, Brownie, my friend and motorcycle companion at Commonwealth, had committed suicide as he reached thirty years of age. She was devastated and had decided to take a trip to Europe in the hope that a changed scene would help her. I met her group and traveled with them on part of the "romantic route" through Rothenburg, Nuremberg, and Munich, for a first glimpse of the south.

Wes and I took bicycle trips far and near, living in youth hostels, riding in all kinds of weather and terrain. We cooked our own meals and sometimes joined with other friends to see vast stretches of beautiful country. I listed once that, within two months, we had gone to Heidelberg, Marburg, Trier, and the area of Rhinepfalz. In addition I had gone for a week with the Akademie students to the cities of the Ruhr Valley, for visits to metal-producing plants.

ANOTHER TRIP TO ENGLAND

Wesley wanted to attend a philosophical congress at Oxford University in England. We decided we could do it and do some sightseeing as well if we took our bicycles and camped out. We had become friends with a British student at Frankfurt who invited us to visit him and his parents in Dorset.

In England we crisscrossed the country six times, each trip taking us farther north, though York was our northernmost city. The Dorset household was our first stop for more than an overnight. We found it somewhat formal for our custom and tastes, and perhaps they found us rather too informal, arriving as we did pretty disheveled after ten days camping beside the river at Oxford. We found meals especially overwhelming—our hostess wearing a hat and gloves to breakfast in anticipation of her post-breakfast attention to her garden. Nor were we prepared to dress for dinner, though we made our best attempt, given our supply of clothes. On our departure we managed, however awkwardly, to tip the maids, as our host had more than once implied we should.

From Dorset we rode as far west as Cardiff, where we spent a few rain-soaked, chilly days, and then set off east again for the next coast-to-coast stage. We were joined by another Frankfurt student, a young woman who brought us news of the immediately upcoming election in Germany—in which, it turned out, the Nazis would make their first substantial gains at the national level. We had planned a trip that would take us back to Germany through Holland and then to Belgium. The one adventure on this trip came in Amsterdam when we sought out the youth hostel where we had stayed on our previous trip; they refused to accept us because we had different names in our passports and therefore could not be married, as we insisted we were. It was late in the evening and we were thrown on the town for accommodations.

My successful application to the Alexander von Humboldt Stiftung (an educational foundation) allowed me to stay on for a second year in Germany. I planned to complete a survey of residential labor education facilities, as well as to cover a major sample of evening adult education schools. Wesley likewise secured an extension of his exchange fellowship and planned to take a degree with Tillich.

Winter Semester in Berlin

On our return to Berlin late in September 1930, the full import of the political news was clear. The Nazis had won many more seats than they had candidates on their lists and were reaching deep into their provincial organizations for people to fill them. Professor Ludwig Bergstruässer had been returned to the Reichstag and offered me a ticket to a seat in the visitors' gallery at any time. I used this privilege to attend the opening day of Parliament and saw the Nazis in uniform march in to their seats as a column at the Hitler salute, under the supervising eye of the now ancient Clara Zetkin. As senior among the newly elected members, she would preside until the dominant party or coalition named its leader to that office.[15] In this atmosphere my political consciousness rose to a fever point that resulted in my inscribing myself, as a student member of the SPD, a commitment to Socialism that I carried over to the United States on my return home.

Wesley and I were now separated again. In contrast to the year before, I was now in Berlin and he in Frankfurt. Paul Bernstein, an active graduate student in the Berlin Hochschule für Politik (College of Politics) had persuaded me to consider spending the fall semester of 1930 in Berlin rather than return to Frankfurt. Among my new friends in Berlin was Fay Jackson, a woman from the British working class. A graduate of Ruskin College at Oxford, Fay had been used as a stump speaker for the Labour Party since she was very young, with her father as her promoter and coach. She had come to Germany to become acquainted with the SPD that Socialists everywhere believed to be the model Socialist Party. We toured political events in Berlin in that autumn when the Nazis put on demonstration after demonstration, stoned the windows of the Jewish department stores on the central Potsdamer Strasse, harassed the SPD, Communist, and Centrist Party meetings, and paraded their storm troops through the central city. The SPD responded by creating their own resistance with uniformed troopers in the Reichsbanner, defiantly displaying the national black, red, and gold flag. When the Nazis won a first provincial government in Thuringia that fall, they celebrated in the Sportpalast, where many of their demonstrations took place. Fay and I went to hear Goebbels speak. We both booed and were threatened by a guard with expulsion if we repeated this behavior.

On one occasion when Paul and I were having dinner, a man walked by the table and dropped a handwritten note near my plate. It warned me against any public appearance with a "dirty Jew." On another night when we were walking through the Berlin streets, police sirens bellowed and Paul threw himself into a doorway, covering his head. Through foghorns the police yelled, *"Strassen frei! Fenster zu!"* (Clear the streets! Close the windows!). Paul recovered enough to apologize for having fallen back into wartime behavior, seeking protection from one knew not what immediate danger, but he pushed me with him into his inadequate shelter.

The police were alert all that fall, as demonstrations brought tensions to the breaking point. I commented at one point, "The Germans live politics as others live sports." Perhaps I came to this view because I was at the Hochschule für Politik, and spending much time with Fay and Paul.

As in my former stay in Berlin, I was enchanted with the prospects of theatergoing. Reinhardt was directing on four different stages; a symphony concert on Sunday mornings was available for only one RM. Yet before I had been there very long, I put all that aside in order to keep up with my visits to schools and my observations of the political scene. I spent many weekends with Lydia and Tasso Tröscher, whose politics at this time were still rooted in the Youth Movement and its back-to-nature goals. Though we shared little in common politically, I found them good and supportive friends and their apartment a home away from home.

Money was a serious problem in our second year. My stipend amounted to only seventy-five Reichsmark, half of which went for our room rent, and Wesley had almost no cash income at all. In November we could say our problems were solved with a loan of four hundred dollars from Wes's sister, Esther, and an offer from Tasso of a three-hundred-dollar loan. Tasso explained that since things were so uncertain in Germany, he would otherwise deposit this money in a Swiss bank; in loaning it to us, he would get it back with 7 percent interest in U.S. dollars.

Everywhere I went, people suggested further institutions for me to visit, where new experiments were going on. One of these spoke to my ever-present interest in what attention was being given to women. I heard of an Academy for Women, organized by the famous early activist, Alice Salomon, who had set up the school five years earlier with the support of another feminist, Gertrud Bäumer. Salomon's purpose was to provide a center where women who had finished their studies and worked at least three years in their professions could look to the future in terms of the special contribution women could make. Since most of the prospective students were in the few professions that admitted women—social work, teaching, and librarianship—the degree to which this early training (in what we might now call empowerment) would influence a broad scope of society was doubtful. Nevertheless, it was my introduction to a new concept in adult education for women. Hilde Lion, the director, welcomed me to any of their classes I might wish to attend.

I studied at the Hochschule für Politik, where I was assigned a paper on the use of political propaganda in the United States. I decided to look at the WCTU's successful effort to attach the Eighteenth Amendment to the Constitution and hurriedly beseeched my mother to assemble the material. She was at a national convention of the organization, where she now had a full-time job in charge of exhibitions and displays that were made available to local chapters. She sent me everything in time for me to prepare the report by mid-December.

By the time the material reached me, the university, though not our Hochschule, was in almost daily turmoil. Nazi students began by attacking Jewish colleagues. Students left classes and professors had to abandon their lectures. I described it as "an extreme lack of discipline and impoliteness." It implied, as I saw it, "an intention of the Fascists to overrun all tradition and authority." There was no doubt that the Nazis were growing in numbers and influence. Although I was doubtful that the Democratic Parties could succeed in forming a parliamentary coalition that could hold a majority in the Reichstag, I still did not think that a dictatorship of either Nazis or Communists could be installed. One began however to hear the Nazi slur of "social fascist" directed at the SPD. Tension tightened hourly, and yet I chose to continue to believe that the Social Democratic trade unions together with the SPD would prevent the ultimate disaster that came only two years later.

THE SECOND CHRISTMAS VACATION

All along Wes and I had expected to find time for a trip to Paris, only a few hours away from Frankfurt. Now we decided to spend the Christmas holiday there. Anticipating a rush to the magic city at this time, we made reservations several weeks ahead for window seats on the express. The reality was that we were almost alone on the train.

A friend from the Akademie der Arbeit had gone to Paris and offered to get us a room at the cheap hotel where he lived. It turned out to be a bit of a shocker. We discovered as we awakened the first morning that we were in a glassed, curtainless space, cut out of the hall, and that anybody walking by had a full view of us. We were able with our feeble French to persuade the manager to curtain us off at roughly head height.

Nevertheless, we were happy with our first view of the great city. The two weeks we spent there were cold and gray, but coffeehouses were our retreat as we walked the streets and visited cathedrals and chapels. Our great discovery was of concerts where only phonograph records of artists were played. Tickets were cheap; seats were comfortable; and classical music, the program.

After our visit to Paris, Frankfurt once more became my base. The atmosphere there was somewhat calmer than Berlin's, although before the summer semester began, students were brawling in this university too, and classes were interrupted again and again. My attendance at lectures and seminars was quite irregular as the semester advanced, for Wesley and I had decided that one of us had to go home and earn some money if the other were to obtain a degree. We could not both hope to get so far. Circumstances clearly indicated that Wesley would be the one to remain, since he was in a more orthodox field within the German system and was further along toward his degree than I. Also, I had no professor who could act as my Doktorvater, since Hendrik De Man was only a visiting professor. We booked my passage for June 6, 1931, and I began by mail to look for a job. My inquiries at the YWCA national headquarters resulted in an offer from Philadelphia for twenty-four hundred dollars a year, a princely sum and one my German friends found hard to believe. I accepted it sight unseen, interview unheld.

In the meantime, I returned to school visiting and went to places that promised to give me new experiences both in methods and organization, among them several cities in the center of the German Reich: Dresden, Jena, and Weimar.

DEPARTURE

Wes and I now faced a whole year's separation. We felt we could well sustain it, for had we not managed our many separations up to now? We each had heavy programs ahead to fill our time, and we would of course write each other openly and in detail about our separate lives.

Wes came with me onto the ship. We walked the decks and had a snack at the bar. I was too tense to swallow and suffered from a severe headache, which I refused to attribute to the prospect of a year alone. At dinner that night I became ill and had to leave the table, although the voyage had begun quietly enough.

Wes returned to Frankfurt and his interrupted classes. I headed for New York to spend the summer with Ruth Sutherland in her Lower East Side apartment, where I would write my report on Germany. The president of the Adult Education Association, Eduard Lindemann, had suggested he might publish it.

5

UNION DAYS, SOVIET HOUSE: 1931–1939

I arrived back in the States in the early summer of 1931 to find that times were bad and getting worse. Unemployment was growing—by no one knew how much. Breadlines were lengthening. Private welfare agencies—public agencies did not exist—were overwhelmed. Banks were failing. Boys left home "to go on the road" and relieve their families of the burden of feeding them. Men, too, left families to seek work elsewhere, sometimes joining the hoboes on the trains and in the "jungles" of the cities. The state of Wisconsin adopted an unemployment insurance scheme, although New York State's Governor Roosevelt was unsuccessful in his attempt to find a regional solution to the insurance problem. President Hoover was unpopular, but the election of Franklin D. Roosevelt was more than a year away.

I moved into Ruth Sutherland's East Side tenement apartment in New York City, laid out much as it had been when the building was put up in the mid 1800s. A toilet in the hall served four apartments on each floor, and in the apartments a bathtub stood beside the stove in the kitchen-dining area. Two cots in another room sufficed for our sleeping accommodations, with space in a minuscule, closetlike room for desk and typewriter. Across the hall lived Harvey O'Connor, at that time the editor of Federated Press, a national press service for labor papers.[1]

I settled down to write a book or thesis on German labor education. The summer was hot, as only New York City can be, and the narrow window of my workroom looked out on a brick wall. The physical circumstances, balanced against the knowledge that I had only the summer for writing, combined to keep me at the typewriter for even longer than normal office hours. On weekends Ruth and I boarded her motorcycle for trips to a Naturfreunde camp in North Jersey, where we camped out in the relative coolness of the woods with newly immigrated Germans who, like us, sought a refuge from the hot, humid city.

PHILADELPHIA

On a visit to Philadelphia a few weeks after my arrival in the States, I met my future coworkers: Eleanor Emerson, head of the City Industrial Department, to whom I would report from the Kensington District where I would work in North Philadelphia; Mary Samson, the executive secretary for the city, to whom Eleanor reported; and Helen Thatcher, Kensington executive secretary, recently returned from foreign service in Turkey. I also met the staff secretaries for two other departments in Kensington, Girl Reserves and Business and Professional Women. I would work with industrial women workers, and Helen had organized a mothers' club. While these various programs did not represent a complete recognition of class divisions among women, the Y approached this crucial issue more openly than most women's organizations—then or now—have done. Certainly the programs took into account the fact of differing work cultures among white- and blue-collar workers, if only in the limited range of career opportunities.

The Kensington community was a working-class district made up largely of Scots, British, and Welsh workers employed in textiles. The Hosiery Union had its headquarters just a few blocks from the Y. Carpets were another major product in the area, and a large lace mill made curtains and tablecloths. Women worked in all these mills, and with its cafeteria, swimming pool, gymnasium, and clubrooms the Y was a welcoming center for those women. Its upper floors offered residence facilities for women who did not live in the immediate vicinity.

In addition to meeting these future staff colleagues, I also met some members of the advisory committees, unpaid volunteers whom the Y recruited to work with staff in dealing with program and administrative matters. Committee members also brought staff information on such other social welfare agencies and their resources as settlements, casework associations, health and hospital agencies, and employment facilities. Many of these women were professionals in their respective fields. The chair of the industrial committee came from one of the Protestant churches, but other members included Gladys Palmer, a research associate at the University of Pennsylvania's Wharton School, and author of *Union Tactics and Economic Change,* on working women members of three Philadelphia textile unions. Another committee member was Emily Mead, the mother of Margaret Mead, who referred to her daughter's research with a mixture of humorous admiration and apprehension.

I learned that the hosiery workers local union had just emerged in January from a long, hard-won strike, marked by the murder of an activist union member, Carl Mackley. The strike had only recently been settled through the offices of the mayor's appointment of a citizens' fact-finding committee, headed by William Fineshriber and including George Taylor, the "Impartial Chairman" for dispute settlement of the organized hosiery industry. Their report had appeared at the end of May 1931.[2] The terms of the agreement (which were agreed upon after my arrival in September) were then bargained by the National Union and the Hosiery Manufacturers' Association and gave the union the closed shop.

Before leaving Philadelphia, I visited Vinita Seward, who with her husband had attended Commonwealth, and they invited me to live with them in a room they had available.[3] I came away from this orientation eager to get started on my new job in September. If I had been allowed to design my new life, it would not have varied much from this reality. It included working people, employed and unemployed, a working-class community, high union membership and commitment—a combination of circumstances that were almost ideal to work with. For my part, I would now have physical facilities for educational and recreational work, a congenial group of staff and volunteer colleagues, and my growing experience as a social worker and labor educator.

Before moving to Philadelphia I had sent Eduard Lindemann a draft of the book I hoped he would approve for publication. To my surprise and disappointment, I never heard from him and so suffered my first rejection—but without the usual letter of criticism or explanation. I began to think of a return to Germany to submit the manuscript for a degree. And indeed, an opportunity seemingly presented itself within the next year as I met Mary Van Kleeck through my Y connections. She was planning to go to Germany for an international meeting in 1933 and would take me as a secretary-cum-interpreter.

I expected I could find a Doktorvater with whose help I would defend my thesis and possibly receive a degree. However, contrary to my hopes and to my belief in the German SPD, Hitler came to power in February 1933 and began to "cleanse" the universities of Jewish students and professors. All my putative professors fled. Horkheimer came to the United States; Mannheim went to England, Bergsträsser to Holland, where the Nazis found him after all. Moreover, any supplementary research that I might have had to do became impossible once the Nazis took over the residential labor schools for training their Hitlerjugend (Hitler Youth). Many of the education directors of these schools were sent to concentration camps, and on May Day 1933 the Nazis abolished the trade unions. To this day, my most advanced degree remains the bachelor's that I received in 1924 from the School of Speech at Northwestern University.

THE PHILADELPHIA Y

But I am getting ahead of my story. I arrived in Philadelphia ready to work on September, 1, 1931. My hope was to make an adult education center at the Y. Of course, my German experience with centers that offered education to unemployed youth and adults was my model. When I discussed this plan with Eleanor Emerson, she was supportive but suggested that such a program had to have interested coplanners and an indication of what students might need and want. She asked whether the young women coming to the Y, employed or unemployed, saw it as a place for study or learning in any systematic way. It would be helpful, she thought, to interview union leaders to gain both their understanding and support.

Thus, I went early to the hosiery workers' headquarters and was referred to Carl Holderman, an organizer for the union and a man with broad social interests, who quickly saw the Y as a community center that could be used by the neighborhood unemployed as a center for their activities. I also met the editor of the *Hosiery Worker*, John Edelman,[4] who signed me up to write articles for his newspaper, which was subtitled *Labor's Tabloid*. These articles appeared as a series on political events in Germany. In them I recounted my growing pessimism by the fall of 1932 about the political fate of Germany, reflected in the increasing number of votes for both Fascists and Communists as election followed election in German cities and provinces. In either case, it seemed to me, the fate of Germany was dictatorship.

I also talked with Bill Pollock, the business agent for the textile workers union and president of the Philadelphia Joint Board of Textile Workers, who later became the national president of the United Textile Workers of America (UTWA). Although his contact with labor education activities so far had been marginal, he readily promised support for any activities we might undertake.

Unemployment

One of my first ventures was to set up an open house for unemployed women, whose numbers increased daily. The Y was a place where they could drop into after looking for work each morning, bring their lunch, and talk with friends. They might use the gym and swimming pool, for which a physical examination was required, which for many of them was a new experience. I arranged for a caseworking agency to send us a woman who could discuss their daily fears with them and the problems they encountered personally or within their families, as well as refer them to available resources. I was able to bring in speakers from the state Labor Office and the Women's Bureau of the Federal Department of Labor. I also recruited a few volunteers who came once or twice a week to help refresh or extend the school knowledge of these unemployed women on a one-to-one basis. At first my advisory committee helped me find tutors, but as the WPA (Works Progress Administration) employment program for unemployed was implemented to include teachers, I drew heavily on its resources to extend the range of educational services we offered.

To this program in Philadelphia came a young woman from New Brunswick, New Jersey, in search of work. She was quite desperate, for she had no money for food or lodging. Our residence took her in for a few nights, but space was at a premium. When she was referred to me, I learned that she had been active in the New Brunswick YWCA. I called the New Brunswick industrial secretary, Marie Elliott, for help, and she offered to come to Philadelphia for a face-to-face talk with Rose and me about possible plans.

Marie had become an industrial secretary in the Honolulu YWCA on her graduation from the University of Nebraska in the early twenties. While there, she had contracted tuberculosis from young women who worked in the pineapple canning factories and had spent several years in a sanatorium for the terminally ill on the island of Maui. She attributed her unlikely survival to her hardy childhood and youth on a horse ranch in Nebraska. Marie was devoted to the young women with whom she worked in the New Brunswick

Y and took Rose back to New Brunswick, where Rose took over Marie's somewhat lackadaisical housekeeping.

When our residence secretary resigned, I suggested Marie as a replacement. She took the job, and we thus shared the years that followed when we both worked with many of the same people both within and outside the Y. She was responsive to the needs of the young women who had come to Philadelphia to find work. Rates for living in the Y residence were arranged to allow women who lost their jobs to remain there while they looked for work, acquired information on local work openings, learned how to write resumes, and were directed to continuing education. Gradually Marie's part of the Y became a residential school, while my section offered daytime and evening living and learning arrangements. Marie remained a close friend all her life and much of mine.

A weekly dance solved one problem of what young women in crowded homes or rented rooms could do for entertainment. Anyone in the neighborhood could come for a minimal entrance fee. The auditorium became the dance floor; the lounge at the entrance to the building became the place where friends could sit and talk. Volunteers from our advisory committees served as chaperones.

Y customs and rules were from time to time put to the test and changed. One such change was the opening up of the building for many community uses. For example, when union organizer Carl Holderman saw that his assignment to bring workers into the hosiery union was reaching its limit—shops were closing down, workers were being laid off—he began to organize the unemployed to deal with the issues that beset them. He set up a barter market where the unemployed could exchange goods that were surplus in one household but needed in another. Once organized, the neighborhood unemployed could help protest or even forbid the entrance of a sheriff sent to expel a family from a house on which the rent was not paid. Meetings of this ever-growing and militant group were frequently held at the Y.

The Y also became a neutral area where labor and management could meet. George Taylor, professor at the University of Pennsylvania and one of the early and certainly most influential designers of labor arbitration,[5] selected the Y as a neutral location for his hearings and invited our staff to visit these sessions. Thus I had an early introduction to this phase of labor relations.

In a more fundamental way the Philadelphia citywide Y was drawn into change as our clientele began to include Italian women who came to us from their workplaces but who lived in a predominantly Italian community west of Broad Street. The Y's bylaws had been those of a Protestant institution. Now the question arose as to whether we could admit Catholic members. The discussions on this issue that took place within the boards and the advisory committees resulted in the admission of Catholic women to full membership. Soon the question was whether our participating club and class members should not be eligible to sit on these policy-making boards and committees as co-decision makers of Y program and policy. Again, the changes took place in many cities, and with quite startling results.

OUTSIDE THE Y

Early on, I made contact with the Philadelphia Socialist Party and with its district branch that included Kensington. As the depression deepened in the late Hoover years, the Socialist Party found more and more adherents. Norman Thomas had emerged as its national leader in 1928 when he first ran for president.[6] By 1932 I was voting the Socialist ticket, as I did throughout the whole New Deal, for the Socialists remained critical of Roosevelt in many particulars. In general we felt that he was not moving far or fast enough to meet the needs of the persons suffering severely under what we saw as the breakdown of the capitalist system.

During the twenties, the Communists who had split from the Debs Socialists following the Russian Revolution in 1917 had mostly worked underground. They had, however, also aimed at finding members and fellow-travelers largely from within the unions at a time when the unions, with a few exceptions, were losing members and influence. In some areas, the Communist Party set up rival unions in mining, textiles, and federal employment, always under a name that began with "National." In relatively strong unions, such as the hosiery workers, the Communists chose to build a caucus within the organization that would gain adherents and in time take over leadership. Such a group existed in the Philadelphia local of the hosiery union under the leadership of Ernie Kornfeld. Communists used this tactic of penetration not just in unions but with liberal groups as well, and established a variety of new committees and newly named organizations (referred to outside the Communist Party as "fellow-traveler groups"), headed preferably by someone not yet associated with the Party.[7]

One such group, the Revolutionary Policy Committee (RPC), which aimed to attract left-wingers in the Socialist Party, was headed by T. J. Matthews, nominally a Socialist Party left-winger.[8] Since the majority of the Philadelphia Socialist Party was very right-wing, made up largely of Jewish immigrant workers in the garment unions, the RPC focused on the Kensington Branch, where it succeeded in creating a severe schism, one that used up time and energy needed for acute social issues. I was for a year or so an outspoken RPC advocate, until I saw that our branch, despite my best persuasion, was losing members rather than gaining influence. I came to the conclusion that I had been used in an endeavor that had anything but the welfare of the Socialist Party as its goal.

The Y itself was not exempt from this kind of penetration—an attractive young Italian woman was sent in to participate in the activities that were directed to public and legislative affairs, and to labor education. At that time the Communist Party's attitude on women differed only slightly from that of society's in general. With the exception of some of the leadership, women were perceived as a group in need of protection at work, but useful for housekeeping chores within the Party. This young woman became an activist within the Y, seeking to promote interest in its legislative and public-affairs goals. If in fact her ultimate goal was to recruit Communist Party members, I saw no evidence of it.[9]

THE Y AND PUBLIC AFFAIRS

In order to forward both state and federal protective legislation, the Y went on record concerning many issues affecting working women. Among these issues were proposals for shortening legal hours of work; providing adequate, clean toilet facilities as well as rest opportunities for women who felt ill; making chairs available for salespersons not occupied with customers; and instituting limitations on lifting heavy weights. These laws applied only to women; under Supreme Court rulings, women required protection against long hours of work because of their reproductive functions. Even though the unions often saw women as low wage earners and thus as dangerous competitors to men's hard-won union wage scales, they also hoped that the adoption of such laws for women would result in a "spillover" to improve conditions for men. They especially hoped that in a period of widespread unemployment, laws requiring shorter work hours might both improve conditions for men and result in enabling the employment of some of the jobless.

At this period all labor legislation was a responsibility of the states rather than the federal government. Massachusetts, Wisconsin, and New York were among the so-called "progressive" states. Pennsylvania had elected Republican governors uninterruptedly from the Civil War until 1932, when Gifford Pinchot, a progressive Republican of the Teddy Roosevelt stripe became governor. Pinchot called on a number of reformers to deal with labor affairs, including Stephen Rauschenbush and women who were active in the Women's Trade Union League and the Consumers' League. The Industrial Departments of the Y throughout the state brought working women to Harrisburg to lobby for new pieces of legislation. On one such occasion, Mrs. Pinchot (popularly referred to as "Flaming Mamie" in tribute to her very red hair) invited our delegation to lunch. To my horror, I discovered on the return trip that many of the would-be lobbyists had appropriated a piece of the governor's table silver. My attempts to collect and return it were not totally successful.

Needing to refresh my information and contacts in American labor education, I attended the annual Workers' Education Conference for the first time in February 1932, where I was asked to present a paper. Out of my consuming interest with what was going on—or had recently gone on—in Germany, I chose to report on "Workers Culture in Germany." [10]

SECOND SUMMER AT BRYN MAWR

As in Chicago, the Industrial Department in Philadelphia established a special committee to recruit students and raise scholarship funds for the Bryn Mawr

Summer School. I had no problem in getting leave to teach there once more in the summer of 1932. Many of the same faculty members returned summer after summer, but new ones were also added.[11]

The deepening depression gave the Summer School a particularly serious cast. Beginning in late May 1932, hundreds, and later thousands of World War I veterans marched on Washington and established "Hoovervilles" in shacks in the southwest part of the city. They remained for ten weeks and eventually numbered about twenty thousand. Everyone followed events there with anxious curiosity, particularly after the president ordered the army to come in, under the direction of General Douglas MacArthur, who was then Chief of Staff.[12] On the morning of July 28, 1932, over a period of fourteen hours the veterans, along with their wives and children were forced out and into Maryland and Virginia. MacArthur's troops' brutal attack on unarmed, unemployed veterans lit the fires of resentment and action among the students and faculty at the Summer School. A group of them traveled to Washington with the hope of talking to some of the veterans. This episode was, I believe, influential in the use of "participant observation" as a research tool during the following summer in 1933, somewhat before sociologists had adopted it professionally. This time a group of faculty and students went to south Jersey, where field workers on vegetable farms had struck against the Birdseye Corporation, in the early boom of freezing vegetables at refrigerating plants near where they were grown. This particular episode was too much for the Bryn Mawr board of trustees, which decided that the school could no longer have the use of the college.[13]

WESLEY RETURNS

Wesley returned in the fall of 1932, his funds exhausted, and still without his Ph.D. While I felt that his personal beliefs and professional aims had in the meantime become secularized, the fact is that he never returned to school thereafter and eventually found his career not in the ministry but in the labor movement, a circumstance I attributed mainly to the opportunities that opened up to him in Philadelphia. During this year of our separation he had had an affair with Greta Lohrke, about which I first heard years later when I looked her up in East Berlin after World War II.

Fairly quickly, Wesley found a job working in a new agency set up to meet the needs of homeless men, many of whom had left home in a vain search for work to support their families and who had become penniless wanderers, dependent on community soup kitchens and occasional overnight accommodation.[14] He joined the Socialist Party and quickly became a strategist with considerable effect on its local programs. My work kept me busy at least four nights a week, but his hours of 8 A.M. to 5 P.M. allowed him to reach out to other Socialist Party branches in other parts of town, to gain their cooperation and support for the Kensington group, and to assess citywide needs on a much broader scale.

Having Wesley back was a wonderful support for my many interests outside the Y. We were finally engaged in something of a joint enterprise in our marital lives. My anxieties about how to face Wesley's ministerial future disappeared. We were founding another life that satisfied both of our needs. We rented a row house in Kensington for a year, furnishing it sparsely with our few things. It was roomy enough to allow us to welcome others to use its second bedroom. The first occupant was Paul Porter and his wife, Eleanor Nelson.[15]

During our year in this house, the Hitlerization of Germany took place. I received several German papers, from which I translated articles I thought deserved English publication. These articles came mainly from the *Gewerkschaftszeitung* (Trade Union Newspaper); some of them formed the basis for articles that appeared in the *Hosiery Worker* or other labor or socialist papers for which I wrote extensively during this period, and an occasional piece appeared in the nationally circulated *Socialist Call.* Each article reported on some aspect of the German trade unions and the Socialist Party's imminent downfall. I often translated at Socialist meetings or other rallies when visiting German exiles spoke. My heart was with this group, in memory and sadness as I thought of my many German friends among students, trade unionists, labor educators, and SPD members. I almost never heard from most of them; at best, I sometimes received desperate news and calls for help.

When I began to look for other ways in which I might help, I found that rescue committees were in the process of being formed to support Jews who were, as of April 1, 1933, forbidden by law from practicing business or any of the professions in Germany. To bring these new exiles into the United States, citizens had to guarantee their support. I felt secure enough in my income to underwrite a number of persons.[16]

I had continued an active correspondence with Paul Bernstein of Berlin. Through it, I knew he had married Johanna Moosdorf and that they had had two children, Barbara, born in 1933, and Thomas, born in 1935. His final letter brought the news that his continued employment looked more and more questionable. Years later I learned that this employment was as a slave laborer at Siemens in Berlin.[17] In 1938 I received a letter from the Quakers indicating that Paul was in danger of being sent out of the city and urging me to send a support letter as soon as possible. I dispatched the letter as soon as I could, but I can only assume that my letter to the Quakers never arrived or came too late for their intervention.

SOVIET HOUSE

During 1933, discussions began among a widening group of friends about the possibility of setting up a Socialist house in Kensington, where a group of us could live together, sharing poverty and intermittent work, as we combined our talents and resources to assist with community efforts to meet the depression and spread the Socialist word. We found such a house on North Fifth Street, only a few blocks from the Y. It was a three-story tenement with four bedrooms on each of the upper floors. Into it moved a varied band of friends, including Paul Porter[18] and Newman Jeffrey (Jeff). Our group also contained Peg Curdy, a nutritionist and child development specialist, and her husband, Franklin, a statistician; an unemployed hosiery topper and graduate of the Bryn Mawr Summer School; a personnel worker in one of the new federal agencies and her husband, an unemployed seaman still in recovery from tuberculosis; a classical music fan who was putting together a Bach bibliography; Phil Van Gelder and Franz Daniel, both of whom withdrew when they married, Phil to Miriam Seaman, a medical student in residence at Philadelphia Women's Hospital, and Franz to her undergraduate roommate at Vassar. Jeff, too, found a wife—Mildred McWilliams (Millie McWillie), a graduate student at Bryn Mawr, who with her friend and fellow student, Ada Stoflet, from the program in social work and policy there, frequently visited us. Millie and Ada will turn up in this story to its very end. We had one African-American member, a former Y secretary who wanted to set up her own small business. We made an early decision that each of us would contribute one week's earnings or income, a plan that identified me as the richest member of the house, but one that sufficed to keep us all going.

With such a group, we were all drawn into many of each other's activities. Phil and Franz were soon deeply engaged in organizing the city's taxi drivers, who shortly went on strike. The nutritionist took over feeding programs, the statistician worked on bargaining demands, the young doctor took on a few families with medical problems and no income, and several others worked as volunteers in the strike's campaign.

The house, which we had thought of vaguely as the "Cookie Jar" (to recognize that it was mainly Wesley's efforts that had brought us all together—I had not yet changed my name from Hanson to Cook) became rather quickly known in the neighborhood as the "Soviet House"—a name that stuck. With this name, our house became known up and down the East Coast, as we attended regional labor and socialist meetings. Visitors from other towns frequently turned up at our door, hoping for a bed for the night or longer.

THE RIGHT TO ORGANIZE

Shortly before we moved into Soviet House, the Roosevelt administration proposed the National Industrial Recovery Act (NIRA) to deal with questions of stabilizing wages and hours, industry by industry. Section 7a of the new law gave "employees the right to organize and bargain collectively through representatives of their own choosing." A new day had dawned for labor. It had acquired legal status with legal rights for the first time, both of which were guaranteed at the federal level.

Under the new law everybody—workers, employers, and even the police—now faced a totally new situation, one that they could neither define nor obey with certain understanding. Kaz Miller, a hosiery union activist, and I were walking a picket line at the Allen-A Hosiery Mill, when the police began interfering. We faced them with a reading of the new law. They retreated to the District Office for a few minutes and came back to say that Captain Dooner was sending them to Washington that afternoon to find out what their rights and obligations were. They were vague about whom they would consult in Washington, and we never learned where they went and what they discovered, but at least the Allen-A picket line was not further disturbed.

With the passage of NIRA, working people were aroused and eager to join unions. When the big Schwedische Kugel Fabrik factory in Kensington organized and went on strike, Ada (who by then was working for a private agency concerned with housing in Philadelphia) and I were on the picket line before our working hours. The police—presumably assigned to keep the peace—grabbed us both and guided us to the paddy wagon. I tried to wave to Wesley as the doors closed and we were taken to the city jail downtown, where, after a "feel-down" by the jail matron, we were put together in a cell. In a few hours we were before a magistrate, facing a charge that since we were not workers at the plant, we were interfering in something that was not our business. The magistrate ordered us to find bail, and put a year's ban on our participation in such illegal activities. Bail was a serious problem. None of us owned property. Then out of nowhere appeared an Italian man who could barely speak English but who offered his home as guarantee of our good behavior for the year. Not the magistrate, not the law (had there been one that fit our case), in fact, nothing other than this action by an unknown "comrade" could have restrained our future activity. For Ada and me, there could be no more picketing for at least a year. However, we both still had to explain to our employers why we were nearly a day late for work. The guarantee that we felt restraining us from repeating the activity may have influenced both these social agencies to forgive and forget.

The problem with labor organizing was not with the workers but with the American Federation of Labor (AFL), after Samuel Gompers's death and under the leadership of William Green. Green was a committed supporter of craft unionism, essentially the organization by skilled crafts as best characterized by unions in the printing and construction industries. The best structural home that the American Federation of Labor could offer these new applicants for organization was a device known as the federal labor union, a local union for workers in various occupations and from a single plant or firm, which was affiliated directly with the Federation. It was meant to be a temporary home from which individuals could be sorted out and sent to the nearest appropriate craft union.

Already at the AFL conventions in 1933 and 1934, John L. Lewis, president of the very deflated but reviving mine workers union, which from the beginning had been organized on an industrial basis, had presented resolutions that would allow the formation of other industrial unions within the AFL. Each time a compromise or delay was found, Lewis had accepted it. By the 1935 convention, however, the experience with federal labor unions, measured by their increasing desuetude, was so disastrous that Lewis came with blood in his eye and derogation in his speech. The latter he directed personally to named members of the executive board and to William Green. I attended that convention, drawn there by my growing concern for the legitimization of industrial organization.

Lewis spoke after the rather conservative and benign defense of the centrality of craft unionism, presented by John P. Frey, the wheelhorse of the molders union and president of the Metal Trades Department. Lewis had been sitting with his union delegation at the back of the enormous convention hall. He rose slowly and walked slowly toward the podium, greeting various friends and familiars en route. Once on the platform he took more time to greet Executive Council members, before reaching the speaker's place. He began softly, but in the silence that enveloped the hall, his voice was audible even in the visitor's gallery where I sat. It slowly rose to a volume that called for no amplification whatever (in any case, microphones were not yet dreamed of). He opened by saying:

> A year ago at San Francisco, I was a year younger and I had more faith in the Executive Council . . . but surely Delegate Woll would not hold it against me that I was so trusting at that time. I know better now. At San Francisco, they seduced me with fair words. Now of course, having learned that I was seduced, I am enraged and I am ready to rend my seducers limb from limb.[19]

He proceeded to do so, describing Green as having experienced a natural growth up to the neck, when he had "just haired over." By then submitting a resolution that would have barred any officer or member of the National Civic Association (NCA) from being a member of the AFL, Lewis also attacked Matthew Woll, a major power on the Executive Council and at the time president of the NCA. That organization was generally distrusted and disliked by unionists for representing a philosophy of cooperation between management and labor and consequently being a betrayer of the labor movement. "If this resolution is not accepted," Lewis went on, "I will accept your judgment . . . as an evidence of the fact that your minds are closed." Lewis's resolution went to the Resolutions Committee, from which it never reappeared.

At this convention, the lines between craft and industrial unionism were finally drawn. The unions, which over the last two years had come into being in steel, autos, rubber, electronics, metal mining, and shipbuilding, petitioned the AFL for affiliation and were rejected. They therefore affiliated with some AFL unions, including the Amalgamated Clothing Workers, and joined Lewis in setting up a Committee for Industrial Organization. The AFL shortly disowned that committee and expelled its members. This action split the labor movement for more than twenty years into the Congress of Industrial Organizations (CIO) and the AFL, who openly warred with one another.[20]

Though Philadelphia was by no means the CIO's central location, the city and even Soviet House became deeply involved in its growth. The United Electrical and Radio Workers of America was founded at the Philco plant on the borders of Kensington, under the leadership of the twenty-one-year-old Jim Carey. The steelworkers in the plants in South Philadelphia and in the steel towns to the immediate west were caught up in the Steel Workers Organizing Committee (SWOC), set up in 1936 by Lewis and his right-hand aide, Philip Murray, under an ingenious and successful organizing plan that called for capturing the company unions to organize the plants from within.

As SWOC became a union toward the end of the thirties, our Young People's Socialist League leader, Michael Harris, a young prodigy comparable to Jim Carey, became regional director.[21] Other activist friends included Johnnie and Annie Green, whose row house in Kensington was back-to-back with Soviet House. Johnnie was a Scots shipbuilding worker, employed at the New York Shipbuilding Company across the river in Camden, New Jersey. His experience with the union in Scotland and his membership in the Independent Labour Party there had made him a Socialist/trade unionist. He drew around him his other Scots and began to build a local union in Camden, which shortly became the Industrial Union of Marine and Shipbuilding Workers, of which he was national president. Phil Van Gelder began to work with him to build this organization and became its national secretary-treasurer. I was tapped to work with a committee designated to write its national constitution, and later became the education director for the Camden Local 1. When Johnnie's third daughter was born, she was named Alice.

The Textile Union

The United Textile Workers of America (UTWA), under the leadership of Francis Gorman, to which the Philadelphia Joint Board of Textile Unions was affiliated, was early approached to join the CIO when it was still an organizing committee. The UTW was neither strong nor large. It had unsuccessfully endeavored for many years to counter the industry's move to the South for its closeness there to the cotton fields and to cheap labor. When the excitement of the NIRA legalization of unions reached the South, violent, often spontaneous, strikes flared and were lost in several company towns, notably in North Carolina and at Elizabethton, Tennessee. Many towns were already aflame by 1929; many others were led by Communists. Gorman, however, was apparently hopeful that the time had arrived to build a strong union under his own leadership. He called a national general textile strike in the summer of 1934.

Wes and I were camping on the Tennessee side of the Appalachian Mountains when word reached us of the general textile strike call. We knew that if such a call came, the Kensington unions would be involved. We felt we must return to Kensington to help out in any way either of us could. In Philadelphia and still on leave from the Y, I was put in charge of the union strike office located in the Joint Board under Bill Pollock. I had to organize the feeding stations, the committees going to the food stores for donations, the scheduling of the picket lines, and the orientation sessions on what pickets were to do and what to avoid.

The strike in Kensington was on the whole directed at companies with established union relations, many of them financially unstable as a consequence of the still deep depression. Wages were the major issue, and not much movement could be expected there. Similar circumstances elsewhere, together with the widespread lack of local or regional leadership of the kind of administrative experience necessary for this national undertaking, soon resulted in a failed strike.[22] However, both the silk workers from Paterson, New Jersey, under George Baldanzi, and the hosiery workers, under Emil Rieve, joined the Textile Workers Organizing Committee (TWOC), and in doing so greatly strengthened it.

When the strike collapsed, Bill Pollock, who saw his own future best served in the TWOC, asked me to become education director of the Philadelphia Joint Board of Textile Workers. Since the Y was already home to a series of classes, I was able to agree to his request, as an extension of services we were already offering. The main change it represented was the influx of male students, who dominated the leadership of affiliated unions. The WPA was a source for teachers, and men such as George Silver (an unemployed teacher who appears again and again in later chapters of this book), became available for these courses, after some training in teaching adults. The Kensington Y became, in addition to its less formal programs, very decidedly the active labor school I had dreamed of after my German experience.

As organization spread to the radio industry, men and a few women from that industry also joined the classes. The central task of the educational program came to be training potential shop leaders in administering the new union contracts. Stewards were taught to handle grievances; chief officers were trained to negotiate for their locals, often with inadequate help from their newly formed national unions.

Emil Rieve of the hosiery workers became head of the rival TWOC and, by 1939, president of the successive Textile Workers Union of America (TWUA). He built a staff to include the new affiliates and brought in Larry Rogin, a journalist, as education director and editor of the union paper.[23] Wesley and I became and remained close friends of the Rogins until their deaths.

Soviet House and the Police

After a year or so, Soviet House had its brush with the local police. One morning when I was at home, two policemen rang the bell. Their mission, they said, was to find the missing daughter of a wealthy Wilmington, Delaware, businessman, and they had some reason to think she might have spent the night at the house. I said that I had no knowledge of such a guest. After some further discussion and questioning, I asked whether they would like to see the house. The answer was "Yes." In the course of our tour I asked why they suspected us, and it then came out that they had frequently observed our goings-on. What had they seen? They had noted, first, that we sang a lot! I asked if there was anything illegal about that. No, they admitted. They had noted too that we had African-American guests and visitors. I repeated my question. Again, they admitted, somewhat reluctantly, that so far as they knew, we were within legal bounds. I asked for a meeting with the chief of the district, Captain Dooner. They promised to make an appointment. When the call came from the captain, I was ready with a support group of neighbor women, some with baby carriages, who walked slowly around the police office, plainly visible from the captain's quarters where we sat talking.

Captain Dooner wanted to be friendly. He insisted that he had nothing against us, especially after his men's visit. The missing daughter was a fiction created to gain entrance. They were relieved to have had an invitation, rather than to have to repeat a visit under sterner circumstances. The captain even boasted that when Norman Thomas came to town on a recent visit, he, Dooner, was proud to have provided him an escort!

Soon thereafter, when Miriam was ready to set up a private medical practice, the household moved to Frankford, the district adjoining Kensington to the northeast. This neighborhood was distinctly middle-class, and the membership of the house began to change with the withdrawal of the originals who went to jobs with the CIO.[24]

In the late fall of 1937 we decided to close out the Frankford House with a celebration. We invited everybody who had ever lived with us, together with many of our frequent visitors, to join the party. It lasted several days and nights in a mood bordering on euphoria. We were in the midst of a labor movement in which we all believed and to which we brought our total commitment. We were sure of a rapidly growing labor movement that would change the conditions under which labor had suffered. We saw no reason why this could not result in a Socialist America. The days and nights were filled with exchanges of experiences, jokes and laughter, singing, dancing, welcoming old friends, eating and drinking. A period was ending, but a broader one was opening.

THE SOUTHERN SUMMER SCHOOL FOR WORKERS

Beginning in the summer of 1933, I taught at the Southern Summer School for Workers, located always in or near Asheville, North Carolina. The school was then under the leadership of Louise MacLaren, a former YWCA secretary who had moved into labor education. Wes would drive me down each year and pick me up six weeks later. We would then set off for two or three weeks of hiking in the Blue Ridge Mountains or the Appalachians.

The Southern Summer School was a smaller school than Bryn Mawr's, but set up very much on that model. During the summers I was there, through 1936, the faculty remained relatively unchanged. I taught public speaking. Economics was in the hands of Professor Lois MacDonald of New York University. She was a born southerner and the daughter of a North Carolina minister. Hollace Ransdell, an independent journalist, who later became a staff member of the *CIO News*, was responsible for writing classes. Bill Wolfe dealt with music and recreation. He led the singing, often composed new songs, and worked with Holly Ransdell in directing skits and plays, thus contributing substantially to a high morale in the school. Our students came mainly from the Y Industrial Departments in North Carolina and Tennessee; among them were some of the unionists who had been involved in the earlier disastrous strikes.

We had no permanent headquarters. The first summer was most favorable at the Asheville Teachers' College with its dormitory and classroom facilities. After that we were quartered for two years in a rundown fundamentalist college, where the president, his wife, and daughter lived in the building and ate at our table throughout the school term. There, at Weaver College, we had our struggles with bedbugs; floors were rough boards; equipment old and barely functional. Another year we were in the facilities of a bankrupt summer camp, built around a large swimming pool that contained (one could only guess how and why) huge snapping turtles, which rather limited its use. One year we were in a bankrupt summer hotel, high in the western Carolina mountains. After the formation of the CIO, and the revival of organizing activity in the South, the new unions put pressure on the school to accept male as well as female students. By the time it ceased activity as a residential school, men predominated among the students.

North Carolina law at the time forbade our including African-American students in the school. The faculty decided that in each session we would set aside adequate time for a presentation and thorough discussion of the issue of race. Many of our students had never questioned the North Carolina law; indeed, they more often saw it as a wise and appropriately considered piece of legislation. The typical response of students was one of considerable initial resistance to the presentations, followed by long discussions of the effects of segregation on the work and family life of both blacks and whites. Despite all the resistance, the process resulted in some mind opening. In several instances it brought recognition of situations in which interracial friendships had been established under cover of an employee/employer relationship—for instance, between maid and mistress. Over time, most students came to recognize the pervasive nature of segregation and the prohibitions that seriously affected the southern African-American communities.

From the Y to the Labor Movement

The Amalgamated Clothing Workers of America (ACWA) had only recently been accepted into the AFL, over the objection of the United Garment Workers of America (UGWA). Sidney Hillman, president of the ACWA since its founding in 1913, had followed Lewis's example of having the Miners Union assume responsibility for organizing the steelworkers. In March 1937, Hillman announced that Amalgamated would support the founding of a Textile Workers Organizing Committee (TWOC).

To give his Organizing Committee a running start, Hillman named each of his Joint Board managers to set up a TWOC in the cities where ACWA was organized. In Philadelphia this task fell to Charles Weinstein. He asked his assistant, Rose Bush, the general administrator of the union's internal affairs, for suggestions. A Socialist Party member and frequent visitor at Soviet House, Rose immediately called Wes and me to her office. On one Sunday morning we phoned friends on the East Coast whom we had met at conferences and seminars, mainly Socialist Party members, to sound them out on their interest in joining such a staff. By midafternoon we had a number of people who could be ready to go to work for the new organization, Wesley and I among them.

I returned to the Y to give a month's notice, with the request that I be allowed to leave sooner if we could find a successor. Alice Overton immediately appeared as an available candidate, and within two weeks I was a union organizer.

Wes and I were assigned together to an office in Marcus Hook, south of Philadelphia, for several months, to organize in a large British-owned viscose rayon plant there. The rayon industry was to be part of a division of TWOC under the direction of Herbert Payne, which would eventually include the many different kinds of rayon manufacture in the mid-Atlantic states—Maryland, Pennsylvania, Virginia, West Virginia, and Tennessee.[25] Wes and I and a few interested rayon workers were often at the gate to the Marcus Hook plant at shift change, handing out organizing leaflets. One Friday afternoon I was arrested with some of the others for "littering and loitering" and spent the weekend in jail, my second and last incarceration.

Soon Herb asked me to become the regional education director for the mid-Atlantic states. Rose Bush and I joined forces to travel from local to local, where active organization had begun. Her job was to set up the financial offices; mine, to meet with local men and women in order to understand their needs for training in various union functions, but primarily in grievance handling. I also had to survey possible community resources for teachers for these classes. Our travel route took us to Lewistown and Meadville in addition to Marcus Hook in Pennsylvania, to Parkersburg and Nitro in West Virginia, and to Roanoke in Virginia; these were the locations of all the plants then owned by the British Crown Rayon Company, which was marked for the first union negotiation in this industry.

Local unions were growing fast in all the plants. Workers were in fact begging for organization. To gain the right to represent the workers in these plants under the newly adopted National Labor Relations Act (NLRA), which set up procedures for a union's recognition, the local first had to acquire a substantial number of application cards from workers there, submit the cards to the regional office of the National Labor Relations Board (NLRB), and then win an election under Board supervision. In Parkersburg, the plant was a little outside the town, and workers used a trolley line for transportation to work. The conductors and motormen on the trolley were committed members of the transport workers union, ready to assist us in signing up new members. One morning I joined Ken Douty to ride the trolley.[26] Passengers piled on at the back entrance and, as they paid their fare, received from the conductor a union card that they filled out in transit. As we arrived at the plant and they left the trolley, Ken and I collected the cards.

Another example of workers' desire to form a union occurred in Nitro, where a local man was in charge. In a town without a motel, I spent the night with his wife in the marital bed, while he slept on the kitchen floor. After the textile workers' meeting, a large group from a local pencil factory was waiting patiently outside the church, the only building in the community where a meeting could be held, to petition me for union membership. I tried to explain that we were organizing rayon workers. I could not think of a union that might be able to deal with their problems. In the end we took them in to the textile workers union. It is from this kind of union organizing history that the employees of the Xerox Corporation to this day belong to the Amalgamated Clothing Workers.

In Roanoke, one of the few cities with a YWCA, I made contact with an active Industrial Department, composed largely of young women in the rayon plant, under the leadership of the industrial secretary, Pat Knight.[27] With her help and with the assistance of the Y, we were able to set up what amounted to a women's program within the rayon union.

INDUSTRIAL DISEASE

Perhaps the most dramatic undertaking I faced during the fourteen months I was assigned to the rayon division began early in Marcus Hook. One of my tasks was to interview workers from the various departments within the plant for the purpose of giving the men in the union who would eventually bargain with the company a picture of the various jobs—including a precise description of what each job involved, its wages, and the shifts that maintained twenty-four-hour, continuous operation.

In the course of talking with men in the department who cleaned the casks in which the rayon fluid was mixed, I learned that many of their coworkers had suffered extreme loss of their mental processes and were in mental institutions in the state. When I reported these findings, the union decided to pursue this problem from several angles, including medical verification, legal information, and publication. We began by asking our friend and doctor from Soviet House, Miriam Seaman, for help. She referred us to a Philadelphia toxicologist, Max Trumper. With their help we set up a program for examining men then working in the department, with the expectation of following their development over a number of years and comparing their progressive states and stages against this baseline.

I went to the State Department of Labor and talked with a man who was aware of the situation and indeed had a file of men who had worked at Marcus Hook and had been committed to mental institutions. He pointed out that they were sent to various places throughout the state to avoid any clustering in its eastern section, near the plant. None of the victims was eligible for workers' compensation, since no law covered industrial disease and compensation was only for injuries incurred on the job.

This civil servant came to my house early one morning to tell me that his files on these cases had disappeared and that he could help me no further. I passed this information on to Herb Payne, who went to the U.S. Department of Labor for help. Secretary of Labor Frances Perkins appointed Dr. Alice Hamilton to make a federal investigation of the conditions in rayon plants using this method of producing yarn. Dr. Hamilton agreed to come back from retirement to undertake the task.[28] Her report included recommendations for fundamental changes, similar to those with which the companies were familiar in their home countries.[29] The result of its publication was the union's support of industrial disease legislation in Pennsylvania, previously advocated almost solely by the miners union in their attempt to gain compensation for victims of "brown lung."

BENNINGTON, VERMONT

In the fall of 1938 I was moved to Bennington, Vermont, where the union had begun to organize in three plants. A local man was its business agent. Wes and I accepted this assignment as part of the responsibility of working for a union. We agreed that as circumstances might permit, we would try to spend weekends together—probably in New York. Nothing was said about how long I might be in Bennington, nor was I given any special instructions as to my probable duties. I quickly discovered that under the elms of this New England town were some twenty-three factories. They included a plant that made needles for the textile mills, a brush factory, and a furniture firm—all of them in various stages of organization into which I was almost immediately drawn. The textile local had an office in a three-story building at a downtown intersection. My first encounters with the local police came in two or three weeks; I was given a ticket for continuing to drive in Vermont with a Pennsylvania license, a practice tolerated for tourists but not for union reps.

Soon after my arrival I received a disturbing letter from Sol Barkin, who functioned in New York national headquarters as the union administrator. The letter said in effect that now that I was settled in Bennington I would no longer receive expenses for living quarters and meals. My salary was fifteen dollars per week. Even in 1938 this was hardly enough to live on. Back in Philadelphia

Wes and I had been sharing two meager salaries to pay for an apartment where all our belongings were deposited. I pleaded my case with Executive Vice President George Baldanzi, whom I had come to know when our travel paths intersected, as we each moved from local to local. I had found George a man of charm, experienced in the labor movement and with a strong sense of justice. With what difficulty I do not know, he rescinded the Barkin decision, and I could once again assume I was on a somewhat limited assignment, with an expense account to defray rooming-house expenses.

In Bennington I had my first experience of participating in collective bargaining, sitting with a committee of workers from the biggest mill, with the assistance of the head of the immediate textile district from Cohoes, New York. The mill's main product was seat covers for General Motors cars. We were hoping to negotiate higher wages, of course, but the company had few orders and hope was not high. The central problem developed around the question of who got to be lead workers or supervisors. I put the issue as between the selection of the nephews and in-laws of management, or selection by merit. None of us had any notion at the time of compulsory subjects of bargaining, and we hung on to this issue for several sessions before accepting the status quo.

Internally, the local union was split, as were the town's residents, between the two predominating ethnic groups: people of Polish descent and French Canadians. This ethnic division influenced elections and positions on all issues. The man who had with marginal success become the union's business manager was French Canadian. When a national auditor uncovered the deposit of union funds into his personal account, the business manager had to go. His departure meant great loss of face for the French Canadian members.

In an attempt to add some recreational elements to union activities, and perhaps thereby to bridge this ethnic divide, I contacted several professors and their students at Bennington College. I first sought help with organizing a biweekly dance at union headquarters, but I hoped soon to introduce educational and research projects. The Chamber of Commerce (COC) occupied the second floor of our building, the union the third. The COC complained to the building's owner about the noise of the dancing and insisted, successfully, that it had to stop. And then a personal change ended my life in Bennington.

PREGNANCY

The first of my reunions with Wes became an intense weekend as we got the news of Hitler's takeover of Sudetenland in October 1938. A war that would include United States participation seemed probable, even inevitable to both of us. A year later, it had indeed begun. Both of us believed that Wes was well within a possible draft age—he had just turned thirty-six.[30]

Within a few weeks of this meeting, it was clear that I was pregnant. I had been told by several doctors whom I had consulted over the years about birth control devices that it was very doubtful I would ever become pregnant, but here it was. I was unsure for a time whether I should try to arrange an abortion and called Miriam for some advice. She had just given birth to her second child. She did not try to influence my decision, but when I told her that this pregnancy was quite unplanned and I did not particularly want a child, she said simply, "Have no anxiety about that; the child brings love with it."

I was influenced partly by this reassurance but also partly by the fact that no one in my immediate circle knew precisely where I might turn, and I had no special friends in Bennington who could help. Moreover, time was passing. I decided to have the baby. I stayed on in Bennington, trying to work both with textiles and the other unions. From time to time I was so overcome with lethargy that I wanted only to sleep. I did succeed, however, during the months remaining, in reading all of Tolstoy's *War and Peace* and *Anna Karenina*.

For me the activity of the thirties ended as I went back to Philadelphia for Christmas. We decided that I should resign from the union and that we would handle the pregnancy as best we could. Thus, my staff connection with the union movement ended for a few years. I saw the pregnancy as a prolonged but not endless period, after which I would of course somehow continue with my trade union career. Toward that end I began writing letters of application to labor papers and workers' education centers for part-time work, which I assumed I could manage while I cared for my newborn. What infant care would really involve remained vague and quite undefined in my forecast.

In my letters of application for work, I summed up my experience and projected it as continuing after a few months' interruption. The forties began for me with the perilous birth of my son in June 1939, the signing of the Hitler-Stalin Pact, and the September march of Hitler's troops into Poland.

6

THE WAR AT HOME AND ABROAD:
1939–1947

When I decided to give up work with the union, Wes and I moved to an apartment in a house in Rose Valley, on the Westchester Line out of Philadelphia and nearer Wes's work in Marcus Hook. I wrote some pieces for the county labor paper and from time to time did editorial work there as an unpaid assistant. However, there was no possibility of a paid job, even as a part-time worker. The future would have to be whatever might turn up. With Ethel Rogin, also heavily pregnant by the spring of 1939, I attended the national meeting of the Textile Workers Organizing Committee (TWOC) when it became an independent union with its own officers and financing. At this meeting, Emil Rieve became president and, to settle an already evident rivalry with George Baldanzi for that office, George became the executive vice president. Wesley was shortly named a permanent staff member and continued to work in the Marcus Hook local of the union's Rayon Division.

PHILIP'S BIRTH

Mother and Father came to be with me shortly before the baby's birth. On the afternoon of June 13, without any of the usual preliminaries of labor, my water broke and washed out the umbilical cord, a happenstance for which neither Mother nor I was in any way prepared. We called my doctor in Philadelphia, and he told us to come to the hospital as soon as possible. A local doctor in Rose Valley joined us to call the ambulance and during the ride of half an hour or more, he asked me repeatedly to feel the cord for any pulse. My reply was always positive.

My doctor met us at the hospital to tell us that he could not officiate at the birth because of an infection on one of his fingers. We would probably require a surgeon for a cesarean section, and he would have to call one who could come quickly. (In fact the operation took place a good many hours later.) In the meantime, Wesley had arrived and been told that my situation was extremely critical. The umbilical cord had been exposed and had had to be drawn back through the vagina to save the baby, a situation that made septicemia a strong probability. Wes must make one of three choices—to save me; to save the baby; or to try to save both of us. He opted for the last.

When I came out of the anesthetic I was in an isolated room with a full-time nurse. The doctors had decided to take me to an unused wing of the hospital to avoid any possible infection spreading from me to other women in the maternity division. This was before the appearance of penicillin. I was treated with sulfa, the most potent drug then available. Septicemia indeed quickly developed, accompanied by a raging fever. I learned when I was conscious that I could not see the baby until I was free of fever. As it turned out, I was in the hospital a month before Wesley could take our son, Philip, and me home.[1] After a few days of my very high fever, the doctors decided I must have massive transfusions, something close to a thorough blood exchange. The word went out to the Teachers Union and to the Party organization, and many volunteers came to the hospital. Donors included my mother and, as it happened, mainly Jewish friends. That fact enabled Philip when he wanted to marry an orthodox Jewish woman to report to her inquisitive grandmother that his mother had Jewish blood!

By early August I felt strong enough to go to Sandy Beach, New Jersey, where our Soviet House friends the McCurdys had built a summer camp for children on the beach. Miriam and Phil Van Gelder had rented a summer cottage there, where she could hang out her medical shield for the summer. I had a room with them. Miriam had a nine-month-old girl and a two- or three-year-old boy, so we established a nursery of second-generation Sovieteers. In my still weakened state Miriam was my tower of strength, both with her reassurances of my eventual recovery and her ongoing medical advice. Wesley came down on weekends and particularly enjoyed caring for Philip, talking to him in a lively way, to which Philip shortly began to respond with coos and murmurs.

THE WAR

All of us were together at the Sandy Beach camp the day Hitler declared war on Poland, September 1, 1939. We spent the evening in anxious speculation over what we feared lay ahead. George Silver had already been drafted, the first of our intimates to join the armed forces, and one who remained in uniform for almost ten years. Before many months had passed, Mike Harris, Ada Stoflet, and Phil Van Gelder from the Sovieteers had enlisted.

THE CHEYNEY HOUSE

Within the year after Philip's birth, we began to dream of having a house. Miriam Van Gelder was pregnant, and she and Phil were looking for their next jobs. They joined us in a house search in the area and helped us with a down payment when we found a typical Pennsylvania stone farmhouse in a tiny village, Cheyney, with a railroad stop on the Westchester line.[2] The house was surrounded by four acres planted with old trees, and the property rose sharply at the rear into woods. At the side we had a flower garden and on the back slope a tremendous vegetable garden, from which I canned literally hundreds of jars of tomatoes, beans, corn, and other vegetables. I once took David Felix, lawyer and urbanite, down to the basement to show off my summer's hard work. He remarked,

"The greatest array of botulism, in my experience." I took it as the ultimate personal and genderwide putdown of women's work.

The institution in the village that was undoubtedly the excuse for a train stop was Cheyney State Teachers' College, the one public college in the state for African-American students. Near it was a post–Civil War Quaker orphanage for African-American children, with an all-white, mainly Quaker board, which I was eventually invited to join. Millie and Jeff with their newborn, Sharon, moved in with us at Cheyney for several months. In the summer of 1941 I was invited to teach at the Hudson Shore Labor School, where Marie Elliott-Algor was now resident director. Attractive as the opportunity was, it seemed impossible. Philip was not quite two; the Cheyney house was big and visitors were always filling it; and vegetables would soon flow in from Wesley's garden. But then, the good Millie offered to care for Philip and the house for the weeks I would be away. I would earn the princely sum of $360, money we badly needed to furnish the big house and keep it going. Wes's own salary, our sole income at this time, became $70 a week when wages were fixed for the duration.

SUMMER SCHOOL AT HUDSON SHORE

Under Marie's direction this school, housed in Jane Smith's old family home on the west bank of the Hudson River, followed the Bryn Mawr Summer School model.[3] At Hudson Shore, space confined us to fewer students than Bryn Mawr had been able to take. As well as women and men from many states, the student body included several German and Austrian exiles, among them Josef Stern, a much revered poet of the Austrian labor movement, some of whose songs and poems I later tried to translate.

During that summer Mrs. Roosevelt, who had long been a member of the Women's Trade Union League and a supporter of the women's summer schools, invited the entire student body and faculty to visit her at Val Kil in Hyde Park, where she had her own home adjoining President Roosevelt's family estate. There she lived with various friends from time to time. As we arrived, she invited us to take a swim and to find bathing suits hung on a long clothesline near the pool. She offered us her famous hot dogs and hamburgers, just like those she had earlier served to the king and queen of England on their visit to the States in the mid-thirties. We sat informally around the outdoor fire while she talked with the exiles from Germany and Austria and with others of us about the school's activities that summer. As we returned to our side of the river, we talked about Mrs. Roosevelt's interest in our work. We had felt her interest to be genuine, part of her well-known curiosity and her search for information.

Then, one morning as I prepared to teach, my brother Fred called from Chicago to tell me that Father had died in California, where he and Mother had retired. Father had been ailing for months from what Mother described as mild diabetes, which, added to a weak heart, had made an invalid of him.

He would be buried later in the fall in a Chicago cemetery, and Fred would go at once to California to assist Mother with the immediate tasks, including finding a place for her to live alone. For a few minutes I considered whether to go on with my class or take this time for thoughtful consideration of what my father's death meant to me and might mean for my mother and brothers. I decided that my job was laid out for me and went to my class.

On my return home at the end of the session, Wesley greeted me with a display of his purchases out of my earnings—a new refrigerator, a full set of Revere cooking ware that I still use fifty years later, and a sofa for the living room. My deep and only regret about this was that he had not waited to allow me to share in the joys of so much shopping! We had always had so little money, so tightly budgeted, that I felt I had been deprived of a rare opportunity to inspect and choose.

WE JOIN THE WAR

Late in the afternoon of December 7, 1941, I heard by radio of the Pearl Harbor disaster and began to realize that our own participation in the war was imminent. I remember resolving that I would protect Philip as much as possible from its consequences, although I was certainly vague about what that might imply. I think I wanted him to have a "normal" childhood, without any knowledge of the death and suffering that war brings.

When Millie and Jeff left us for Detroit where they had been offered jobs with the Auto Workers, I found a student from the local African-American college to live with us and take care of Philip when I was away in the evenings teaching union classes. She went with me in the summer when I was invited again to teach at the Southern Summer School in Asheville and Philip, just getting sure of his feet, was running about on his own explorations. It was her first trip to the South and her first experience with formal race segregation, for which I had tried to prepare her, however inadequately. When she graduated, I had to make a new search. My difficulties with finding child care during the war were about to begin. Her successor from the same college was much less dependable, and we severed connections at the end of a semester.

I was invited to take a job as secretary of the Amalgamated Clothing Workers of America (ACWA) Philadelphia Joint Board, a very tempting offer, but my search for a woman who would come every working day was still ongoing. When I finally found a young mother from Westchester whose husband was in the service and who would bring her three-year old boy as companion for Philip, I felt I could take the job.

THE ACWA AND ITS MANAGER, CHARLIE WEINSTEIN

Charlie Weinstein was the shrewd, tough, likable manager of an ethnically mixed union, himself a product of the men's clothing industry and part of its Jewish leadership from its founding days in Chicago. He was utterly loyal to its national president, Sidney Hillman. Hillman had sent Charlie in to Philadelphia several years earlier with instructions to free it from the local leader, an Italian member of the Mafia. Charlie accomplished that task by paying him to leave the city, under threat of legal pursuit should he ever return. Charlie then replaced some of his predecessor's local business agents with men, mainly Jewish, whom he believed he could trust. After this housecleaning, Charlie's election to the post of Joint Board manager was immediately accomplished. His staff was, on the whole, an ethnic representation of the members of each local union, of which there were about twelve, each organized by one of the crafts in the industry. The most powerful politically within the Joint Board were the cutters, the most skilled workers, who were all male. The least influential, for a variety of reasons, not least because of their gender, were the buttonhole makers, all Italian women. The two women on the staff were Sarah Fredgant, a Bryn Mawr Summer School graduate, who was education director for the Joint Board, and Rose Bush, the union's business manager. At this period, the national union was still an avowed Socialist organization that made May 1 a holiday, in the manner of many European unions.

Charlie's need for a secretary and general maid-of-all-work had been served for years by a competent young Jewish woman.[4] In contrast, I was 100 percent WASP, with no ethnic or personal claim to membership in the union's inner circle. Charlie called me in for a friendly, get-acquainted interview, making plain that I had Rose Bush to thank for being there. He hired me at once.

With that introduction, I began the most instructive job I had held so far. Charlie shortly added to my title of secretary that of assistant to the manager, thus establishing me with his male staff as one of his inner circle. In a relatively short time I was representing him at community meetings, at inner-union meetings, with local politicians, at the United Way, and with arbitrators who, he insisted, had to be recommended by George Taylor. It became clear to me that Charlie was a power in the city. Reformers sought his endorsement of their candidates, who were running against an entrenched and corrupt political hold on city government, a move that succeeded.

Charlie was not only manager of the Joint Board; he was, in fact, manager of the Philadelphia industry, "the market," as the local territory was always referred to in this union. Employers came to him, as did politicians, for his endorsement of their new plans. Whether shops were large or small, he knew them all well. Most of the small enterprises were "contractors" who were former union members, often out of the Cutters Union. Quarrels and tensions between the bigger, independent shops and the contractors were typically settled in Charlie's office. He knew their financial status, their loans, their marketing, and their profits.

If a particularly interesting visitor came to the office, he would open his door, beckon me to come in, and sotto voce tell me that the topic would interest me.

I never took notes, and I think it was understood that no notes existed on these meetings. Charlie's head was big enough to keep all these files and to cross-reference them.

After a year and a half, it all came to a sudden end. My housekeeper had recently told me that she was receiving no GI payments from her husband. I assured her that she could ask for them, perhaps through the Red Cross; she had followed my advice and had begun to receive a monthly check from the army. Without any notice, she did not come in one Monday morning. When I went to look for her in Westchester, the only result was that I was now without a caretaker for Philip. Wesley was constantly traveling and could not fill in. Charlie called in the janitor of the union building and directed him to find me somebody, assuring me that I would have help. Nothing worked, and I was forced to remain at home. I retreated to Cheyney and thought of looking for part-time work.

Just at this point Ken Douty asked whether I might take his second son, Tommy, for a while. Ken's case was particularly poignant. Tom had been born just nine months before Philip. When he was only a few months old, Mary had disappeared and was found days later in New York City, where she was in search of her obstetrician, who, she felt, needed her. She was hospitalized, and her brother, Walter Pugh, and his wife, Ellen cared for Tom. Ken's older son, Michael, was first looked after by a family friend, Una Corbett, a teacher; when Una had to begin teaching again, Michael was sent to a progressive boarding school in New York State, where Una's daughter was also enrolled.

Ken's situation became critical again when Walter Pugh, a reserve officer in the army, was called up for duty and his wife Ellen could not care for Tom properly. As a baby, Tom had spent months in a hospital crib, becoming more and more lethargic, almost autistic. Una took him in the summers, but this was only a temporary solution. Tom was four years old and I was at home when Ken turned to me for help. I saw Tom as a companion close to Philip's age and thought it might work. At Christmas Mike came to us for his vacation and begged to stay. We added Mike to the family. And then one morning I had a call from Liz Ross who told me that Margie Harris was desperately ill in the hospital with a tubal pregnancy, from which she had had excessive bleeding. It was by no means certain that she would pull through. Liz had Margie's three-year-old, Susie. Could I possibly take Susie at least until her father, Mike Harris, who was in the army, could be alerted? I said, "Yes," of course, and found myself with four children, three of whom were three or four years of age. My time was completely filled.

I had become acquainted with a neighbor up the hill, Eva Cherry, who ran a children's summer camp. She would take my four as day campers in return for my doing the bookkeeping and some administrative work. Eva was looking for a doctor who would be available, and I suggested Miriam. This meant that Miriam's two children were added to the day camp enrollment and that our household expanded further to include them.

Ken Douty established the custom of coming to Cheyney from his Washington job in the Department of Labor every two weeks to visit his children. Wesley was usually home for weekends. Thus the Cheyney household became a familylike assemblage, at least on weekends. As the summer progressed, Margie slowly recovered and came to join us for the duration of the war.

When Philip was three, I enrolled him in the Rose Valley School's nursery division, and I now took on the job of school secretary to earn his tuition. When the Douty boys came to live with us, they too went to Rose Valley School. Parents were deeply involved with the school, and through it I met many congenial people who lived on the commuter train line. They included a family who had taken several British children, sent to America for the duration, as well as Claire and Glen Milliken, with their three boys.[5]

Teachers in the school became personal friends as well. Among them was Margaret Rawson, a particularly valuable teacher and healer of young students suffering from dyslexia.[6]

BACK TO PART-TIME WORK

With Marjorie Harris as another adult in the household, I looked for evening classes to teach. I was hired by the Penn State College Labor Extension Program, as well as by the Philadelphia Schools' Labor Extension classes, headed by Dr. Ben Barkas, an active member of the Teachers Union and a man deeply interested in labor education. The federal government financed special wartime programs for union stewards and local officers who could be trained to handle grievances and arbitration cases in the interests of labor peace, thus avoiding the interruption of production. Both these institutions were offering such courses, and I was kept fairly busy with their evening classes in Philadelphia.

In addition, the CIO encouraged their unions' establishment of local community relations programs with the training of community stewards, a new kind of office in local unions. These new in-plant officers were to be trained in the availability of community resources, such as child care, children's summer camps, elder care, casework agencies, health programs, and the like. These programs would help both male and female wartime workers under heavy overtime assignments to present their problems to community agencies for needed assistance.

The United Way began to function at the time as an umbrella agency for raising local funding for many social services. A United Way staff member was nominated by the local labor movement to act as an intermediary between these newly trained stewards and the social agencies affiliated to United Way. This union representative was also meant to enlist unions' support for workers' payroll deductions to United Way's member organizations. The new director of community relations for the CIO, Leo Perlis, asked me to write the training manual for this new kind of steward. Immediately thereafter, I was busy training such stewards in many of the Philadelphia unions. This experience gave me the groundwork for the project with which I began my career at Cornell a decade later.

THE AFFILIATED SCHOOLS BOARD

I was invited to become a member of the board of what was now called the Affiliated Schools for Workers, still under the direction of Eleanor Coit and her assistant, Fannie Turkel. This group had taken on a variety of services, other than the central administration of resident summer schools. Conditions in wartime were such that workers could no longer leave work for several weeks under the excuse of pressing family demands. Everybody was needed at work, including many hours of overtime.

A new function of labor education was providing experts to work in cities or with a group of unions that wanted experienced assistants in setting up local programs.[7] The Affiliated Schools continued the Washington's birthday conferences held in late February, which provided a meeting place for labor educators from both the AFL and the new CIO. These organizations had become fierce rivals in organizing, lobbying, political activity, and international affairs. I remained a board member until the Affiliated Schools had to wind up its affairs and cease to exist in the early fifties.[8]

MY FIRST VISIT TO ITHACA

I was invited in the fall of 1945 to go to Ithaca, New York, for an advisory meeting at the newly opened State School of Industrial and Labor Relations at Cornell University. The agenda called for a discussion of its projected curriculum and its extension activities, particularly for labor unions. The dean of the school at that time was State (shortly to become U.S.) Senator Irving Ives, the legislator who had conceived of such an institution. The faculty consisted only of Maurice Neufeld, whom I first knew through Rose Bush in the early thirties when he was working for the Amalgamated in Philadelphia, and Jean McKelvey of Sarah Lawrence College, one of the few early arbitrators. Faculty were added during the first year, including Milton Konvitz, Pete Jensen, and others with War Labor Board backgrounds. Phillips Bradley, who had written the school's charter under Ives's direction, was serving as general administrator during Ives's frequent absences from Ithaca. Within two years Eleanor Emerson had been invited to head the Labor Education Extension Program. Al Smith became director of management education, and Ralph Cambell was director of the extension program.

For this meeting, the school succeeded in bringing together the top people from the labor education movement. These included Mark Starr, education director of the ILGWU-AFL, Larry Rogin, Eleanor Coit, and Tony Luchek, the director of the Pennsylvania State University labor education program that had preceded the founding of the school at Cornell.[9] Our group of twenty or so worked together for a few days in this newly established institution at a major university. We learned about the new school's legislative charter, which called for an undergraduate program leading to a B.S., graduate courses leading to either a standard M.S. or an M.I.L.R. (Master of Industrial and Labor Relations, a terminal degree for practitioners) as well as a Ph.D.

The extension program would offer nondegree classes and conferences in consultation with labor, management, and public groups. In terms of staff, teachers, and administrators, these classes would be modeled on the statewide services long available in agriculture and home economics to the agricultural communities throughout the state. We were hopeful that we would, like the agricultural community, receive federal assistance. Hilda Smith spent many years in Washington advocating and lobbying for such a program, and for a time this appeared to be near adoption. However, management in major industries successfully opposed it.

A third aspect of the school's program was to include research and publications that would feed into the extension and resident programs and become available to the entire industrial relations field. The original charter still covers the now greatly expanded research activities undertaken by the school.

We ended the meeting with the sense that a new phase of labor education had been established, one based strongly in the universities. Although at least two universities had preceded Cornell—Wisconsin and Penn State—we knew that this program was based on legislative recognition and the fulfillment of a postwar need; indeed, many universities, both private and public, soon followed with similar programs.

An Invitation to Work in Germany

After the war was over, a delegation of American educators was charged with making recommendations to the occupying U.S. army in the American Zone of Germany about restructuring the German educational system. As the adviser on adult education, Larry Rogin recommended that a labor education expert be sent to work with the German trade unions, an institution that the army and its State Department advisers had already seen as an aid to the establishment of a postwar German democracy. He knew of the study of German labor education that I had made sixteen years earlier and suggested my name.

In the early spring of 1947 I received an invitation from the army to go to Germany as a "visiting expert." After long consultations with Wesley and the boys—Mike, Tom, and Philip—as well as with Ken Douty, it was decided that I could—indeed, should—accept the invitation. The boys would all go for a while to Una Corbett in Baltimore. Ken suggested wisely that I come to Washington a few days before my departure to Germany to visit Val Lorwin, then in the State Department, who could introduce me to people knowledgeable about the state and goals of the occupation in the American Zone, where I would be stationed. It was a very sound piece of advice, which I was happy to follow.

The boys and Wesley accompanied me to the train that took me to Washington, where I was to report on May 1 for what was to be a two-months' assignment in Germany. In Washington, I stayed with Ada Stoflet, no longer in uniform and back at her Labor Department job.[10]

In my first meeting with him, Val Lorwin offered me a wealth of information and useful contacts. I met with several well-known German immigrants, among them Otto Kirschheimer and Herbert Marcuse. Thanks to their introductions, I would be able to meet Germans who had already returned to Germany from the United States. Kirschheimer and Marcuse had written reports to the State Department on the reviving trade unions. Just as important, they filled me in on the Americans in the American Zone who were responsible for labor affairs. In short, they gave me the background and provided contacts sufficient to fill in for the sixteen years of my absence from Germany.

At the official meeting of the group assembled to travel together, I met my companion visiting experts. We were a miscellaneous group of about ten, including a minister of the Missouri Synod of the Lutheran Church, two athletic coaches, and the dean of the School of Journalism at the University of Missouri. On May 1 we took off for Westover Field, where we expected to find an army plane ready to take us to Frankfurt. We would all receive "assimilated" army rank, which would allow for our accommodation in billets, our use of PXs, and transportation once we arrived. I was an "assimilated colonel."

On arrival at Westover we found that no plans had been made for us; since we had to spend the night, I was assigned to a WAC barracks. My companions there were a group of "dependent" wives of men stationed at Thule in Greenland, who were also outbound, expecting to leave the next morning. They invited me to their farewell party, at which they all shortly became hysterically drunk, mainly because they were apprehensive about the unknown that lay ahead in the isolated, frozen north. It became too noisy to sleep and too sad a display of fear and anxiety to disregard. The party went on most of the night. We spent several days at Westover, during which we were briefed on over-ocean travel and our group was augmented with an assembly of army men with various destinations and missions. Some of our members began to exhibit their own anxieties.

Late in the afternoon of May 4, we were ready to go. Among our new companions were a sergeant specialist in dealing with corpses and a young corporal headed for Paris where his would-be bride was waiting for him. Although our pilot told him that he had no orders for Paris, the corporal nevertheless was on the boarding list.

This flight across the Atlantic, to my amazement, seemed entirely in the hands of our pilot, who made his own decisions about our route and landing places pretty much as we went along. As we boarded the plane, it was clear that the pilot had multiple assignments. One side of the plane was filled with seats, while the other was filled with cargo. I was the only woman aboard. The sergeant who acted as flight attendant instructed me to give him a special signal when I wanted to go to the toilet, so that he could "clear it out." The Lutheran minister declined to remove his safety vest (we all had to put one on for takeoff) and flew the whole journey wearing it. My seatmate was a State Department courier with his bag of mail locked to his wrist. He roused me after an hour or so to point out the window where I could plainly see that one of four propellers was dead. We landed at a Canadian base for a couple of hours and then, presumably repaired, we took off for Goose Bay, where we unloaded again for our first meal at the officers' club. We had an hour or two to walk about in this bleak land.

At sunrise we landed in the Azores for breakfast. As we reboarded the plane, the pilot asked me whether I would like to sit with him and the copilot as we headed for Lisbon. Once more in flight, he asked me whether I had ever seen Mont St. Michel. I said, "No." "Well," he replied, "Let's go to France that way!" So up the coast of France we flew, encircling the islet in beautiful weather, with beautiful views, then across France, high above the destruction left by war. The Paris-bound corporal was led to believe our trip had been rerouted. Now we were clearly bound for Charles de Gaulle airport. Should we go down the Champs Elysées? Why not? We descended to perhaps a thousand feet, which felt like five hundred, and flew up the Champs Elysées and over the Arc de Triomphe. After Paris, I was a normal passenger again, and at the end of a twenty-four-hour trip we were in my familiar German home, Frankfurt.

While waiting for transportation to a billet, I phoned the Manpower Division office in Berlin to see whether I might stay in Frankfurt. No, they replied, headquarters were in Berlin, where I must report first for briefing. They were waiting for me, and I was to take the first plane in the morning.

Berlin Briefing

Germany was divided into four zones, British, Russian, French, and American. My assignment called for me to visit the three provinces in the American Zone, as well as Bremen and Hamburg, port cities located in the British Zone but under American jurisdiction. In each case, I was to meet with the labor officer through whom I would locate the trade unions. I was to visit their meetings, talk with their officers, visit functioning factories, and estimate the various educational and material needs of workers and unions. Berlin, the capital of Germany, was also on my list, though its structure was unique, since it functioned under the rule of all four Allies, each having responsibility for one sector, just as the country itself was divided. Military police, for example, traveled throughout Berlin in parties of four in a jeep, one from each occupying country. Sector borders defined administrative areas only but were not yet impenetrable barricades. We went easily to museums, opera, and theaters in the Russian Zone of Berlin, which included the old cultural city center.

In Berlin I met with Leo Wertz, a Labor Department civil servant, now director of the German office. I learned that George Silver was traveling in the Zone and that I would see him when I arrived in Munich in a few days. Captain Mullaney, formerly a unionist from the West Coast, and now the chief of trade union affairs in the American Zone, alerted me to problems that concerned him and that were to some extent part of current American policy. Among these were the rivalry between AFL and CIO interests in the future German unions and the questions of Communist infiltration.

During my briefing in Berlin, I was also told that I was to meet with women workers assigned to bring order into the piles of brick and rubble lying everywhere in bombed German cities. These *Trümmerfrauen*, as they were called, were for the most part heads of households because their husbands were dead or still severely wounded or in Russian prisons. In any case, these women had had perforce to assume what German tradition told them was the man's job in the family. One woman, for example, said, "When my boy came home one day with a bicycle that was not his, I so much needed that bicycle that I could not even ask him where he got it. If I had told him to take it back, he would not have obeyed me, as he would have had to do if it was his father's request."

Again and again, I heard of men suddenly returning, unable to assume their roles as provider and parent. I frequently saw men in ragged, dirty uniforms, their feet bound in whatever could substitute for shoes, who had walked from Russia to their home city. One such family, whom I quickly came to know, was that of the woman head of women's affairs for the newly revived Berlin trade unions. When her husband appeared, he was half crazed, and neither he nor she could reassume their traditional roles after years of his absence, during which she had taken over full economic and parental responsibility for both children and survival.

I saw my early days in Berlin as a chance to look up old friends and acquaintances, if I could find them, to hear from them personally about their experiences, their survival, and their hopes and plans for the future of the SPD, the party we always called Socialist (see chapter 4, page 63), and the trade unions. On one of the several German holidays in May, which the Americans also took as a holiday, I was allotted a car and driver and set out to locate the Tröscher family, but I found that the last address I had was just inside the Russian Zone where an army vehicle could not go.

I did find Luise Hüls, a student who had been on an exchange to the United States when I was first in Germany and whom I had met at a conference short-ly before I left. She had written her thesis on adult education in the United States. Luise and her mother were living in their old apartment, badly dam-aged in the bombing but providing a roof over their heads. Their stories of life in Berlin during the several hundred air raids and of Frau Hüls's shipment to the countryside, where presumably she would have sufficient food and be out of the war, were my introduction to a whole series of tales of extreme suf-fering. I heard stories of escape by foot over long distances before the advancing Russian army; reunions under great difficulties with other family members; nights in bomb shelters; and the deprivations of the last two post-war years.

On another occasion I found a former fellow student now in Berlin, who had taken advantage of the Nazi encouragement of women to increase child-birth rates by deciding to have a baby of her own, though she was not married. The baby girl was born a few days before the Russian occupation of Berlin. When she decided to take the infant to a friend across the city, she experienced Russian soldiers' concern for children firsthand. They repeatedly offered her rides in Russian vehicles as she progressed through the city, and she especially remembered with what reluctance the last soldier host lifted her baby down to her as he gave the child a good-bye kiss.

Such war stories very early gave me some understanding of how German civilians had lived through the war and postwar years.

To the American Zone

In the American Zone, I would visit in turn Munich, Stuttgart, and Frankfurt, capitals of the three provinces Bavaria, Württemberg-Baden, and Hesse. As I began my travels, I went first to Munich, where I met with George Silver, still in uniform after almost eight years in the army. He had conceived the plan for my trip. He was accompanied by Abe Kramer, the local Berlin labor officer, and we three went to see Franz Loriaux, the Manpower Division officer for Bavaria, and Herb Baker, his young assistant.[11] George and I set out to visit some of the restored trade union schools in the mountains. To reach one, we had to climb a kilometer or two beyond where the car could get through to find a class of young workers under the leadership of a prewar unionist. A major issue for this man was the unification of the revived trade unions into a complete industrial structure. This would mean several basic changes: a limitation of national unions to about fifteen broad industrial structures (metal, textiles, public employees, chemicals, etc.); a single federation, in contrast to the pre-Hitler model of several ideological groupings; the inclusion as equal members of skilled, semiskilled, and unskilled workers. It would mean not only including the former Catholic unions but also finding representation for them on executive boards and as heads of functional departments (education, women white-collar workers, and youth). Finally, it would mean loosening the federation's ties to any one political party.

When George and I arrived at the school, we found that the teacher that afternoon was a Catholic, who spoke of family as the building block of society with "the man at the head, and the woman as the heart" of this basic unit. I was invited to speak and after a few sentences was flooded with questions about the United States in general. These young apprentices had so little experience of unions that my attempt to talk about the American labor model and tradition was hardly heard and certainly not understood.

On our return, we took with us a young staff member with whom we shared refreshments at an officers' club as we neared Munich. He was almost speechless at the amount of food from which we could choose, and although we encouraged him to eat as much as he could, he found it impossible as he thought of his hungry sister with whom he could not possibly share these riches.

I had an address for Eduard Weitsch, the prewar director of Dreissigacker School where I had met Paul Bernstein. Eduard's wife was now Ilse Theiss, a former fellow student at Frankfurt, and I wanted very much while I was in Munich to find them both. George helped me persist until we found them in the village of Deisenhofen, to which they had moved during the war. Like Luise Hüls, they had trouble remembering who I was, since we had known each other sixteen years and a revolution ago. Eduard was ill and near death. He was writing his autobiography as a memoir for his children, now in their teens, who had never known the days before the Nazis took over Germany. Ilse worked at the Munich radio station in the women's department and signed me up at once for an interview broadcast. Our reconstituted friendship continued for about ten years and was constantly renewed as I returned to Germany again and again during the fifties. She died much too young in 1957, as a consequence of the deprivations of war.

Among the schools I visited was one well established by the Railroad Workers Union in a building that the Nazis had made a youth leadership training center but that the local government, with American help, had now returned to the union. The railroad workers were employed, as many other industries were not. That, alone, contributed to their considerable optimism about the future and provided the means for the operation of a better-furnished school.

Although unemployment was high, mainly because the factories still lay in rubble and the economy was completely disorganized, everywhere I went I found workers with the urge to work, even under the most trying circumstances. In a metal working factory that had been totally destroyed, the former workers were endeavoring to produce much-needed household articles out of the twisted metal they found in the rubble. Reforming it into household pots and pans was an attempt to make a few pennies in response to the huge demand. German money was practically worthless, and in any case there was little to buy.

The Germans lived in a cigarette economy to which the Americans contributed massively. Germans, both men and women, went about with little boxes in which they collected discarded cigarette stubs, from the crumbs of which they made their own cigarettes. Though forbidden to buy or sell in the German market, Americans, in or out of uniform, carried on an active trade in German antiques and art, paying with cigarettes. At my meetings I sometimes passed around a package of cigarettes, from which women put one or two in their worn purses "to take home to their men." One American told me that he believed he had the world's most complete collection of Käthe Kollwitz original prints, all bought with cigarettes. Although dollars might have been even more desirable, the American side of this surreal economy was to issue us scrip for use in American installations. The value of this scrip might be changed from time to time without advance notice, which made these dollars worthless. Germans who had scrip were presumed to be criminals and treated as such.

THE INTERACTION BETWEEN AMERICANS AND GERMANS

The cigarette economy was only one measure of the ways in which both Americans and Germans accommodated themselves to one another. If many Germans could have chosen between Russian and American occupation they would have preferred the latter. Nevertheless, they had many complaints about our shortcomings. These complaints began with our feeding programs, which often included our big shipments of corn. Germans saw corn as fit only for animals and perceived our sending it to mean a derogation of them as a conquered people.

The Germans were going through what was called de-Nazification: those who had been or were suspected of having been members of the Nazi party were held in camps, many of which I saw in my travels, where hundreds of men walked about aimlessly in the summer weather, waiting for their hearings and possible clearances or sanctions. All former teachers, government officials, and other public servants were presumed to have been Nazis and, if they were to continue working, had either to be cleared of this past delinquency or punished for a crime. One spoke of *"braune Flecken"* ("brown spots") on those who could show that they had had little responsibility for policies and decisions. In such cases one might receive a *"Persilschein"* (a laundry soap certificate) that cleansed one's record. At the other end of the spectrum was a full-blown trial and imprisonment, which reached its zenith in Nuremberg with the trials of Nazi Party leaders.

In union meetings, I often listened to expressions of great resentment against Americans and particularly American unions. The complaints had a strong political source. The Morgenthau Plan, for instance, was well known for its aim to make Germany once more an agricultural nation and to bar any possible restoration of its industrial complex, which had supported the Nazi system and supplied its arms. Sidney Hillman, adviser to President Roosevelt and president of the CIO, was known to have given his support to this plan. Most trade unionists, however, earned their living in the manufacturing industries that under the plan would presumably have been closed or not rebuilt. They were Socialists who saw the German peasants as hopelessly conservative, still throwing all their support to the right-wing prewar parties.

The reviving unions, as I saw them, needed everything—paper, mimeograph machines, furnishings for their meeting rooms, housing, schools—to make them effective organizations. But Americans, the members felt, were suspicious of their leaders, oblivious to their needs, and acting like exploitative overlords, making little distinction between those who had been active Nazis and those who had been opponents of the Nazi system. Particularly, they charged us with making no distinction between Socialists and Communists, and thus distrusting both kinds of local trade union leaders. Because of the long, lost war, most Germans were bitterly anti-Communist, although in many sections of the American Zone there was no doubt that the Communists had successfully placed themselves in local leadership of the unions. These Communists were determined that when the labor movement achieved national federation status across zone lines they would be able to establish themselves in decisive roles and offices in the more powerful national unions.[12]

STUTTGART

I had promised to look up the relatives of several Philadelphia friends in Stuttgart. Within the first days there, two of these visits were possible. One friend's sister was still in her old home but was now a war widow essentially without resources. Since the house was hardly damaged, all but two of its rooms had been taken over by the city to house refugees from the lost eastern provinces who had moved by the millions westward. She spent my visit denouncing the Allies, who had allowed Germany to be the victim of the Russians, and complaining about her unwanted housemates who imposed on her kitchen, her bathroom, and her well-furnished home, which they were gradually destroying. She wanted no comfort. She wanted only a return to what had been the good old days. By contrast, another older couple welcomed me warmly as an emissary from the United States, bringing word of their family there. They were now filled with hope that they might soon get to the United States themselves.

An outstanding experience was a provincewide women's conference held at Bad Boll in the undamaged buildings of the Protestant Academy, where I met a former fellow student, Irmgard Rexroth-Kern, now working as a freelance journalist and living in Frankfurt with her four-year-old son. Prewar feminist leaders, some of whom I had known as students, appeared here, much older but eager to make connections with post-Nazi women, who had experienced sixteen years of denigration under Hitler.

Found: The Tröscher Family

As I was driven back to the hotel in Stuttgart one evening, I saw a man gesturing in my direction and could not believe he really wanted to talk to me. I had the driver stop and wait, however, and my welcomer introduced himself as Tassilo Tröscher, the young agronomist who had married my dear friend Lydia, whom I had met through my first job at the Chicago YWCA. Wes and I had renewed our friendship with the Tröschers when we were students in Berlin. I told the driver that the day was not over, as I took Tasso into the car, and we set off for the suburb of Leonberg, where the family had been reassembled with his mother-in-law, who had always lived there, and where Lydia had been born. Tasso had heard over army radio that I had arrived in Germany and knew that I was shortly due in Stuttgart.

As we came in, the family was sitting down to a meager supper of potatoes and green applesauce. The table was extended to include not only four Tröscher children but a young cousin as well, plus a Jewish family of older parents and a grown daughter, whom the family had sheltered and cared for during much of the war, until they themselves had been sent to rural Thuringia away from the air raids. The oldest son, Gerhard, had been sent to a church school in the southwest, where he had spent several years away from the family, and had not yet returned to the crowded household. Tasso had escaped being drawn into the armed forces by working as an agricultural expert for a private company that contracted his services to the agricultural department of the government. He had often worked in the captured territories, where his task had been to survey agricultural output and introduce modern techniques or new products. That morning the children, Kristin, Hans-Jörg, Adelheid, and Ursula, had been sent out to a nearby farm to buy what could be bought that day to eat—the results of the expedition were on the table. The applesauce was bitter, made as it was from the newly formed apples in mid-May.

For me, it was like a return to family. The old ties were quickly reestablished, and I discovered that Adelheid had been born in the same year as Philip. I also learned that Lydia's younger brother, for whose university education Lydia had come to the States to earn money, had been killed in the war, as had all of Tasso's brothers. Lydia, who had wanted a large family, had had six children, the first of whom died at birth. Gerhard, the second-born, had been named Gerhard Lincoln, in tribute to their American years. After our first meeting, I met Tasso several times during this trip. He was now in business for himself as an agricultural consultant.[13]

REUNIONS IN FRANKFURT

My visit to Frankfurt, the last of my field visits, was particularly poignant. It was the city where I had lived as a student and I felt I knew it well. But it had been 90 percent destroyed, and most of the landmarks I had known lay in ruins. Dust from the rubble blew in clouds. I was billeted in one of the hotels on the central Bahnhofplatz, with a view of the shattered main station, still one of the busiest in Germany. I came in on the weekend, eager to spend a day or two looking up old friends and places. As I walked the streets to the Römerplatz, hardly a building was standing, yet people were living in the rubble. I learned that an SPD rally was in progress in the historic, once picturesque Römer, with Kurt Schumacher as the speaker.

Schumacher was the leader of the reviving SPD. A wreck of a man, he had lost an arm in World War I, suffered imprisonment under the Nazis, and was thin, worn, and hardly able to get about. And yet in the heat of the full sun, in the destroyed center of town, he spoke with fervor for more than an hour to a plaza filled with people. He spoke of "Volksgenossen" (Peoples' Comrades) a word with strong Nazi overtones. He was apprehensive about Eastern Europe, because of the terror there under Stalin, and almost equally apprehensive of the West, because of its capitalist dominance. He was appreciative of the British Labour Party, and seemed to think in terms of an isolated German middle ground between a dictatorial Communism and an as yet unrealized Socialism, based on something peculiar to the German people.

In Wiesbaden, the capital of Hesse, and the seat of American authority in the province, I found a skepticism among American officers about German unions and schools, as well as about the Germans' ability to do anything satisfactory to change their circumstances. This skepticism existed together with the assumption that American social, economic, and political institutions were to be the given model. My impression was one of a distant, cool relationship between Americans and Germans, one in which suspicion on both sides was a major ingredient.

Many of the Americans came from small cities and towns in the Midwest, and all had moved in relatively small professional and political circles. Most of these men were abroad for the first time, and some of them were recently demobilized from the army. Almost none of them spoke the language. The stereotype of an evil German nation had been created by wartime propaganda in the United States, when the German language vanished from its schools, towns changed their German names, and all forgot German scientific achievements and denigrated German universities. Beyond the stereotype that truthfully characterized Hitler's reign, no clear statement of American postwar policy for Germany existed until the announcement of the Marshall Plan, which came in the last days of my stay.

From a German's point of view at the end of two long, dreadful postwar years, money had lost its value, food was scarce, housing was crowded and often built on rubble, cities still lay in ruins, and de-Nazification was moving at a snail's pace. Many Germans now saw the "Amis" as imposing their own institutions on a land with a long history of noble traditions and educational and scientific leadership, for which the Americans had no appreciation.

I drove back from Wiesbaden through Taunus villages, whose hills I had once hiked as a student, and stopped to attend a nonpolitical meeting of a Women's Association, where I met Irmgard Rexroth-Kern again. After the meeting, on the drive back to Frankfurt, she told me of her war experiences, the death of her Nazi husband the year of her pregnancy, and her decision to have the baby in the countryside around Thuringia. There she worked for the Americans, who eventually brought her to Frankfurt, though they had no job for her. I told her of my interests, and she introduced me to Maria Borris on the faculty of the revived Akademie der Arbeit, again dedicated to training top officers of the trade unions. I visited there and met its postwar director, Josef Furtwängler. He was struggling with all the shortages that plagued the union movement but had assembled a staff with which he was satisfied.

Students were difficult to accommodate since there were no vacant rooms for them to rent, and the Academy had had to set up its own food program.[14] When I visited a class, I noticed there were only two women among the students. Furtwängler told me he had appealed on the radio for women to enroll, since they currently made up the bulk of factory workers. He had received a stack of applications, but many of the women would have had to bring their children with them, which, given the unlikelihood of finding suitable housing, made it impossible for them to attend the school.

Furtwängler set up a meeting for me with Willi Richter, the future head of the Deutscher Gewerkschaftsbund (DGB) of Hesse. Furtwängler would be meeting Minna Specht, the former head of the Internationaler Sozialistischer Kampfbund (ISK), whom he admired.[15] I assumed Richter was one of this group. Furtwängler also invited me to join him and another "comrade," an ISK member, Anna Beyer, on this trip. Anna wanted to repossess the Walkemühle and open an advanced political training school for union and SPD leadership. Under Minna's leadership, surviving ISK members had allied themselves, often as postwar leaders and officers, with the SPD.

From them I learned that the German trade unions, although still without a national federation, had been invited by the CIO representative in Germany, Elmer Cope, to join the World Federation of Trade Unions (WFTU). This was a Communist-initiated and, so far, the only postwar international trade union federation. Richter and other German leaders were holding back, not so much because the WFTU might be Communist but because their AFL connections with U.S. labor had given them the information that the CIO was itself heavily Communist. The CIO shortly broke with the WFTU to join the non-Communist International Confederation of Free Trade Unions (ICFTU) as a founding member. As soon as the all-German federation of trade unions was founded, it too affiliated with the ICFTU.

During my stay in Frankfurt, Irmgard told me about the fate of some of my former fellow students. One of the most tragic stories was that of an American woman, Greta Lohrke-Kuckhoff, whom I had met in Wisconsin in 1928 on my way to Bryn Mawr. She had indeed gone to Germany, as she had then planned, and, in 1933, had married a theater director and Communist, a member of the von Harnack family, who played a major part in the Nazi-opposition group called Rote Kapelle, usually referred to as the Schulze-Boysen-Harnack group. When I visited Greta, she told me that she had joined the Communist Party and had worked with her husband in Rote Kapelle. They operated a hidden radio station for several years, but in 1941 their group was infiltrated and all of them arrested and condemned to death.

She spent seven months in solitary confinement, expecting, as she said, to have the hangman enter after every knock on the door. Along with all the other members of the group, her husband was hanged—"strangled"—as she put it. She was retried and sentenced to ten years at hard labor, of which she served three. After the Russians liberated the concentration camp of Sachsenhausen, she walked to Berlin. The Russians made her food director of their section of Berlin. Her child, who had been four years old when Greta was arrested, had been adopted by a family that settled in Poland. Once freed, Greta advertised on the radio for her boy. Only a few months before my visit, a Russian soldier with a small boy had appeared at her door. The child spoke no German, but, as he entered the house, he saw a carousel horse that had belonged to him. He rushed toward it, put himself on its back, and wordlessly insisted on remaining there. Shortly after that, Greta was given a ministerial post in the East German government.

When I visited Irmgard one Sunday at her home, she asked me whether I would be willing to talk with some of her neighbors whose stories involved escaping from eastern cities as the Russians approached. She explained that all of them had been through such terrible experiences in the war and in the following two years that they could not help one another, consumed as each was with trying to find food and means of heat and other necessities for living. Without any premonition of how stressful this experience would be for me, I agreed. Each story seemed to me more dreadful than its predecessor. One after the other, these women (there were few men about) poured out their fears, their adventures, their narrow escapes, their brushes with death. Several of them expressed some relief at doing so. For me, however, this accumulation of horror was so overwhelming that when I returned that night to the hotel, I was unable to walk. I fell from the trolley, worn out by the realization of what these people had had to endure behind the front in wartime.

I was received most graciously by Frau Epstein at the Frankfurt Adult Education Center. She granted me free entry to any class that interested me. When I went to an all-women's class, however, the students were suspicious of an outsider and an American, fearing that they could not talk as freely as they wanted to either with the teacher or each other. I did my best to explain my interests, my historic connections with Frankfurt and its Volkshochschule, its university, and its unions, but I was politely invited to leave. With other classes, I had a friendlier reception.

While still in Frankfurt, I had the first inkling that some Germans had heard that I was a Communist. The hint came when Irmgard took me to a radio station for an interview with the woman head of women's affairs in Hesse. It was an uncomfortable meeting. Bit by bit, she withdrew her invitation for me to speak, and hinted in the end that a negative report had reached her about me.[16]

FINAL DAYS IN BERLIN

I returned to Berlin for debriefing, report writing,[17] and a short trip to the British Zone. George Silver and his companion (and later wife), Hannah, met me and took me to his billet in a mansion of a house in Dahlem, the section of Berlin where the American headquarters for the Zone were located. In the house lived at least three other Americans, including an old acquaintance, Nels Anderson.[18]

Life in the Dahlem house was intense. George had made contact with trade unionists and SPD activists in Berlin and had become particularly friendly with the mayor of Schöneberg, Ernst Reuter, who later became the mayor of all Berlin. George was also in constant communication with unionists and Socialist Party members in the United States, organizing help for his German friends who lacked everything for both themselves and their organizations. He was known beyond his household as "APO Silver," in recognition of his daily receipt of bags of mail. He frequently spent the night working into the small hours on replies to this mail and on the distribution of its contents. (Needless to say, I joined his relief organization; once I returned home, I organized all the comrades from Soviet House and others interested in my firsthand report of conditions to take over some piece of aid for an individual German family or local union.)

George was also in touch with musical artists struggling to make a living in their professions when no one had any money. His Berlin friends included people who had lived through the Nazi period in concentration camps and were now trying to find a place for themselves in what they hoped would be a Democratic-Socialist country. Among these was Jeannette Wolff, who had been in more than twenty different concentration camps. She had been arrested early in the Hitler period, having perhaps come to the attention of the Nazis because her husband, a fairly wealthy man, had given her a printing establishment so that the town where they lived could have a Socialist press. In the camps, she had registered her occupation as a seamstress, had become a uniform maker, and credited her survival to her possession of this useful skill. Once, on a forced march from one camp to another, she had passed a group of marchers and recognized her husband among them, going in the opposite direction. It was their final meeting. She had tried to hide an infant granddaughter in one of the camps, but the child had cried inopportunely and was taken from her. Jeannette and a daughter were the only survivors in her family. We celebrated her fiftieth birthday at the June solstice in the Dahlem house garden. Each of us was expected to leap through the solstice bonfire, which Jeannette did with great élan.

BREMEN AND HAMBURG

On a short trip to Bremen and Hamburg in the British Zone I met the British officers in the Manpower Division. In Bremen I met Anna-Marie Nevissen, whom I had known as a student in the ISK School in 1931. She told me about many of the ISK people I had met at that time, who were now active in the British Zone.[19]

In Hamburg, I met the men in charge of labor and adult education, one of whom, a former Austrian, Karl Stadler, had gone to England in the pre-Hitler period and was active in the Workers' Education Association (WEA).[20] I quickly became aware that the British civilians in their zone lived a very different life from the Americans in theirs. They were tightly rationed for food, as were those at home in Britain. At the same time, under a Labour government they had a fraternal tie with the burgeoning labor and Socialist movements in Germany and, indeed, sponsored the future head of the Deutsche Gewerkschaftsbund (DGB), the German Trade Union Federation, Hans Böckler. Several trade union schools had already been established.

These short, crowded days in Bremen and Hamburg gave me some insight into the distinctly British concept of their function as occupiers in a defeated land: a more fraternal and, in labor relations, a more comradely philosophy than that held on the whole by our former AFL or even CIO officers.

BACK IN BERLIN

Once again, Leo Wertz, the head of the Labor Department's German office, invited me to his home for a conversation with Fritz Tarnow, a pre-Hitler member of the SPD-influenced trade unions (ADGB) and their economic expert. Wertz's hope in talking with Tarnow was to understand why and when the former unions had agreed to try to continue to live under the Nazis by depoliticalizing themselves and restricting their activities to collective bargaining, a strategy that had totally failed to save them. General Lucius Clay's interpreter was borrowed for the occasion. It was clear to me after a bit that, good as this interpreter might be for the general's purposes, he did not understand much of what Tarnow was trying to convey. I began to add details that I felt he had overlooked or misunderstood and eventually took over the job of interpreter for the evening. Tarnow told us that when the final vote on the Executive Board of the Federation had taken place, early in 1933, only three votes were cast against the change. Essentially his story was that, if the unions were to endure at all, they had no other choice than to reserve this one essential function, collective bargaining. Wertz pushed him hard on this but Tarnow still continued to justify what they had done.

It was already clear that the administration of the occupation would soon be passing into civilian hands. The chief of trade union affairs, Captain Mullaney, told me that under such circumstances the position of the Manpower Division was by no means certain; a number of forces seeking to control American policy did not support the idea of relying on the unions as a major democratic force in the new Germany.

In the few days before my departure, I saw some more people with whom I had worked in my student days. I still had no definitive word about Paul Bernstein. George Silver suggested that I put a notice in the papers about a meeting for former labor education people, which he would arrange through Ernst Reuter at the Schöneberger Rathaus. About twenty-five people turned up, among them Walter Raue, Paul's close friend, who told me that Paul had been sent from the concentration camps at Theresienstadt to the death camp at Auschwitz, where he had probably died in a gas chamber in 1944, although this had not yet been certified. He gave me the address in Leipzig where his wife, Johanna Moosdorf, and his children were living. It was too late in my stay to arrange for a trip there, but I immediately wrote to Johanna and received her reply after I got home. Walter told me that, although Johanna was a member of the Sozialistische Einheitspartei Deutschlands (SED), the German Socialist and Unity Party in the Russian Zone, and had been given a journal to edit, she was in trouble and wanted to move to West Berlin if she could find a way.

Eberhardt Schulz, Wes's friend from the Theological School in Berlin in our student days, came to the meeting and later came to breakfast at the Dahlem house. He had become a journalist with the *Süddeutsche Zeitung* and kept us spellbound with stories of his assignments during the war.[21]

Another figure from the past was Walther Pisternik of the Hamburg Carpenters Union youth section, with whom I had exchanged English lessons for German lessons in the summer of 1929. He turned up to tell me that he was living in the Russian Zone because he believed the Russians better represented working-class concerns than did the Western powers.

Since George's efforts to extend my visit were ineffectual, on June 30, the end of the American fiscal year, my contract expired and I boarded a plane for home. The plane was nearly filled with fiancées of American soldiers. For them, too, it was the last opportunity to get free transportation to the United States. They were bundled into fur coats on this hot June night and loaded with all their other possessions.

In New York we were all herded into a hot and airless room where each German passenger was to be identified by her would-be husband before being allowed to enter the country. We "experts" were quickly released and put on a plane for Washington for a debriefing there. My seatmate was bound for Alabama and an African-American husband. I have thought of her dozens of times since and wondered about her experience there, fur coat and all.

NEW ASSIGNMENTS

Once home, I worked frenziedly. I sent messages to friends whose relatives I had met and wrote letters and made telephone calls to other friends, urging them to send CARE packages to German friends and detainee families whom I had met in camps. I also made attempts to get local unions to adopt German schools or local unions and to supply some of their needs. With Agnes Douty, I visited a steelworkers' school at Penn State and the Wisconsin Workers School, where I talked about the revival of the German labor movement and their schools. I corresponded almost weekly with George, as his list of persons and institutions needing help grew. I felt I was a pipeline between Germany and the United States at a level where almost no one else was working.

This short but intense trip to occupied Germany dominated my activity and my thinking during all the next year and a half, until Wesley was appointed labor attaché to Austria under the Marshall Plan. His appointment there meant we would be back in Europe together. In fact, a whole new turn of events there would mark my life to its end.

7

MARRIAGE ENDS, NEW WORK BEGINS:
1947–1952

At the end of the summer of 1947, the three boys came home from their visit to Baltimore, and I resumed my old routine, augmented now by my continuing concern for the people and institutions I had come to know during the crowded trip to Germany in the late spring. But things at home began to change. Mike Harris came back from the Pacific, and Marge and Susie left our family to live in a house not far away on the same railroad line. Susie continued in the Rose Valley School.

Ken Douty remarried, this time to Agnes Martocci, long an acquaintance and now a closer friend. Ken was now in Atlanta, where he joined a new labor education institute located there to serve unions in Georgia and other southern states. Tom was the first of the boys to join them. He had presented the most problems while he lived in our household and was really attached only to Ken. Mike followed in a few months. Phil Van Gelder returned from Europe and rejoined the Shipbuilders Union in Camden, as its national secretary-treasurer, an office he retained for many years.

Thus by early 1948 Wesley, Philip, and I were again a nuclear family. Philip was almost nine years old and still a pupil at the Rose Valley School, where I was secretary.

Though 1948 was an election year, I engaged in little or no political activity. I still remained loyal to a Socialist Party that hardly existed once Norman Thomas was unable to run for office. We had moved to the suburbs, and I had gradually lost close touch with Philadelphia local Socialist activities. Still, everyone was keenly interested in politics, and we and our friends were unhappy with the apparent assured victory of the Republican governor of New York, Thomas Dewey, whom all the polls foresaw as the clearcut winner. Wesley and I sat in a bar watching TV returns the night of the election and went home somewhat depressed that Dewey appeared to be our next president. This, together with Congress's passage of the Taft-Hartley Act in 1947 over Truman's veto, indicated to us a decided turn to the right after all the years of the New Deal and of Truman's appreciation of the labor movement. This direction was also supported by the institution of the Cold War in earnest, when Poland and Czechoslovakia had been forced to withdraw their initial acceptance of invitations to join the Marshall Plan. It was a reassuring shock the next morning to hear that, despite the polls and all the major political commentators,

Truman had won the election. We were very aware, however, that he was by no stretch of the imagination a Socialist.

OFF TO VIENNA

In 1948 Wesley was nominated and confirmed as a labor attaché in Austria under the Marshall Plan. The week before Christmas we were ready to go on the *Queen Mary* to France for a briefing in Paris and then on to Vienna. Philip and I spent the week in Paris sightseeing and buying books at the stalls along the Seine. The trip to Vienna itself was on the revived Orient Express, its former luxury and cleanliness now considerably diminished.

We arrived shortly after the new year to a darkened city. Herman Brotman, the embassy's labor attaché, and his wife were our hosts for the first few days and treated us as part of the embassy. We were shortly billeted in a roomy hotel of sorts in the eighteenth district. My status was now that of "dependent wife."

Many of our friends were already in Europe in various capacities, or were shortly to come. Ken and Agnes with their new daughter, Nina, came to Paris (Jeff had been there earlier); Pat Knight was also in Paris, with the organization that later became the Office for Economic Co-operation and Development (OECD); Paul Porter, who had been in Greece with the Truman Plan, had now moved to Geneva with his family; Jim Stern of the Auto Workers, whom we knew slightly, was a supervisor of labor attachés under the Marshall Plan and visited us from his Paris office; and Victor Reuther became the CIO's representative in Europe.

My first task was to look for an apartment that we might renovate and rent. Our car had been shipped over, and this allowed me to spend many days getting acquainted with all the sections of the city, in a way that Wesley never had the opportunity to do. I visited the historic spots sacred to the Socialist Party's nineteenth- and early twentieth-century history: the city cemetery where its heroes were buried; the Karl Marx houses, whose occupants had defended themselves—hopelessly, as it happened—against the attacks of the "Green Fascists"[1] who had preceded Hitler; and many of the housing projects for which the city's Socialist government was famous after World War I.

After several weeks, I found a place only slightly damaged in the bombing, where a woman and her daughter lived. The owner wanted to leave Vienna, but her daughter worked in the city and needed to remain. We arranged that the daughter could from time to time use the maid's room when she had to stay in Vienna overnight. The apartment was light and roomy, on the edge of a little park and not far from the east side of the Ringstrasse, near the Belvedere Castle. Repairs and refurbishing as well as furnishings had to be dealt with. I hired a cook and a housemaid. The cook was a Hungarian refugee;[2] the housemaid was an Austrian who somewhat resented having to work with an efficient Hungarian; I developed a friendly relationship with her, though, which extended to her family and gave me considerable insight into working-class life.

When the apartment owner objected to my suggestion of coming to her home to negotiate the final terms of our lease, I learned about the Viennese custom that called for doing business in a coffeehouse. I had heard of a cabinetmaker who would build necessary furniture for the bedroom and living room, and we set a date for the furniture's delivery on the day—still a couple of months away—when we could expect to move in. I planned a little party of newfound Vienna acquaintances and American coworkers for a few days after our moving in, only to find that the furniture was by no means ready. When I asked the cabinetmaker why he had promised delivery if he knew he could not deliver, his answer was, I was told, typically Viennese: "Because Madame very much wished it!"

In these early months Wesley was extraordinarily busy, acquainting himself with trade union leaders and with the governmental ministries concerned with social affairs with which the Marshall Plan might be associated. His budget allowed him to make grants to agencies that fell within the Plan's range of assistance.[3] Rita, Wesley's Austrian assistant, an old friend of Karl Stadler, was a young woman whom we both found knowledgeable and lively. She had spent several years in England and spoke English without any accent. Moreover, she came out of the Socialist Party, knew many of the trade unionists, and could help Wesley with access to both groups.

Early on I was entertained by wives of other embassy officers, who enjoyed a regular lunch together. We all strove mightily for common ground without my finding very much to put my feet on. I realized that I would much prefer to seek an occupation for myself that stemmed from my months in Germany in 1947 and from my continuing interest in adult and labor education. I sought out the trade unions' education office and visited their resident schools and became acquainted with the head of the Vienna Volkshochschule (Adult Evening School) where I could take some classes and visit others. Among other things I decided to improve my school French, which had never enabled me to speak the language with any ease. I enrolled in a French class and found that the teacher also taught German classes to foreigners. I employed her as a private tutor in German with the resolve to perfect my German. The French instruction proceeded slowly, but the German tutoring was most successful. We became friends and saw each other frequently. She gave me an introduction to the pre–World War I history of the Austro-Hungarian Empire as well, when her father had been an officer in the imperial army. As a consequence of her tutoring, I began to feel really assured about my use of German.

Wes and I sought friends among old Socialists who had gone into exile during the Hitler and Green Fascist periods and had now returned to edit the socialist daily paper, *Die Arbeiterzeitung* (The Workers' Paper), to codirect the Volkshochschule, and to direct the city housing office. One of these newfound friends invited us to view the May Day parade from the mayor's balcony at the Rathaus on the western Ring in May 1950. As we walked into the office, we met the colorful mayor, a man who had never left the city during its Russian occupation during and after the war, and who had used the time to learn Russian so as to deal with his overlords.

Like Berlin, Vienna was under the control of four different powers. Our apartment was in the British Zone; my German teacher lived in the Russian Zone and I visited her there many times without incident. On one occasion, however, my car with its diplomatic license plates was observed for some time. That one incident was enough to persuade me to make these visits by public transportation from then on.

A TRIP TO AND FROM SWITZERLAND

During our first few months in Vienna, Philip was enrolled in the American School. He was learning no German, and I very much wanted him to acquire this second language at an age when presumably he could pick it up accent-free. However, he had resisted all my early devices to achieve this end. I had hired an Austrian student to teach him, but this resulted only in Philip's helping the student with English conversation. On the ship coming over to Europe, we had met a family with two boys in his age range, bound for Switzerland, where the boys were to attend a Swiss boarding school. In May I decided to take Philip to that and other schools in Switzerland. I hoped he'd like attending either a French- or German-speaking school.

Vienna was surrounded by the Russian Zone; the American Zone began at the edge of Salzburg, about one hundred miles to the west of Vienna. We lived under an instruction, in the event of a hostile Russian action, to be prepared to make our way to the American Zone. This meant never letting the gas tank go empty, always having transportable food supplies in the house, and always having some suitcases packed. To leave Vienna, we went through an American checkpoint, which noted our car license and time of departure; this information was then wired to the first westward American checkpoint.

In the Russian Zone we had to stop at two Russian checkpoints for inspection. At St. Pölten we were asked by the Austrian who interpreted for the Russians to take two Russian officers with us to the next Russian checkpoint. I demurred. I was a woman alone with a young boy. He persisted. The Russians, he said, even the officers, unlike the Americans, had no jeeps or other transportation. The situation was pressing. I saw no way out, if I were to proceed at all. Philip, as though instructed, rolled over into the back seat of the car, and the two officers piled in, one beside me, one in the back with Philip. For several kilometers we rode in silence, after I had tried out English and German on them. Somehow I came to the conclusion that they were unaware I was driving with a diplomatic license, a point I had turned over in my head for its possible meaning to them. Finally I decided that we could not ride for the distance we had to go without at least an attempt at conversation. I pointed to a decoration on my front-seat passenger and asked what it was for. He was able in pidgin

German to say that it was a badge from an outfit like the SS troops in the German army, by which I took him to mean an honorific branch of the military. We went on from there in an interchange that never showed any curiosity on their part about my identity. When we arrived at the next checkpoint, they immediately offered to get out. I thought I had learned that their billets were some distance from there and I offered to drive them to their destination. Quickly it was clear that that would in no case be allowed. They would go on foot. The whole incident thus closed on a relaxed note.

We visited the school and saw the boys Philip had come to know on the *Queen Mary*. After a visit to classes and a friendly interview, we then went on to Geneva, where Paul Porter and his wife and two children were living, and stayed a few days with them. Their children were in a French-speaking school, which we also visited, along with perhaps two others, before we began the trip back to Vienna. En route in Austria we had planned to stop at one of the lakes for Easter weekend with Barent and Louise Landstreet of Philadelphia, who had been in Germany and Austria with a relief organization since 1946. They were then living in Munich. At one of the first Austrian towns where Philip and I spent the night, his developing cold and general state of unwellness clearly became measles. The inn where we were staying immediately mobilized to help me. When Philip had to go to the toilet, I was to call the desk and someone would appear and carry his blanketed form there. Meals came up to the room for both of us. I had an hour each afternoon for a walk and shopping. A pleasanter arrangement could not be imagined. Of course I ran out of books I could read to Philip (for days he was beyond reading for himself) and I searched the shops for anything in English. All I could find was *I, Claudius*, the book that later became a Masterpiece Theatre serial, familiar to millions, with its details of Roman misdeeds and lewdness. Philip listened enthralled, understanding and retaining nothing of the characters' sex lives. For years, however, he was able to recite the long list of Roman emperors, ending with Claudius. I learned from this experience that children deal with what they can and overlook what they do not know.

Wesley joined us for a pleasurable weekend with old friends. We repeatedly visited the churches, picturesque and ancient, now filled with chanting women, praying for themselves and celebrating the rebirth of Christ. We picnicked. With Philip restored to health, the children became reacquainted. We adults brought each other up to date on our lives and present occupations. And then back to Vienna with Wesley at the wheel.

Enjoying Cultural Life in Vienna

Wesley and I had decided to enjoy Viennese opera and theater. There were frequent musical festivals, and we sometimes went out many nights in a row. I could sleep in in the mornings, but Wesley began to insist he could not keep up this degree of attention to the arts and still get to work each morning at eight as was expected. We often took Philip to the Volksoper (light opera), where his lack of German disturbed those around us as we tried to help him with the story line, which he very much wanted to follow. The classical Opera House itself had been so damaged in the bombing that the opera company had to perform at the Theater an der Wien. As for theater, I especially enjoyed the Theater in der Josefstadt and saw many of its plays.

As a dependent wife, I was expected with the others to assist at some embassy functions. At advance briefings we were told what would be appropriate dress—"a simple navy blue dress, white gloves, no hat"; we were assigned to our stations—"bottom of the stairs, entrance to the library"; and we were directed, as the concluding hour approached, to point the way toward the front door with a wide and inviting gesture and some casual remark about the hour.

I decided to inform myself about the new city housing policy, which had come to replace the widely famous effort in building public housing between the wars. This policy consisted of restoring housing that existed within the city but had deteriorated, either because of the war or through neglect. It meant retaining residential quarters within the city at the same time that the great public housing complexes existed on its rim. I sent off an article on this current policy to the *Survey Graphic*, but it was not accepted. Longing to get back to work, I decided to explore whether any opportunity for employment still existed in Germany with the Manpower Division and was invited to return on a short contract.

A JOB IN GERMANY

In the fall of 1949 I arranged for Philip to enter the Odenwaldschule, a boarding school in Heppenheim, near Frankfurt. Wes brought him up in the car, and we took Philip to Heppenheim and settled him in there. Wes left the car with me, and I set to work on a new project evaluating the unions' work with youth.[4]

In the year and a half since my first postwar visit, things had changed radically. The American Zone was now under civilian control, with John J. McCloy as the director of the High Commission, Germany (HICOG). Again, I went first to Berlin headquarters. The intervening period had seen the successful conclusion of the airlift that supplied the city of Berlin, which the Russians had closed to road and railroad access. This had resulted in a thorough politicization of the citizens of Berlin, and the development of a strong pro-American sentiment throughout the Western Zones of Germany as well as in Berlin. In addition, a monetary reform had been introduced and stores were once more filled with goods. Life had begun to settle into accustomed prewar routines.

In Berlin I found Paul Bernstein's widow and children, who had been able, not without some risk, to leave Leipzig and come to Berlin. They were living in an almost bare apartment with Gerhardt, a male friend of Johanna's who had worked with her in the publication of a magazine in the Russian Zone to which she had been assigned as editor. Johanna had decided the time had come to leave the Eastern Zone when an article she had written about the experiences of some workers in factories who had expressed dissatisfaction with their circumstances had been censored. She had been able to send the children to feeding programs in the Western Zone, and with them momentarily safe, she had taken her typewriter and little else on a series of trolleys that enabled her to arrive in West Berlin. Tom, then twelve, and Barbara, fourteen, belonged in secondary school, but West Berlin still had a tuition charge for anything beyond the compulsory elementary school. Hanni had no money for this or indeed for much else. I arranged to pay tuition for both children to join Philip at the Odenwaldschule, where they shortly dubbed themselves "the three twins."

I decided this time to begin fieldwork in Bavaria where Ludwig Koch, with whom I had worked so satisfactorily in 1947, was still in charge of youth work in the unions. I was warmly welcomed into the Bavarian unions' program dealing with apprentices in industry. These apprentices were mainly young men, for although programs existed for women, they were limited to the women's trades and were largely in retail sales, office work, and cosmetology. Most of the women's programs did not exceed two years in length and were decidedly less exacting than the journeyman training that was generally offered to males. The schools attached to the training program were now better staffed and supplied than I had found them earlier. I concentrated, however, on the training of these young people for union activity and spent much of my time in the resident schools where this training occurred. I spent a particularly memorable period of time in Nuremberg, observing the evening courses that formed the basis of this trade union approach as well as acting as the center of much of the organization of leisure time activities such as chess clubs, hiking groups, and the like. The aim of this program was to reach young apprentices early so as to initiate them into a totally Socialist life, a workers' culture that would fill their leisure time.

THE FOUNDING OF THE FEDERATION OF GERMAN TRADE UNIONS (DGB)

The Western allies by 1949 had agreed that the time had come for the German trade unions to form a national federation, and a date had been set for the fall. I heard that Dave Saposs, a veteran American trade union historian, wished to observe the meeting and needed an interpreter. I decided to fill that position. I was to sit with him and translate as he needed me to.

Hans Böckler was the presiding officer, as we all knew he would be, and was destined to emerge from the meeting as the federation's elected president. It was clear very early on that he would direct the elections of an executive committee that would precede his own crowning. His goal was to establish a single federation of all German unions, a goal that meant including the former

Catholic federation. This goal implied the politically judicious inclusion of Catholics on the executive committe, and Böckler intended to give them the posts in charge of youth and women.

His concept was that the number of national unions affiliated to the federation would be few but totally inclusive of all workers employed within a total industry. This meant combining white-collar workers with manual workers, skilled with unskilled, in broad aggregations of chemical, metal, food, textile, public employees, transportation workers, teachers, and so on. For all his political savvy, Böckler was challenged. The white-collar workers wanted their own industrial union, one that would contain not simply white-collar workers in public employment but also those in insurance, banking, and in industry. Böckler held firm against them. This caused a large section of white-collar workers under the aegis of the Deutsche Angestellten Gewerkschaft (German Employees Trade Union) to withdraw. An important part of their argument for a union of their own lay in labor and social law, which provided for special protections and procedures for white-collar workers. Only now in the 1990s are there discussions looking toward a possible unification of this independent union with the federation.[5]

The next oppositional move came from the leaders of the youth sections of the unions, who clearly did not want to give up leadership in this important area to the Catholics. The opposition in this instance was strong enough to prevail. When the women's leadership came up on the agenda, their opposition also spoke out, but Böckler made clear that he had compromised as far as he could or would. The women were unable to prevail and in the end accepted his handpicked leadership. Thus began the internal organization of the DGB, and the role of the women's section, which I continue to follow and with which I have dealt at length in my book, *The Most Difficult Revolution: Women in Trade Unions,* which was published by Cornell University Press in 1992.

A TRIP TO EGYPT

I went back to Vienna shortly before Christmas to prepare for a trip to Egypt. Wes and I had agreed that this would be our first major travel while we were in Europe. It would be a trip of the kind that had not been possible for us when we were students. Wes was earning what was for us the unbelievably large sum of ten thousand dollars a year, and we felt that, together with the money I had just earned, we could now afford to do this.

We had chosen Egypt, largely because the country had been of intense interest to Philip as he had begun to study world history just before leaving his Rose Valley School. As soon before Christmas as Wesley could free himself from his job, we set off by train from Vienna to Rome, loaded with sweets from our Hungarian cook. Immediately as we crossed into Italy, the train became tightly packed with soldiers free to go home for the holiday. We could not get through to the dining car many cars away, and we dared not try to reach it by getting off the train and running along the platform as we made innumerable stops. We were thrown back on to our sweets, which began to cloy, and we arrived in Rome almost twenty-four hours later, half sick and thoroughly exhausted.

We had a day or two in Rome, which we were intent on using for sightseeing. It was well that we did, for I later never had an opportunity to become acquainted with that city. From Rome we took a plane to Cairo and stayed at Shepherd's Hotel, then the pride of Cairo. In taking a walk with Wes after Philip was in bed, I saw the sickening sight of utter poverty as people along the streets around the hotel were preparing to bed down for the night. As we approached, they surrounded us with their hands out, begging. I had no skills for handling this kind of thing and fled back to the hotel, never to try a casual evening walk in Egypt again.

We found a guide who took us to all the tourist sights—including of course the pyramids—and for a short ride on a camel, to the museums, and to temple ruins. We boarded a train for an overnight ride to the upper Nile and Aswan. Again, at stops, we found our window surrounded with beggars of all ages, sick, half blind, eyes covered with flies. When on the return trip we stopped at Luxor, Philip and I were both ill and Wesley visited the temples alone. I recovered before Philip, who arrived in Cairo barely able to walk. We delayed our return home for a couple of days until he had recovered enough strength to travel. I was deeply impressed with the artifacts of antiquity and deeply upset by the poverty we encountered everywhere. Our guide was enormously helpful in making the trip a genuine learning experience for us all, but I had seen a third world that depressed me in the extreme.

During the trip Wesley and I had several long talks about our own relationship, from which I emerged apprehensive about his continuing love and regard for me. He repeatedly denied that our marriage was in any danger, but I came back to Vienna with the strong sense that things had changed in an unhappy way. An early call came in from Rita, his assistant, who had apparently been ringing the apartment frequently in the last few days when we had delayed our return. As I turned the phone over to Wesley, my apprehension focused for the first time on his relationship to her.

WESLEY ASKS FOR A DIVORCE

It was not many weeks before Wes came home late one night to say that he had been with Rita, that they had fallen in love, and that he had promised her to ask me for a divorce. My worst anxieties were realized and I was devastated. We had had what was then sometimes called "an open marriage," in which I accepted that he might from time to time have a casual relationship like the one he had had with Greta in 1931, the year when I came home from Germany ahead of him. I might also, if I wished, have a casual relationship. Although our marriage was important, perhaps even central to me, it was not in itself enough for me. Since I needed to be able to work in my fields of interest, I had again and again led a life separate from his, always assuming that he accepted and understood my decisions. Obviously, something had shifted. He had changed. He loved Rita. What might have been another casual relationship had become his life's center and I did not belong there. He had to choose.

Rejection is perhaps severely hurtful in any form. I found it unbearably difficult to accept. Through all this, we made an effort to see me as "best friend" to both of them. As a result, from time to time Wes brought Rita to our apartment, where they occupied the erstwhile maid's room. One such night I heard Philip get up and call for Wes. I went to Wes to arouse him, for we had agreed that Philip, who was shortly to leave for school, would not yet be told that his parents would be divorcing.

I came to realize, as I looked back over the past twenty-four years of marriage, that in our frequent absences from one another, we had lived almost as many years apart as we had lived together. Yet for the most part, the magic had held with each reunion, nor had the differences between us ever been great. Still, in the last few years I had perhaps relied too much on this long, ongoing, loose, and mutually independent existence. Particularly it came to me that in a discussion as to whether he should take a union assignment in the deep South, I had said quite emphatically that I would not take Philip to the South and expose him to all the racial prejudices endemic there. Could this have rung in Wes's ears as a total declaration of independence on my part? In retrospect, I was not very sure of what I had meant. Perhaps that remark had not played any part in this decision of his—I was completely unsure. I sought for months, then and thereafter, for an explanation, at the same time that I wrestled with the finality of his decision. My best advice came from my lawyer brother, Fred, who had handled dozens of divorce cases. He wrote me to cut off any relationship and to focus with Wes on the terms of the divorce.[6]

I turned again to my friends in Germany in the hope that once more there might be a temporary work contract there. I remained meanwhile in the Vienna apartment, although I knew I had to leave, but where would I go? The full meaning of "dependent wife" came home to me. I had no claim even to a room of my own. Should my destination be to go home or back to Germany? In a search for a sympathetic ear, I turned to Lydia Tröscher for advice and made a trip to Leonberg, from where I decided to go again to Frankfurt to spy out the job situation there.

The Manpower Division took me in again, but it was clear that this would be the very last of these short-term contracts. For a time I worked on an assignment that came with an apartment in Berlin; I succeeded while I was there in finding a job in the department for my friend Luise Hüls. I sought out my old professor, Max Horkheimer, now returned from the United States to the Johann Wolfgang von Goethe Universität, where he had just been elected Rektor; I wanted to talk with him about the Ph.D. that I had been unable to work for in 1933. He welcomed me. At last I had an alternative in case further work in Germany would not be available. Indeed, when the current contract ended, I was told there was no possibility of another.

Mother had written that she was coming to a WCTU international meeting in Britain in the summer and would join me afterward, but where? It was a difficult question.

PUZZLEMENT AND SOLITUDE

I was puzzled and very much alone in Germany the summer of 1950, without a job and far away from the large circle of friends to whom I had always been able to turn, at least for company and sometimes for guidance. I needed someone now, quite desperately. But all my friends were also Wesley's friends. How would they look upon our separation and imminent divorce after our twenty-four years of marriage? I decided that Ada Stoflet would be the friend from whom I would find out. I wrote to ask her permission to allow me to turn to her with my problems and puzzles and to expect from her that my problems would be hers—not that she would not be in touch with Wes if she wanted to be but that I could count on her, to understand and respond to me. I am no longer at all sure why I chose her unless it was because she was the unmarried woman in the group, who would not have to keep our relationship somewhat away from a husband. She responded at once that I could count on her and that she would come to Germany in the summer if I wanted her.

I do not remember how I heard that I might apply for a position with the Education Division of the High Commission, Germany (HICOG) that might begin toward the end of summer. I applied for the job and decided this was a summer I would spend in Scandinavia. I wrote to Esther Peterson, whose husband, Oliver, was labor attaché at our embassy in Stockholm and to my Swedish friend from summer school days in the States, Mai Larssen, that I was coming and hoped to see them. Mike Harris was also in Stockholm, as labor attaché under the Marshall Plan, although Margie, Susie, and a new child, Katie, had remained in the States.

When Mother arrived, Philip was through school for the term, and we three set out in the car for Denmark, Sweden, and Norway.

SCANDINAVIA

Esther told me as we arrived in Stockholm that she and the family were about to leave for a vacation trip to Norway, to visit the homeland of Oliver's ancestors. We could live in their house during our stay. She also arranged for a lunch with a number of prominent Swedish women, including several members of parliament, trade union and Socialist Party members, and leaders of other women's organizations. It was at this gathering that I heard for the first time of these women's dissatisfaction with the slowness of the progress they had made and of the piecemeal approach in Sweden to women's problems. One woman made the cutting observation, "Women are still Sweden's 'niggers'." I was shocked. I had come to think of such measures as then existed—including child allowances and the assignment of a man to advise and assist single mothers with receiving available assistance beyond the allowance (such as aid with housing supplements for large families)—as part of a more enlightened program than existed elsewhere. I now had to deal with this critical set of observations in estimating women's needs and their remedies.

The reunion with Mike Harris was a pleasure after his long absence in the war when Margie and Susie lived with us. Mai was a great help in taking us sightseeing in and around Stockholm. Mother and I spent one day trying to find Grandmother Hanson's old home in the vicinity of Stockholm. We were searching for a farming village named Kalmae. Grandma had told Mother stories of her childhood there and that it was a day's distance from Stockholm. We had decided that we should measure this distance by foot travel, and we located a village of the right name. Indeed, we found a farmhouse on a small lake with an island in it that we decided had to be the one where Grandma had pastured the cows in summer and rowed out twice a day to milk them. We tried talking to the farm wife on the property, but language was an impassable barrier. We sought out the pastor and hoped his church records would show us whether Grandfather as well as Grandmother Hanson might be registered there, but they had been born when men and women were known as Hans, son of Peter, or Carlotta, daughter of Peter. We did not know the first names of our earlier ancestors, except that Grandma was a Petersdatter. The search had to be given up. Still, we had had a glimpse of what might well have been the landscape in which Grandmother had grown to adolescence.

We moved on to Norway and stopped in Oslo. Mother had heard of the park where statues of people of every age were devoted to a portrayal of the changes we all undergo throughout life. We were both very deeply impressed with the portraits of old people, and for Mother it was the highlight of her Scandinavian trip.

Mai left us in Bergen, and we decided to take the overnight boat to Trondheim and return by train through the mountains to Bergen, where we would pick up the car again. Philip and I shared a cabin. During the night I heard him get up and leave the cabin, presumably to go to the toilet. I dropped back to sleep and roused perhaps a half-hour later to realize that he had not returned. I woke Mother next door. He was not there. I found an officer of the boat and told him of my concern for the boy who was, I thought, half asleep when he left his bed. The officer, with me at his side, made a thorough search of every cabin on the boat. He simply opened every door and turned on the light, and I searched every surprised face as I sought my son. Cabin after cabin, and no Philip. I began to word a telegram to Wesley that would break the awful news that Philip had disappeared. And then in a presumably unoccupied cabin, not far from the ones we had reserved, we found him sound asleep in an unoccupied bed! The depths of loss and the heights of recovery are the way I recall this whole experience.

Our return trip by train on tracks laid down along the ridges of mountains sealed my love of Norway's geography. It would be thirty-five years before I would return to Norway to take a coastal trip that carried Fran Herman and me into the Arctic Circle to reconfirm and extend this experience.[7]

When we returned to Stockholm a telegram was waiting for me at the embassy telling me that I had a staff appointment in the Education Division of HICOG in Frankfurt and should return as soon as possible to Germany. We immediately began the return to Germany and to a genuine job for me, not just a short-term contract.

CHIEF OF ADULT EDUCATION IN THE AMERICAN ZONE

I now had the right to an apartment with a housekeeper; I would once again travel a great deal, so that it seemed right that Philip should continue in the fall at the Odenwaldschule, which was only a few kilometers down in the area of Bergstrasse. For the first time since we had gone abroad, I had a defined role and a function; I would be earning my own salary; I would have a desk, a small staff, a task and the responsibility for carrying it out. I would be working with many people on the German side whom I already knew. The unease of the past months, and to some extent the despair, were mitigated.

I was located first in Bad Nauheim, outside Frankfurt where the Education Division was then situated. Later we were moved into the I.G. Farben building with most of the rest of HICOG in Frankfurt, and I was assigned a new apartment near the Dornbusch section of town, with a housekeeper to take care of me and my guests. Philip could live with me during his holidays. Up to that time I had had to send him to Wesley in Vienna. This had involved a change of trains in Munich, where the Landstreets, now living there, would meet his train and keep him with their family for a day or two before sending him on to Vienna. For a year and a half my Dornbusch apartment in Frankfurt represented home and security.

Wesley kept me informed of his steps toward getting a divorce and, still in the "best friend" spirit, invited me to use the same lawyer. He pointed out that to do so would be in the interest of hurrying up the process, but I declined and employed my own. When I received his draft of the divorce document, I found that he had made no provision for support of Philip. When I challenged him on this point, his reply was that it had worked out all right so far, meaning that he had been contributing. I pointed out that we had many years of support to face after we both returned to the States. He agreed to make a monthly payment that would see Philip through college, presumably through age twenty-two. Since Rita was already pregnant, this was the most he felt he could do, and I accepted it. We were granted an Austrian divorce.

My current assignment was considerably broader than my previous work with trade unions. To deal with the whole adult education movement in the American Zone, however, I knew I would need to build on my previous experiences and my earlier contacts. In Bavaria, for example, my relationships both with my American counterparts and with the Germans heading adult education schools in towns and cities had been close and cooperative, whereas in Württemberg-Baden they had been somewhat distant and superficial, and in Hesse rather formal. On the other hand, my connections with trade unions in all three provinces had been fairly strong and complete. Here, I first wanted to acquaint myself with both residential and evening schools and with their province-wide associations. In addition I assumed I was to collaborate with my counterparts in the British and French Zones on projects that might cross zone lines.

I soon found that I had control of a large sum of German money that could be used to aid specific projects that supported the American goal of reeducating adult Germans to take up citizenship in a democratic society. These funds derived from the "selling" of food and other U.S. material support sent to German governmental institutions for distribution. The new German money (Deutsche Mark or DM) they received was used to make repayments to the United States and redistributed by various HICOG departments to further democratic programs initiated by German organizations. I began my first year with about a million and a half DM for adult education projects initiated by the German adult schools. These sums diminished substantially in the two succeeding years until 1952 when the West German state took over more and more functions of self-government.

I soon had to decide whether I could support projects that might come to me through contacts in the other occupied zones, specifically from the British Zone. I decided to risk giving money to a movement in Lower Saxony, led by Adolf Heidorn. He was education director for the unions there and a prewar member of the ISK group. His hope was to provide general educational opportunities for workers who, under the established school system, left the Volkschule at twelve or fourteen to take up apprenticeships and begin their life's work. Heidorn's plan called for an alliance between the unions and the adult education movement throughout Germany, operating mainly through evening classes in the Volkshochschule. The name of the new alliance was to be Arbeit und Leben (Work and Life). The idea caught fire in the unions of Hesse, though in Württemberg-Baden only a few of the affiliates signed on. I attended planning conferences on themes and procedures with Heidorn and was able to help substantially as the German leaders set up a sponsoring organization. Similarly, it was possible for me to aid in the establishment of a national adult education association.[8]

My requests for such appropriations had to go through the chief of the Education Division, with whom I worked smoothly enough until early in

1952, when he rejected a fairly routine request for release of funds to the Bavarian Adult Education Association, on the grounds that that organization had already received numerous items of support. The rejection was a shock to me, since the association and its director had more than fulfilled the program and accounting requirements that these grants demanded. When my own pleadings did not change the decision, the director, Josef Baudrexel, came to Frankfurt to plead his own case and achieved a degree of success. I had the impression that the division chief had had up till then little direct contact with the Germans themselves and had suddenly realized the impact of their needs, their interests, and their accomplishments.

The funded project had begun with a trip I took with Baudrexel and some of his colleagues in a Volkswagen bus along the whole stretch of the eastern border between Bavaria and Czechoslovakia. We started in the north at the town of Hof and proceeded to the south, from county town to county town. In each place we met with the town clergyman, the school superintendent, the mayor, and other influential citizens, along with the Kreisresidenzoffizier, the American resident officer, stationed in each county of the Zone. This last person was always of special interest to me, as the visiting American. He was often a former GI or officer, now, in 1951 or 1952, in civilian clothes. After a year or two in his county town, he had fully identified himself with it and appeared very much in the role of a local Chamber of Commerce secretary. He knew the town's economic base and its postwar problems, including finding itself with its eastern boundary totally cut off. Often this meant its former road or railroad cut, with no new transportation yet open to the west. It might mean that its products were cut off from markets as well. Czechoslovakia had withdrawn everyone from an area of several kilometers east of the border and set up army stations with watchtowers in the empty areas. Frequently, our road took us within a few feet of the border and in sight of the watchtowers.

Our aim was to assess the adult education needs and plans within these quite isolated towns. For me it was new territory never before visited, in a unique rural setting, a very needy area, with many refugees from the east, as well as disoriented long-time residents, all with few resources. Above all, these communities were now artificially isolated from long-established sources of employment and markets. It was unquestionably the most impressive and the most intensive learning experience of this part of my work in Germany.

In Hesse I slowly gained the confidence of the man who had succeeded Frau Epstein as postwar director of the Frankfurt adult education association. He was a somewhat rigid Socialist, who followed the Party line in distrusting and, in so far as he could, distancing himself from the capitalist Americans. He worked hard at reestablishing the adult evening schools in every district of the city, but he was neither imaginative nor very intelligent about adult pedagogy nor in anticipating immediate and future needs. As I have suggested earlier, his American counterpart was quite unfamiliar with the past of pre-Hitler

Germany and saw the future pretty exclusively in terms of replicating American institutions in Germany if democracy, as he envisioned it, were to be established there.

I met the American woman, Betsy Knapp, assigned to the Hesse Office on Women's Affairs in Wiesbaden, who with her German assistant, Antje Lemke, was in touch with women's organizations and their needs throughout the province and who began to set up an umbrella organization in that area. Betsy Knapp had served for several years in the League of Women Voters in Washington, D.C. Her approach to political education was like that of the League, nonpartisan and urging that women inform themselves about their urgent political issues and concerns. Through her, I came to know several women especially engaged in the education of adult women. They included a woman who had set up a resident school for one- and two-week courses on issues of special concern to women emerging from a generation that had experienced sixteen years of National Socialism with its derogation of girls and women. This meeting with Betsy was an important opening for me in my German contacts. It was also the beginning of long-lasting personal friendships with Betsy and Antje, friendships encouraged by the fact that they both later came to Syracuse to live, only fifty miles away from me in Ithaca.

One of my several functions during this period was to bring experts from the United States and Scandinavia to Germany to work with adult educators on problems of methods and administration. Among the people I was able to invite were Eleanor Coit, director of the Bryn Mawr Summer School both years I taught there and the founder of the Affiliated Schools, and Eleanor Emerson, my supervisor in the Philadelphia Y and now head of Labor Education in the Extension Division of the new Labor Relations School at Cornell University. Both these women were students and advocates of John Dewey and his participative methods in adult learning.

They called this approach "the discussion method" and used it to acquaint themselves and their fellow students in the teaching group with each other's experience and expertise. They approached subject matter as a set of problems that the group of students with the assistance of its leader would endeavor to learn about and solve, using experience as well as book learning in their movement toward understanding. Since much of the teaching in German adult education had always been through lectures by "experts," most of whose knowledge was derived from the theoretical and academic world and rarely from experiential encounters, it was often extremely difficult for persons without considerable formal education to learn from such classes.

Eleanor Emerson invariably worked with her students or staff as equals, considering that they contributed as much to her education as she to theirs. I invited her to Berlin to help with the establishment of a resident school there in which George and Hannah Silver were especially interested. They had succeeded in taking over the mansion of one of Hitler's close coworkers for use as a trade union school. In a conference for future teachers and administrators in that school, we introduced the "discussion method." The effort called for infinite patience, with which Eleanor was always well supplied. I cannot say that we came away from this one meeting at all certain that we had made ourselves either clear or convincing. But I did feel that over the months of working with many groups and with expert help, we left some mark.

Eleanor Emerson was with me at exactly the time that it became clear that I had a critical choice to make about my future. I had first met Eleanor when I went to Philadelphia in 1931, and over the many years of our joint work in the Y we had become close friends.[9] Now HICOG was nearing its end in only a few months. If I were to remain in the Foreign Service, I would have to prepare to take the difficult examinations that would determine whether I could become a Foreign Service officer with the State Department. Several colleagues had already made this choice and were being assigned to countries in the Middle East or Africa. If I were to follow them, Philip would not be able to find the equivalent of high school education there; it would mean boarding school somewhere in Europe or England for him, and separation from both Wesley and me. He had gone through a period of extreme distress at the Odenwaldschule after Wesley had told him in my presence of the impending divorce, and he had spent several weeks in Freiburg in therapy. I wanted above all to be able to have him near or with me, and the outlook for that—if I decided on the Foreign Service—was not good. I felt strongly that I should get back to the States.

I considered taking this opportunity, instead of continuing to live abroad, to start a whole new career. My solution was to go to a completely new section of the country, perhaps the Southwest, to teach in a high school or otherwise to "re-Americanize" myself. All this was still vague, as I talked things over with Eleanor.

Nevertheless, when she returned to Cornell, she talked to her dean about possibly appointing me to a project in the Cornell Extension Division.[10] Dean Catherwood wrote to ask for my curriculum vitae, at the same time noting that a visit to the school and meeting with its faculty usually preceded appointment. I replied that, given the circumstances of terminating my job, I could not make the trip. I pointed out, however, that Professor Maurice Neufeld of Cornell's faculty was now on leave in Italy and might be able to interview me. The dean replied by sending me a letter of appointment for September 1, 1952.

Ithaca, New York, was to be my American home. In the summer of 1952 I began to wind up affairs in Germany—final visits to the Tröschers, reports to my superiors, final meetings with my French and British counterparts, farewell parties with coworkers, a long talk with Betsy Knapp about our future meetings in New York State. I sent Philip to a summer camp in Switzerland where, toward the end of August, I would pick him up on our way to Genoa and our departure by ship for New York.

8

AT CORNELL UNIVERSITY: 1952–1955

THE PROJECT YEARS: TEACHING IN EXTENSION

When Philip and I arrived in New York, we reclaimed our new Hillman station wagon from the ship and went to visit George and Hannah Silver, who had arrived in New York before us. We drove to Ithaca at the end of August. When we stopped for lunch en route, I remember being shocked at the price of sandwiches, which was well above the PX and army mess amounts that I had been paying for years in Germany and Austria. It was the first of many adjustments I would have to make as I began to live with a decided cut in salary from the $10,000 a year I had earned in Germany to the $6,600 a year Cornell was going to pay me.

At my request, Eleanor had found a room for us with a woman on Aurora Street, where we would stay until we found an apartment. Philip was enrolled in school, and I reported to Eleanor and her superior, Ralph Campbell, assistant dean for extension in the New York State School of Industrial and Labor Relations (ILR).

THE SCHOOL OF INDUSTRIAL AND LABOR RELATIONS: HISTORY AND STRUCTURE

Cornell University, almost alone within academe in the United States, is a combination of private and state-supported colleges (the former known as endowed, the latter known as statutory). The ILR School was the fourth statutory college in the University, and with seven other colleges made up Cornell's Ithaca campus. The Medical College, also endowed from its founding, was located in New York City. The School of Industrial and Labor Relations (ILR), founded in 1945 by an act of the New York State legislature to provide undergraduate, graduate, and extension teaching on labor-management relations, had only recently been located at Cornell, where it was the newest college in the university. Faculty members from the three "divisions" of the school—teaching, research, and extension—would participate. My work would be located in the Extension Division, where I would report to Eleanor, a replay of our relationship in the Philadelphia YWCA, twenty years earlier.

The school, then and for the next ten years, was located in quonset huts on what would later become the Engineering College campus. Crowded into three of these huts were the library, already notable for its holdings, as well as classrooms and faculty offices. The first dean had been the school's founder, State Senator Irving Ives, but when in 1946 Ives decided to run for U.S. Senator, the acting deanship had passed temporarily to Phillips Bradley, who, as Ives's assistant in Albany, had drafted the school's charter. It then passed to Martin P. Catherwood, former professor in Cornell's College of Agriculture, and more recently Industrial Commissioner of the State of New York. The school had opened in the fall of 1945 with Maurice Neufeld and Jean McKelvey as the first two faculty members. Professors, Extension staff in administrative positions, and professionals elsewhere in the school were part of the ILR faculty, while teaching professors within the school belonged also to the university faculty.

The school's teaching faculty in 1952 was not yet departmentalized but covered about six areas considered germane to this newly defined field of industrial relations. Many of the faculty in the school's first seven years had come from service on the War Labor Board, whose work and regulations had in a very real sense first codified concepts in the field. The subjects taught in all three divisions of the school included labor economics, personnel, statistics, organizational behavior, international labor relations and labor history and collective bargaining. It was to this last that I was attached.

In Extension, Effie Reiley headed the New York office and Lois Gray, the one in Buffalo. Soon thereafter, with Ardemis Kouzian as director, the Albany District office was inaugurated. In the areas surrounding New York City, Buffalo, and Albany, Extension staff offered courses for labor unions, management, government agencies, and the public generally. Classes organized in consultation with their sponsoring groups could be held in or near factories or other places of employment, in schools or other public buildings, or in the offices of the Extension Center. Extension staff were largely engaged in administrative work and public relations. It was their job to find teachers competent in the subject matter from the Cornell School, or from a nearby university or college, or from selected practitioners, as approved by the appropriate teaching faculty.

The school had already founded what became the leading journal in the field, the *Industrial and Labor Relations Review,* shortened in school and field parlance to the *ILR Review.* The school's charter also provided for a publications section, which would reprint articles published by faculty and was soon to publish books in the field accepted from outsiders as well as faculty.

By no means were all of these elements clear to me as I joined the school. I knew of course that I was a temporary addition to ILR's faculty, but in the first year or so I felt no sense of hierarchy in which the resident faculty were seen or felt themselves to be a notch above the persons working off campus. Indeed, there was some effort to attach these field people to one or another of the resident groups within the school. Those in the Extension Division were either labor or management experts. Eleanor Emerson was the head of the labor union side; Al Smith was the head of management education. I was clearly attached to the labor side. Maurice Neufeld was back from his first leave in Italy and, together with Eleanor, assumed the role of my mentor. Through them I quickly became acquainted with faculty members and with women on staff in the library, the business office, and the publications department.

THE PROJECT'S BEGINNING

The project I was to direct was entitled Integrating Labor into Community Affairs, one of eight experiments in labor education to be carried out by eight different universities, each under its own title, each in its selected field of research and teaching methods.[1] This consortium of universities, known as the Inter-University Labor Education Committee (IULEC), was funded for three years by the National Adult Education Association, with funds received from the Ford Foundation. Its Committee, headed by Ralph Campbell, was composed of representatives from the universities, as well as four members from each of the labor federations, among whom I had many friends and acquaintances.

IULEC became the outstanding source of labor education research on program organization and teaching. It could never have functioned as quickly and successfully as it did in all of its locations and under the eight-university consortium without the history of university extension work with unions that had taken place in the twenties, thirties, and forties. It also profited from the work done in wartime training programs, which had used teachers and directors from the WPA in many industrialized states. Perhaps above all, IULEC profited from the leadership Eleanor Coit had given to all these efforts through her organization of the Affiliated Schools and the "Washday" conferences, where labor educators from both federations had met as educators rather than as partisans.

I spent my first weeks consulting with faculty, with members of the school's Labor Advisory Committee who were drawn from unions throughout the state, and with Extension staff. I was looking for one or two cities where we might be able to interest labor leaders and their unions in working with us and helping us to become involved in community affairs. I was also looking for community leaders who might be interested in working with labor unions on particular local projects.

I knew about the CIO's concern with community affairs through the program they had established during the war, for which I had written a handbook on training union-community stewards. This program had included establishing a link between labor unions and the Community Chest by putting a designated labor representative on the Community Chest staff, thus encouraging workers' contributions to Chest drives, as well as legitimizing workers' increased use of social services supported by Chest appropriations. Our search for communities where leaders and unions might collaborate ended in our choosing Syracuse and Utica as two cities where we could find the kind of interest we sought.

I was quickly given a competent secretary and two graduate students, Wally Wohlking and Jack Flagler, as field staff.[2] We soon had a smoothly operating team. Jack was a native of Utica, which suggested his special assignment there. Wally worked closely with me in Syracuse, and when we later added the smaller city of Olean to our program, I asked him to assume much of the day-to-day work there also.

I soon ascertained that relationships between labor and Community Chests already existed in both Syracuse and Utica. In repeated visits to these communities I began to get a picture both from labor leaders and from Community Chest officials of their views of problems that were affecting wide areas and many citizens; I also learned which organizations and persons were seen to exercise decisive power in these areas. Somewhat later a book by a North Carolina sociologist presented an analysis of community power structure that I found formative for my own thinking on the subject. As I employed teachers for classes with union members, I strongly recommended this book on community organization and power for their background reading.[3]

The labor movement was still sharply divided between the AFL and the CIO, with raiding and counter-raiding part of each group of unions' organizing strategy. My central problem became that of finding local leaders in each city from each affiliated group. Syracuse was predominantly a CIO city, with the head of the Steelworkers Union a recognizable leader of a very large number of organized workers, including the auto and electrical unions. At the same time the Laborers' Union in the AFL became actively engaged in the program in Syracuse as well. For our work in Syracuse, it was possible for me to call on two members of the staffs of the national CIO and AFL education departments, who were also members of the IULEC board. Larry Rogin and George Guernsey of the CIO visited the central body of Syracuse CIO unions to favor its endorsement of the IULEC project.

Utica, on the other hand, was in the process of a painful economic transition from a predominantly textile city whose products—bed and bath linens—were widely known and involved many women in their manufacture. But the textile industry, which had fled to Utica from New England exactly one hundred years earlier, was now fleeing to the South. A great many of these women, particularly those who were Italian and Polish, had slipped back into their family structures without signifying any intention of continuing in the labor force by registering for unemployment insurance. What the future might hold was unclear, but unions as well as city leaders had to some extent joined in trying to attract new higher-wage, higher-skilled industries, where men might well predominate. And indeed over the next few years they were successful in this endeavor.

In Utica, a local officer of the Printers Union and an active member of the Machinists Union, both AFL affiliates, became leaders of the program. I was able to ask for help from John Connors, education director of the national AFL, whom I had known when we were both active in the Teachers Union in the thirties. I could also ask for advice from Art Elder, now with the

International Ladies Garment Workers Union, and Otto Pragan of the Chemical Workers, all three of whom were now on the IULEC board. As the city of Olean was added to the program, all three branches of the labor movement, including the railroad workers, formed separate classes in community structure and organization.

We found teachers for these classes among the faculty members at nearby universities and colleges. I asked Betsy Knapp, a graduate student on her way to the well-known Maxwell School of Public Affairs at Syracuse, to join us. And a decade before the Civil Rights Act, I was able to find a first-rate black professor of sociology, Charles Wylie, also at Syracuse. I hired a number of graduate women students from ILR, as well as professors from Colgate University, the University of Rochester, and from several of the former teachers' colleges, now part of the State University of New York (SUNY). I also sought consultants from city and state governments, some specialists in matters of the environment and in the administration of social programs, and a journalist, all of whom, as interest developed in action programs, were able to give us guidance. These activities took several months of my first year.

LIVING IN ITHACA

In addition to getting things going on the ILR project, I had to find a place for us to live. Tom Bernstein, Paul Bernstein and Johanna Moosdorf's son, was planning to come and visit us. His actual arrival depended however on the speed with which he might be granted a visa. In fact he arrived in January 1953. But in the fall of 1952 Lydia Tröscher arrived as one of the early community leaders to observe community organization and the work of voluntary agencies here. She herself was engaged in Germany—in addition to her many familial duties—in setting up one of the early senior citizens centers there.

By the time Lydia came, I had found a roomy apartment on East State Street, not far from the university. The furnishings I had acquired for our Vienna apartment had remained with Wesley and Rita and were now in storage in Washington, where Wes once more had a job with the textile union. After I arranged to have the furniture picked up, I learned in a phone call from the truck driver that Wes had never paid storage on the load and that the driver would have to come back to Ithaca in an empty truck. So Philip and I camped out until we could get this move worked out. The consequence was that the furniture and Lydia arrived almost simultaneously. At this time, demands on the project were keeping me very busy, with the result that Lydia, ever the helper, spent her time between meetings with local community leaders and putting my apartment in order. Among many topics that she and I discussed was the possibility of her daughter, Adelheid (Adi), who was the same age as Philip, coming to the United States for a year at high school. Philip would be in high school in another year, so it seemed like a good idea for Adi to come soon.

A further time-consuming problem in these months involved the early arrival of Gerhardt, Johanna Moosdorf's coworker from her time in the Russian Zone, who had joined her in Berlin. The plan we had agreed upon in Germany was that with some help from me, Gerhardt, as well as Tom, would shortly come to Ithaca, that he would find work, and that he would be responsible for bringing Johanna and her daughter, Barbara, to Ithaca as soon as possible. This plan had the great advantage of bringing Tom and his family together on this side of the ocean. It also meant my taking ultimate responsibility for them all, should they not be able to sustain themselves economically. I had several consultations with the family social work agency about how this system of certified immigration worked and what my financial responsibility under it might be.

I had to spend time consulting the Ithaca high school about Tom's placement there. He would come with some English acquired at the Odenwaldschule, but his basic language training in the Eastern Zone had been in Russian. His Odenwaldschule papers showed him considerably ahead in some subjects but lacking in American social studies. To give him the least stress, we agreed to enroll him as a freshman whenever he might arrive in the second semester.

I celebrated my new situation, new friends, and new work with a party during the holidays to which many people, both staff and faculty, came. It was in part my return of hospitality to those at the school who had invited me to their homes and whom I found congenial, welcoming, and stimulating. This group included graduate students Val and Madge Lorwin, who had been very helpful as I had set off to Germany in 1947, and Ed Beal, whom I had discovered there as chief labor officer in Stuttgart. Both Val and Ed were using their GI rights to study once they were out of uniform, and both had come to the new ILR School for Ph.D.s. Many of the new, young faculty at ILR were in a similar position, having just finished their Ph.D.s elsewhere or still busy with their final stages at nearby universities. Somewhat later, Matt Kelly, another coworker from Germany, turned up on our Extension staff in New York, while various others, with whom I had worked less closely in Germany, were in other colleges at Cornell.

Eleanor began to introduce me in the town and to her women friends on the faculty of the College of Home Economics. We went to the local chapter of the United Nations Association and participated in the women's club, which was busy at the time in raising the money for a women's building in the community, a goal achieved a few years later. There, women's groups of all varieties could meet and rooms for transient women and newcomers were available. The club also offered a roster of adult courses, planned mainly for women.

I also joined the Business and Professional Women's Club, in the hope of finding friends and getting to know the community. There I had my first contact with Constance Eberhardt, a graduate of the Cornell Law School, who had recently come to Ithaca to set up a practice. In a few years she married Alfred Cook. As Constance Cook, she became first the staff assistant to a state legislator and then his successor as a member of the state assembly. There she wrote New York State's abortion law, one of the most liberal in the country. In the seventies she was the first, and until 1994, the only woman vice president of Cornell.[4] Connie and I have remained friends over the past forty years, as well as coworkers on a number of projects that we continue to the present day.

Tom came to live with us in January, eager to be an American. He was quickly taken under the wing of a teacher of German, who was delighted to have a native speaker at his side. He did well in school and at the end of the spring term was advanced to sophomore status, with some junior courses, so that in 1955 he graduated with his age group. All that remained of his German accent by that time was a tendency to make "z's" out of his "s's". His mother soon began to complain that his letters to her were "translated English." Indeed, during Tom's years with us, he did, in effect, become my other son, a place he has held ever since.

Among the many pleasures that were now part of life in Ithaca were our Sunday hikes. I had started them when Tom came as a way to introduce him to Ithaca's natural beauty spots, and I kept them as a memory of the routine that I had adopted in Germany when I was a student of walking with friends on Sundays. A small group of women staff at the school, including Doris Stevenson, the financial officer, and Lee Eckert, the librarian, often picnicked with Eleanor and me on Connecticut Hill. There we could enjoy discovering the remains of its farmhouses and settlements, its abandoned cemeteries, its wild berries and overgrown orchards, as well as its views of distant hills and lakes.

In our first weeks in Ithaca Philip and I had discovered its waterfalls and state parks. We had also visited Betsy Knapp in Fayetteville, where she lived with her parents and Antje Lemke on land granted to one of Betsy's ancestors for his service in the Revolutionary War. Her father was engaged in planting a small forest of evergreen trees in a meadow near the house and up the hill in back of it. The place was known as Indian Oven Farm because, legend had it, Native Americans had migrated through these hills and stopped here to use small caves for preparing and storing food. Sometimes we met Betsy and Antje to explore a neighboring state park with its area of primeval forest, its round lakes, and its glacier-marked cliffs and streams.

On one of our Sunday expeditions, perhaps on the way to Betsy's, I promised Tom a view of a Native American reservation. In those years, Interstate 81 was not yet built and the road to Syracuse was a two-lane route through the Oneida reservation. Tom, who had been raised on stories of Native Americans written by Karl May, a German who had never been in the United States, much less known a Native American, was bitterly disappointed at the undistinguished housing, the glimpses of poorly dressed people, and the general shabbiness of reservation life that bore no visible relationship to the heroic tales he had enjoyed.

When spring came, I was quickly aware that our apartment was on a very noisy street. The by pass, Route 13, had not yet been built around Ithaca, and all east-bound traffic, or so it seemed, rattled up State Street's brick pavement. I was homesick for our Cheyney house with its trees and gardens, and I set out to look for a property I could afford in the nearby countryside. The place I found satisfied all my demands, though in somewhat different dimensions from the Cheyney house. I had acreage, room for gardens, a wood, and a stream that ran through one side of the property. I also had a second floor that would house the boys comfortably and give them their own bathroom. I could take over a very favorable GI mortgage. The property was on Turkey Hill Road just beyond the settlement of Varna, about four miles east of the campus. Neighbors were close but not too close. The boys could ride their bikes much of the year. Without any prospect of permanency in Ithaca, but with a very great sense of having found the kind of place I loved, I took that risk, became a home owner with a large mortgage, and moved in—as it turned out, for twenty-five years.

My job called for work during the summers. What to do about the boys in school vacation? That summer Philip could go to his paternal grandparents and work on their cherry farm when the harvests came in, and Tom decided to join him. Perhaps my tales of bicycle trips in Europe in my student days influenced us all to let them go off to Chicago and upper Michigan on their bikes. Both boys returned in August with money in their pockets and their first experience at earning it.

The following summer Tom Douty wanted to come to us from Atlanta. He and Philip once more took to their bikes for a several-hundred-mile trip to Grandfather Cook and the cherry orchards, while Tom Bernstein remained in Ithaca to work at a local business. They had been gone two days when Eleanor and I caught up with them on the road to Buffalo, as we were driving to our first experience of the Stratford Shakespeare Festival in Canada.

I had heard about this festival at a dinner party with a family devoted to theater who had gone to Stratford its very first summer in 1953. I had caught their enthusiasm and had persuaded Eleanor to join me in going to the festival's second year. The theater was then housed in a magnificent tent and was still very much an experiment both artistically and financially. We saw only one play, but were so caught up in the experience that as we drove back we promised ourselves to come the following year for several nights. I have followed that schedule—except when I was not in the States—until this very day. The festival has presented Shakespeare as nineteenth-century and modern drama; as faithful to its original text and form; and at other times with daring innovations that have not always pleased me. Nevertheless, the Stratford experience has been part of living during the last forty years, always with friends who came to share my enthusiasm.

An early piece of political advice was given me by Arnold Tolles, professor in the ILR labor economics group. He and his wife invited the boys and me to Thanksgiving dinner in 1953 and told me about the local political situation from Arnold's view as a member of the city council. His wife was a member of the League of Women Voters, in which she played an active role. "If you are interested in political office," he began, "be sure to register Republican. It's the dominant party here and you can't get elected as a Democrat." I had neither time nor sufficient interest in a political career in upstate New York to pay much attention to this well-meant admonition. I have thought of it often, however, as I have observed over the forty-odd years since that dinner that Ithaca has become predominantly Democratic and that most recently the Democrats achieved decided majorities in both town and county governments.

ACTION PROGRAM

My weekday activity on the project continued to be one of a personal education for me in many respects. In one particular case I made great strides in that education as I learned how to deal with a problem raised by Ralph Campbell, assistant dean for Extension services. His questions arose at the end of the first year as study groups became ready to do something about the problems they had been studying. Labor groups are generally organized to act on problems that face them, and an old labor adage is that a strike is the best learning experience for trade unionists. Ralph's background, in contrast, was that of an army bureaucrat who had dealt with personnel problems during the war years, an experience that left little room for self-initiated or any action that went beyond "going by the book." He had in fact little knowledge of labor as an activist organization. Nor was he acquainted with adult and labor education that combined action with learning, and how these two elements could be made compatible by each supporting the other so as to lead to more learning.

For my part, I was unfamiliar with aspects either of adult education or of academic research that might respond positively to Ralph's concern. As I understood it, Ralph was concerned that we stood in danger of involving the school—even the university—in programs that might be seen as more political than educational, thus alarming the school's management side. In my work in the Y and at the summer schools, I had of course faced such issues when they arose and considered them as occasions for finding alternative solutions. The Bryn Mawr Summer School had had to leave the Bryn Mawr campus, when summer school faculty and students had supported strike by employees of the Birdseye Corporation in New Jersey. But the summer school had not blamed its students or faculty, nor had it ceased to exist. It had moved elsewhere and continued its work. When the YWCA was faced with protests from its members about the narrowness of membership eligibility and the lack of participating members on its boards and committees, it had included representatives of the "club girls" in these bodies. When industry representatives in the Community Chest opposed the Buffalo Y's Industrial Department's program with working women, the Y did not change its program; rather, it raised its own funds within the community, until it was invited to rejoin the Community Chest program of joint fund-raising. Indeed, the YWCA's long history has been one of adapting programs to its members' needs as women have moved from positions of dependence and oppression and begun to aspire to equality and justice.

My training and experience made me unwilling in any way to abandon the action component of adult education. In addition, I had not yet heard of the ways in which students in sociology and anthropology, when trying to understand cultural and social aspects of their subjects of inquiry, became "participant observers" and thus learned how people found their own solutions to life's problems.

The early fifties were a very tense and troubled time, however. McCarthyism was not limited to a congressional witch hunt of the State Department's civil servants, where it had begun; it had been extended to the moving picture industry, to other industries, to labor unions, to libraries, and to universities. It penetrated everywhere, setting up a Cold War norm—one that not only defined explicit behavior but also had a chilling effect on activism of many kinds in long-established, quite legal organizations. Cornell University had already had to deal with allegations against two of its scientists who had been engaged in the creation of the nuclear bomb, with results that had polarized and divided its faculty. Outside its walls, radicalism expressed as allegation or rejection was, in this atmosphere, attached particularly to labor unions, many of which were not only suspect of harboring Communists but of being controlled by Communists.

The CIO itself, at its 1949 convention, had counted the cost of further inaction on such matters and had expelled a number of its affiliates suspected of operating under Communist leadership. Now it was attempting to rebuild non-Communist, even anti-Communist unions in the jurisdictions that alleged Communists had occupied. The growing auto union had throughout its first years been an ideological battleground over which radical, sectarian armies had fought to elect their own leaders. The recently elected non-Communist president, Walter Reuther, was attacked by opponents who pointed to the year he and his brother, Victor, had spent in the thirties working in Russia. Conservative opponents likewise cast a shadow by insisting that Reuther's Socialist Party affiliation was a cover-up for his basic adherence to Communist ideas.

The AFL, for its part, took political cover by noting that some of its powerful unions consistently supported Republican candidates in elections and that it had a long history of anti-Communist activity going back to its abandonment of the Brookwood Labor College. The AFL attacked the CIO as a political organization that had abandoned the historic Gompers position of political nonpartisanship by conveniently supporting Democrats through its Political Action Committee, which had been founded in the Roosevelt period and headed by Sidney Hillman of the Amalgamated Clothing Workers. (This was the committee that generated the Roosevelt "clear-it-with-Sidney" phrase, which had become a by-word.) The postwar decade was indeed a parlous time.

This confrontation with Ralph Campbell forced me to examine my own commitment to espousing action as one outcome of learning. Within a few days I had called a meeting of the teachers in the program, and together we discussed the issue of education of working adults as it relates to, or moves forward through, action to solve the problems studied in class. On the basis of that discussion I addressed a paper to Ralph which, in another long discussion, he accepted.[5]

Professor Jack Barbash of the University of Wisconsin, who, at the end of the projects, was asked to evaluate the work of each of the eight participating universities, dealt at some length with this issue at Cornell in his book published as the projects ended. In it, he described how our group leaders had encouraged the worker-students to:

1. explore the field;
2. identify a problem;
3. do fact-finding on the problem;
4. recommend a policy; and
5. attempt implementation of a policy.[6]

In *Labor's Role in Community Affairs*,[7] which I wrote at the conclusion of our project, I went into considerably more detail to outline eight steps, beginning with a survey and leading to continuing education, based on the observation that "community problems are never ended."

How study groups or local unions decided on an action program varied considerably from city to city and, in fact, raised no hackles in any of the communities. Indeed, the programs tended to conform to widely acceptable conservative standards of community behavior, with no trace of radicalism, even of the least problematic kind. Where strategies failed, it was in one case at least because of inadequate consultation within the unions themselves.

Three examples will illustrate this process. In Syracuse, the fact that many steelworkers were also members of the Rod and Gun Club led quite directly to a concern with cleaning up polluted Oneida Lake, a program the city and some of its suburbs in the county bordering on the lake sorely needed and wanted. In deciding on its own role, the CIO council's Community Committee consulted with a variety of interest groups and a professor of sanitary engineering. It then brought a resolution to the CIO County Council for its endorsement. The council in turn named the committee its representative in future hearings on the subject of lake pollution and its cleanup. However, when the county produced its plan, the CIO committee opposed it on several grounds. Nor was the CIO council persuaded that its representatives were wrong. Its committee turned to Syracuse's mayor, asking him to veto the county plan, an action he took. The CIO plan was to call a citywide conference in support of the mayor and of its own program, but that failed to materialize and the issue fell to a low place on the city's agenda. Despite the lack of success, these activities remained a positive learning experience for these union members. They continued to offer support on the issue as it arose again in later years.

In Olean we had begun to work with three labor groups—AFL, CIO, and railroad workers. The Chamber of Commerce invited all three to work with its committees on a series of local projects, including support for a new airport, rent control, and technical training for semiskilled workers. (The decision of three companies to close down their Olean operations had created a citywide crisis.) A joint labor–Chamber of Commerce committee agreed on a proposal for rent control as proposed by realtors and homeowners. The labor organizations, however, repudiated the agreement. The lesson here was one in the requirement of representative democracy within their own organizations, whose interests had run counter to a majority of union members who were in this case renters.

Utica had better success. There, the AFL council in Utica decided on a two-step program: first, a series of lessons in public speaking, the better to carry their message; second, a study of the community need for employment of the handicapped, a matter that had concerned the Community Chest board for some time. A second group, a joint Labor-Management Committee on bringing new industry to Utica brought in a series of outside experts to talk at open meetings, and the professor who had worked with this labor group became the joint committee's adviser. The whole experience is reported in the handbook, which was reissued at least once and distributed for the next twenty years.

ILR's judgment on the value of my project was expressed by its supporting its continuation into a third year. In the spring of 1955, as the third year was drawing to a close, the dean invited me to lunch. He told me that Mark Perlman, who together with Maurice Neufeld had been teaching the labor history courses, had decided to leave the school, and that Maurice had been granted a much-wanted extended leave of absence to go to Italy and write the book on Italian labor he had started in Ithaca. Maurice was leaving in the fall. The dean badly needed someone to take over the labor history courses. Would I consider a position on the resident faculty?

I JOIN THE RESIDENT FACULTY

I am no longer sure how I answered immediately. I must have hesitated in some respect, for the dean began to bargain with me. It would mean a professorship, he said, and if he could persuade the faculty to go along, it would be a tenured position. If tenure were not immediately possible, then he would endeavor to work that out after one year, during which we could all see how my teaching went and generally how I fitted in to the resident faculty. I was still an innocent insofar as fully comprehending all that the dean's offer implied, beyond realizing that it was generous and that I had his strong backing. I felt that he meant the best and that, because he badly needed someone and I was at hand, he wanted me. Within a few days of considering my experience with the labor movement, I accepted his offer.[8]

What I had agreed to do was to teach a required course that would in its first semester cover American labor history. The first semester would begin with Commons's nineteenth-century shoemakers and progress through to the Taft-Hartley Act of 1947 and the union federations' amalgamation negotiations that were currently in progress.[9] In the second semester I would deal with union structure in its various forms throughout the AFL and the CIO.

Only after I had accepted the offer did I face the task that lay before me. To be sure, I had for many years worked closely with organized labor. My most direct and lasting experiences had been with the teachers, the clothing workers, and the textile unions. My teaching of union members had taken me into many different unions—electrical, bakery, shipbuilding, railroad. I also had extensive knowledge of the German unions and their very different history, structure, and function. All of this gave me considerable assurance about handling the second semester of the program on union structures and functions.

I had nevertheless to face the fact that I had never taken a course in labor history, nor had I systematically read the classics in the field, as they had been produced both at the University of Wisconsin under John R. Commons and in the Johns Hopkins series, "Studies in American Labor History." As for course administration, I would need to select textbooks and prepare a syllabus that would include topics and assignments for each week of each semester. I would have about eighty students in the course, most of them juniors.

Questions of exams, term papers, and reading assignments took me to Maurice. He generously gave me his syllabi over several years. A lecture pattern for at least two hours a week with a discussion period at the third meeting, in smaller groups with my teaching assistants as leaders, seemed a reasonable structure. This last would involve some work with the TAs to cover the reading, select themes for discussion, and hear weekly reports on troublesome areas. It became clear not only that I had an enormous amount of reading to do during the summer weeks but also that my best efforts would mean that I ran the risk of being only a few weeks ahead of my students in systematic study.

THE SUMMER OF 1955

Indeed, it was a summer of intensive reading. As I began to sum up the attempts of workers to protect their interests and their livelihoods in the nineteenth century, I saw these as a long and painful series of attempts to build organizations that could effectively deal with the problems that early industry in the United States had presented to its workers. Most of these workers were immigrants—propertyless, often illiterate people, penniless on arrival. They began to form an urban population in a country still dominated economically and politically by agriculture. Labor history began then with native tradesmen and specifically with Commons's shoemakers, while the immigrant masses that industry recruited or who came out of their own desperation were so divided by language and hampered by poverty and exploitation that they were considered unorganizable. The few immigrants who came with a quasipolitical experience of solidarity began to try to replicate it in their own national enclaves in this country. They established European-like institutions—Lasallean, socialist, anarchist, cooperative—but these gained little foothold in a country that proclaimed its societal goals as classless, democratic, participative, and opportunity-rich, the very goals that had drawn Europe's exploited to these shores and hinterlands.

The labor movement that established itself by the 1880s was expressly nonpolitical. It was purely an economic organization set up to deal with economic questions in the workplace, questions limited to wages, hours, and working conditions. It was therefore made up of skilled workers and included few immigrants; these instead were drawn into the expanding factories and mills that were the forerunners of post–Civil War high capitalism. Major industries established themselves in and near cities—or created new cities—around the plants that produced oil, steel, coal, clothing, rubber, and lumber, as well as handling meat packing, flour milling, and lumbering. All these activities were unorganized and deemed unorganizable. In short, the problem was so vast as to defy control by the then trade union formulae that primarily applied to skilled workers.

The result was a viable labor federation of labor aristocrats, the skilled workers who could establish something of a monopoly of employment and skill learning for their own members. Membership numbers were limited by the unwritten rule underlying this concept, namely to maintain a membership at a level of fewer workers in the trade than might be needed, thus guaranteeing something like full employment through control of the available workers and jobs within a trade. (I presented this overview to classes in a simple algebraic equation in which x represented full employment, and x minus one equaled "the maximum number of available workers.") Since the industries reached by this system of organization then had to deal with multiple craft unions— as they did in construction, printing, railroads, marine work, and harbor work— it was important to try to develop a kind of skilled worker loyalty, in which unions in difficulty with contractors or other employers could count on the support of fellow unionists in their strikes and boycotts. This was a far cry from classconsciousness or worker solidarity in European Marxist terms. This creation of limited inter-union loyalty resulted in the sanctity of union jurisdiction, the necessity for the federation to attempt to mediate jurisdictional disputes, the federation's opposition to industrial unions, and the war between the AFL and the CIO as it developed in the 1930s and continued until late in the 1950s.

Among the unions in the AFL were nevertheless a small minority of unions that were organized not by crafts but by specific industry. These unions included both skilled and semiskilled workers, as well as the unskilled. Of primary importance here were the coal miners under the leadership of John L. Lewis, whose union was in serious decline. In the Great Depression of the 1930s, Lewis called together other unions that were built on an industrial basis, such as the garment and textile unions, together with new ones trying to fasten a foothold in autos, steel, rubber, shipbuilding, and electrical products. They formed a committee within the AFL that would sponsor the organization of unskilled and semiskilled workers who had either never been organized or only locally and inadequately so.

The result was the creation of two rival federations by the end of the 1930s and a state of war that continued bitterly for twenty years. These rival federations espoused diverse policies on issues such as politics and social programs, membership loyalties, differentiated coalitions with nonlabor organizations, and international programs.

My own espousal of Democratic Socialism, with its intimate relationship between party and unions, had come to seem inappropriate in this country, both because of the history of unions and because of political structures. My own Socialism had never been friendly to Communism, even before my German and Austrian postwar experiences. The behavior of Communist-dominated trade unions in Germany under Hitler in turning on the Socialist-led unions and the Socialist Party, the subsequent appalling history of Stalinism in Russia and East Germany, together with the opportunism and infighting of the American Communist Party, had all seemed to me hostile to concepts of worker solidarity. Rather, the idea of industrial democracy, as developed in the progressive period in the United States in the early years of the twentieth century, followed by the legitimation of trade unionism in the National Industrial Recovery Act (NIRA) and the Wagner Law in the early thirties, now seemed to me developments that met the special needs and history of U.S. workers by recognizing the right of those workers to organize and bargain collectively.

Thus, I entered on a learning process that has not ceased from that time forward. I wanted to make some contribution of my own to the field of labor education by adding to the understanding of what has happened to working people in the contexts of the different and varied economic, cultural, and political systems controlling their lives.

THE FAMILY

During that summer the constitution of the family changed again. Tom Bernstein had applied to several colleges and was accepted with tuition grants at Harvard. To replace him at school and at home, Adi Tröscher was coming shortly before Tom left, and would spend a year and perhaps more with Philip and me in Ithaca. Gerhardt had arrived a year or so earlier, and while he was often with us, he had a room in town and a job with the telephone company. In his case it would shortly become clear that he had neither desire nor intention of bringing Johanna and Barbara over; certainly his income could not finance such an undertaking. Presumably, he would devote himself to writing and would work at jobs that would hold him above water but provide no surplus. He began to display psychotic behavior that culminated several years later, during my absence from Ithaca, with the police sending him from Ithaca to Willard Psychiatric Hospital a few miles away.

I met Adi at the boat in New York one day in August 1955. She came filled with admonitions from her mother aimed at making her a good and helpful daughter to me, as indeed she was. We helped Tom pack for college and took him to Cambridge to see him established in a freshman dormitory in Harvard Yard, without quite realizing that with this break he was leaving us for his own life. He shortly became eligible for the German government's pension for surviving victims of fascism and received a grant that enabled him, with some student work opportunities, to remain at Harvard and to graduate cum laude in 1959. He spent his upper class years at Eliot House, majored in government and political science, and moved on to do graduate work at Columbia.

Adi entered high school in the junior year and quickly made friends and was invited to join the girls' leadership organization. She became a neighborhood baby-sitter, joined the Methodist Church, and in all the recognizable ways became a normal high school girl.

Philip was also a junior and beginning to demonstrate the talent for political activity that has become a life's work for him—namely that of successfully backing selected candidates for office. He was a good, though not outstanding student, who expected to go to college—probably to Cornell, since one of my benefits as a faculty member was that of free tuition for my son.

With these new arrangements, and stuffed with as much preparation as I could manage through hours of daily reading, I moved into permanent status as a member of the Cornell and ILR faculties and, as well, into citizenship in Ithaca and its surroundings.

9

BEGINNING A FIFTH CAREER IN ACADEME: 1955–1962

When I accepted an academic appointment, I had only the dimmest notion of what this involved. I assumed of course that it meant teaching, but I had not yet distinguished between undergraduate and graduate courses—though that was one of the first things I learned as I went to a department meeting in labor history, labor law, and collective bargaining, my home base. As the beginning of the term drew near, I realized I would also have considerable advising to do, mainly of undergraduates. I had to learn about required and elective courses, as well as the distinctions between courses in ILR and those outside our school. Early in the semester I was assigned to my first faculty-student committee. I had to learn about its past actions in order to evaluate what might need to be changed. Later, the dean of the university faculty named me to a university committee where I learned to recognize the movers and shakers from the other colleges in the university. Drawn to them perhaps by my well-developed political interests, I eventually become a member of that group.

It was also not long before I became a member and then even a chairperson of a Ph.D. committee. I inherited my first student when Bob Risley went on leave just as his student was coming up to defend his thesis in personnel (not at all my field).[1] I found that I had to do almost as much preparation as the student in order to test him. That experience certainly taught me that I would need to work closely with my own doctoral students throughout the whole period of their thesis development, from finding a topic to presenting a final work.

TEACHING

In the first month of this, my fifth, career, my attention in the summer of 1955 was focused mainly on the required courses. My sons have both told me that their memory of that summer is of my constant reading. I had not yet developed any hypotheses to explain the wide differences in the way different unions were organized, which officers performed which internal or external functions, under what circumstances members had power, or what forces internally or externally brought any of these officers or functions into prominence. I realized over the course of the summer that I wanted some answers to these questions, and I looked both in history and in reports of current events in the labor relations field for hypotheses that might offer some of those answers.

In the end, I selected two major texts. For the first semester in trade union history, I chose the new book by Foster Rhea Dulles, *Labor in America,* which came out first in 1949 but reappeared revised in 1955. For the second semester in structure and function of trade unions, I chose *How Collective Bargaining Works,* the study of types of unions' collective bargaining, a Twentieth Century Fund publication edited by Harry Millis.[2] As a result of my new focus on differences among unions, the history of their structures, and their manner of functioning, I came to see the scope of their bargaining as determinative. This central thesis rested on two very different factors: first, the origin of the industry's raw materials, which in turn strongly influenced its location; and second, the scope of the industry's market. Construction unions, for example, were primarily tied to a local market, while autos were made and sold nationwide. For purposes of bargaining, the several craft unions involved in construction had formed a department at the national level, often replicated at regional and local levels, and suggested joint bargaining of a number, or even all, of these unions. On the other hand, autos, produced on an assembly line, were represented by an industrial union of semiskilled and skilled workers that bargained nationally with each of the three or four major manufacturers in turn. Thus, I was concerned with what became their pattern of bargaining: At what level of the structure did bargaining take place? How were union members consulted about goals and achievements, and were they participating in the process in any regularized way? What specialist staff might be needed and what was their relationship to the union's political structure? Overall, did union structure, particularly for the industrial unions, necessarily replicate the hierarchy of a company?

Another powerful factor in designing this part of the course was the fact that the years leading up to 1959, when the Landrum-Griffin Act on union democracy was adopted, had produced a public debate on issues of democracy in union structure and behavior that dealt with the rights of union members. These issues harked back to the findings of a series of congressional hearings that began in the depression years of the thirties. The hearings continued in the aftermath of McCarthy's anti-Communist attacks on radical labor organizations such as the Industrial Workers of the World (IWW), the Socialists, alleged Communists, and, in fact, progressives of all kinds. The debate centered on an issue usually identified as "union democracy."

Soon after I began working on this phase of my teaching assignment, I also began to design research on union democracy, which resulted in several later publications. This move into research and publication was of course a standard component of academic life. I knew vaguely that it would be expected of me, but I was not yet clear that my promotion to a tenured position hung on it. Indeed, the dean had told me that he would endeavor to persuade the faculty to appoint me at once to tenured rank, but at the beginning of the semester I did not know whether the process had begun, nor was I, at that point, much concerned about rank. My interest in research arose from all the systematic reading I had been doing and from my far-reaching concern with democracy within unions. That topic was in a way a spin-off from the McCarthyism that had been a major approach to political problems from the early fifties onward.

Like all professors in ILR, I was also expected to teach these topics in a 500-level graduate course for students seeking either a terminal master's degree (M.I.L.R.) or an M.S. that might also be terminal or lead to further study for a Ph.D. Both types of students came from other colleges and had not taken our required undergraduate courses in the ILR field. Thus, each of us was expected to develop a seminar for M.S. and Ph.D. students majoring in labor history, collective bargaining, and labor law.

STUDENTS

Without any formal assignment, I came to be the adviser of two types of students in addition to my assigned undergraduate advisees. I was sought out by Asian foreign students, whom I met again many times in my later travels and who helped me immeasurably in understanding their countries. Among these were Tedjasukmana, a minister of labor in an early postwar Indonesian government, whom the Rockefeller Foundation had brought to the United States when threatening political changes occurred in his country, and Tamboenan, a railroad union leader from Indonesia. Philip Se-Sun Oh was a Korean economics student, whose inadequate grasp of English barred his getting the degree he sought with us. He left after a disappointing year, but he and I have remained in touch to this day. Ichiro Yamamoto, like many other Japanese students, was sent by his company to ILR for a year. Another Japanese student was going to head a branch of a Japanese company setting up a lumber business in Alaska; since he was going to manage American workers, he needed to become acquainted with American labor institutions and law. Hiroko Kageyama was on the management ladder with the Telecommunications Corporation in Japan. She first came to ILR in the mid-fifties, and then, in her retirement role as a professor of management, spent a sabbatical at Cornell almost forty years later.

The second group of students who played a similar but different role in my academic career was made up of U.S. women. In these early years the number of women in ILR's freshman class was limited to about fifteen, out of an admission of eighty to a hundred. This number was limited by the number of beds reserved for women in the college dormitories, and home economics had the major intake. The result, of course, was that we turned down many women who were better equipped for admission than some of the men whom we accepted. Many of these women turned for advice either to me or to Jean McKelvey, since she and I were for many years the only two women on the tenured faculty; Jean, however, commuted from Rochester, usually spending only three crowded days a week at the school.[3] Many of these students have remained close friends whose names, like those of the foreign students, will appear again as I continue my story.

FRANCES PERKINS AT CORNELL

In the spring of 1957 the dean tapped the school bell on his desk to call me in for a new assignment. Over the years of his deanship his habit was to give each new faculty member a task that had to be performed alone and outside the school. What followed, I have always believed, was his testing of me.

He told me that he wanted to persuade Madame Frances Perkins, the secretary of Labor under Roosevelt and the first woman in a U.S. president's cabinet, to become a member of the Cornell faculty. Frances Perkins had been a visitor at the University of Illinois for a semester, a fact that had undoubtedly persuaded the dean to propose a more permanent relationship for her at Cornell. He had already had some correspondence with her that suggested her interest. My task was to go to New York and discover her terms. I was to assure her that we would arrange living conditions to meet her needs, provide an office and a secretary, and allow her time to get acquainted with us before deciding what she would like to do as an ILR professor. We would certainly hope that she would want to lecture on some phase of her experience as secretary of labor, and we would be delighted if she wished to give a course in this area of labor history.

With some trepidation and a great deal of anticipation, I undertook the assignment. Miss Perkins (as we always addressed her when she was at Cornell) lived with a friend on the Upper East Side, where we began our discussions. At her suggestion, we then moved to the Women's City Club, and she pointed out to me the sofa under a corner of the stairs where she had taken John L. Lewis away from reporters' eyes while they discussed the possible ending of one of the wartime coal strikes.

I returned to ILR with a positive reply from Miss Perkins, as well as with several assignments, including finding living quarters for her. Our discussion of teaching had resulted in a plan for me to teach a course with her, perhaps to be called Labor and the New Deal. When, after her arrival, we planned the course in more detail, she agreed to do the lecturing, while I would handle the administration: the admission of students, assignment of papers, midterm and final examinations, and grading. Miss Perkins came to Cornell and remained, with a few short breaks, until her death seven years later.

She quickly became an important guest of the university. President Malott took a special interest in her presence, and she was in demand as a lecturer in several departments. A popular visitor while she was there was Professor Dwight Perkins of the University of Rochester and his wife, who were guests of the Law School. The two Perkinses became close friends and even established that they had a distant blood relationship.

Her course, which was first offered in the fall of 1957, is still vividly remembered by its participants—a few outstanding undergraduates, as well as graduate students. Miss Perkins began with a brief statement of her work as industrial commissioner in New York State when Roosevelt was governor. She referred also to an earlier time when she was a factory inspector for the Consumers' League.

She then told the class about the discussion she had had with the elected president when he finally called her to his New York City apartment, very shortly before his inauguration, to tell her that he wanted her as his secretary of labor. She was neither surprised nor unprepared, though genuinely doubtful that he was making a sound political choice of a woman candidate who had no close connection with organized labor. Her background as a factory inspector and her association with Florence Kelley, organizer and head of the Consumers' League, had led Miss Perkins to see labor as not simply composed of unionized workers but as composed of all hourly waged and salaried workers—indeed, all employees, both those at work and those seeking work. The upcoming president was aware of these problems, but he made it clear that he had nevertheless decided, on the basis of their association in New York State, to proceed with her nomination.

Miss Perkins had brought with her to this meeting a list of legislative improvements she wished to see enacted as administration policy. These included a prohibition of child labor;[4] the institution of a minimum wage;[5] and the establishment of unemployment, health, and old age social insurance.[6] She told us that despite the problems she and Roosevelt both knew were attached to such legislation, his response was nevertheless positive. He did, however, make the condition that she remind him of the list well before the end of his term of office, so as to provide time for the necessary bills to be drafted, introduced, and debated within Congress.

Miss Perkins's recollections were vivid. She recounted how, at the beginning of her term of office, she had to deal with the elementary matter of occupying her physical office. Her predecessor was still at his desk when she entered; he apparently believed he could take his time to wind up his affairs, which had been mainly concerned with immigration policy. Both he and she were sharply aware that she had another agenda. She made it quite clear that she needed to come in without delay and without further discussion. It was her first, but far from her last, encounter with male assumptions of authority.

When she had set up the Committee on Social Security, she selected Professor Ed Witte of the University of Wisconsin as its chair. The committee had necessarily moved slowly, but as the end of Roosevelt's first presidential term neared, and under pressure from the White House, she set a deadline for the completion of its work. She invited the committee to her home for what had to be its final meeting; seated them around her dining table; produced a bottle of whiskey, which she placed in the middle of the table; and, clearly on her way out, said, "Gentlemen, I am locking the door. I need a finished report."

In any current sense, Frances Perkins was not a feminist. I believe that she would probably not have supported concepts of affirmative action, nor did she express any sense of her own subordination, except to the president himself. In dealing with critical issues, official opinions, and commission reports, she relied on the power of her office and on the superior power of the federal government over state and local rules and practices. When she went to Pennsylvania to see for herself what the coal and iron police were doing to workers in the steel mills and coal mines, the companies forbade her access to local halls. Miss Perkins simply walked to the local post office (a federal building, of course) and, standing on its steps, addressed her audience.

The Women's Party, headed by Alice Paul, opposed protective laws for women in favor of equality with men; Miss Perkins, however, was clearly on the side of extending and enforcing such protection.[7] She saw it as a necessary policy if the growing number of working women were to be protected from utter exploitation; but she also wanted to be sure that men were included in minimum wage legislation and maximum hour restrictions. As industrial commissioner in the State of New York, she had experienced the limitations that the market set, state by state, on dealing satisfactorily with these matters, and she pioneered the introduction of federal legislation to deal with the regulation of working conditions.

Her concepts of race relations were still influenced by her early reading of the doctrine of the white man's burden in his dealings with the darker races. She spoke with deep appreciation of the African-American caretaker she had employed to care for her ill husband, but she believed that he was inherently limited in the range of his occupational possibilities.

As a politician, she was devoted to her party. In 1928 she had volunteered to campaign in the South for Al Smith, when the basic issue was whether this country could support a Catholic for president. She had worked with Smith when he was the most prominent member of the New York State Legislature, and some of her friends still believed that she thought more highly of him than of President Roosevelt.

Frances Perkins was deeply religious; immediately on her arrival in Ithaca, she sought out the Episcopal Church and its rector. On occasion, she visited an Episcopal nunnery for extended periods for rest and contemplation. She was in fact there when she had the stroke that led to her death. She once asked me what church I belonged to. When I explained that I was not religious and had withdrawn from any church affiliation, I had the impression that such a state was beyond her understanding. Her grandson, then a preschooler, and his religious development were of deep concern to her. In preparation for one Christmas she asked me to help her find records of hymns that she could give him.

She carried with her always and everywhere a black leather envelope bag. When I told her in the summer of 1957 that I was going to Germany and Italy, she told me that she very much needed a replacement for it and recalled that she had bought it from "a little man" in Florence. She described his location in precise detail—near an ancient chapel, just north of its plaza, on a street near certain other tradespeople; she located it in relation to the river and to one or two notable public buildings, though she had no names for any of these landmarks. It was all so exact, however, that when I searched for the shop, I found it easily. What was more, the "little man" spoke enough English for us to communicate; he recalled Miss Perkins, though he had no idea, I thought, that she was at that time a high official in the United States government. When I returned with the bag, almost an exact copy of the one she was ready to discard, she told me that it would contain all her personal papers. This meant they would be immediately accessible to her executor in the event of a severe accident or illness, when she might be unable to give instructions. This was indeed the circumstance of her demise, for she never recovered speech, perhaps not even consciousness, after the stroke that took her down.

Miss Perkins settled in to Ithaca socially as well as professionally, and from time to time returned the courtesies offered her by faculty and university officials, as well as by members and priests of her church. She usually gave dinners, held for several years mainly at the Ithaca Hotel, where she could rely on good service from a staff of waiters who knew exactly how to take care of her and her guests. Conversation on these occasions never failed to move broadly through political events, both national and statewide. She could be persuaded to talk about her own experiences, but she could also defer to and draw out her guests. She became an appreciated member not only of the university community but also in the town.

Her lectures continued to be a delight. She limited herself to a narrative—what happened, how it came about, what part she played or was allowed to play, what her friends, supporters, and opponents said or did. For students who, for the most part had no insight into the workings of politics at the level of decision-making, diplomacy, and compromise, these hours were a revelation about how government works. When, several years on, she was living at Telluride, a high scholarship house on the Cornell campus, she would invite one after another of the still-living Roosevelt cabinet members to the campus to meet and talk with students and faculty.

One of her anecdotes concerned the writing of the Wagner Act of 1935. The National Industrial Recovery Act (NIRA) was before the Supreme Court on the question of its constitutionality, an issue unrelated to its Section 7a, which legitimized trade unions and collective bargaining. Challenges to collective bargaining had precipitated this crisis, and several powerful groups of supporters each sought to draft replacements for it that would not weaken its provisions regarding union organization and collective bargaining. Miss

Perkins was not included in any of these undertakings. She heard, however, that a group chaired by Senator Wagner of New York, whom she knew from her work in the state, was holding late-evening meetings in the Treasury Building and that this group was close to a decision.

When Miss Perkins went to the president with this information, he directed her to attend the Wagner meetings to assure that the emerging bill would be acceptable to her and to him. Unaccompanied, she knocked on the meeting-room door and was somewhat coolly received. She took a seat to join the group. Of particular concern to her was the retention not so much of Section 7a on collective bargaining as of the minimum wage and maximum hours controls imbedded in the old NIRA. In the end these measures were handled in the Fair Labor Standards Act after it came into being in the summer of 1938. She lost on the issue of the location of the National Labor Relations Board, the enforcement agency of the NLRA. She wanted and rather expected to have it within the Labor Department, but it became an independent agency, made up of rotating terms of presidential appointees, and has remained so to this day. Roosevelt decided to embrace the NLRA's provisions, and signed the measure on July 5, 1935. With its adoption, the attitude of government toward labor moved from toleration to strong support and the recognition that government had a positive interest in labor's power to negotiate with management over conditions of work.

Her lectures never went beyond the events of the first term of the Roosevelt administration. During this period she had succeeded in introducing all and gaining some of the items she and the president had agreed upon when he nominated her to the Labor Department post. My original hope was that, as we repeated the course, we would reach well beyond the achievements of the first term and into the growing difficulties her program met as the war neared and anti-Roosevelt strength crystallized. I was able to express this hope to her, but in the three years in which we gave the course on Labor and the New Deal, we never went any further than 1936.

When Miss Perkins first came to Cornell, she had made it clear that she was engaged in writing a book that would compare Al Smith's and Roosevelt's influence on labor reform. She had, in her years as lobbyist and factory inspector for the Consumers' League in New York, worked ever more closely with Smith. On one occasion she conducted him on a trip across the state on the New York Central Railroad, stopping in several towns where she introduced him to workers and their working conditions, thus gaining his support for a variety of progressive labor laws. She saw these two men as essentially of one mind, at least on the subject of protective labor legislation, and she was still deeply puzzled by Smith's bitter opposition to Roosevelt, expressed in Smith's adherence to the America First Movement's opposition to Roosevelt's prowar program. It was a problem she never solved.

She interviewed many of her contemporaries for a key to the estrangement. Among others, she met with Eleanor Roosevelt, returning disappointed and, incidentally, critical of the way in which Mrs. Roosevelt was then living. Her mood and her recounting of this incident made me wonder whether their relationship had always been cool or whether the present distance between them was a momentary product of Miss Perkins's failure to solve her central problem concerning the estrangement of the two men. In any case, after Miss Perkins's death, her secretary told me that, despite Miss Perkins's continuous concern with Smith, she had in fact written very little on her proposed book during the Cornell years.

The university president attended Miss Perkins's funeral in New York City, inviting a number of her friends and coworkers, including the ILR dean, several of the Telluride House students who were her pallbearers, and a few faculty members, of whom I was one, to join him on the university plane from Ithaca to New York City and back. The ceremony was a high Episcopal mass and was also attended by many celebrities of the Roosevelt era. Miss Perkins's portrait hangs today prominently on a wall of the ILR faculty lounge.

Opening the Faculty Club Lunch to Women

When Val Lorwin, then a Ph.D. candidate in ILR, first showed me around the campus soon after my arrival in Ithaca, he pointed out the faculty club in the Hotel School building, noting that I would find it difficult to use, since it was barred to women at noon. He and I both treated this as a bitter joke on the times in which we lived. I spent much of my first three years off campus and considered the exclusion merely an expression of the university's disregard for equal treatment of its women. At that time most women on the faculty were in the College of Home Economics, which had instituted an excellent lunch service in its own building.

After I became a resident faculty member, however, and was on campus six days a week,[8] I found the club rule hampering and improper. In 1957 I decided to do something about it. I discovered that the time to act was at the annual club meeting in May, when members were offered free desserts if they came to the meeting in order to vote on club officers and carry out any other business the retiring executive board might have on its agenda. I decided to send a memo to all the women I had met, with the information that I would introduce a resolution to open the lunch period to women faculty. I was amazed to discover that my list ran close to a hundred names.

Shortly before the meeting date, I was visited at home one evening by two young professors of mathematics. They told me the club had other objectionable rules, such as requiring men to wear jackets and ties there until a date in late spring. They offered to encourage their colleagues in mathematics to vote to admit women at lunchtime if they in turn could count on women's support for a resolution they would be introducing to abolish the dress rules for men. I had to tell them that I represented no organized caucus and could not be a negotiator with women on their behalf. We would both have to see how the meeting addressed these two separate grievances.

About seventy-five members attended the meeting, the majority of them women. Both resolutions were adopted, with the help of two well-known professors, who rose again and again to test new wordings for the desired new rules. The discussion, which was sometimes heated, revealed a great deal of stereotypical bias against treating women as equals—our "tender ears," for example, "might be violated by the language men used at the club," said a gentle botanist, perhaps seeing himself as our genuine protector.

The adoption of the resolution admitting women faculty to the sacred precincts of the Rathskeller at lunchtime resulted in a rather unpleasantly worded sign at the entrance. In effect it read that admission to the Rathskeller was limited to male faculty members of all grades and to women at and above the rank of assistant professor. At that point, Jean Blackall, then an instructor in the English Department, came to me seeking help in extending the new rule to include all grades of faculty for women, thus including instructors, lecturers, and research assistants. At the next year's meeting this amendment was rather easily adopted. After that, Felix Reichmann, the assistant director of the university library, called me to say, "Now you have to include my librarians!" That, too, was accomplished, and we felt we had now covered all the women who had faculty status.

I must, however, add that like many issues of exclusion, this matter of women's eligibility for universitywide benefits, specifically for membership in the faculty club, is a demand that arose again in the early 1990s among the administrative and secretarial staff, who are still predominantly women. In behalf of this large group, it should be noted that at the time of the original struggle, professional men from the town—mainly doctors—were club members and arrived every day at noon to occupy "their" round table at lunch. On the matter of the female administrative staff, the club's board, after a year's hesitation, voted unanimously to open membership to all these women. The reason may well have been a need to increase membership, which had fallen off sharply in recent years, as much as a commitment to diversity. In 1983, on the occasion of my eightieth birthday, I received an award from the Women's Studies Program to commemorate the original faculty club coup.

MCCARTHYISM AND VAL LORWIN

One of my young colleagues, Bob Aronson, told me that Val Lorwin was on the list of one-time State Department employees whom McCarthy denounced as a Communist on the basis of "evidence" that a former fellow student in Val's undergraduate days at Cornell had put in McCarthy's hands. Once charged, Val had hired a lawyer, taken a leave from his professorship at the University of Chicago, and returned to Washington to fight the case to clear his name. He needed money for legal expenses, and he had to gather testimony from all his friends and former colleagues that might help him and his lawyer to demonstrate his innocence. Bob took the lead in forming an Ithaca defense committee, which I quickly joined.

It took Val several years of full-time work to assemble his case and in the end to win it; it also took stamina, patience, and the knowledge of a host of devoted, supportive friends for him and his wife, Madge, to endure those years. Once cleared, he responded to a call from the Department of History at the University of Oregon, where he lived and worked with distinction until his death in the early eighties.

RETURNS TO EUROPE

In my early years at Cornell, once Tom and Philip were busy during their summers, I felt free to take summer trips back to my work in Germany. I wanted to see how Arbeit und Leben was flourishing, how individual schools and their directors were getting on, and how the young Tröschers were growing up. I was able to make several such trips during the fifties, often speaking at conferences or schools.

Iceland

One year I traveled to Germany on Icelandic Airlines with Alma Molin, professor of European history at Vassar, who had also been invited to continue her contacts with women's groups in Germany. In Reykjavík we were held up for several days because of mechanical trouble with our plane. Our stay fell on the very days of the solstice celebration. People came from all over the country to the capital, older women dressed in their native village costumes, children and adults dancing in the streets all night, students in their characteristic caps celebrating the end of term or university life.

We took a bus one day to a point near the village where the first democratic parliament had met in the fourteenth century. Walking several kilometers, we saw a somewhat bleak countryside, laced with hot streams and sparsely populated with hospitable people. In our short stay, we lived through days when the sun never set, people were always in excited motion, and during which we slept and soaked in hot baths exactly as the spirit moved us.

Italy

In the summer of 1957 Lydia Tröscher and I took the trip to Italy we had long promised ourselves. I bought a VW bug in Germany with Richard Molin's assistance, and shortly before setting out, we were joined by my long time friend, Marie Algor. At the Tröscher home in Wiesbaden we carefully packed our belongings and ourselves into the tiny car, and the three of us set out with the ominous blessing of Tasso's chauffeur, who assured us we were in for trouble: "The Italians steal like the ravens." His meaning was clear. Three women needed a man for protection.

We planned to limit our first trip to the northern part of Italy. We visited Florence for a week (it was on this trip that I purchased the leather bag for Miss Perkins)—reveling in the museums, the city's public art, its open squares, its bridges, and the villages in the surrounding hills. We moved then to Venice where we were engulfed in a heat wave that made the canals stink and persuaded us after a very few days to leave for some of the higher towns in the foothills of the Alps. There we climbed on little-used roads into the Tyrol, once German and now annexed to Italy. Lydia left us to get back to her busy life at home, while Marie and I turned east again into Austria, to stay in an adult summer school at Salzburg that Karl Stadler was directing. It was my first meeting with his wife, Regina, and his daughters, then schoolgirls, who had been born and lived their lives in England where their parents had gone as refugees from the "Green fascism" that preceded Hitler.

I gave one or two lectures at the school, and Marie and I attended the Salzburg Festival and visited some of the resort towns on the many lakes east of Salzburg. On our return to Wiesbaden and Frankfurt, we could happily report that no "ravens" of any breed or nationality had in any way interfered with our travels. On the contrary, the trip had been a happy summer, plagued by nothing worse than the extreme Italian heat.

PHILIP IN TROUBLE

By 1959 I was truly feeling at home at Cornell. I had registered in two courses in the Arts College and was beginning to be acquainted with professors across the campus. Maurice Neufeld had even nominated me as a faculty representative to the Board of Trustees. Our assistant dean, Arnold Hansen, who had become dean of the university faculty, had appointed me to a universitywide committee of faculty and students that dealt with questions of what today would be called those of racial diversity on campus.

My relationship with Philip had been growing more distant since his junior year in high school. Sadly, I assumed I was experiencing the usual behavior of adolescents working out their problems with parents. As long as Philip lived at home during his freshman year, he constantly stretched the rules in the name of independence—staying out into the early morning hours, taking Wes's monthly support check as his due, and telling me, for example, of his desire to open a coffee shop—then a new, popular type of enterprise greatly sought out by students. I was unable to sleep until he came home and suffered greatly from lack of sleep and from my growing concern about our relationship.

The summer between freshman and sophomore years, Philip attended a program sponsored by the Ethical Culture Society near New York City, from which he had returned politically very radical, carrying the *Communist Manifesto* in his jacket pocket so that its red cover was clearly visible. When I tried to involve Wesley and Rita, Philip decided he disliked his stepmother. One day, Proctor George, in charge of student behavior, came to my office. I assumed he wanted to discuss one of my students, but the subject of his visit was my son, who had been accused of selling marijuana. I was in a state of shock. When I got in touch with Philip, I urged him to get a lawyer and recommended one whom I knew vaguely. Philip called me from the lawyer's home that night to tell me that the fee would be twenty-five hundred dollars. I had planned a trip abroad that summer, but the demand for this sum of money immediately wiped out that possibility.

I insisted that Maurice withdraw my candidacy for the Board of Trustees. In a state bordering on panic, I went to a psychiatrist for counseling. His judgment, after one session, was that not I but Philip should come to him for help. I sent Philip, who shortly refused to go any longer. He was in the meantime expelled from Cornell but still had to face trial in the local courts. His lawyer prepared him for going unaccompanied before a grand jury. In the end he was sentenced to a year's probation, but he had neither a job nor any occupation. He went to live with Wesley for a time and began counseling there but was shortly forbidden to come to the house by his stepmother.

He began to talk to the army recruitment agent about volunteering before waiting for the draft. He chose a three-year enlistment because it would allow him to name where he might be sent after basic training. He chose Korea first, partly because Michael Douty, his old brotherlike friend from the Cheyney days, was there serving out his draft duty. Later Philip would be sent to Germany. I was not happy with this outcome but hoped that army discipline might have some positive effect.

With Tom and Philip both gone, I undertook some changes in the house. I converted the second floor into an apartment that could be rented. To make it useful either to me or to tenants, I had the roof raised at the back of the house, put in two large picture windows for a view into my woods, tore out walls, and created a large open space for my study. I added a stove and refrigerator at one end to complete the apartment. When I left for my first sabbatical shortly thereafter, I rented the downstairs to a young family, while my old friend, Marie Algor, now retired, moved into the new apartment when she came to Ithaca to teach in Extension programs.

Sabbatical Leave Plus

In 1961 I had my first sabbatical leave and moved to the New York City District Office, now headed by Lois Gray, who had gone there from Buffalo. In the course of that visit, she and I became fast friends, as we cooperated in writing up our joint research on labor relations in the public sector in New York City.[9] My special concern, however, was to undertake a study of large local unions—of which there was a considerable number in the city—to see how their structure addressed the issue of union democracy, on which the industrial relations field and Congress had focused in the adoption of the Landrum-Griffin Act (1959). I had begun work on this project in 1959 and by 1961 was ready for field study.

I had selected several unions and used this semester in New York to make contacts, hold interviews with union officers and members, and observe the unions in action not only around collective bargaining but in their internal and external relationships both in and outside the labor movement. The unions to which I gained access were Local 3, International Brotherhood of Electrical Workers (IBEW) with 33,000 members; Local 65, then affiliated with the Retail, Wholesale, and Department Store Union (RWDSU) with 25,000 members; Local 6 of the Hotel Employees and Restaurant Employees (HERE) with 25,000 members; and Local 32B of the Building Service Employees with 40,000 members. Each had its own types of subdivisions, some geographic, some representing degrees of skill, some by major employers or employers' associations. At these intermediate levels there were possibilities for membership participation. Hence such representation from those levels to the top governing structure was critical to the formation of both legislative and executive bodies.

I looked upon these organizations as examples of private organizational government, which to some degree were modeled on public government. Among the few students of this subject, this model was indeed a widely accepted criterion. Hence the question arose among these theoreticians, and to some extent within progressive unions, of the absence in them, as in most private organizations, of a judicial body. The Auto Workers at this period adopted a Union Review Board, made up of outside experts labor leaders and arbitrators, to hear and determine members' complaints about alleged violations of the union's constitution by its executive bodies. This review board continues to function today. I supported the adoption of such an institution as a needed element in union democracy, and applied it, along with other measures, including the degree of membership participation, majority rule, and representation, as criteria for my analyses.[10]

During that semester, I lived with Ethlyn Christensen, who had so impressed me in my YWCA days. She had left the Y at that time in order to work with the local government union, the American Federation of State, County, and Municipal Employees (AFSCME) in organizing New York City's social workers. She laid the groundwork for an organization that still exists as a model for unionism in this semiprofessional field.[11]

By 1962 I had spent ten years in Ithaca, the last seven as a resident faculty member. I was not the only faculty member to come into resident teaching from Extension, and like the others, I had felt ambivalence from certain quarters of the faculty. I had, after all, arrived on campus late in life, and it was my experience rather than long years of study that had qualified me for a professorship. Yet I had many friends among the faculty, as well as in Extension, and an active social life within the school. Often I was the only female faculty member in much of this life, and when wives and husbands typically and informally broke into separate groups after dinner, I sometimes found my proper place hard to locate. I came to realize that the usual women's discussions held little interest for me. On the other hand, I enjoyed having other faculty members visit my classes, and I took one or two courses within the school, including one in labor law.

In general, then, I was so content with the work of teaching and with my life in Ithaca that I was not anxious about academic hierarchy at the university. During the year I was due to come up for tenure, 1962 to 1963, I was living in another country and facing other problems.

10

THE FIRST YEAR IN JAPAN: 1962–1963

APPLICATION FOR A FULBRIGHT TO JAPAN

Ever since Anne Edelman, my Philadelphia friend of Teachers' Union days, had taught in Japan in the mid-fifties and had reported on her experiences there in detailed letters, she had awakened my interest in that country. I had taken a course on Japanese society taught by Professor Robert Smith, had come to know him and his wife, Kazu, and had begun to think about going to Japan myself. When in 1961 an announcement from the Fulbright Commission of an opening in industrial relations at Keio University came across my desk, I saw this as my opportunity to make that trip. But I had already taken my sabbatical in 1961. I asked Dean John McConnell whether an unpaid leave might be possible. He thought it could be arranged, and I sent my application off. Early in 1962 I received word that I was an alternate to Phil Garman at the ILR Center at the University of Illinois, where an exchange program with Keio's Industrial Relations Center had been operating for some time under the direction of Sol Levine. Phil had been born and had grown up in Japan as the son of missionaries, spoke fluent Japanese, and was a strong member of the Illinois labor relations program. I knew his qualifications well exceeded mine, and I counted myself out.

Then, in June I received word that Phil had withdrawn his name because of illness in his family. I was appointed in his place. Exchangees were to leave for Japan in the early fall. How was I best to prepare myself in these few months? I went out to Champaign to consult University of Illinois colleagues. Their advice was to read a bibliography they gave me, but not to attempt to learn the language—the time available was much too short for any degree of proficiency. I learned that the labor attaché in our Japanese Embassy was Lou Silverberg, formerly of the NLRB staff, who, they promised, would be very helpful. They told me, too, of the Japan Institute of Labor (JIL), whose staff was hospitable to visiting American scholars.

We discussed a possible research project. My proposal was to acquaint myself with the structure and behavior of Japan's unions, for a possible comparison with those in the United States and Germany. I learned that the founder and director of the Keio Institute had just died and had been succeeded by Professor Kawada, who had lived in prewar exile in the United States and, more recently, had spent a considerable period at Illinois. I believed he would surely be helpful in assisting me on the United States/Japan side of such a comparison.

I came home feeling that I had had the best available advice and immediately began to prepare myself for a year in a totally new country. This appointment meant another summer of intensive reading such as I had undertaken when I began to teach at Cornell. Bob and Kazu Smith gave helpful advice on living in Japan. Anne Edelman wrote letters to her former students at Wakayama University and particularly recommended me to a young woman whom she had brought to Temple University for a master's in education.

Settling in, in Tokyo

When the Fulbright exchangees arrrived in Tokyo, we were taken to the International House of Japan, with its pleasant accommodations and its spectacular Japanese garden in the Roppongi District. On the next day our group began to travel to our separate destinations throughout the country. Only a few of us remained in Tokyo. Finding suitable housing there was a critical issue. I was given the name of a family accustomed to receiving Fulbright exchangees. My former student, Hiroko Kageyama, who had spent a year at ILR in the mid-fifties, accompanied me to their home on local transportation. The family lived in a traditional Japanese house with a garden, near the Meiji Shrine and Park. Hiroko made it clear that the hosts and the house were treasures, so I rented two rooms with a door leading to the garden and remained there during my Fulbright year. Moreover, I returned there for several summers, when I came back to Japan to continue my study of Japanese trade unions during the sixties.

In preparation for the trip to Japan, we had been invited to Washington in September, where State Department officials on exchange programs sought to prepare us for a foreign culture. We were warned that life in Japan would be very different culturally and physically from that in the United States. But once I was in Tokyo, I experienced only friendly hospitality and helpfulness. I settled in at once and without a day's upset. In fact, I felt very much at home throughout my entire stay. After all, as I have noted earlier, I have never experienced homesickness, no matter where I have traveled. Indeed, I have enjoyed the experiences of mobility.

New Friends, Old Friends, and a Research Project

Life was made comfortable and interesting by the assistance offered by many former ILR students as well as by several of my new Japanese students, members of my graduate seminar. Their suggestions ranged from Sunday trips to beautiful or historic towns in the Tokyo area to the possibility of undertaking research projects within their companies. I discussed my proposed research with Professor Kawada and with Professor Shinichi Takezawa of Rikkyo University. I also discussed my ideas with Hiroko, since she was engaged in various aspects of working women's lives within the Telecommunications Corporation.

I finally designed a study of some fifteen unions, selected from among the four labor federations. I planned to interview the union leaders at various geographic locations and levels of union hierarchy. I wanted to gain an understanding of their relations with political parties and their emphasis on a variety of action programs, as well as to acquaint myself with problems of internal administration covering the division of responsibilities between national and local unions. The annual organization of wage "struggles" conducted by the major federations, Sohyo and Zenro, would provide an example of how these unions conducted strikes as well as negotiations. Since most Japanese unions have their national headquarters in Tokyo, I did a great part of my work there, conducting some twenty-three interviews with federation officers that fall—with the help of two interpreters, Chie Adachi[1] and Kazunobu Cho.[2]

I was in touch early with Lou Silverberg at our embassy and with Harry Pollak of the United States Information Service (USIS), both of whom quickly became friendly mentors, inviting me to their homes to meet their wives and children. Lou saw that I met Ted Cohen, the American labor specialist during the occupation, when General MacArthur was the molder of American policy. Ted had stayed on in Japan after the occupation ended[3] and was a mine of background information on the founding and early history of the Japanese unions.

Another new friend and assistant was Setsuko Koga, a former student of Antje Lemke's, who soon after her arrival in the States in 1952 had become a professor in the Library School at Syracuse University. Setsuko was now teaching in the Library School of Tokyo's Aoyama University. Anne Edelman's former student, Setsuko Itaba, also got in touch with me.[4] Among the fairly large group of Fulbrighters in Japan that fall was Eleanor Hadley, recently a professor at Smith College but with an impressive history in Japan.[5] She became my close friend. In the course of the year we took many weekend hiking trips together in the mountains, and also spent time together in Tokyo, where Eleanor was very much at home.

Many American friends and acquaintances with whom I could discuss my research plan came through Japan during the year I was there.[6] In the late fall, Mitzi Bales, my student in a two-year ILR program that trained American trade unionists for work abroad, came as part of this program to work in the Tokyo office of the International Confederation of Free Trade Unions.[7]

Philip came from Korea in the early fall to stay with me for some R&R. I finally got some feel for his experience in the army after the Korean war, as well as a report on Mike Douty, who had preceded Philip in Korea. We walked long distances around the city and at last began to establish a relationship satisfactory to both of us. Before I left on my intersession travels in Southeast Asia, Philip came again on a troopship, while he was being transported to his second selected location, in Germany. This visit lasted only a few hours while the ship docked for refueling. I had waited on the pier for him to appear, but after an hour or so, I spoke to an officer there to inquire how and when I might meet my son. He immediately produced Philip, and for the few hours allowed us, we walked the streets of Yokohama and drank a cup of coffee together. Philip has never been a good correspondent. In his three years in the army I might have received five short letters. These visits, therefore, were all the more important for me.

As the year passed, part of my pleasure in finding these new friends and meeting with the many old ones who came through Tokyo was that most of them contributed in some way to my research project. I also thoroughly enjoyed what might otherwise never have come my way—the music, the hiking in the country, and the enjoyment of a hospitality that gave me many insights into Japanese culture.

FIELD RESEARCH

In December I made my first trip outside Tokyo. Back in the States I had met the president of the Steel Enterprise Union at Hakata, near Fukuoka on the south island of Kyushu, who had then invited me to visit Nippon Steel. I went down by overnight train to Hiroshima, and then by daylight to Fukuoka, where I was to be the guest of the American consul. Although the Steel Enterprise Union presidency had changed since I had met this local officer on his trip to the States, I was received hospitably by the new officers. I was invited to visit the plant and to talk with the personnel manager of the company about the custom of hiring a "class" of high school graduates each year for blue-collar jobs, whether they were immediately needed or not. This practice, he explained, was dictated by the fact that each class of young men would remain with the company all their working lives, and hence hiring was done with the projected needs of the next twenty-five to forty years in mind.

The consul provided me with an interpreter from his information staff, on whom I was able to count whenever I later came to Kyushu. Indeed, Lou Silverberg at the embassy was often able to make such an arrangement for my other local trips. Frequently, the quid pro quo was my availability for a lecture on some phase of American labor relations. I often spoke to employers' groups, at universities, and in public meetings arranged by local USIS offices in the consulates. This system allowed me to get out of Tokyo and travel fairly widely throughout the country. Thus I got to know and to work profitably with Kazunobu Cho, with whom I have remained in contact ever since.

In Fukuoka on the south island of Kyushu, a young woman, Hiroko Hayashi, introduced herself to me as a student of labor law at the Imperial University of Fukuoka. She then introduced me to her parents, who presented me with a pearl necklace, which quite overwhelmed me, for I had nothing to give in return. Yet in spite of what I experienced at the time as an embarrassing situation, we two shortly became fast friends. I later visited her home. In a traditional ceremony that it is difficult for me to describe, her mother and I became "sisters," and in another summer her mother arranged for Hiroko and me to travel right around Kyushu from Fukuoka and Nagasaki in the north to Kagoshima with its active volcano and palm trees in the south.[8]

Hiroko's parents knew little of my research, but they looked after me and helped greatly in my understanding of Japanese culture. Some years later while Hiroko was still a student, her parents gave a dinner for me to which they invited the law faculty of Kumamoto University. The occasion was on one of the first days of spring, and the party was held at a river inn. I was familiar with and enjoyed the chef's particular handling of the first courses, but then came a surprise with which I had no notion how to deal. As guest of honor, I was served first and saw that I was expected to consume small live and lively fish, flipping about in a sauce. With my chopsticks I captured my servings one by one, and quickly masticated them. Normally I enjoy raw fish, though I found these something of a problem. Later, Hiroko told me that instead of chewing them I should have let them take a last flip in my throat before swallowing them alive.

THE U.S. STUDY ON UNION DEMOCRACY

Before leaving the States, I had turned in to the ILR Press a manuscript of my New York City study of democracy in large local unions. In early December 1962, the manuscript came back to me in Japan, with an acceptance letter that, however, included a detailed critique from the editor, Don Cullen. It was obvious that I had a great deal of rewriting to do during the holiday period immediately ahead. Thus, during the prolonged New Year's university vacation, I set to work at home at my desk (the one piece of Western furniture in my Japanese room), to complete the job. Accomplishing it, in fact, took several weeks of both day and evening hours. During the afternoons I tried to take off a couple of hours to walk through the surrounding Tokyo streets and parks. When I was tired, I would flag a taxi to return to my task.

In mid-January I sent the revised manuscript back to Don just before classes resumed. It was published shortly before I returned to Ithaca in 1963 as *Union Democracy: Practice and Ideal.*[9]

TRAVEL IN ASIA

In December, at Tokyo's International House, the Japan Fulbright office held a meeting of all exchangees. The cultural attachés from our embassies in Taiwan and Korea each invited me to visit their countries and promised me contacts with union leaders there. In addition I had an invitation from the labor attaché in the Philippines, Tony Luchek, to visit the labor education school he had established at the University of the Philippines, where he had aimed to duplicate the Penn State Labor Extension Program.[10] This combination of opportunities suggested the chance to discover any similarities among Pacific Basin trade union movements. I began to plan a trip that I called my "Asian tour" and scheduled it for the university intersession of March and April.

Okinawa

I decided to go first to Okinawa, then as now one of the Japanese Ryukuan islands that were under American occupation. Jerry Daniel, an American trade unionist, represented the International Confederation of Free Trade Unions (ICFTU). He met me and took charge of the program for my visit. He included interviews with various American labor officers in our civilian administration; the Ryukyuan labor minister; several university professors in the labor field, one of whom had studied for a few months at Cornell; about twenty local trade unionists; and a group of thirty or so women, all of whom were members of the government employees' union.

I found Okinawa dominated in every way by the American presence, as represented both by army and civilian staff. It was a view of American colonialism in the raw. The army employed at that time about fifty thousand Okinawan workers, half or more of whom had formed their own unions on the Japanese model. Jerry's job seemed mainly to consist of helping these workers deal with their American employers.

The army commander apparently had the last word on every subject, whether military or civilian, and was the focus of Okinawan dissatisisfaction, as I saw it. There were in fact three layers of bureaucracy in island government, with the U.S. Army commander at the top, able to veto any actions by the U.S. civilian administration as well as those of the Okinawan government, the GRI. This army commander addressed the opening session of the Ryukuan legislature, where he laid down proposals for legislative action.

The twenty-seven-thousand trade unionists were loosely associated with Japanese unions, were vocally anti-American, and sought full integration with Japan. Apparently forgotten were the days when Okinawa belonged to Japan and Okinawans had received very much resented subordinate treatment. Okinawans, they said, were restrained by the United States from going to Japan. The unionist named as a delegate to the last ICFTU meeting in Tokyo had never received a visa in time to get there. Again and again I collected information that illustrated how trade unionists were caught in restrictions based on varying interpretations of customs and laws, coming from one or another bureaucrat in Japan or from the U.S. authorities.

The capitol area in and around Naha had been devastated both by the war and by typhoons. Off the main street were dirty, dreary, small streets of stalls and bazaars, "teahouses," bars, and brothels—altogether a depressing view, fifteen years after the end of the war, and apparently unchanged from the time the U.S. military had moved in to occupy the island.

Jerry gave a farewell party for me at a geisha house where I was in the care of the oldest geisha. She was totally attentive and wanted a photographer to take our picture, my head on her friendly shoulder, her loving arms around me. It was my first experience of a geisha.

Taiwan

I arrived in Taipei on a Sunday afternoon. No one met me, and there was no message at the passenger counter. My one contact in the country was the cultural attaché, who had issued what I had taken as a cordial invitation. The embassy was closed on weekends. I inquired about a hotel and took a taxi, hoping I could be accommodated. This lack of attention to my letter to the cultural attaché, informing him of my arrival and reminding him of my interest in interviews, signaled all that did and did not follow. This attaché was a mainland Chinese by birth, and in the days that followed he seemed to have regretted his invitation to me.

He had not set up a program, nor had he made any contacts with unions. All that was possible for me on Monday morning was an interview with mainland "government" (Kuo Min Dong) representatives, whom he reached in an instant. They presented Taiwan as still a province of China, operating under prerevolutionary Chinese law as one of many provincial governments, responsible only for strictly local affairs, and in no sense an independent country. At the attaché's insistence and with his interpreter, I also met with the Free China Relief Association and the Free China Anti-Communist League. I emerged from both laden with slick paper publications mostly about the mainland government as reported by its government-in-exile in Taipei. Soon thereafter two Industrial Labor Organization (ILO) experts came to me in the hotel lobby and wanted to talk with me there—they believed their rooms and probably mine were tapped.[11] They gave me as unpleasant a picture of labor relations as I had heard in all my travels.[12] My national government interviewees had maintained that labor laws were those of mainland China from the early thirties, when Taiwan was a province. They had discussed the situation as though these laws were properly operational, although admittedly they were set aside for the duration of what was called the "emergency," i.e., the exile of the mainland government to Taipei. My ILO friends' task was to attempt to codify these laws, together with their later overlay of amendments, regulations, and exceptions that were brought about by the "emergency." It was their judgment, however, that, codified or not, the laws had no more than a cosmetic significance for the foreseeable future, being applied like makeup for visitors from abroad but not applied in domestic situations. In fact, the unions in Taiwan had the right neither to strike nor to bargain. Indeed, in an interview with a local union leader, he asked me to suggest the sources of the unions' power in the United States, "aside from these factors"!

I visited five modern factories in a twenty-four-hour visit to Kaiosung, a rising industrial center in the south. In these new industries, the presumably joint worker-employer committees administered welfare programs based on funds accumulated through a tax on company sales, but nothing of the kind seemed to exist in the cottage industries where most of the labor force worked.

In an interview with the head of the Transport Workers' Union, I mentioned that I had decided to go by air to the east coast and to return along the national highway to Taipei. He insisted that I should not go alone and assigned one of his union members, Jade Swallow—Jennie to westerners, a bus conductor who spoke English—to go with me on the trip. I dread to think what that trip might have been without her!

It began well enough. However, once off the plane and in the bus for the westbound trip, we were in uninhabited country on a narrow mountain road, facing our first landslide, the result of an earthquake of the day before. In the mountains, fog and rain closed in. Jennie kept our spirits up by singing, having everybody sing, telling stories and jokes. After dark we reached a landslide with no bulldozer operator nearby to open it up. The bus driver disappeared for an hour and a half, while Jennie kept people alert. He returned in a Jeep, and we were transported in ones and twos to the nearest rest house, with which Jennie was completely familiar. She got the two of us a bedroom, although most of the passengers slept on the floor in the lounge.

The morning was bright and about noon a bus appeared, but our ride was short. Another landslide. We were told to take our baggage and walk past it. The walk became several kilometers long through territory I was sure had not been traveled except on foot for many weeks. At its end and with a bus in sight, another landslide was still moving. Dozens of men were busy, however, pushing boulders over the edge, where they jumped and banged down several hundred feet to a stream. I saw us walking back, but it soon became evident that we were supposed to go through this moving earth. And so we did, with the help of the highway workers, who formed a human chain to help us across. They were the remains of the defeated Chinese army that retreated to Taiwan and were then removed from sight and mind by being sent to work on finishing and constantly repairing the national highway begun under Japanese occupation. Seven hours later we were back in Taipei.[13]

The Philippines

I had been invited to teach at the Asian Labor Education Center that Tony Luchek had founded. It was located in several buildings, including a dormitory, on the campus of the National University, where it was a pleasure to work. Despite the center's isolation from other buildings on the university's enormous campus, and despite the difficulty of getting from there to the city of Manila, I managed to visit my former student, the Jesuit priest, at the Ateneo (the Catholic University) and to get from him an appraisal of the labor union situation.

I had a discouraging morning with the woman who headed the women's and children's division of the Labor Ministry, where it became apparent she neither knew nor cared about workers' conditions. She asked me what I thought of reducing the child labor age to ten. When I expressed surprise, she said, "Well, it would bring the age into conformity with the labor statistics, which report on 'all those in the labor force 10 years of age and older'." I pointed out that it would contradict the ILO child labor convention, a fact she knew nothing about although the Philippines was a subscriber to the convention.

I spent a weekend in Baguio, the summer capital, with a former ILR student. The trip there from Manila gave me a good opportunity to observe life in the countryside between Manila and the hills. Up in Baguio I hired a car to take me into the backcountry, where I saw very primitive tribesmen working on terraced farms of great beauty and with magnificent views across the mountains.

Korea

I had met a Korean trade unionist, Pak Yung-Ki, at Cornell when he visited ILR among other labor centers in the United States, and he had cordially invited me to visit his country. Thanks to his assistance, I began there with a direct connection to the unions. In the spring of 1963 conditions were still as tense as they have remained between North and South Korea, under the postwar division of the country. The North, under Communist leadership, was totally cut off from any possibility of a visit, but, rebuilding was going on in the South. A very large number of the United Nations military force in the South was made up of Americans, which provided for considerable stability there.

Our ambassador there was Sam Berger, a man I had known slightly through the Socialist Party in the States. Sam asked me to dinner at the embassy, where he gave me his view of the current status of labor law and the unions.

To some extent Korean unions had adopted the Japanese structure, since early attempts at organization and independence dated back to the Japanese occupation of Korea that had ended only with the war's end. Father Robert Ballon, of the Jesuit Sophia University in Tokyo, had suggested I meet his colleague, Father Basil Price, at Sogang University in Seoul. I found Father Price keenly interested and knowledgeable about labor affairs and relied on his background information. He helped me to a considerable degree in meeting with labor leaders in the city. When the unions came under attack from a conservative government a few years later, Pak joined Father Price at Sogang.

My conclusion was that although the South Korean unions were by no means completely free legal agents, they were growing in numbers and in influence. Pak introduced me to several national union leaders and to the national federation staff. Among the latter was a young woman, Sunny Sung, in charge of the trade union library.[14]

My former ILR student, Philip Se-sun Oh, was now married with two young sons, and was an economics instructor at one of the many universities in Seoul. I met his family and profited from his help and advice during my visit. I spoke at several Korean universities but particularly remember Ewha, the largest women's university in the world, where the faculty was largely made up of women. At a lunch given by the president I had an opportunity to meet with several of them and to capture in this short encounter their desire to offer an education to women equal to that offered in the major national university.

Undertaking this "Asian tour" had not been part of my plan for my year in Japan. As the trip ended, I felt the time would have been better spent in Japan, pursuing my original agenda. Of the countries I had seen, Okinawa and Korea alone had come strongly under Japanese influence, but both were presently hostile to these origins. It turned out that the short stay in each country, and the fact that so many of them were in considerable political turmoil, had provided mainly accidental and anecdotal information.

Subsequent Travel in Japan

I came back to the second semester at Keio clear that my research should be limited to Japan and be intensified there. Moreover, I would need to include considerable travel during the months remaining, during which I wanted to get into the provinces to talk to local leaders, where the center of organizational power seemed to lie. That was where collective bargaining on the implementation of national agreements took place.

I undertook my first journeys in Japan after the beginning of 1963. I was able to employ Adachi-san for a memorable trip to Hokkaido, the north island. We traveled north by train and ferry (the present tunnel connecting the islands was then only a plan). Once there, I learned that the United States had historically had a strong influence on Hokkaido's character and its economy.

Until shortly after our Civil War, Hokkaido had had few settlers from the main island and was largely inhabited by a native race, the Ainu. At about that time, land grant colleges were being introduced in the United States.[15] A secretary of agriculture in the Grant administration had come to Hokkaido and introduced the organization of the American farm to the new settlers from Honshu, who were being encouraged to take up land in the north. The farmer would live on his own land, surrounded by his farm buildings, his silo, his animal barns, and his farm machinery. He would send his sons to the new State College of Agriculture at Sapporo to learn scientific farming, and his village communities would become sales and distribution centers. The American founder of this new way of life coined the slogan, still repeated to the upcoming student generation, "Boys, be ambitious!"

Our first visit was to the former school of agriculture, now Hokkaido University. There it became clear to me that local universities serve their own useful purpose for the would-be practitioner, even when the universities are not particularly distinguished. Students come to appreciate these professors for their lifelong availability and assistance, which is often given personally as well as through extension programs.

As we traveled through the winter farmland, people asked me again and again if I did not feel very much at home in Hokkaido. Indeed, it was true that the countryside strongly resembled that of New York State. In Sapporo our consulate helped me meet trade unionists and organized a few meetings at which I spoke to local unionists and personnel managers. Unfortunately, there as elsewhere in the labor world, independent farmers and employed wage earners had few interests in common, and organizationally were often at odds.[16]

Another memorable trip taken this time on my own was to Kanazawa on the west coast of Honshu, a castle town undamaged by the war, where there was an American consulate. The consul and his wife took me into their home and provided me with an interpreter. The town was beautiful, and the consul's wife was familiar with many of its institutions and its women's organizations and had become an expert in several periods of local Japanese art. On the evening of my departure, we learned that heavy rains had resulted in mudslides across the tracks of the east-west railroad. Since my work there was essentially done, I was free to go with her to a private exhibition and sale of art and to attend a Japanese tea in the home of one of her friends. I was also able to take several long walks through the town and to see the castle at leisure.

JAPANESE FRIENDS AND ASSISTANTS

Early on I made the acquaintance of Ryoko Akamatsu, then director of the women's bureau in the Ministry of Labor. She helped me greatly in making contacts with women in the labor field and in understanding working women's social position in the workforce and the unions of Japan. She has had a brilliant career that has allowed our lines to cross again and again, and our friendship to deepen during the thirty years since our first meeting.[17] Late in the 1950s she was the author of the Equality Law in Japan.

At the Japan Institute of Labor I met Professor Hanami, Ms. Akamatsu's husband. He was at the time and has remained helpful with all my Japanese research, not least because he is a lawyer but also as a member of the Tokyo Labor Disputes Mediation Commission. He was one of a circle of young men in this new field at JIL, who were known as the "Japanese Mafia" and whose membership included Professor Taishiro Shirai and Yasuo Kuwahara, who later earned his master's degree at Cornell. They worked at the Institute under the direction of Dr. Ichiro Nakayama, a highly regarded Conservative, who acted as a protective cover for the financing of the Institute's rather liberal and influential organization. As my Illinois colleagues had called to my attention, the Institute was indeed welcoming to foreign visitors, and I was shortly invited to give lectures under its auspices.

UNIONS, JAPANESE STYLE

After interviews with many of these outstanding scholars, I endeavored to summarize what I had learned about union structure and function. I focused particularly on the ways in which Japan appeared to me to be unique. Chief among these were their scheduled spring struggles, which mainly dealt with issues of wage increases, and the collective bargaining that followed at the enterprise level. I was also interested in their selection of officers mainly from among the men who were on the white-collar or even management ladder; their ghettoizing of women in the women's divisions, where they had little power, representation, or money; the fact that each plant was almost 100 percent organized; the scheduling of the spring struggle into more and more sensitive times and areas; their pay systems; and—at least in the large companies where most union membership was located—the employers' assurance of lifetime employment. All these were totally new concepts, which I had observed as well as discussed with union representatives. I felt I still needed to know how and why they had come about.

As these issues arose, I came to realize that I would have to prolong my research beyond my sabbatical year. Such an arrangement would be made possible by my going to Japan in the summers of 1963 and 1964.

CULTURE CLASH

Although I had believed that I would not and certainly should not impose my American judgments of "best practice" on this new and hitherto unknown country, I found myself doing it again and again. At a Japan Productivity Center lecture, I spoke out categorically against employers' manipulation of "second unions" in their plants as a means of setting up competition with the standard union there. One consequence was to see several of my audience of Japanese managers ostentatiously walk out of the room. In a conversation with Kageyama-san immediately following the lecture, she made clear to me that I had gone too far. She softened her reprimand by explaining it as her sheer puzzlement at my lack of understanding of Japanese labor relations strategies. On another occasion, I was asked as a newcomer to report on my impressions of Japanese strike tactics. My audience was patient and polite, but they found my premise of a fundamental difference in goals and values between unionists and management as unrealistic as I found some of theirs. My framework, I soon realized, was that of my homeland, not theirs; my analysis was too innocent of their reality.

I was deeply interested by all that I had found so far. I began to see it as based in large part on the job security promised by the system of lifetime employment. That situation demanded a live-and-let-live acceptance of a relationship that could exist only if the company had an ongoing life as a profitable organization, one in which the future of both parties could be certain: labor with work and ever-increasing wages, and management with workers in whose skills they could continuously invest.

An example of the far-reaching implications of the lifelong employment system occurred during my first months in Japan. The coal mines had for some time been in the final stage of coal production—one of Japan s few native mineral resources. Thousands of miners, mainly in Kyushu, faced unemployment. Demonstrations moved from there to Tokyo, where crowds of miners in work regalia met daily at the Ministry of Labor, rested in the downtown parks, or set up picket lines before company headquarters. The matter became a national issue with an understanding that government must and would come to the rescue, as indeed it did. The solution was worked out in mediating sessions between local and provincial authorities. I wrote two articles on the subject, as illustrations of the workings of the Japanese system of labor market justice.[18]

In my occasional interviews with personnel directors or other representatives of management, I tended to bring up the case of the steel workers in Fukuoka that had interested me from the beginning—namely, the recruitment each year of a new class of young workers, whether they could immediately be put to work or not. Repeatedly, I was assured that hiring was not against immediate needs but against the projected needs of the next twenty-five to forty years, when these young men would become skilled workers with a wide range of experience throughout the company. If work were not immediately available, they would be schooled and trained. Workers with more seniority might even be loaned out to subsidiary companies.

WOMEN'S PLACE

It was early apparent that the form gender discrimination took in Japan was to consider that women were outside the system. Although research on women's roles as workers, working mothers, and coparticipants in the building of dual careers, lay several years ahead, my interest in them lay just below the surface and derived I believe from my intimate history of working with women in labor education and at the YWCA. I knew little more about Japanese women than a hazy notion that they were treated socially and economically as secondary and even oppressed creatures.

Japanese professional women frequently asked me how I was received by trade union men. I had to reply that I seemed to be regarded as a member of a third sex. Certainly through their Japanese eyes, they did not view me as one of their own culture. The American occupation had faced them with many unfamiliar ideas—democracy, gender equality, and concepts of labor market policy among them—and it was difficult for these men whom I interviewed to know where I fit in. I was not a visiting male American; nor was I a woman in the Japanese sense; I was simply something else. I would often be received formally and without much help from my interviewees. I would explain that I was a foreigner and largely unfamiliar with Japanese goals and ways. But I then had to be specific about what I wanted. They had no way of guessing at what I knew or didn't know, or what I needed to help me understand them and their unions.

Interviews customarily lasted about two hours, and not a minute longer. At that point, some body language told me (if I had not had my eye on the clock) that the agreed-upon time had passed. Frequently, however, at this stage, an invitation to lunch or coffee would come. I slowly came to understand that this invitation was given out of their interest in the possibilities of being able to satisfy their curiosity about the United States. One day in Tokyo, the man on my left at lunch asked if it were true that American men often carried pictures of their wives and children in their wallets. Yes, I said, they often did. My thought was, why is he asking me this particular question? Perhaps it's his custom too? I asked him if this were so. Sure enough, he pulled out his wallet and showed me his pictures.

In the parks where I spent time on Sundays walking and observing, I saw small family groups picnicking on the grass in the shade of magnificent trees. Fathers played with children, cuddled babies, watched toddlers. My early impression that fathers had little or nothing to do with their children, leaving that sort of thing to the mothers, was not the family picture I came to observe. That men had little time for their families during the week was, however, painfully evident. They spent long days at work, socialized with their work peers at the end of the day, and only then undertook the long commute to distant employee apartments, miles out of the center of the city.

Job segregation ran very deep. Young women were recruited into the textile and electronic industries and were almost exclusively in demand for work—not always behind the counter—in retailing. Attractive young women bowed to customers as they set foot on the escalator or entered the department store door. Only young women were acceptable in broadcasting. Training for incoming women usually took a shorter and more limited course than was the case for men. Men's wages frequently moved upward at shorter intervals than did those of women. Married women, on the other hand, presumably ruled the home. Women were considered employable at best until marriage. Firms even set up classes for them in flower arranging and the tea ceremony, which might augment their marriageability. Marriage to male fellow workers was encouraged, and the female employee's boss might even be recognized at her wedding as having successfully played the part of matchmaker.

Japanese law at the time allowed only fourteen weeks' leave after childbirth. If a mother did not return to work immediately at the end of this period, she sacrificed her right to return to her job. Lifetime careers were only rarely open to women in any case. In the government, for example, the only career possible was in the Ministry of Labor's women's bureau. In the public industrial sector, Kageyama-san, on the management ladder at the Telecommunications Corporation, was a notable exception.

A small number of radical women lawyers, loosely associated with the Socialist trade union federation, Sohyo, made up another group of working women, as did a few women journalists and broadcasters. Thanks to Kageyama-san I heard about and even met some of them. She worked with a committee of such women, who were endeavoring to set up a defense fund that would allow them to support complaints from women alleging discriminatory dismissal. One evening when I met with this group, I was invited to match their substantial gifts, and I promptly did so, glad to be included.

Hiroko Hayashi, on a first visit to Tokyo after our Fukuoka acquaintance, introduced me to an unusual woman in the labor relations field. Fujiko

Hongo headed what might be seen as a rival institution to JIL, a labor relations institute that she, a widowed mother of a young son, had founded after the war and now directed. I was invited to lecture to her staff and members. Whenever Hiroko came to Tokyo and could interpret for the two of us, we invariably had dinner together.

ANOTHER TRIP TO SOUTHEAST ASIA

As my year in Japan drew to a close with the end of the summer semester in July, Mary Taylor, an art historian with particular interest in Japanese painting of recent periods, agreed to accompany me to Southeast Asia as I began my travel homeward. Our trip would include Vietnam, but our special objective would be Cambodia, with its temples in the jungle.

In Saigon it was already apparent that many Americans were there as "advisers," dressed as civilian on the streets and filling the hotels. Saigon was still very much a French colonial city, and in our short time there we toured markets, temples, and monasteries—including the temple where a monk had recently immolated himself. We had excellent food in Saigon's restaurants and felt safe enough as we traveled in our pedicabs as visiting foreigners.

The Cambodian temples were something quite new to us both, although Mary was better prepared than I to understand what they represented of a totally different religious and national culture. The "jungle" seemed very open to me as we walked from temple to temple, sometimes with a guide and sometimes quite on our own. From a child, I bought a little ivory bell that made a monotonous sound as we walked and presumably protected us from wild animals and snakes. We saw of course many temple ruins completely engulfed in roots and vines, hidden and perhaps never even tampered with.

Mary was an ideal traveling companion. She called my attention to art I might easily have overlooked. She was as interested as I in the streets and homes and people we observed. She tolerated my special concerns, both personal and professional. We both parted with regret, and although we wrote thereafter of other possible joint travels, they never took place.

Back in Ithaca, I had to discipline myself to the requirements of university life and to a private life without the boys. Tom was now in graduate school in the field of public law and government at Columbia University, with Professors John Hazard and A. Doak Bennett, who would serve also as his sponsors for a doctorate he was to complete in 1970.

Although he had started out with an interest in the Soviet Union and the Russian language, a course he took with Alan Whiting convinced Tom to switch his language studies to Chinese and his focus to China. While completing work on his dissertation, he served as an assistant to Zbigniew Brzezinski, who ran Columbia's Research Institute on Communism, and who later became President Carter's national security advisor. Tom's dissertation was published as *Up to the Mountains and Down to the Villages: The Transfer of Youth from Urban to Rural China.* I visited him and his wife at the University of Indiana soon after they went there for Tom's first teaching appointment. From there he moved to Yale University. His daughters, Anya and Maia, were born six years apart in Bloomington and New Haven.

Philip was finishing his army enlistment at a base in the Bavarian Alps. He soon returned to the States, but not to Ithaca. Rather, he went to Buffalo to work in a steel mill. His ambition was to follow his father's career as a labor official. At that time his choice of a career path was to rise from the ranks and aim first for the office of shop steward, as a popular grievance handler for his fellow workers.

My own future would take me on several return trips to Japan, during the summer vacations of the next two or three years.

Alice at Cornell University, circa mid-1950s.

Alice with Frances Perkins, after graduation ceremonies at Cornell University, circa late 1950s.

HIGH NOON AT THE RATHSKELLER

Alice depicted breaking the male barrier at the Rathskeller, the Cornell University faculty dining room, in 1958. Dorothy Hom, the artist, called the drawing "High Noon": "Presented to Alice H. Cook on her 80th birthday, November 28, 1983, in commemoration of her many successful battles on behalf of women at Cornell, by her friends and colleagues in Women's Studies."

Alice knitting with mother, Flora Hanson, sewing, circa 1968.

Alice with friends Eleanor Emerson (left) and Fran Herman (center), at Turkey Hill Road, Ithaca, 1969.

Alice in Connecticut with granddaughters Maia (unseen, on couch) and Anya, March 11, 1972.

Alice in Fukuoka, Japan, in 1973, with formerly unemployed workers now in government programs. Photo: Terue Ueno.

Alice celebrating with translators in Fukuoka, Japan, 1973: Hiroko Hayashi (left) and Chizuka Saiki (right).

Alice in Fukuoka, Japan, in 1973.

Alice in mid-1970s

Alice, circa 1975.
Photo credit: Rose Goldsen

Alice with Jean McKelvey (left), founding faculty member at
the ILR School and world-famous arbitrator, and Barbara Yaffe,
wife of Byron Yaffe, professor at the ILR School and second
ombudsman at Cornell University, in 1974.

11

NEW TASKS, OLD AND NEW FRIENDS: 1964–1972

SUMMERS IN JAPAN

During the three summers I spent in Japan in the mid-sixties, continuing my study of trade unions there, Haruo Shimada, a graduate student in economics at Keio, was of immeasurable help to me. In addition to acting as my interpreter, he took charge of housing and recreation as we moved about the country.

When I visited the Japan Travel Bureau in Tokyo to get our tickets for a provincial town in the mountain country between Tokyo and Kanazawa, I could not understand the agent's refusal to consider my request, until he told me that the area provided no accommodations for Westerners. Haruo-san at once offered to buy the tickets and shortly returned with them. From earlier trips with me he had no doubt that I would fit comfortably into Japanese on-the-floor furnishings and would be at ease with a Japanese diet. Yet when it came to room reservations, he had to check whether I wanted to share a room with him, since that would be considerably cheaper than paying for two rooms. And when we had a "western" breakfast, he was puzzled that I did not order a lettuce-and-tomato salad as he did.

In all but one town on our itinerary, Haruo-san found classmates who on graduation had joined a company in that town. Knowing that I was fond of sushi and sashimi, Haruo-san would ask his local friend for directions to the best shop and, once we were there, introduce me to the sushi cook, who would at his request teach me the local cries of welcome and farewell. In the next sushi bar I would be shown off to those customers. In a town in Kyushu Haruo-san's former classmate was the "commodore" of the company "fleet." On a hot Sunday in August, we had the one-boat fleet to ourselves and swam in the sea for hours until the jellyfish drove us back into the boat.

At the same time as I was enjoying these fascinating adventures in provincial life, I was keeping appointments that related to my study of trade union structure and function. I usually had two meetings a day. In the hot weather we typically entered a union office to find it filled with men in their freshly washed white underwear. The men with whom we had appointments would shortly reappear in jackets and ties. Only when they returned fully dressed would introductions take place.

Travel Home

Remembering the satisfactory tour I had with Mary Taylor three years earlier, I decided at the end of my 1966 summer in Japan to return to the States via Europe, where I had not been for five years. I planned first to visit Singapore, where Abe Kramer was now the labor attaché; Malaysia, where Abe's old friend in Germany, Franz Loriaux, was now a representative of the International Secretariat of Chemical Workers; Indonesia, where two former students, Tamboenan and Tedjasukmana, were available to give me insights into labor relations there; and India, where Murray Weisz, accompanied by his wife, Yetta, was labor attaché. Then I would go to Greece for some sightseeing and to Israel, where a Cornell colleague, Gerd Korman, had Histadrut connections that would enable me to acquaint myself with labor relations in that country. Finally, I planned to have a reunion with Luise Hüls, then with our embassy's Manpower Division office in Germany, at her vacation spot in Switzerland.

In Singapore Abe introduced me to the powerful heads of the unions, with whom we had lunch. As was customary with Abe, he had integrated himself with these unions here, however, not merely as a trustworthy friend but as an invited mediator in a number of their labor disputes. I also met Abe's Mexican wife, Alicia, and their new baby. Abe had recently learned in the course of a routine physical examination that he had cancer. He subsequently asked for and was given a transfer to Mexico. He was soon stationed in the consul's office at Guadalajara, where I visited him and his family about four years later. He asked me then to be available to his wife after his death, should she want advice about educational plans for the boy. I spoke last to Abe by telephone on what I later learned was his deathbed. No call ever came to me from Alicia.

Franz Loriaux included me in his visits to several union centers in Malaysia, ending in Kuala Lumpur, and allowed me to sit in on the discussions of the reports from his local union leaders. In honor of this visiting union celebrity, the local unions had planned parties with competitive games that were delightful to watch. We were on the road for about a week, with Franz "lecturing" much of the time, in between dealing with how to cross the shallow rivers and conversing with workers and their superintendents. Driving through rubber plantations and seeing canals in the process of being built provided us with some understanding of the people, mainly Chinese, who were doing much of the work in this area.

In Indonesia I stayed a few days in Jakarta with the Tamboenan family, some of whom I had known when they were students at Cornell. Tamboenan was no longer directly in the field of labor, and so I saw a good deal of the city's middle-class life. I went shopping with his wife in pedicabs, from which we also saw the poor literally living on the city streets. Since Tamboenan was still an officer of the Railroad Union, he took me up country to visit a local union. On the way we decided to stop at a teahouse in the hills for a cup of tea. The proprietor, a graduate of the School of Hotel Administration at Cornell, apologized almost in tears that he could not serve us—he had no water! He felt himself utterly neglected by his employer, the Indonesian government; he had no customers in this benighted spot and foresaw the eventual closing of his establishment. He was touchingly grateful to sit for a few minutes with people who shared his happiest memories of life at Cornell. Though I did not learn much about labor relations in Indonesia, meeting with former Cornell students was enjoyable.

In India Murray Weisz arranged for me to speak at a labor relations center, several of whose faculty had studied in England or the United States. He also arranged for me to visit Chandrigarh, with its beautiful new government buildings and, on a weekend, to visit the Taj Mahal. I was left with the strong impression of a crowded working-class population and, again, of people living in the streets, by begging. China had recently made its first attempts to take over Tibet, many of whose citizens had fled to India to establish their businesses within all the major cities. Thus, the fate of refugees within a developing Pacific Basin country was early exemplified by India's reception of these Tibetans.

From the point of view of my research, the most thorough and useful of these trips was to Israel, where Gerd Korman's friend gave me the first female commander of women in the Israeli army as a guide for my whole trip. We traveled from north to south, following the growth of the water system that enabled the development of cities and the flowering of deserts. My guide had been one of the pioneers from Russia to Palestine in the early part of this century and was able to introduce me to founders of kibbutzim, the army, and the government. She arranged my trip to include a visit to Ben Gurion and his wife on their home kibbutz, south of Ba'er Sheba. I opened that conversation by asking Ben Gurion when the desert between those two points might bloom as his kibbutz was obviously doing. His reply was, "That will come when we have more Jews." I replied, "But I spent yesterday looking at new housing in Ba'er Sheba where bedroom space for children is limited to two in a narrow room that can only make space for one cot above another." He said pointedly, "We shall have to make more Jews! The two nations with the most Jews are Russia and the United States. From Russia they can't come and from the States they don't want to come. We need more Jews and we must make them. If the present space is too small we will just break out the walls we have built!"

My guide told me of women's special place in the Israeli army: their somewhat segregated training for and assignment to "women's tasks"; the fact that when they married they no longer belonged to the army's reserve and so did not have to continue training and service. I had already heard something of these attitudes in Ithaca from Bila Zamir, an Israeli woman who had studied at Cornell. Unmarried, she had by continuous training risen to the rank of lieutenant and served as such in the war of 1966. Bila and my guide both told me that it was considered almost obligatory for married women to provide the state with the "more Jews" whom Ben Gurion saw as the salvation of Israel.

At Histadrut, the organization of Israeli trade unions, I met Aliza Tamir, the recently elected young woman responsible for collective bargaining for women in the unions. I also met the director of the women's division of the unions, whose members included the wives of male unionists. Her task was to establish a variety of educational and social work programs for women in the growing cities and among the growing number of women in the factories that were now being established even in the kibbutzim.

Histadrut was unique in its internal structure in that it was made up of trade unionists from each of the political parties, with the Labor Party holding the majority of offices and thus in control of the federation. Unlike any other labor federation, it was also an employer of the transportation workers, as the owner of the railroad and bus companies. These unique qualities stemmed from the early days of immigration, before Israel was an independent state.

Teaching

After my return from Japan I began teaching again, but with a new view of the world in general and particularly of the place of American unions in it. I needed to look at those unions anew, historically, as shaped by their founders, their self-set goals, their successes and failures, the sources and markets for their products, and their affiliations with the AFL or CIO. On these questions several new books had been written, both about individual unions and the CIO federation, now almost twenty years old, years during which the CIO had severed from the AFL and then in 1955 rejoined to form the new AFL-CIO. In the last seven years since the amalgamation of the two rival organizations into one federation, the CIO had retained its identity by becoming a department of the federation and providing a number of departmental heads. From my point of view, both Larry Rogin's appointment as head of the new federation's Education Department and the inclusion of the CIO's Community Services Department in the reorganization signified an acceptance of areas in which the old AFL had not implemented programs.

Such changes demanded that I read at least enough to bring me up to date. I wanted, too, to join with other members of my faculty in exploring new developments within the American labor movement, such as those that were occurring in the health care field and, to some extent, in other semiprofessional areas, including teaching and social work. The health and hospitals union was growing rapidly from its original core of hospital pharmacists to include all kinds of workers in those areas. Laws had been passed protecting collective bargaining by public employees, who were already organized in professional organizations such as the American Nurses Association (ANA) and the National Education Association (NEA). Unions in these fields were now challenged as to how they would take over collective bargaining functions within, or in rivalry with, these organizations. A pattern was beginning to be visible that consisted of adding a collective bargaining department to other functions in those local chapters eager to enter a particular field. A contrary development occurred in the UAW, however, as skilled workers created a special department to deal with their particular problems in an industrial union in which the bulk of members were semiskilled.

In collaboration with other professors, I offered new courses that dealt with such developments both structurally and historically. Questions raised in these discussions led to the issue of whether these semiprofessionals and professionals might demand more democracy in union government than the traditional immigrant blue-collar workers had. By the time of my second sabbatical leave in 1968, I was ready to study large local unions to see how they might have responded to such demands from their members generally. New York, I thought, offered an especially interesting source of information, with its adoption of the Taylor Act.[1] I arranged with Lois Gray, the director of the New York City Extension office, to spend the second semester of the academic year, 1967–1968 in the city, acquainting myself with a number of firmly established, large local unions there, none of them in the public sector. I planned to deal with those later, to note the contrast between the long-established unions in the private sector and the new unions of public sector employees.

THE EAST ASIA PROGRAM

In the meantime, another new area of interest opened up, as I became friends with other women scholars at Cornell in the East Asia program in the College of Arts and Sciences. I was soon invited to give occasional lectures for them on women in the Japanese labor force. My name was passed along to new faculty as they joined the program, and for two years or so I gave lectures for Jim Nickum until he left Cornell for the East-West Center at Honolulu. He was followed there by his wife, Glenda Roberts, a recent Ph.D. graduate of Cornell, who had written her thesis on her experience as a worker in a Japanese factory that employed women. Her book was the first study of this subject of which I am aware. Glenda later became the assistant to the director of the University of Hawaii's Japan program.[2]

A NEW DEPARTURE: MEDIATION

Very shortly after the staff were appointed for the Public Employment Relations Board (PERB), the enforcement agency set up to implement the Taylor Law in New York State, they invited experts in labor relations to a meeting in Albany. Many of the participants were recruited to work as mediators for settlements between parties in a labor dispute where both negotiators certified to PERB that, unaided, they had been unable to reach agreement.[3]

Although I had had no particular experience in this field, I agreed to become a mediator and was consequently involved in a series of disputes, mainly those between teachers and their local school boards. My work in mediation continued after my retirement. In 1972 I was a member of a small panel of mediators and arbitrators available to a section of the New York City School Board and to a part of the city's massive teachers union. Later, when I was in Hawaii for a few months each year, I was appointed by the Public Employment Relations Board there to work on several cases involving firefighters and university professors.

RESEARCH AND PUBLICATION

I was also eager to write on my research in Japan and produced a good many articles during these years.[4] Some of this writing was done in collaboration with other Japanese scholars, but a good deal of it was on my own observations of special events during my several visits to that country in the summers of 1965 and 1966.

VISITORS

Travel that I undertook for my own interests often had the side effect of encouraging the persons I visited to come in turn to Cornell in their turn. Hiroko Hayashi came for her first visit to Cornell during this period, to work with John Burton on what had become her special field of expertise: workers' compensation systems in the United States. During the year she spent at the university, after our many discussions, we decided to write our book together on discrimination against women in Japan. We completed the book several years later, after we had met together many more times, both in Japan and the United States.[5]

Hiroko was followed by several other friends from Japan. Among them was Yoko Sano, a young woman economist at Keio, who had made clear to me how difficult it was for a mother of young children to have a professional career in Japan. The fourteen-week limit on maternity leave meant that women had to return to work or lose their employment. In Yoko's case, both her mother and her mother-in-law had taken over the care of each of her three infants, immediately after they were born. On this visit, which was to the Illinois Center, she brought a preschool child with her.

Still another visitor from Japan was Yasuo Kuwahara, whom I had known at the JIL. Yasuo chose to attend Cornell University and received a master's degree in labor law, labor history, and collective bargaining from ILR.

CORNELL FRIENDS WHO MADE A DIFFERENCE

Of course, American friends were equally important in aiding my own work and career. As examples of these friendships, and rather than trying to include everyone on the long list that in fact exists, I will introduce three of many women whom I have deeply appreciated and loved.

Eleanor Emerson is first because her friendship and our joint work goes back furthest and covers most aspects of the labor relations field. Eleanor lived her pre-college life in Buffalo as the second oldest of four daughters. Her father was prominent in business, a longtime director of the School Board, and active in lay religious life. Eleanor and I first met when I came home from studying in Germany to work in the Philadelphia YWCA's Industrial Department. She was head of all the Industrial Department work in the city, and my superior in the Kensington Branch. She had prepared for this with her first job in Bridgeport, Connecticut, where she joined the staff of a church-sponsored new organization to assist the many young women coming into the munitions plants in 1917 when the United States joined the Western Allies in fighting Germany. Later she moved into the newly established women's bureau in the federal Department of Labor. There she became closely allied with the women who were founding the Bryn Mawr Summer School for Working Women, along with members of the Women's Trade Union League and with trade union men and women concerned with the fate of unemployed workers. During the Second World War she had been the personnel director of a steel plant near Pittsburgh, from which she was recruited to the ILR School in its Extension Division, when the school was established at Cornell in the fall of 1945. She was director of the Trade Union Division in the various Extension offices, at that time in Albany, Ithaca, Rochester, and Buffalo.

She was instrumental in bringing me to Cornell and, once I was there, she introduced me to ILR women from the library and finance office, as well as to many in what was then the College of Home Economics, where most women professors in the university were clustered. A small group of us hiked and explored the nearby countryside on weekends.

Eleanor captained a tight ship, keeping a close eye on appointments as the program grew and needed both line and staff people. From teachers, she expected full reporting on their content, teaching method, and materials. She also offered training sessions from time to time. She employed several women who had been associated with the women workers' summer schools, because they had the background in adult education that she desired for her staff. Thus Cornell was prepared to be one of the early universities (Penn State and Wisconsin preceded us) to take over labor education in the sixties and thereafter, when the summer schools no longer existed.

Through a set of unhappy circumstances, Eleanor and I came to live an even closer personal life. She broke an ankle in a fall in her apartment. After long stays in the hospital and in a recovery center, she was dismissed from care, only to find that her landlord wanted her apartment for his own use. Since she was in no state to look for a suitable place to live, I invited her to stay with me until she could get about more easily. Both boys were permanently gone from home, and we ended up living together until her death in 1979.

She was the quiet, thorough one; I the more explosive. Her advice was never admonitory, but again and again as I faced choices in meeting problems with colleagues and acquaintances, her model served me well.

ROSE GOLDSEN

A very different person was the woman who for a dozen years was my closest friend. I first came to know and appreciate Rose in the late fifties after I had become a professor and when she was still a research associate in sociology. I was happily impressed with her colorful, direct, and sarcastically humorous approach to her topic, whatever it might be. I learned that she had worked earlier at Yale as a Ph.D. candidate under C. Wright Mills and had known Theodor Adorno when he came from Germany to Columbia. Her thesis was on the migration of Puerto Ricans from the island to the United States. She had learned Spanish in order to make this study and spoke it colloquially ever after. She developed a consuming interest in Latin-American countries, working in Argentina and later with the Ford Foundation team in northern South America, mainly Colombia and Venezuela.

An early struggle for her was to get her own department to consider her for a professorial vacancy. In the end, she had to nominate herself as a candidate. It was in the course of living through that episode that I saw her indefatigable and forthright way of winning an issue against rather formidable odds.

Rose was an innovative and popular teacher and most liked to teach freshman seminars. In her seventies she taught these seminars with other professors, among then Peter Kahn in art history and Linda Waugh in semiotics. She brought many Argentinean and, later, Colombian students to Cornell for graduate work. She influenced students' ways of thinking, by demanding exactitude in reasoning and expression, an effort that, while it required her identification with her students, went well beyond the merely pedagogical.

Her special field of study was the imprint that radio and television left on American society, not just as communications media (though they were powerful in that regard) but for their influence on the behavior of both children and adults. She developed a weekly local radio program entitled "What Our Children Know Is What We Show Them," in which she called attention to the way these media extended their influence, both by selling the characters that populated children's programs to toy companies and by favoring the companies that advertised on them by supporting those companies on public and political issues. She made it her business to acquaint herself, usually by long-distance phone, with government officials. She bought shares in the TV companies that sponsored these programs and so was able to speak up to other shareholders at their stockholders' meetings. She gave public testimony and appeared on TV news documentaries. She used her graduate students at home and abroad as research staff. A vivid picture I can still recall is of coming into her house in Bogota to find Rose and her housekeeper lying on their stomachs watching soap operas from the United States, while Rose used this opportunity to interview Maria as the latter drank in this U.S. neocolonization of Latin-American society.

Rose wrote vividly, with care and feeling for written language. She devoted at least a full day each week to the composition of her weekly five-minute radio program. Her best writing, however, was never published. It consists of a series of articles on the Colombian jungle near the rise of the Amazon. She spent at least two prolonged trips in that area, to which she devoted scientific care and personal attachment.

Rose was fully conscious of being a Jew, though from childhood onward she had not practiced any form of religion. She served for many years on the board of Cornell United Religious Works (CURW).[6] Her close tie there was to Jack Lewis, originally a fundamentalist Baptist from Texas, who over the years had found his own way to a humanist religion. After Jack retired from the directorship of CURW, Rose worked closely with his successor, the Presbyterian minister. She was drawn, after a few years, to join Ithaca's Temple Beth-El, mainly to identify herself with the Jewish community, but in the end accepting all its demands upon her. She died in 1984, just as she was about to retire from teaching, from cancer of the spleen. After a few months of increasing suffering and finally of loss of any hope for recovery, she gave up the struggle.

My total knowledge of Latin America was gained with her help. We traveled together to Mexico, Guatemala, Colombia, Venezuela, and Brazil. Perhaps the most memorable trip was a Christmas holiday in Brazil. Rose wanted to use the days there to acquaint herself with Portuguese, and used every opportunity to converse with people we encountered—the hotel's shoeshine boy; the head of a group of fishers who spread their nets and hauled them in, in the very early hours as we walked and talked with them on the beach; the desk clerks at the hotel; the clerks where we went shopping. She did not gain much fluency in the language, but in every instance she was fully accepted by these new friends. The fishers offered a share of their meager catch. The shoeshine boy's family, in an unannounced visit to them New Year's Day at the other end of Rio, shared their holiday meal with us. His siblings and relatives were every color from African black to Latin blond. I soon learned that a by-product of my friendship with Rose was adventure of a kind that I had never before opened myself to. I have had to remind myself as I write how directly and easily she engaged in it.

I introduced her to my friends Harold Coy and his wife, Mildred Price, in Mexico City, where they had fled after pressure from the McCarthy witch-hunt of the fifties. Harold was my friend from the Commonwealth days, when he had been a journalist, while Mildred had been my assistant in the Chicago Y during my last days there. Mildred had fallen under suspicion during the McCarthy hearings because she had worked with the China Relief Committee, a quasi-Communist organization that attacked Japan's occupation of much of the territory defended by Chiang Kai-shek's armies, which in turn were conquered by Mao Tse Tung's Communist armies. Harold established himself as a writer of children's books on Mexican history, and whenever we visited Mexico City he traveled with us, pointing out the vestiges of pre-Colombian, colonial, and modern Mexican history as they co-mingled in the city and its environs.

Rose made friends everywhere and shared these friends with me. When I went to Bogota for the first time, I met her Colombian best friend, Gabriela Samper, a filmmaker and daughter of a man who introduced the telephone to Colombia. The subjects of Gabriela's films were the outcasts of Brazilian society, the brickmakers and the saltmakers, the latter of whom worked illegally since salt was a national monopoly. She took us to visit some of them and their extended families, where men, women, and children worked long hours for pittances. I still have a snapshot of the hands of a brickmaker, fingers covered with mud too thick to clean off.

During Rose's assignment in Bogota, Gabriela was arrested as a political leftist. For days, neither her family nor Rose had any idea where she was, until an anonymous voice told her daughter that she was in a military prison. Gabriela, like Rose, was a chain-smoker; in addition, she was an epileptic under medical treatment. Overnight Rose, in identification with Gabriela's deprived and perilous state, broke her own addiction to tobacco and stopped smoking for the rest of her life. When Gabriela was finally released, Rose succeeded in bringing her to the Committee for U.S.-Latin American Relations (CUSLAR), CURW's organization for work with and on behalf of Latin Americans. Gabriela's lectures and films became a central element of that program during the months she lived in Ithaca. Our separation from her came when she was diagnosed with cancer and flown back to Bogota to die.

A final story about how my life was intertwined with Rose's. She went one evening in the late seventies to a meeting, sponsored by the Center for Religion, Ethics and Social Policy (CRESP), of a group of young people who wanted to recruit those interested in setting up a cooperative housing project. She called me immediately on her return to her trailer home, to say, "Alice, this is something for you. Promise me you will go to the next meeting." I joined her for that meeting, and we both joined the group.

Within a remarkably short time this group had bought farm land and had put up a group of ten houses, in a common living organization that we called Longhouse, as an indication of our commitment to cooperative living. Longhouse is the background for all the following chapters. In Rose's last years we both lived at Longhouse, and I lived there afterward until I moved in 1996 to Kendal in Ithaca, where I shall end my life.

FRAN HERMAN

The third friendship that has been very important to me is that of Fran Herman. Fran and I met in the winter of 1968 when we had each responded to calls of the Democratic Party for volunteer help in preparing written material for the presidential campaign. Fran was widely known at this time for her daily radio program, called "A View from the Kitchen Window," in which she reported with interest and fidelity on topics she found on any of her trips to nearby communities. She wrote well, though in a style very different from

Rose's, and had a good broadcasting voice. Fran went to graduate school in 1970 and subsequently became a professor at Cornell's School of Hotel Administration.

Fran's specialty was recording how communities made their lives more interesting. In searching out material for such reports, she came upon Stratford, Ontario, just as that town undertook its annual Shakespeare Festival. She reported how in a relatively short time these efforts met with success and how, as a result of inspired and devoted leadership among the Festival's volunteers and staff, it began to draw audiences from all across southern Canada and the bordering United States. From among them came a large body of supporters who returned for a week of theater year after year. Fran and other Ithaca friends believed that Ithaca could do something comparable. They organized a committee to raise money enough to build a stage, bring actors for the summer to Ithaca, and locate a strong group of local Shakespeare scholars and fans from the colleges to work with management on selection and presentation of plays. In the end Ithacan local opposition was too strong to bring the plan to fruition, but interest in theater has prompted the organization of local troupes ever since, and in some of these Fran played a leading organizational role.

On our political assignment she and I worked well together. As a result I became a deputy delegate, along with Dr. John Ferger of neighboring Dryden, to the 1968 Democratic Convention in Chicago. Because I was staying with my brother Ted and his wife in Evanston, rather than in one of the downtown hotels, I missed several of the dramatic events spurred by the radicals at the convention. I came home, however, a convinced left-winger and an enrolled Democrat. Fran and I continued our joint work in public relations activities for the Party. We quickly grew to be friends and traveling companions. She joined me for years on trips I took for research purposes as well as on trips just for pleasure. She met me several times in Japan and once in Australia, Norway, and Canada, and she joined me in Israel when I was finishing a study there. With Adi Tröscher, she met me in France, and from there we went to Corsica on a New Year's holiday. As I began to go to Hawaii for the winters and stayed with Ted and his daughter Sue, I worked at the university in its Industrial Relations Center; Fran came along after a few years and found her own place there.

We were both avid Scrabble players. Once, leaving Germany with a stopover in England, we heard an announcement that our plane would be delayed several hours. So we started a game of Scrabble on a travel board with magnetic disks. A later announcement caught us when we were deep in the game. Rather than give up the game, Fran organized all its elements so that we could continue it on the plane, while I handled the baggage. We caught the attention of the flight attendants as we boarded the plane, Fran carrying the game board on the palm of one hand like a waiter with his tray. They moved us to better seats near their workstation and then laid their bets on us. I have no recollection of who won; indeed, we have remained over thirty years pretty evenly matched, though she has long since outdone me in solving double crostics, our other field of competition.

THE BOYS

Neither boy, once they had gone off to college, ever lived at home again. Our contacts even by phone were infrequent and very rare by letter. Visits at best were during the winter holidays. My relationship with Tom was more formal than that with Philip, but neither was a confidant. I went to Tom's wedding to Ellen, largely, I think, because Ellen very much wanted it. From the beginning of her acquaintance with Tom, she and I were good friends. Philip was married and wrote me about it when I was abroad on one of my extensive study trips, and I only met Marjorie some months later. We were friendly but never close. She was not a mature personality, and I thought for some time that her attraction for Philip was precisely her dependence on him. He had grown up with fairly strong and independent women who had not given him an independent sense of his own self.

As each of the boys entered on careers and had children, the mother-son relationship gave way to that of mutually appreciative and admiring adults, and the daughters that were born in both families became my grandchildren. When my sons divorced and then remarried, I readily established an enjoyable colleagial, as well as a familial, relationship with each of their second wives.

It was in Tom's second graduate year that he met and married Ellen, a recent Smith College graduate, who had come to New York after graduation to find work, and who turned up one day for a tour of the Columbia campus where Tom was earning pocket money as a guide. Ellen and I quickly became close friends, and although a divorce followed after more than twenty years, we remain in close touch. In 1968 their first daughter, Anya, was born. Tom's first job after earning his Ph.D. cum laude was as an assistant professor at the University of Indiana in China studies. He was invited thereafter to Yale, and still later, moved on to return to Columbia, where he has served two terms as head of the government department. His second daughter, Maia, was born in New Haven; somewhat later they bought a house at the shore on Long Island Sound, and the girls both graduated from Guilford High School.

Anya went on to Barnard College, while Maia in her turn opted for Columbia but waited for a year to begin while she worked in a doctor's office. After her sophomore year Maia took another year off, working in the university library, but she is now continuing her studies at Columbia. Anya accepted a fellowship at Harvard in government, and although her first semester was full of problems, not least that of falling in love, I urged her not to make any decisions until she had completed her first year. By that time she had become engaged and had made a good academic start. She has now earned a Ph.D. in government and recently presented a paper at an annual meeting of the

American Association of Political Science (AAPS), as did her father. They believe that they may be the first father-daughter pair in AAPS history to have read papers in the same year! Now a wife and mother of Benjamin, Anya follows the academic path as a part-time faculty member at Brown University.

PHILIP

Philip, who had enlisted in the army for a three-year period, ended that career after spending his second half of it in Germany. Posing as a German friend, he phoned me one day, ostensibly to inquire when I could expect him home. His German accent was perfect and his vocabulary far above anything he had learned in the Oldenwaldschule. For a minute I was totally deceived about my caller.

The Castro Revolution had just taken over Cuba when Philip met a group of people who were going there and attached himself to it. When the return date passed with no word from him, I worried that all kinds of things might have happened. In fact, he had stayed on a few days to meet the brother of Fidel, Che Castro, and came home with hopes rather than plans of a return to Cuba. He went to Buffalo to get a job in a steel mill there as the first step to identifying himself with the working class of this country, in order to follow his father's footsteps into a career as a trade union official. His plan changed, however, after he was injured in a serious industrial accident. The index finger of his left hand was caught up by the chain from a crane, and he was dragged over molten steel and lost the first joint of that finger. He then changed his plans and decided to return to school. Because of his poor academic history at Cornell, the University of Buffalo insisted on his going to the extramural evening school until he had proved himself ready for a more disciplined program. After he earned his B.S. in government, he decided on graduate study in a new government institute and, considerably later, won his Ph.D. with a study of ethnic politics in Buffalo. In the course of that study he became acquainted with the local political boss of the Democratic Party and emerged as the treasurer of the City of Buffalo. From there Philip moved to Albany and took on the political job of budget director for the legislature. From this position, he assumed a variety of informational tasks for the Democratic Party within the state so that he came to know people and to assist with party problems.

MY WORK ON CAMPUS

During the mid- and late sixties, I served on a number of university committees. One had to do with the university's growing concern for the number and isolation of its minority—mainly African-American—students after the adoption of the Civil Rights Act in 1964. Vice President Summerskill, in charge of student affairs, set this up as a mixed student-faculty committee. We focused on the fraternity-sorority system's general prohibition of African Americans for membership, a prohibition that in some cases extended to the admission of

Jews. The presidents of the fraternity and sorority councils became influential members of the group.

We concluded our work with resolutions supported by the faculty, requiring these bodies to abolish rules that forbade such exclusionary policies, giving them a limited number of years to do so. Most of these organizations had faculty members as advisers, many of whom did not agree with the committee's recommendations. On the other hand, students for whose "benefit" these decisions had been accepted were impatient with the time allowed for favorable action on the part of the national organizations or their local chapters.

After serving on two other committees, I became chair of both. One was the University's Speakers' Committee, which had the use of several long-established funds to bring outstanding speakers from American and foreign universities to the campus. I endeavored, once these visitors had been selected by rules laid down by the donors, to attend their lectures in order to evaluate both the speakers and the surrounding circumstances, such as the suitability of the assigned auditorium, and of the time of day or evening. The job also involved providing a luncheon or dinner for the speaker to meet with his or her sponsors. As this experience drew to its end, I estimated that I had spent about twenty hours a week throughout the term on this activity alone, in addition to teaching courses and carrying advisory and other committee responsibility within the ILR.

The second of my assignments was to chair the school's Committee on Teaching and Curriculum, its purpose to integrate resident and Extension faculty in the patterns established by Cornell University in agriculture and home economics. The faculty eventually accepted our recommendation, which called for assigning Extension teaching staff to resident faculty departments. However, after a few years this decision fell into disregard and even into disrepute. One resident faculty member saw it as a process of "dumbing down" teaching within the university. Although this language was not repeated publicly, the negative attitude toward Extension faculty persisted among resident faculty more and more widely as time passed.

Still another universitywide committee chair fell to me as plans developed for the 1965 centenary celebration of the university's existence. This work included planning a dinner for well over a thousand members of faculty and their wives and students, together with trustees and council members. Barton Hall, the largest building on campus, had to be the locus of this event, but it had no kitchen. We decided to have a complete trial run-through of the caterer's transferring hot dishes to Barton and serving acceptably warm and presentable food to the guests. The rehearsal paid off.

THE RACIAL CRISIS AT CORNELL

President Perkins had come to Cornell in 1962. One of his goals was to increase the number of African-American students at a time when both

Malcolm X and Martin Luther King, Jr., were calling the nation's attention to the continuing oppression of African Americans and offering quite different goals to abolish it. The assassination of both men resulted in many programs to overcome the ills of which they had complained. With the president's active support, the number of African Americans recruited to Cornell had constantly grown. The university was not alone in this effort. Many universities in the country undertook similar programs, and black militancy early took over large sections of their campus communities.

In 1968 some sixty African-American Cornell students took offense at the views of a visiting professor of economics and held the head of department in his office for several hours. As a result of these and succeeding events in which the libraries in several schools were attacked under the slogan, "These books have nothing to say about us," the students' demands came to include an Africana Center with its own budget and director. The president acceded and designated a house on campus for that purpose under the headship of a highly regarded liberal (albeit white) professor, Chandler Morse, while a search was begun for a permanent African-American director of this new institution.[7]

The spring months were marked by one crisis after another. The new Africana Center was burned. Individual classes and professors were disturbed or threatened, and some of these men moved their families out of their homes. Many professors were outraged by these interferences with school life, and some professors left the university, never to return.[8]

Apparently judging that any other choice would be unacceptable to the students, the search committee decided to appoint as the director of the Africana Center a young candidate, James Turner, a known militant from Northwestern University, where he had not yet finished his Ph.D. thesis in anthropology. At the meeting at which this decision was made, four masked African Americans appeared to demand much more—a black college and a million dollars. This request the president found excessive and denied. Turner, however, came as director and remained in that post for many years, during which he duly received a Ph.D., though not from Northwestern.

On parents' weekend in May, African-American students occupied the student center, Willard Straight Hall. Steve Muller, a university vice president, took over negotiations with the students. Three days later the students agreed to leave the building. They came out carrying guns and saying that a group of white students had entered or tried to enter the Straight during the black students' occupation. They claimed that these unidentified students had guns and that they had therefore sent out word to the African-American community to bring them guns as well. Immediately on their release, a meeting of students of all colors began in Barton Hall and went on day and night for four days under the leadership of a white leftist. Their demands were for students to share in many issues that had been solely faculty or administrators' decisions. Such a change could occur with the establishment of a "free university."

This whole episode resulted in sharp divisions within the faculty. At a meeting soon after the African-American students left the Straight, more than three hundred faculty members voted by a two-thirds majority to support the promise of a vice president that there would be no reprisals or discipline. A few days later, in a somewhat smaller meeting, they reversed themselves and supported a disciplinary approach. But when a newly formed disciplinary committee of faculty and students identified a number of African-American students who were to appear for a hearing, these students failed to appear.

Meanwhile, a small group of sympathetic faculty, headed by Bill Whyte, saw an opportunity here for teaching by applied learning. They set up the Human Affairs Program (HAP) to offer courses that would, they believed, attract students concerned with "real world problems." HAP opened storefront headquarters downtown and established connections with several community agencies. Bill was able to get Ford Foundation money to start the project, and during three or four succeeding years interested many students in action-oriented endeavors. The faculty continued to be a divided body over such matters as granting academic credit for HAP courses and gaining the support of some deans for using school funds for employing directors for such undertakings. In his autobiography, Bill describes faculty behavior within the colleges as it began then to show itself, and in some instances continues to do so to this day.[9]

My own relationship to all this flurry of activity was remarkably marginal. I had had my second sabbatical in the fall of 1968 and had spent it in New York City, working on what I saw as my second study of large local unions, this time those in the public sector. But then the ILR dean asked me to stay in New York during the second semester to take over the directorship of a new labor school established between our Extension Division and SUNY's Empire State College. Under this arrangement, Empire State could offer a B.S. degree in labor-management studies, for which all the professional courses would be given by teachers from the New York City Extension Division of ILR and our resident Ithaca faculty. This work resulted in my being on the Ithaca campus only occasionally during this disturbed spring. On one such visit shortly after the Straight takeover, I met my colleague Bill Friedland, who spoke of the meeting going on in Bailey Hall as the "revolution" and suggested that I visit it. The truth was, however, that by that time, the participants were worn down. The tone of the meeting that I attended was more wordy than activist.

Although I had attended both faculty meetings, I no longer remember how I voted in them. However, I had become acutely aware that President Perkins, the avowed protector of black students, was now one of their chief targets and that a swastika had been burned and the black students' center torched. The president's attempts to mediate faculty differences from the platform of the second faculty meeting had received little attention and were, each time, futile. On May 31, 1968, he resigned.

The university closed before examinations, leaving faculty to decide for themselves how to grade students. Some sympathizers with the militants gave everybody A's; others refused to give any grades because, they said, they could not find bases for judgments of students' work. Tension was high throughout the university.

An immediate search committee was established to find a new president who could take over on July 1, the beginning of the university's fiscal year. Apparently, the committee quickly agreed that it would best choose a man from within the established circle of experienced and well-known persons at the university. The lot fell to Dale Corson, who had been dean of the College of Engineering, and more recently university provost.

PRESIDENT CORSON ESTABLISHES AN OMBUDSMANSHIP

As part of his attempt to heal wounds and set a new course, President Corson named a committee headed by Alfred Kahn, dean of the Arts College, to look into the desirability of establishing an ombudsmanship. Such an office had already been established in many of the universities that had had experiences similar to Cornell's. The office that emerged from the committee differed, however, from the office established in most other institutions, where a student held the office and dealt only with student complaints. At Cornell the Kahn committee proposed an office that would deal with any complaint of a misuse of authority within the university. Thus the office of ombudsman was clearly an office for mediation between a complainant and anyone in authority over him or her. The only power the ombudsman could exercise if mediation did not result in settlement was to give such a case full publicity.

Early in August I had a call from the president's office. He asked me to take on the new office, using the Kahn report as a charter for its performance. I was surprised, indeed overwhelmed. I asked for a few days to think it over and consult with friends. Assuming the position would postpone other work I was doing, I wanted to figure out how I could reorganize my projects—particularly the study of government in large local unions. The offer had described the job as half time, for which I would receive an extra $1,000 a year. The length of service was not mentioned, nor was staff beyond a secretary. Neither the president nor I had any idea how much work might be involved. The atmosphere suggested, however, that the office would mainly deal with student demands, including those from the African-American students as they arose, and thus spare university officials further disruptions.

I felt strongly challenged and only marginally prepared. My experience with mediation was minimal and mainly gained from a few months of recent practice as a panel member with the newly established office of the New York State Public Employment Relations Board (PERB). A few days later, I met President Corson again to tell him that I had decided I would take on the post. He asked me whether I would want to attend his Monday morning staff meetings. Out of no experience I said, "No," explaining that I might have cases that direct-ly or indirectly concerned him or his staff, and that I thought it essential to remain independent of any relationship with Day Hall. The president accept-ed my decision, but it was later questioned persistently by the attorney for the university, who was in charge of charting the university's organization under the new president. The attorney wanted to show the ombudsman as part of the president's staff. I repeated more than once to him what I had said to the president and assured him that the president had accepted my reasoning. I heard one day at the faculty club that the matter had been settled by attach-ing me to the president on the chart with a dotted line!

In a few days before the fall term began, I hired as secretary for the ombudsman's work Dannilee Poppensieck. But since no office had been provided for us, my academic secretary, Elsie Cole, with whom I had worked for years in happy harmony, welcomed Dannilee into her own narrow space, and for the first year we operated under these crowded conditions.

The weekend before classes began, I was asked to describe this new office to the university's trustees and council in a filled Statler Hall. I dared to out-line a position based carefully on the Kahn report and was welcomed by many individuals, who in effect were moving the burden of dealing with a militant, and somewhat frightening, group of unassimilated students from their shoul-ders to mine. I attempted to emphasize that none of us had any idea how this might work out, or indeed whether the "culprits" would under any circumstances turn to me with any more assurance than they had responded to the past pres-ident, the faculty decisions, HAP, the new disciplinary board, or the Africana Center's temporary director. And, if they should try, would my attitude, my limited action, and powers be any more satisfactory to them than their pre-vious experiences with university officers? Thus began two years of a very time-consuming and expanding job, one that fully absorbed me and the two staff assistants who eventually helped me run the office.[10]

THE OMBUDSMANSHIP

Once the ombudsman's office got underway, I turned more and more to the original Kahn Committee report. I particularly used the following elements as guidelines: First, the office was to be available to "all members of the uni-versity community . . . wishing to present any grievance that may arise against the university or anyone in the university exercising authority." Although a num-ber of other universities had already established ombudsmen, Cornell was, I believe, the first to open the office to "all members of the community" and not only to students. We were also among very few to decide that a full pro-fessor should head the office.

Second, the office was to be independent of any administrative office with-in the university, including President Corson's office. Third, appropriate information from anywhere in the university was to be available to the office.

Fourth, the office, in endeavoring to settle what appeared to be justified complaints, was to rely on methods of persuasion, fact-finding, and conciliation. The office had no judgmental or punitive power. As a last resort, where these procedures failed to bring about a settlement, the ombudsman could resort to giving the case full publicity. I decided at once to use the publicity option very sparingly, and indeed never used it in dealing with an individual case. I believed that its use would endanger our promise to clients of confidentiality, and that its worst effect would be to enable readers to identify individuals without offering much chance of systematic improvement of a bad situation. Fifth, and finally, the report suggested the further possibility of establishing smaller or sub-offices within each of the colleges. However, in a meeting I held with deans, there seemed no need for such an elaboration. The mathematics department had established such an office before the universitywide office had been proposed, and it was left to deal with matters within that department.

An advisory committee to the ombuds office, composed of faculty, students, and any others concerned with its operation, was never established, for it seemed to me to violate the promise we were to make to all applicants of confidentiality. The office was originally set up only for nine months, after which a new legislative body was to decide whether to continue the office or whether to find some other way of dealing with grievances. At the end of nine months, a senate that might possibly take over this function was still being discussed. In fact, as the end of the spring term approached, the president asked me to continue for a second academic year.

During the first year, we had accepted help from two student volunteers and hired two staff members, Joycelyn Hart and Alan Sapackie. We were assured of adequate separate office space in Barnes Hall for our second year. Joycelyn remained with the office for several years, until she was invited to become assistant dean of the graduate school. With the extension of civil rights legislation, she then became an assistant vice president of the university for the administration of civil rights problems, where she remained until her retirement in 1996. Alan was a recent graduate of the College of Engineering.

Danilee remained as indispensable secretary and receptionist in the office, until her experience there justified her promotion by one of my successors to assistant ombudsman. In my years in office, it was the rule that after every interview we staff members dictated a full report for our private record, under the promise to the complainant of full confidentiality. As secretary, Danilee adhered to this requirement as did the three staff members. I have no doubt that her promotion to assistant ombudsman was well deserved. When a new office of victim advocacy was recently created, it was placed in her hands at the ombudsman's office. Danilee is the only person who has remained in that office throughout the twenty-seven years of its existence.

We began to operate on the basis of two classes of appeals to us: (1) helping people who wanted information that would allow them on their own to find the person(s) who could answer their question(s); (2) receiving complaints against someone in authority. Concerning these latter, we kept a full report of the interviews undertaken to meet the complaint. We took no anonymous or secondhand reports.

In the first semester complaints came mainly from undergraduate students. By the second semester the number of graduate students coming to the office had increased considerably. Faculty and staff complaints also began to appear. We were clearly operating as the Kahn Committee had foreseen, namely, with all elements at the university.

I was constantly bombarded by colleagues with questions about how we operated and how successful our interventions were. Some were concerned with their fear that we were or could be "used" by the "militants." To the extent that the militants either felt they could handle their own problems or that they did not believe we could give them the kind of help they wanted, they did not turn to us in these early months. Therefore the possibility that they "used" us to strengthen their complaints against the university had no basis.

In my first report to the university constituents, my assumption was that:

> Most organizations have within themselves the self-direction, commitment, resources, and leadership necessary to make them self-sufficient, autonomous bodies, able and eager to handle their own affairs. They do not need or want the intermediation of the Ombuds in drawing up, adopting, or implementing their programs. At most, they may request access to us for information about the people who could help them. If they get into trouble, they may want help in getting out of it, but small, weak, and new bodies are a different matter. With them as with others, the Ombudsman is concerned about issues which affect open communication, due process, and issues dealing with the purpose and policies of the University.

Under these guidelines, we responded to a certain number of quite unanticipated problems. Among these were: as election watcher in the referendum on the senate; as a hearing officer at the request of both parties in a case in which a student brought charges against his professor on grounds of political favoritism; as a repository for documents of persons who anticipated future need for them; and as referee on problems arising out of the grading legislation adopted to deal with that problem when the university in 1969 closed before final exams.

The Kahn Committee had also proposed that at the end of an appointment period, the office make recommendations to the administration and faculty for changes or improvements of their established procedures. At the end of the first year we made six recommendations to the president and provost. At the end of the second year we could report progress on all of these: (1) a student grievance procedure had been instituted and is still in place; (2) the Advisory Committee to the President on the Status of Women had been established in response to our proposal that "systematic attention go to the recruitment and promotion of women to tenured professorships; (3) the appointment of persons below tenure rank had been regularized by requiring that a letter of appointment include specific statements about all its terms, although we had to note that a number of aspects of working conditions still needed attention for this growing group of sub-faculty; (4) communication lines to the dean of the graduate school had been established such that students could go to the dean when intractable problems arose between a student and committee members.

In addition, we noted that (5) a grievance procedure for teaching and research assistants and all graduate students had not been achieved. However, the Personnel Office had agreed to hear grievances of work-study students, although its powers did not include redress in cases of academic appointments. We could now add newly revealed problems that included: the need to make more and better athletic and recreational facilities available for women; the need for further study and redress for students who had reason to believe that the university was delinquent in fulfilling all points in its housing contracts with them; and that while all women and men of color recognized that some progress had been made in affirmative action on their behalf, much dissatisfaction still existed.

As early as the spring term of 1970 I announced that I would not remain in office past June of 1971. My belief was that the university should experiment widely with the administration and scope of this office and that I should therefore remain in the post no longer than two years. I believed that fairly short terms of office would be a way to bring in other approaches and procedures. I followed this promise and asked the president to set up a search committee early in 1971 to ensure that there would be no break in the office's ability to deal with complaints.

In the spring of 1971, as in the first year of our operation, student uprisings again took place, this time for the most part in protest of the United States's invasion of Cambodia. The university's response was again to close before final exams. Since more than five hundred students had poured into the office in 1970 with complaints about the lack of a grading system, I had had perforce to set up a procedure, which sent them to their professors, then to their department heads, and finally to their deans before coming to our office. In the second year, under similar circumstances, seven hundred thirty students were referred to this procedure. In this year, too, both town and gown had become uneasy about what protesting students might do, and after rumors reached us that an army unit was on its way to Ithaca, we set up a rumor clinic that functioned day and night. With the assistance of a single student, Alan Sapackie recruited more than a hundred students and faculty to staff the clinic, in two-hour shifts around the clock for about two weeks.

After my retirement, I did not return to the office (moved permanently to Stimson Hall) until I prepared to write this chapter. It was of course very satisfying to hear Danilee say that very few changes had been made over the years in any of the procedures we established during the first two years.

Although the work of heading this office had been described as half time, in fact, I spent a good deal more time than that on it. I never finished my research on large local unions in the public sector. I no longer had responsibility for the required courses in labor history and administration. During these years many new faculty members were brought in to fill places in all departments as the "founders" began to go into retirement. I find myself still thinking of these recruits as the "newcomers," although some of them are now beginning to retire themselves.

RETIREMENT

My own retirement loomed. My last year of teaching ended in 1972. Dean Bob McKersie, with the help of some faculty and the administrative hand of Fran Herman, who was at the time an M.S. student at ILR, organized a party at the faculty club. Colleagues and TAs made some honorific speeches. After the speeches and the food, I was invited to walk across the way to the lower quadrangle of what we still called "the new ILR" campus, although it had been our home for almost ten years. We saw new redbud trees under the library windows, labeled "Cook Grove," where a plaque honored my contribution to the school and the university. The trees, of course, have grown and now completely cover the plaque, but if I brush branches aside, I can still show it to family and personal friends.

I was somewhat taken aback, however, when the assistant dean came to me in mid-June to announce that he would need my office as of July 1. At that time, the few already retired professors had severed their connections with the school, and no facilities were available for retirees. I had mistakenly assumed that I could take my time in packing up. Not so. I was rescued by my long-time secretary, Elsie Cole, who immediately undertook the task of making my files ready for storage, while Richard Strassberg, the school's archivist, provided space for them. In any case, I knew by this time that I would be leaving Ithaca for a considerable period. I felt very fortunate to have an intriguing new job to look forward to. Indeed, the summer looked all too short for the preparations I had to undertake for my next assignment.

STUDYING WORKING MOTHERS IN NINE COUNTRIES: 1972–1973

In the early spring of 1972, Barbara Wertheimer,[1] a professor in the New York City Extension Office of Cornell University, and a mover and shaker among trade union women, told me that the Ford Foundation, which had underwritten several of her projects, had asked her to undertake a comparative study that would examine and evaluate policies of European countries responding to the special needs of working women. Susan Berresford, now the president of the Ford Foundation, was then the responsible figure within the foundation for this assignment. Barbara herself felt too closely attached to the credit program she was developing with trade union women in the Institute on Working Women that she had founded to take on this new project. She asked me for permission to pass my name on to Susan, and I soon received an invitation to take on the project.

I began to plan my itinerary. One of the many decisions to be made was whether the study could be done as a comparison of Communist and non-Communist countries. This appealed to me because the two groups apparently differed sharply in their views of women's working lives. Communist policies strongly encouraged women to work continuously in paid employment, even when bearing and rearing children. Policies in non-Communist countries varied both about women in the labor market and about their ongoing responsibilities for maternity and the household. I wanted to test whether policies in non-Communist countries where women's employment was growing rapidly were moving toward the Communist model. There seemed also to be some particular reason for women to enter the workforce, since some countries abroad were experiencing selective labor shortages. Some of these countries had tried to solve their problems by recruiting guest workers drawn often from Eastern and southern European countries. These were thought of originally as semiskilled men who would return to their homelands when the crisis had passed. But many of these men soon brought their families, and their arrival presented the receiving countries with a variety of social problems, including health care, housing, and the education of children.

A second problem was methodological: what information did I want and what sources of supply should I seek out? I decided to go first to the International Labor Organization (ILO) in Geneva, Switzerland, for I assumed that they would have substantial information on all the non-Communist countries and many of the Communist ones. Moreover, our ILR librarian, Gormley

Miller, was working there, on invitation to modernize the ILO's library. Even in this library, however, I could find very little information about the dependents of these migratory workers, and nearly none on migrant women workers.

I set off on September 1, 1972, just as my colleagues were beginning the fall semester of teaching. I felt no loss, but only the challenge of the new assignment. My route of travel was to be determined by the countries responding to my exploratory letters. Sweden was to be the first of these, and I knew I would go there after three weeks with Gormley Miller in Geneva.

The ILO, Geneva

I met first with the head of the ILO Women's Division, a woman who introduced me at once to one of the problems of comparability studies. Her division, she said, was dependent for its information on reports from member countries. These typically suffered from a lack of any prescribed systematic or comparable way of presenting their material, mainly by failing to state the assumptions about women's lives and work in each society and hence incapable of measuring progress or its lack. Most of the reports, moreover, were simply descriptive and non-analytical, nor were they written with an eye on other countries' policies. After all, she pointed out, international discourse is often meant to conceal or to provide a basis for agreement, rather than to analyze and solve problems. She advised that I ascertain as best I could in each country I visited whether women are assumed to exist for the family or as part of the family, indeed, as an equal part of the family. With regard to Communist countries, she urged me to look carefully at child care, as a necessary element of aid to employed women in countries where women were expected to work. She suggested that I attempt to discover how much employers, the government, and parents contribute to the cost of child care; she suggested also that I evaluate the scope of vocational guidance, training, and retraining available for women.

During these weeks in Geneva, Gormley Miller also offered very useful assistance. Early in my visit he invited me to a lunch with Mr. DeAngeli, the ILO representative of the World Federation of Trade Unions (WFTU), the Communist-oriented labor federation. With him I was able to discuss the problem of getting into Eastern Communist countries. DeAngeli had come out of the Italian trade union movement, known at that time and for years later for developing a progressive Communism. He said at once that he could not help me with many Communist countries, but that he could reach unions in East Germany, Romania, and Russia, all of which he did. With that, some of my visa problems were on their way to being solved, though disappointments were still frequent.

I spent much of my time at the ILO in the library reading materials that Gormley set on my desk from day to day. On weekends, Gormley also took care of my sightseeing interests with trips into the French Alps, as well as to several Swiss peaks. On my own, I vacationed briefly in Germany. I had sent my heavy luggage to my old friend, Tasso Tröscher, in Wiesbaden, where he was now minister of agriculture for the province of Hesse. He and his second wife, Edith, whom he had married shortly after Lydia's death from cancer, had invited me to make their home my base in Europe, as I moved through seasons and countries. Nearby Frankfurt, a city I had not seen in several years, seemed very modern as it rebuilt itself to cover most of the scars of war that I remembered so vividly from my visits in the early fifties.

Admittedly, I came to the Ford Foundation study with a certain bias. I was someone who had been for many years a working mother and a single head of family. Even prior to my divorce, my paid employment had been interrupted when I was unable to find child care for the household's children. It is not surprising, then, that I chose to look at working mothers rather than at working women generally, since it seemed to me that the experience of working mothers concentrates and epitomizes problems that most women have to face. I knew I would find among working mothers all the circumstances with which women have to cope in the world of work plus the additional burdens of housekeeping and child care.

Fundamentally, the study needed to uncover the assumptions about women's lives and functions in each country. I believed that I needed to learn from government officials and others how these assumptions underlay policies fixed into law in recognition of the special needs of working mothers. Were these policies based on the assumption of biological differences between men and women, and thus, to some significant degree, mainly natalist? Were problems of support such as child care, maternity leave, and the like, directed solely to women's reproductive function and their responsibilities as homemakers? Or was the issue one of equality, not only of conditions in the workplace but also of those in the household where the male parent needed to be encouraged to assume equal parenting and homemaking duties?

To carry out these inquiries, I wanted to interview women at work in factories and offices, so as to understand the degree to which they accepted the common familial divisions of labor and to discover the impact of women's family responsibilities on their workplace performances. I needed to meet both local and national trade union officers to discover how far unions recognized the increasing numbers of women in the labor force and also how much the double burden of work and family responsibilities imposed on women. To do this, I would need to understand union structure in each country, as well as the jurisdiction allotted to the unions in terms of dealing with issues directed to meeting the needs of working mothers, especially for child care, whether in publicly sponsored or voluntary institutions.

As for work, I was concerned with issues of gender segregation on the job, separate wage scales for women, and women's participation in unions and workers councils. I was concerned also about the opportunities provided for women's promotion in firms, or for their access to vocational training that could lead to improvement in both their status and wages. And I wanted to inquire about reentry into the labor force after maternity leave or some other temporary withdrawal from employment.

I conveyed this outline well in advance to my sponsors in each country, so as to use my time most profitably. I hoped to have a program ready on my arrival that responded to my requests, amended perhaps with items added by my hosts. Such additions might well indicate significant areas of emphasis.

By the end of my stay in Geneva, I knew that after I left Sweden early in November, I would go to Israel for six or eight weeks before the new year. I hoped to spend January in the Deutsche Demokratische Republik (DDR), as East Germany called itself, if arrangements could be completed in time. Thus, the Ford Foundation study was about to begin. How it would proceed had still to be worked out as I went along. Planning for future countries, while I studied the countries I was temporarily residing in, made for an element of double focus to the entire experience. More or less fixed, however, were the kinds of information I would search for in particular locations in each country.

In all I visited nine countries, in the following order: Sweden, Israel, East Germany, West Germany, Romania, Austria, Russia, Japan, and Australia. Without in any way diminishing the importance of each of them, I have chosen here to write in detail about three of these visits: to Sweden, East Germany, and Japan. A complete account is available in my book, *The Working Mother*, second edition (Ithaca, New York: New York State School of Industrial and Labor Relations, Cornell University, 1978).

SWEDEN

Through the Swedish Institute, the Swedes traditionally and very systematically take over the organization of programs for visiting foreigners. When I reported there, I was introduced to Brigitta Linner, whose book on sex roles had implanted the phrase in Swedish thinking about the two genders and their differential social assignments in family, economic, social, and political life, and how gender segregation resulted from traditional but no longer valid assumptions.

For trade union contacts, I relied on Birger Viklund, an officer of the Metal Workers Union and former Swedish labor attaché in the United States. He referred me to Ms. Lagby, head of a Women's Committee established in an agreement between the LandsOrganisationen (LO, the blue-collar labor federation), and the employers' association in national collective bargaining. The Women's Committee had been seen as a response to the entrance of increasing numbers of Swedish married women into the labor market, a shift that had followed a trial period of foreign workers recruited to fill a shortage of labor in several European countries in the mid- and late sixties. But the thousands of foreign males who came to Sweden brought their families with them, with the result that education, housing, health care, and transportation had become overloaded. The Swedes then decided to cease foreign recruitment and, instead, to encourage the employment of one group of adults not yet in the workforce, namely Swedish married women. Moreover, these women were to be promised equality with their male fellow workers, a promise that quickly raised the issue of women's responsibilities in Swedish families. Thus the Swedes moved to rethink their policies on child care, child support, women's assignment to women's work, the low pay for women's work, the length of maternity leave, the typical responsibilities of women also for the care of elderly family members, the regulation of part-time work in which women predominated, even the legal status of children born out of wedlock. It became clear that all these issues would need to be addressed if women moved from their traditional place inside families to the labor force. As these issues surfaced, the Swedes decided to abandon Women's Committees in the unions where they had existed, as well as in other labor market institutions, in favor of Committees on the Family, designed to include both men and women, a change fostered by both the unions and the employers' associations.

A New Definition of Equality

I visited Alva Myrdal[2] because the Socialist Party (VPK) had asked her to write a proposal covering the Party's commitment to gender equality. She drafted it first for discussion within the Party throughout the country. As was common with new proposals, discussion took place in more than 3,000 Party study circles, including most of the local unions. Some unions, accordingly, had already abandoned Women's Committees, and instead had set up local committees, including men, for the implementation of family policy. Based on reports from these groups, the Socialists had drafted a bill that circulated to other parliamentary parties and to such major voluntary organizations as churches, employers' associations, the traditional women's organizations (including the Frederike Bremer Association), with the expectation that each organization would then submit a paper on their reactions to the revised proposal. The Swedes call this whole process *remiss*.

At the same time, at the request of the unions, an economist at Stockholm University had written a study in response to the concern for the solidarity wage. He offered a program that would raise the wages of low-paid workers so as to narrow the gap between them and high-paid workers. His study had revealed, moreover, that low pay was not primarily a men's problem, as had been assumed, but that the vast majority of low-paid workers were women, and hence, that bargaining for special increases for this group would largely affect women's wages. This report had been circulated to unions and employers but, to my surprise, had not been published. When I visited the professor, who was a former metal worker, he was unable to satisfy my curiosity on this point.

Despite its limited circulation, and thanks to a timely United Nations resolution on the status of women, there was wide acceptance in Sweden of what came to be known as the Equality Report. It had stressed the significance of instituting equality in every social relationship, including the family, the place of employment, the care of disabled persons, housing for large families, and education at all ages and for both genders.

After my meeting with the economist, I went next to visit the Labor Market Board (AMS), concerned with maintaining full employment,[3] several local housing authorities, two communities outside Stockholm, the minister of education, and several child care centers.

My first visit to a child care center was to one headed by a man. He was, I believe, unique in his position at the time, a first measure of the Swedish effort to bring men into women's work, as well as to train women for men's traditional jobs. Very early on, the Swedes had recognized the necessity for establishing publicly sponsored child care, staffed with qualified personnel. A requirement for training young women candidates for these positions included spending a year in a family as a mother's aide. Now the Swedes were trying to convince families to accept young men in this capacity. The woman who introduced me to Swedish child care had had a young male helper in her family for the past year.

I was indeed impressed with the quality of child care in the public centers that I visited, but again and again I heard from parents and staff members that the supply so far achieved was quite inadequate to meet the growing demand.[4] Staff members complained of receiving low women's wages and welcomed men into the occupation in the expectation that they would successfully demand higher pay if they were to make a career in child care.

In the education ministry, both the minister and the head of Vocational Guidance and Training were disappointed by the slow pace of practical acceptance of their efforts to open schools to older workers as well as to young people, and to open exclusively male occupations to women. However, I visited a paper factory where an apparently successful experiment was in progress. A class of thirty women had trained together for work there, where previously no women had been employed. After instruction, they were brought into the line, two to a department and shift. As I came into the pulp room, a machine had broken down and the people on it had to clean up the pulp before mechanics could repair the machine. A dirty job, but both men and women were in it up to their knees. In the mixing room, a woman showed me bags of chemicals, all of them weighing about fifty pounds, that had to be dumped into the vats. I asked who lifted them. "Those who can" she said.

I learned from several women that part of the training had included asking the women how they would prefer to deal with unfriendly, even sexist responses from men. The group had decided to do nothing for the first two weeks, and then, were the responses to persist, to make clear that they were not acceptable. Ever since their initial employment, the women had continued to meet at regular intervals for a discussion of work problems. They offered that, generally, after a few weeks, the unfriendly behavior had ceased. For all of them, it had been a positive demonstration of how to deal with what might now be considered sexual harassment.

Trade union structure and policy in Sweden were complex, for the influential LO was not the sole labor federation. Although some white-collar workers belonged to unions in LO, generally they belonged to their own federation, Tjanstemhannens Central Organisation (TCO). A third federation represented various grades and occupations of supervisors and managers in the civil service. As a matter of principle, TCO had no political affiliation, nor did it share general attachment to the solidarity wage principle, accepting instead wage adjustments based on merit. It was through such observations that I began to see that for LO and the Socialist Party, equality had to do more with class than with gender. With respect to wages, LO had won the agreement of the National Employers Association to narrow the gap over the years between low- and high-paid workers, men as well as women, by awarding the latter an additional and higher percentage of increase. It was generally admitted that this approach was possible only because of the disciplined adherence to the concept of equality among the skilled male workers, based on their commitment to the Socialist doctrine calling for the abolition of class.

Having noted that low wages were mainly a problem for women, closely related to job segregation, the Swedes directed attention to the parental responsibility of men as well as women and to the whole panoply of family life. This consideration had already resulted in a host of programs including men's sharing of parental leave after the birth or adoption of a child, and the rights of both parents to shorten their workday to six hours until a child had reached school age. Joint marital tax returns were abolished in favor of individual taxation of each worker, so that a working wife's earnings did not risk putting the family's income into a higher tax bracket, thus diminishing the benefit of her earnings for the family. As for part-time work, where women predominated because of their family responsibilities, the Swedes made a distinction between long-time part-time and short-time part-time, with twenty hours a week the dividing line for women's eligibility to public social benefits. Such considerations included giving large families the assurance of housing subsidies, if they were necessary, to allow them to live decently; the payment of children's allowances to all families regardless of income; provision of care for sick as well as healthy children. For older people, it meant the provision of home help to enable them to live in their own apartments for as long as possible.[5]

In education and vocational training, reform meant the elimination of differences in the treatment or in the curriculum offered to boys and girls, and also the introduction of new textbooks to reinforce an understanding and rejection of gender segregation in public and private life. Further, reform included vocational guidance, assistance in job searching and placement, using a kind of affirmative action to bring men into formerly women's jobs, and women in those formerly ascribed to men.

By the end of my stay in Sweden I had talked with leaders of three distinct women's groups: Socialist Party women; traditional women in the Frederike Bremer Association; and a radical feminist organization called the Red Stockings. The lines separating them seemed quite firm and impassable. On the one hand, the Socialists indeed strongly advised their women members to have nothing to do with the radicals, and on the other hand, clearly abjured the traditionalists as middle class. The Red Stockings were hostile to both other groups, for they saw them as not moving with modern needs, and, in the case of the Socialists, as too dependent on legal action through legislation. I had to conclude that there was no inclusive women's movement in Sweden.

During this visit, I was particularly impressed by the months-long study and discussion within the thousands of rank-and-file adult study groups, as well as the inclusion of the views of various voluntary organizations as part of the legislative process. I saw this as a grassroots approach to achieving democratic consensus. I was also impressed to find that within the family there was concern for the care and rearing of healthy children, especially through the recognition of parental rather than solely maternal responsibility for family life. By the end of my time in Sweden, I knew that I had viewed not only a new but a positive approach to working mothers' problems. As I traveled across the Swedish landscape observing the efforts being made nationwide to meld the needs of all in the family and the workplace, I moved from the outskirts of feminism to its center. Sweden became the model against which I measured every other country. It remains that way still.[6]

THE GERMAN DEMOCRATIC REPUBLIC (DDR)

In the German Democratic Republic (DDR), I was met by a group of heartily welcoming women under the leadership of Frau Klewe,[7] who would be my companion throughout my visit to my first Communist country. The program that had been prepared for me would involve a good deal of travel, visits to factories, interviews with women workers and with trade union leaders at local and regional levels, and toward the end of the trip, an interview with the woman in charge of the Women's Division of the trade unions, Margarete Müller. The program, I was assured, could be altered, if I wished; I had only to ask and Frau Klewe would endeavor to meet my wishes, as indeed she did whenever I brought new queries to her.

We headed first for Dresden and remained there for several days, visiting factories producing pharmaceuticals, textiles, and office furniture. A pattern for these visits emerged during visit number one. We were taken to the manager's office; in two cases the plan was under the management of a woman. Gathered there were the trade union chair of the plant; the head of the Women's Committee, who administered cultural and social benefits; the director of the Trade School; and, in some instances, the Party representatives in the plant, and perhaps a regional officer of the Party or the union or both. These meetings consisted of a report from each participant on his or her functions in fulfilling national or regional plans for this branch of the industry. Such a meeting could last an hour or more. Then we all gathered for a trip through the plant. In some cases, women were called away from work to speak to us; during one or two visits, I was urged to speak to any woman I selected.

Invariably, we visited the child care center of each plant. These were seen as key to women's full-time employment. Many of them not only provided day care but boarded children during the week, particularly for single mothers. On Saturdays, these mothers could pick up the children, together with food and fresh clothes for the weekend. Parents of children could in some cases return their household laundry with the children's laundry on Monday morning.

We also visited the clinic and the doctor's office, where preventative work was emphasized, and in the pharmaceutical factory the doctors reported that they made regular inspections of chemical exposures and their control. We went to the canteen and were often invited to share a meal there. The canteen also served meals to workers in nearby shops and prepared food for the child care center as well as for a nearby school or two. During school vacations, children of workers could eat their noonday hot meal at the factory. Plants were encouraged, I was told, to adopt a nearby school and, there, to organize children's sports and vacation programs. As they grew older, the children would be given small tasks in the plant in preparation for apprenticeships, perhaps conducted under the industry's vocational program.

Most plants had playing fields, a bowling alley, and sports clubs, while large plants had their own vacation homes. Most of these programs, as well as the administration of certain social insurance, were in the hands of the union. An officer helped with housing, and since transportation was admittedly an inadequately solved problem, factory-supplied housing near the plant was an objective. Factories often ran stores at which workers could buy basic groceries. Many factories provided laundry services for workers. At the time of my visit, household washing machines were not available under the production plan. One of the few complaints I heard came from women workers who found public laundries careless with clothes, which came back many weeks later, gray or with some articles lost. The alternative, however, was for women to do laundry at home in the bathtub. Indeed, most apartment balconies in January were filled with clothes hung out to dry during the short winter days of cold and cloudy weather.

The staffs of child care centers consisted of certified educators and technical people, all women. When I talked with one of the educators about her methods and goals, she showed me her lesson plans prescribing the teaching of the names of colors, and sought proof of her success through questioning the children. I noticed that some children were restless and inattentive and so I asked about whether special assistance might be provided for them. This was not in the plan, which assumed that, at given ages, the assigned topics were to be dealt with uniformly. The curriculum was apparently uniform throughout all child care centers and was to be followed without exception. Groups of children of similar ages advanced from crèches (available for six-month-olds) through nursery school, to kindergarten. Some centers received school-age siblings during after-school hours. School principals were supposed to hire assistants assigned specifically to work on after-school programs.

On the issue of on-the-job skills training, in one plant I chose to interview a middle-aged woman, mother of several children, who had come back to work only a few years ago. She had just completed one section of a training course, she explained. She had at first resisted taking the course, then had been tapped for it by her works leader and the union, and had also been encouraged by her collective, who were aware that they had to take on her work in addition to their own, while she was in the training course. She reported that she had felt proud of her achievement, once accomplished, even looked forward to the next stages of training, was grateful to her teammates, and still somewhat surprised that she had been the object of their choice.

We made several visits to institutions providing workers' benefits, including a vacation home, a supermarket, a department store, a research center on labor market issues, as well as several cultural institutions, including the former concentration camp at Buchenwald, the Goethe and Schiller museums in Weimar, and the Brecht theater. In addition, I spent an evening in the home of the director of the Buchenwald Museum. This was a very relaxed evening with good wine and cakes, in a home that could meet Western middle-class standards of living, in contrast to the much narrower confines of workers' housing and the limited choices of goods available in the markets or department stores.

The research director for Women's Affairs in the National Academy of Science, Dr. Herta Kuhrig[8], arranged for me to use the National Library, where I spent an afternoon with the librarian responsible for the card catalog, searching for materials on women, labor markets, and trade unions in other countries. The material available was very thin. Under "Women Workers in the DDR," Dr. Kuhrig's paper was the only entry during the past four years. There was nothing from Britain; from the United States, I found several leaflets from the Department of Labor's Women's Bureau; from Sweden, one paper by Annika Baude.

On the last morning of my visit, I had breakfast with Margarete Müller, the director of the Women's Division of the trade unions, who was also a member of Parliament. The main work of women's organizations in the unions, as she described it, was to make sure that women, particularly those with children, were adequately housed, and that they received the many benefits to which they were legally entitled: child care, a half day off on Saturdays, maternity benefits, abortions as women themselves desired, and with special protections against chemicals that might affect the health of their reproductive systems. She pointed out that the DDR had adopted the Leninist program of socializing many of the traditional women's home tasks not specified in law, such as laundry, and that it had eased shopping and provided for feeding children in schools and during holidays. Women's representatives in the workplace were also presumably notified by teachers about difficulties with students and were urged to offer help, especially to single mothers.

My overall impression of the DDR's policies affecting working mothers was mainly positive. The men I met seemed fully accepting of women and used no sexist innuendoes, allusions, or cheap jokes, a reflection of the official position in which they had been successfully schooled. Considerable training was also evident in the way local women leaders spoke freely and knowingly about their jobs in the Party or the union. What they had to say was well organized, if a bit hard-edged and somewhat awkward, but they were clearly in command of their areas. Moreover, each local official was committed to encouraging women to undertake further political as well as vocational training.

I found the approach to on-the-job training both pervasive and uniform. First, candidates needed to be confirmed by a vote of fellow workers; second, the programs were broken into parts so that goals could be achieved rather quickly, and could be conceived also as a means for continuing further.

The thorough going provisions for child care were charged to large industries as one of their costs for doing business. Women saw child care as an entitlement, and hence were willing to have their children early in marriage, but seldom did they have more than two. On the other hand, the divorce rate was high, as was the proportion of single mothers who headed families. At every level of discussion about child care, I was told that parents were frequently involved as aides to teachers, as members of parent councils, as workers in factories that adopted schools. Parents of delinquent children were often visited or required to attend formal hearings on their children's behavior. Activists know everything about such a child and his family, I was told. With both parents working full-time, it was hard to believe—and I did not beleive—that there was much time for the volunteer activity of such activists.[9]

Planning in the DDR was done nationally, industry by industry. The governing cabinet was largely made up of commissars of the major industries. Plans were conveyed from the ministry through regional officers to local managers. Plant earnings were expected to cover the benefits that I had observed above in addition to something like lifetime security of employment, which existed even where choice of employment did not. Promotion, however, depended upon good performance, as measured by supervisors, and comradely behavior, as measured by the collective. There were apparently fairly frequent periods when the plant closed, either because of shortages of supplies or the breakdown of machines. A few women reported that they used these breaks to catch up on their shopping.

It was also clear that workers enjoyed little input into collective bargaining. Indeed, bargaining was not a union function as it was in the West. The union, like other organizations within the plant, was notified of the National Plan for the factory; its function then was to animate its members and cooperate with management to fulfill the Plan as handed down from the industry's ministry.

JAPAN

My frequent visits to Japan in the preceding decade had accustomed me to many aspects of social and industrial organization that made it possible to begin interviews, listen to speeches, and take part in discussions at a moderately well-informed level as I looked at problems through the eyes of women workers. I was able to move both far and fast because of many friends who were ready and even eager to help with contacts all over the country. Ultimately, Japan's was the most extensive and thorough study among the group of countries I visited. I recorded toward the end of my time in Japan that I had interviewed local and national union representatives from all four federations, personnel managers in several firms, women activists, reporters from three of the four national newspapers, freelance experts, women in public and private employment, local and national representatives of the employers' organization, representatives of small businesses, social workers, heads of child care centers both publicly and privately supported, directors of training programs, officials in at least four ministries and in several cities, and academics in sociology, anthropology, economics, and labor relations.

On the whole I found the situation for women still very tradition-bound, with arranged marriages still very common, and both men and women convinced that marriage and motherhood were the proper goals for women. Although their employment was accepted during their premarital years, women's opportunities for training were very limited, their scope confined chiefly to nursing, shopkeeping and other retail employment, elementary and nursery school teaching, and some types of social work. Jobs in which women dealt with the public in banks were beginning to multiply. Everywhere, however, I heard the complaints of working women that, if they were to be recognized, they had to be twice as good as men, and destined to advance both in rank and wages much more slowly than the men who started with them in full-time employment. There was, in fact, very little flexibility for married women, and almost no part-time work available. Or, rather, what was called part-time work meant temporary full-time employment at slighter wages and without benefits of any kind.[10]

Although my friend, Ryoko Akamatsu,[11] had been successful in 1972 in recommending and seeing adopted an equality law for women, it was not mandatory; rather, it aimed to set a normal standard for employing women. My interviews repeatedly revealed that, as the provincial Women's Bureau's representatives visited large and small firms, employers often said that they had never heard of the law. One reason, perhaps, was that Nikkeiren, the employers' association, had opposed the law and, even after its adoption, had never informed its membership of its existence. Some employers said that they first heard of it only when the union in their plant raised demands under its umbrella.

My interviews with unions, however, did not suggest much enthusiasm for, or understanding of, the purpose of the law. Indeed, union representatives tended to agree with personnel directors, who believed that women were not much interested in work, since their minds were always on their homes; that women frequently took leaves from which they did not return; and that women did not want to take responsibility for others and felt no commitment to their working lives, for even when training programs were made available to them, women rarely seized these opportunities.

Employers, moreover, were scornful of the vocational training offered by the Labor Ministry and preferred to organize their own training programs, so that their workers under lifetime commitment to their firm might usefully command a variety of skills as needed in various locations. In general, they claimed that wages were justifiably low for women, given the tasks they could undertake. Since women were expected to retire upon marriage, employers often provided programs in the social arts—tea ceremonies and flower arranging—which would contribute to essential feminine skills. Employers were also frequently present and honored at weddings in recognition of these services.

The chief remedies used to protect women against total exploitation took the form of protective legislation: limiting night work and working hours for women, and offering paid maternity leave of fourteen weeks. But unless women could return to work thereafter, they were considered retired. Child care, however, was legally available only after a child had been toilet trained at about two years. The result was the private establishment of illegal infant care. I visited one such institution where, in the tiniest space imaginable, infants were swaddled and laid side by side on shelves between feedings and diaper changes.

Altogether, there was general agreement that the number of those women in employment—married and awaiting marriage—was rapidly growing in response to a labor shortage. There was also general agreement that, whenever a downturn in the economy might occur, women would be let go first. In any case, employers who did not want women as workers were free to build all-male organizations.

On the positive side, cases on sex discrimination were coming before the courts. An impressive group of women lawyers, associated with the Sohyo Labor Union Federation, were available to carry these cases. I talked with two of their alleged victims and their lawyers. It was clear that, unless a woman could gain the support of a women's organization as well as a pro bono lawyer, she had little chance of building a case or of carrying it through many years in the appeals system of the courts. One woman I talked with had been fired when her union was voted out in the fifties. The defeated union, which was Communist-dominated, immediately put her on its staff, where she was able to remain throughout the long, drawn-out procedure, finally won in the Supreme Court while I was in Japan. We met at least twice while she told her story both of infinite patience on her part and of unwavering support from the union. The second case was of a woman broadcaster in Nakano, who had been let go on her thirtieth birthday and told that she was too old to attract viewers. She had won in the District Court and in the Appeals Court, but was waiting for outcome of the company's appeal to the Supreme Court. The company, in the meantime, had been forced to rehire her but had provided her with no office. She had to spend her working days in the ladies' room. Many other cases had to do with the differential ages for women's and men's retirements.[12]

As I consider the conditions for working mothers in Japan, I am aware as well that, in many of the other countries I visited, conditions were as limited. In some countries, small steps had been taken, but in most countries much remained undone. The most positive sign on the horizon was the growing internationally aware women's movement at work both inside and outside trade unions.

EIGHT PROBLEMS PECULIAR TO WORKING MOTHERS: MY FINDINGS SUMMARIZED

Early in the study, I identified eight problems peculiar to working mothers, and as I went from country to country, I collected material on each of these: (1) the extent of job segregation, specified often as the distinction between men's and women's work; (2) the limited opportunities for education and vocational training open to women; (3) equal pay for women and men; (4) how women's responsibilities as wives and mothers cling to them even when they work outside the home and thereby undertake a double burden; (5) child care for preschool children and for older children after school hours; (6) the advantages and disadvantages of part-time work for women; (7) the effect on women of such labor market policies as protective legislation and social welfare programs; (8) women's place and effectiveness in trade unions, as indicators of the degree to which unions are concerned with women as members.

In the early seventies, while gender equality was beginning to be widely accepted as a goal for treating the problem engendered by women's massive movement into the labor market, still the meaning of equality differed not only in Communist and non-Communist countries, but also in Nordic countries and in the United States. In the United States, the goal of equality meant that ideally women were to achieve equal status with men, whereas in Sweden and most of the other Nordic countries, the ideal aimed at setting new goals for both women and men with reference to both family life and the workplace.

As I visited each of the nine countries in this study, I searched for the ways in which each of them set or aligned policy to one of these distinct messages. I based my observations on the insights I had gained first in Sweden, where I had noted the systematic effort to change gender segregation in the workplace by encouraging men to take on "women's" work and women to qualify for "men's" work. I noted also as even more significant those aspects of employment policies that directly affected family life.

JOB SEGREGATION

In nearly all the countries I visited, it was quite customary to recognize men's work as distinct from women's work. In construction, men dominated almost to the point of excluding women entirely, whereas in textiles, where women were heavily employed in Western countries, spinning was apt to be a man's job and weaving largely a woman's. (In Pacific Rim countries, on the other hand, men were chiefly the weavers.) On the whole, however, in every country, men mainly worked with men and women with women. In many cases in the West, women may routinely advance to the supervision of women at the shop or department level, whereas within the Pacific, it is extremely rare for women to gain even shop-level promotion. As noted in Glenda Roberts's unique study of a Japanese shop producing women's undergarments, all shop-level supervisors were male. (In the United States, shortly after this study had been completed, the phrase "glass ceiling" was introduced to describe the limited promotions available to women, who could see male coworkers moving steadily up the management ladder.) In most countries, certain production and service jobs, in both public and private sectors, were widely perceived as suitable only for men at any level. Included in this category were police work and firefighting, and much of the apprentice system in the printing, machine, and construction trades.

The Communist countries took a somewhat different view, while at the same time maintaining a job segregation of their own. Since long before the 1917 revolution women had traditionally been dentists and to some extent doctors. After that time the number of women doctors steadily increased, but it is generally men who are surgeons and heads of hospitals and heads of many departments, with the possible exceptions of gynecology and pediatrics. Since training for all occupations in these countries is linked in all fields in a given year to the current needs for workers, women appear from time to time in fields that in the West would usually be offered to men—the physical sciences, engineering, architecture. In the DDR I met a woman harbormaster, but men mainly staffed the ships, although the cooks aboard were usually women. Whatever deviations from Western practice may occur country by country, the generalization still widely holds: men work with men, and women work with women.

In the West, remedies for the more rigid cases of job segregation have come through the courts. In many of these cases the complainant has been supported by a women's organization that expanded its agenda to set up a special defense fund for such women. The resulting successful court decisions have had the effect of opening up job opportunities to qualified women applicants.

EDUCATION AND TRAINING

Until recently women's general education and vocational training everywhere have been severely gender restricted. Recent studies have also shown that both women and men schoolteachers in the classroom give preference to boys by responding to them more frequently and more encouragingly than to girls.[13] Vocational training courses open to girls and women are mainly preparation for food service, household management, retail sales, clerical work, and cosmetology. Although child care would seem to be a useful area for training of high school girls, until recently women were thought to be "naturally" equipped to care for children, both boys and girls, until well into adolescence. Hence, when women worked outside the home, they retained in the public mind this special ability and were expected somehow to continue to carry the complete responsibility for their children's welfare. That attitudes have changed in this regard is largely a product of more women working outside the home, as well as of the high rate of teenage motherhood. Boys in many school systems are now very widely eligible for and even recruited to high school classes in cooking and parenting.

Some women's organizations have centered the struggle for equality on breaking restrictions on work for women, so as to prepare them for entry to what have up till now been male-dominated occupations. I found two approaches to achieving such opportunities: one was to prepare women to qualify for entry to training; the second, to open some of the requirements for training itself. These efforts have shown that there are very few occupations that women cannot enter if qualifications are defined by the genuine demands of the occupation. This has meant abandoning such qualifications as height or weight or high school graduation when these have been shown to bear no relation to the job description itself. A further problem arises as it becomes clear that if women's equal access to "men's work" is the goal, then a high percentage of men must similarly move to women's jobs. Here a major concern is that men have no incentive to move voluntarily in this direction so long as women's wages remain lower than wages for men.[14]

Protective laws forbidding the employment of women for late-night work or at heights or underground were clearly based solely on gender and had their effect on the number and quality of openings available to women. Such laws still exist in many Asian countries such as Japan. In the United States these laws were taken off the books when the Coal Employment Project (CEP) was formed by women who went to court citing the Equal Employment Opportunity (EEO) law and won access to employment in the mines. As a result some five thousand women are today working in coal mines in the eastern United States and metal mines in the West, areas that had previously allowed almost no opportunities for women's employment, or employment only at wages that did not provide for decent, independent living.

In comparison with other countries, the United States adopted civil rights equality legislation early, in 1964. At the time this legislation applied only to the private sector and was motivated by concerns for equal employment opportunities for African-American workers. The clause extending these rights to women generally was added only after a Southern senator submitted it as an amendment to the bill. He did this, he said, because otherwise African-American women, but not white women, would gain equal opportunity. His expectation was that such a provision giving equal rights to all employed women would meet certain defeat. He was wrong.

The enforcement of this legislation in the United States has depended largely on presidential executive orders calling for "affirmative action." Further legislation in 1972 extended these laws and orders to nonprofit, educational, and various public institutions. In the seventies, Britain, Canada, Australia, and New Zealand followed this pattern. In the seventies also, women in Italy, France, Germany, and even Israel began to press for similar action in their own countries. As I moved from one country to another, I raised questions about this movement for affirmative action and women's rights more generally, and I tried to meet the responsible women leaders in each case. I also tried to meet women who had taken advantage of these efforts, usually aimed at far more than moving women upward on the occupational and wage scales. Usually I found these efforts tied to other efforts on behalf of the empowerment of women, frequently manifested in such new laws as might define marriage as a partnership, rather than an agreement about property controlled by the male partner.[15] To the extent that elements of these programs have been embodied in law, they presumably represent more enduring progress than the unquestionably exemplary work of private agencies in their localities. The work of the regional women's voluntary organizations is not only exemplary in this connection, but essential. Without it, male-dominated legislatures rarely put feminist programs on their agendas.

West Germany is widely credited with having the earliest and best established apprenticeship training programs, linked, as they have been since World War II, to general schooling for two days a week for three or four years. Students spend the other three to four days of the week with apprentice masters in the factories. This arrangement begins with a contract made between the parents (until 1958 the father only) and the business where students will be trained. Satisfactory completion of the training is attested to by the guild to which the master workman belongs. The apprenticed students emerge as journeymen.[16]

Up until the late 1960s, Germany expected a very low percentage of elementary graduates to prepare for university attendance. The high school, which students began at ten years of age, was divided between a terminal course ending at sixteen that prepared students for transfer to the semiprofessional and administrative positions, such as optometry and accounting, and the classical gymnasium course of nine years' duration, which was the appropriate preparation for the university. Very few girls expected to attend a university. Since the early 1970s, Germany's postwar development has been more like that of the United States in terms of the overall proportion of university graduates, including the proportion of women to men. University education is at the cost of the state. Germany has also developed one or two bridge universities for adults who early in life took one of the other educational choices and who now wish to obtain a university degree. I have followed with pleasure the development of a woman friend, now fifty-two years old, who took this route to a graduate degree.

Trade education considered appropriate for girls has mostly been considered to be satisfactorily completed in two years. The fact was, and to a considerable degree still is, that girls in some countries undertake this training but then work only rarely or intermittently. This happened especially in Israel, as I observed—particularly among women who were trained in cosmetology. The United States includes some vocational training in its high schools, until recently offering auto mechanics only to boys, for example, and typing and other office skills mainly to girls.

The Communist countries not only expected women to work, but each year determined where trades needed replenishing and set a regional quota of admissions to training for both academic and nonacademic skills. As postwar industry increased and more and more women reported for work because of the heavy loss of men in the war, they had to be trained on the job. I observed that East Germany responded to this need by dividing training into short terms. As I indicated earlier, candidates might be selected by their fellow workers, who had additionally to do the work of the man or woman in training, since replacements were not available. Twenty years later, after the wall was down, I interviewed East German women in Potsdam. They and their mothers had worked a lifetime. They could not imagine what life for them would be like without the amenities with which their state had provided them—full health care, child care, subsidized housing, food, and transportation. The future was beyond their grasp. "How can they expect us to work without these benefits?" was as far as they could go. The simple answer was that the West—now in charge of their lives—expected them to "to manage" on their own, mainly by carrying a dual burden of work and domestic responsibility.

EQUAL PAY

The demand for equal pay for women is long-standing in labor history and was usually read into the slogan, "equal pay for equal work." To the unions that supported the phrase, it meant that women working at the same job as men should receive the same pay. The unions wanted to be guaranteed that lower rates for women would not result in drawing down men's pay. During the late seventies in the United States, a new concept of equality began to be discussed, in part as a consequence of a case brought to the courts by nurses in Denver. The nurses had studied the wages paid to male workers in Denver hospitals as compared to nurses, almost all of whom were women. The males in the hospital worked as bakers, gardeners, and truck drivers, all of whom were paid more than the nurses, although the nurses had trained longer and had skills beyond those of the men. The case went to federal court under the Equal Pay Act (1963), calling for equality based on jobs as measured by skill, effort, responsibility, and working conditions. The nurses lost precisely because theirs was not a case of men and women working side by side on the same job, but rather an example of the strict job segregation that existed in hospitals.

Shortly thereafter, women workers began to speak of this problem as one of comparable worth. This terminology had the advantage over "equal pay for equal work," since it offered a method of comparing skill, effort, responsibility, and working conditions by breaking each of these into its subelements and giving them an arithmetical value that, when totaled, gave a numbered value to each individual job. This value could then be shown on a scale comparing it to other jobs assigned by the employer to his or her workers.[17]

As I worked in Germany in 1973, several women called my attention to a study, initiated there by the federal minister of labor. He had asked two compensation specialists, Josef Rutenfranz and Walter Rohmert to develop a scientific method of breaking wages into payment by a system that would evaluate the components of jobs so as to achieve a numerical value for each job. It could then be placed on a scale comparing it to all other jobs paid by the same employer. Soon after the study (popularly known as the Ru-Ro Report) was published, the political scene changed. The succeeding federal minister of labor buried the report in a file from which it has never been exhumed.[18]

By 1979 the U.S. Women's Bureau and the Office of Equal Opportunity (OEO) had called a conference of women's organizations at which Eleanor Holmes Norton, then the chief of the OEO, made the keynote speech in behalf of this new definition of wage equality. I attended this meeting and became persuaded that this was the rational approach to equal pay for equal work. The argument on behalf of this interpretation rested on the high degree of job segregation in the labor market and on the lower wage scales for women who did work comparable to that of men working for the same employer.

My own work henceforward centered on recording the introduction of comparable worth in all levels of public agencies in the United States. By the mid-eighties I had published two booklets and several articles on this subject. I did not have the mathematical or statistical background to do studies of this kind myself, but I was closely in touch with women who were able to deal with the problems of job evaluation, as well as the introduction of comparable worth in compensation strategy.[19]

WOMEN'S DOUBLE BURDEN

I first came on the phrase "women's double burden" in Sweden in 1972 when I met Brigitta Linner, who had introduced it in articles she wrote in the late sixties and early seventies. In these pieces Brigitta greatly influenced Swedish thinking about gender equality, through her analysis of society's assignments of tasks to women. She described the many, varied occupations women were expected to undertake over long hours of the day and night without remuneration. While these tasks were essential to society, they were taken for granted, never enumerated, evaluated, or valued. In her work as a family counselor, she saw that despite the wide acceptance of the traditional women's role, the Swedes felt little guilt about the decline of traditional marriage and the increasing acceptance among young married couples of their joint responsibility for parenting. She dated the beginning of this lifting of old social pressures back to the 1950s.

Other countries I observed over the next year and a half, including the Communist ones, had only begun to consider legalizing changes that the Swedes had long since learned to live with. In those countries, the conception of women's role was still generally accepted without examination or critique, as is still in the nineties very widely the case. Its cost is that women alone bear the double burden. Women are still expected to be housekeepers, even when they take on full-time jobs. And since housekeeping has no money value, it is disregarded both for the time it consumes and the contribution it makes to society. When a woman today responds to a query about work by saying, "I am only a wife" or "I am only a mother," she indicates her own devaluation of her work. Women who carry the double burden of work in the home and in the workplace pay a high price in physical exhaustion as well as lack of sleep.[20]

In her book on modern marriage, Arlie Hochschild makes clear how young couples, married or unmarried, may well enter the parental state with an agreement to divide housework and parenting equally. Only rarely does such a partnership become a reality. In fact, divorce is a not uncommon consequence of the failure to do so.[21] The birth of a child puts the marriage agreement to its most critical test, one to which the U.S.'s Family and Medical Leave Act (FMLA, 1992) was meant to respond. But the leave granted by this act is unpaid. The consequence is that while the wife is pregnant and recovering from childbirth she may be paid under maternity leave insurance.

In this country, however, paid leave is frequently limited by the insurance companies to eight weeks, divided between pre- and postnatal time. The husband, who is often the better earner of the two, cannot take the FMLA unpaid leave, and rarely does so. He consoles himself for his absence at this time with the belief that the child "naturally belongs to the mother." He does not see that housework, aside from child care, covers a wide variety of tasks, some of which cannot be neglected: laundry, food shopping and preparation, and bill paying remain as the most urgent.

It might be useful to remember at this point that Sweden pays parental leave for more than a year at 90 percent of normal income. The result is that some 20 percent of fathers there take some advantage of their right to parental leave. Several Communist countries began early to offer three paid years to new mothers who wished to remain at home with preschool children, though nothing to fathers.

CHILD CARE

Because it is clear that if mothers need to work—either as single women; or as the wives of unemployed, underemployed, or disabled men; or as women who have been deserted or divorced, as such women often must do—their most imperative need is for child care, whether it is for preschool or after-school children.

Societies where women are expected to work provide child care as a cost of women's full employment. In some cases, under capitalism, private agencies or small businesses offer infant care. In Japan I observed infants laid on shelves and moved only for feeding and diapering. Somewhat older infants were put in a cart during the afternoons for a trip outdoors. Mothers with no family resources who had to work used such facilities because, under the law, women who failed to return to work after fourteen weeks' maternity leave (paid in full in Japan) had no right to or expectation of reemployment. I could not discover how many of these child care facilities were in operation.

I found during my study that after-school centers, where children could spend afternoons until a parent or relative picked them up, were being widely introduced in Communist countries. Indeed, working women in Communist countries, who made up a much higher percentage of the labor force than women in non-Communist countries, could count on infant care at very little or no cost, as well as on other amenities, including the boarding of children during the work week, and the providing of diapers and laundry services, as well as after-school programs for older children. In addition, women had free access to birth control and to abortion. Most families consisted of no more than two children. Missing altogether was provision for family leave of any kind.[22]

PART-TIME WORK

Despite the problems inherent in working part-time, many mothers in their attempt to lighten the double burden, or to find time within the twenty-four-hour day to complete all the work, paid and unpaid, that has to be done, have undertaken such work. Some countries I visited met the need to recruit married women into the labor force by taking a favorable view of part-time work. They began this process by legitimizing shorter hours for mothers of young children, who found full-time work almost impossible so long as children were in elementary school. Many European schools close at one or one-thirty in the afteroon when children are dismissed and are expected to return home for a hot meal. Mothers are expected to oversee the large amounts of homework assigned to fill the afternoons.

Employers could also be persuaded to accept women's working part-time, for they would not need to pay benefits to employees working fewer than thirty-nine hours per week. Sweden and Norway faced that question almost alone by breaking part-time work into "long part-time" and "short part-time." Short part-time consisted of nineteen hours, and benefits proportional to hours worked above that amount were required. All countries were not uniformly interested in this pattern. Communist countries, for example, showed no interest. And Israel showed little interest in drawing women into part-time work because of pressures from conservatives to encourage married women to remain in the home and have many children, in response to the policy in place of increasing the population as rapidly as possible. Moreover, when extra workers were needed, Israel could draw at will on members of the Arab population in Gaza and on the Left Bank, who came into Israel by day but returned home at night.

At the stage when industry restructured from manual work on machines to computer-controlled operations, employers became interested in offering part-time work, as occupations changed. These structural changes meant in many cases that part-time work could be placed in facilities that were open all night or in the home under computerized supervision. And work might be organized as full-time evening or night jobs. In such cases, change might mean savings for the employer in rent and supervision, as well as in benefits to employers stemming from employees' isolation from union organizers and thereby from information about fellow employees' conditions and grievances.

The ability to work at home has been suggested as a way to save on child care costs. In reality, working at home has often meant very limited or unsatisfactory working hours for women, often after the children are in bed. Such a situation compresses the double burden into late-night hours, particularly if deadlines are attached to work assignments. Supervisors can measure through electronic detection whether this kind of work production equals that done at a standardized workplace.[23]

When faced with an option of a four-day work week of nine-hour days or a five-day work week part-time, many women prefer the four-day week, despite the fact that several women I have interviewed admit that they spend most of the fifth day sleeping off the stress and weariness of the four long days. They seem to prefer the sense of control they derive from three full days away from work.

LABOR MARKET POLICY

The United States has so far left legislation on women's role largely to the states. Abroad, smaller and more homogeneous countries have turned to national law-making. Thus, on the issues I was investigating, as well as on social policy in general, U.S. history traces a different development of labor market policy from that of Western Europe. In one particular, however, we all share a common historical concept of women as developed during the period of early industrialization. This is the concept that woman is a weak physical body whose strength must be conserved for the production and care of children. She must be protected: hence "protective legislation." Her hours of paid work must be limited in total per week or month; she must not work a night shift; she must not work underground or above certain heights. As a consequence, job training was strictly divided between training for "men's work" and "women's work." This division of labor occurred in a period when children worked at early ages and women's work was compared to that of children. When regulation of children's labor began to take place, women's wages and working conditions were judged as more or less equivalent to those of children.

As more and more women flowed into the sections of the labor market that were understood to be suitable to them—food preservation, preparation, and service; garments; tobacco; hairdressing; and retail sales—they were as much pulled by employers as pushed by their own initiative to augment family income. The need for women in all kinds of work had increased rapidly, especially during World War II, as men were drawn into the armed forces. By the time they returned to take up their old jobs, the nature of production generally began to change rapidly from mechanization to computerization. Concepts of what constituted women's work did not greatly change, however. The constant increase in the numbers of women in the labor market from the mid-fifties onward was a result of rapidly rising inflation rather than any continued opening of new occupations to women in the first postwar years.

For this reason, the concept of equality in work—arising from the civil rights movement and designed originally to bring African Americans into equality in the workplace—became the goal among feminists and women's organizations. The goals included women's equality with white men, not only politically but in the labor market as well. The Equal Rights Amendment (ERA), introduced as an amendment to the Constitution, was adopted by Congress in 1972. For the next ten years, its supporters sought adoption by at least three-fourths of the state legislatures. But by the deadline of June 30, 1982, only thirty-five of the necessary thirty-eight states had ratified the proposed amendment. In the last three states in which votes took place, the ERA failed by less than a total of ten votes. In the years since the failure of the ERA, more and more women's organizations have shaped their programs to include reforms that will enable women to achieve labor market equality, not at the price of the family but through partnership within it.

The Trade Union as an Instrument for Equality

The Communist trade unions, as I became acquainted with them in this study, seemed to be of considerable help to working mothers, though in very different ways from their namesakes in the West. The unions carried out semigovernmental functions as they monitored the social programs of housing families and checking on the child care programs in or near the factory. Unions also administer social insurance. The Women's Divisions inform members of their social rights, including the factories' feeding of children during school holidays.

These functions have their very positive side, but the unions' scope and efficiency in these matters are mainly in the hands of men who, much like male leaders in other economies, are caught up in other activities, their powers subordinated to other, mainly political, concerns. The unions do not bargain, and thus the reason for unions' existence in the West is invisible in the East.

In non-Communist countries, the unions, as early as the days of Clara Zetkin in the last half of the nineteenth century, set up Women's Divisions, whose leaders were usually, but by no means always, women. Of these, West Germany beginning in the early 1970s, may have had the best example of a structure for women that reached from the local to the national organization of every union's Women's Division. A paid, female staff representative claims a seat on the National Executive Committee and at least twice in modern times has also been the first vice president of the Federation, the DGB. Yet this Women's Division has no budget of its own. The efforts in recent years to specify the Division's power and its work have not succeeded in changing the statement of its purpose and power from that described in the 1949 postwar reconstitution of the West German labor movement. In effect then, the actions and programs of the Women's Division remain subordinate to the votes, permission, and decisions of the male majority. In spite of these limitations, many unions, through the pressure of their own Women's Divisions, have included equality provisions in their own constitutions and structures.

The "Ru-Ro" study was strongly supported by the entire DGB and many of its member unions. Since the Women's Division is a member of the Frauenrat (the national Women's Council, an umbrella organization of nearly all women's organizations in the country), which lobbies the federal government on women's issues, many of its non-union members joined with the unions to support this wage program.

I attended the national convention of the Women's Division of the Metal Workers Union in 1988 when the union's president was scheduled to speak. The women delegates expected him to address what they considered to be his violation of an agreement the union had made at its previous convention, namely to fill staff vacancies, as they occurred, with women in proportion to their membership in the union. In two recent incidents, he had failed to do so. His explanation, which seemed very reasonable to me, was that in each case the local unions were made up entirely of men. No woman existed in the membership who had worked with the problems that had to be negotiated with the employers concerned. This was an insufficient explanation for the women. Suddenly the air was filled with balloons, which they had released. I turned to the woman next to me in the observers' gallery and asked what this meant. Her reply was "Blah! Blah! Blah!" Although rumor had it that the president never again spoke to the chair of the Women's Division for allowing (perhaps even encouraging) this demonstration against his authority to happen, she continued in her post.

In Britain, an agreement in 1920 between the Women's Trade Union League (WTUL) and the Trade Union Congress (TUC) resulted in an amalgamation of the two, whereby women were given two "protected seats" on the Council (a number increased to five in 1981). As a result women have from time to time been presidents of the TUC.[24]

In Israel, the unions' Women's Division, which includes wives of male unionists, functions like Hadassah and other women's organizations in taking on child care, youth work, and prevocational training for girls. Its head office is located in the Histadrut headquarters. Shortly before I visited Israel in 1971, the first woman, Aliza Tamir, had recently been appointed to the Collective Bargaining Department of Histadrut, to work mainly for and with women members of the unions on issues of wages and working conditions. She continues in that position today but with no additional staff. The Japanese arrangement within unions is much like the Israeli, with the exception that, since textiles are a major industry in Japan, many more women are involved in that union than in comparable Israeli unions. Japanese unions play a larger role politically and economically than their Israeli counterparts.

Australia's trade unions resembled those in the Unites States more than any other country's. Australia's growing women's movement, led by the Women's Educational League (WEL)—somewhat comparable to the National Organization for Women (NOW) in the United States—supports some of the demands of the women trade unionists.[25]

Women trade unionists, sent by trade unions themselves, were richly represented at the Fourth United Nations Conference on Women in Beijing (1995). They succeeded in noting that unions can be centrally important to the achievement of the reforms recommended for working women generally. Altogether, the close interweaving of work and family problems whenever women work for wages was amply evidenced at Beijing. Women in every country, large or small, are concerned with bringing about change for women workers. This concern was expressed in the Platform for Action, the document produced by the international conference and signed by almost all the world's nations, thereby binding themselves to implementation. The Platform for Action defines the critical areas of concern and proposes strategic objectives and actions to be taken with regard, for example, to domestic violence, sexual harassment, conditions of wages and work, job segregation and training, and the care of children. There is to be a progress report to the United Nations in the year 2000.[26]

DEEP CHANGES

This round-the-world study of working mothers affected me deeply in unexpected ways. I decided to focus my hitherto varied experience on the problems of working women. I wanted to devote myself, for whatever time was left to me, to writing about their problems and to working to achieve remedies for them. I had previously thought of my life as made up always of interesting choices and events that often happened to center on women, even when women were not my central theme. Now I saw my life as directed to a single cause. I resolved to express my activism as widely as I could push it, certainly maintaining its international themes, searching for remedies among early experiments in various situations. My activism would perforce be expressed locally, wherever I might be—on my own campus, in Ithaca, where I planned to go on living. It would be expressed through many quite different organizations, for I believed firmly in group action, directed toward my newly acknowledged and verbalized feminist goals.

13

WINNOWING, HARVESTING, RESEEDING: 1974–1979

My first task on my return to Ithaca was to produce an overall report for the Ford Foundation. I looked about for a secretary-assistant who could put my thousand pages of notes in order, and feed them to me as I wrote.[1] I was lucky to find the right person in Mary McGinnis, who began a file I have continually added to over the more than twenty-four intervening years. I worked in the upstairs apartment of my house, since neither assistance nor space for emeriti was available at the school at that time.

During my time as ombudsman, when I had withdrawn from all campus organizations, and my later total absence from the university, Judy Long-Laws had joined the faculty of the Sociology Department and had drawn about her an informal group concerned with women's questions. I heard about this group late in 1971 and had asked to join it, if that were possible, although I was spending much of my time on my research in New York City on large local unions in the public sector.

What Judy had in mind was the reestablishment of a Cornell University Women's Studies Center. Dean Kahn of the Arts College, she had learned, would welcome it. I attended the college faculty meeting where the establishment of the Center was approved, and Jennie Farley became its first director, established in a small, three-room office on the fourth floor of Mann Hall. We formed a board that began work with a small appropriation from Dean Kahn's budget. Board members might come from any of the university's colleges; they needed to be offering courses about women. As I took off for Europe that summer, the Center was in business. We celebrated our twentieth anniversary in 1993.

WRITING THE FORD FOUNDATION REPORT

As I began writing, I was full to overflowing with my new insights and my wealth of information. In the fall of 1974 I announced a course in the comparative study of women and work, which attracted ten or so students through an announcement in the recently created Women's Studies Program.[2] I repeated it the following year. It served to show me where the United States stood in regard to what was going on elsewhere in the industrialized world, and thus helped me to rank women's issues in this country in the order of their importance.

As I began to deal with remedies, I advocated "A Maternal Bill of Rights," drawing on the GI Bill of Rights for certain suggestions. The GI Bill had allowed millions of men and a few women, who had served in the armed forces in the very years during which they would normally have been engaged in training or advanced education, to achieve that education. This had produced great benefits not only to them but also to the economy. In the fifties many of my male students were there on the GI Bill; they were among the most highly motivated students I had taught.

My Maternal Bill of Rights would award similar grants to mothers who had interrupted their careers to bear and raise their children through the preschool years. These grants would similarly open up advanced education and vocational training to working women, so that their loss of years of experience in the labor market would not result in a permanent handicap to promotion and age-equal earnings. In advocating such a plan, I argued that,

> A detail in planning would permit women to carry on some of this training part time while they were still mainly occupied with child care and thus to cut short somewhat the time needed for full-time training at re-entry. It could be linked to the unemployment insurance system in such a way that it covered work experience before the "interruption" and thus could be carried forward to ensure support during training that had received the approval of the labor market specialists.[3]

Within a year after the publication of *The Working Mother,* the book that resulted from my report to the Ford Foundation, the ILR Press asked me for any revisions I wished to make. Mary Cullen was now my assistant, and I put her to work revising tables while I expanded some of the ideas I was pursuing in my class, my reading, and my increasing discussion with groups outside Cornell on the many aspects of this subject.

DISSEMINATION

I began to receive requests for conference papers, contributions to edited books, and testifying before state legislative committees.[4] I saw all these requests as evidence of interest in and growing concern with the topic of working mothers, with which I had now become identified. Responding to them, on the other hand, postponed my working on any other monograph-length reports. I read widely, however, as the problems of working mothers were attracting the attention of an increasing number of scholars.

As conferences began to address these issues, I decided to attend them if possible and to offer to write papers for sessions announced in what I considered my field. Often I was the only representative of labor relations on issues of equal treatment for women in the labor market. Perhaps the first such meeting was in 1974 in Toronto, called by a group of Canadian scholars, including Janet Salaff, whom I had met in Hong Kong a year before. I found there an international meeting that included women from third world countries as well as the industrialized countries, to which my study had largely been limited. It was there that I first met Arlene Daniels, with whom I later did a great deal of work when she coedited two books for which I was mainly responsible.

In the summer of 1975 two meetings offered me the possibility of travel: one was the Groves Society meeting in Yugoslavia; the other was what became the first of a significant series of United Nations–sponsored meetings on the legal status of women throughout the world.[5] I did not foresee that Mexico City would be the first of an ongoing series. I had long wanted to visit Yugoslavia and indeed had a personal invitation from a woman scholar there, given when she visited Cornell. To me Yugoslavia represented a distinctly different kind of Communism than the Communism with which I had become acquainted on the Ford trip. I chose to go to Yugoslavia partly because I had been invited to organize a panel whose papers would perhaps be publishable and partly because several Cornell friends were going, including the Feldmans. Harold Feldman was in the Department of Family Life and Child Development in the college still called Home Economics; his wife was a psychologist at neighboring Ithaca College. Harold had early joined the group of women who set up the original Women's Studies Project; he had taught the first course in Women's Studies at Cornell and was a member of its executive board until he died. Before I left for Yugoslavia, I consulted several people who had worked there. I also lined up a woman interpreter and made an arrangement whereby I could receive trade union sponsorship, for a study there either before or after the Groves meeting.

YUGOSLAVIA

All this advance work came to naught. The interpreter had recently learned that she had cancer and was unable to work for me. The government had attacked the national sociological association, particularly its journal, *Praxis,* so that the meeting that ensued in Dubrovnik was under a cloud, the nature of which the local sponsors were unable or unwilling to discuss with us foreigners. At one point I was more or less stranded in Bucharest, although one woman there received me kindly and introduced me to several professional men and women living in the massive new suburbs built as cities for as many as two hundred thousand people. I was entertained in several homes and able through those contacts to get a picture of the self-management employer-employee committees that presumably managed every factory, office, and agency. I was told that my acquaintance in Sarajevo did not know what to do with me if I came there, and that she would meet me later at Dubrovnik. I acquired something of a picture of the organization of work in Yugoslavia, and I received the strong impression that the many different ethnic groups in the country were living in friendly and cooperative fashion under Tito.

I had an interesting experience with the medical system there when I had a problem with heart palpitations and asked the hotel clerk to get me a doctor. Two visited me, but we could hardly communicate. Neither spoke English, and they professed not to speak German. The desk clerk, who spoke fair English, helped out with translation. They prescribed a medication, which the clerk procured for me, and told me to rest in bed. On the second day, only one doctor came, who did after all speak some German, which he had learned in school when the Germans occupied the country during the war. He made it clear, however, that nominally no one in Yugoslavia would now speak German in protest against the German occupation, from which the Russians had liberated them.

A few days later I decided to use the time until the beginning of the conference to take a trip along the coast to Split, and from there to Dubrovnik. The days in Split were a revelation of the legacy left behind by the Roman Empire during its capture of the city. Split also had a two-thousand-year-old collection of Egyptian sculptures. I attended an open-air performance of *Aida*, where I could see, outlined against the evening sky, one of these magnificent ancient displays for which the city is known.

In Dubrovnik, at the hotel to which I was assigned, I found a man openly reading *Praxis* on the veranda, despite the official ban on the paper. I enjoyed visits to the ancient walled city itself, which really glowed in the nightly illumination of its marble-paved streets. One morning I walked the top of the wall with a newfound friend, where I browsed in boutiques and shops and bought a few mementos.

Adi Tröscher joined me in Dubrovnik as the conference ended. We rented a car to visit neighboring mainland towns, including Mostar, which we had been urged to visit because it contained a Muslim community. As I write, all these names have brought up old memories, for the recent war in Bosnia has pounded most of these cities to rubble.

A New Research Project In Europe

In the summer of 1975 Val Lorwin returned to Cornell to teach European history during summer school. We were having dinner at the Aronsons one night when the discussion turned to the subject of women in trade unions and how their interests were represented. Before we parted that evening, Val and I had decided we would seek funds to do a comparative study of trade union women in at least four European countries. I was hopeful we could get support from the recently established German Marshall Fund.[6] Here, at last, was the possibility of detailed research on one of my topics.

The U.S. State Department, named as the recipient of the fund, had established it as a private institution with a former American consul in Hamburg as its director. He had come to Cornell the previous year to talk with me about setting up a division of the fund that would support comparative studies of women in selected European countries and the United States. Val and I prepared a proposal to fund travel for us and an assistant in Europe as we studied unions and their women members in four countries. Our assistant was a new doctoral student at the University of Oregon, Roberta Till-Retz, who was working with Val as her adviser on a historical study of Austrian women. We decided Val would go to England, where he still had close ties from his days with the Office of Strategic Services (OSS) during the war; I would work primarily in Sweden and Germany; and Roberta would first assist Val in England and then work in Austria, under my supervision.

We received the grant and set up its administration under Jennie Farley in the newly established Women's Studies Center at Cornell. Early in 1976, we decided to visit all four countries for a short period to meet our main contacts and make further plans. We would select three or four unions in each country for intensive study.

PRELIMINARY TRIPS

We went first to Sweden, where we decided to work mainly with four unions: the Metal Workers, the largest and most influential union in the LandsOrganisationen (LO), the Labor Federation; the Food Workers (also an LO affiliate) whose headquarters were, rather exceptionally, not in Stockholm but in Malmo; and with one or more white-collar unions in the Tjanstemhannens Central Organisation (TCO), the White-Collar Workers Federation.

Since my previous visit to Sweden, the Metal Workers had invited Berit Rollen, later director of the Labor Market Board, to do a first study of women in their union. She had recommended the establishment of a Women's Division within the union, and a director had been appointed, a development that greatly aided our later research, as well as establishing a concern with the female minority of union members in this important organization.

The Food Workers had a much higher proportion of women among their membership, though most of them were in the lower grades of employment. Their affiliation with LO suggested strong political ties with the Socialist Party, as was the case with the Metal Workers.

White-collar workers in public and private employment were in separate unions, both affiliated, with TCO, but many more women were members in the public employees union than in the private sector. In all these unions, men predominated in the leadership. LO and its affiliates were still committed, as they had been since 1972, to family-oriented policies rather than the simply women-oriented policies of earlier years, and had set up implementing committees composed of both men and women.

We moved then to England and met the woman in the Trade Union Congress (TUC) who headed its Women's Division.[7] Women were originally organized in their own Women's Trade Union League (WTUL), which only became part of the TUC in the early 1920s when the latter body agreed to reserve two seats on its executive board for women.[8] Nevertheless, the "female labor question" had agitated many unions of men as early as the 1840s. The result was the adoption of a considerable number of protective laws, which still remained—including barring women from night work. The Factory Bill of 1844, for example, limited the number of hours for women workers in the textile industry to twelve per day. Later hours of work in other industries were specified, and employers in certain chemical industries were prohibited from employing women until four weeks after childbirth. Male union workers supported this legislation, particularly when it banned women from working in certain industries such as mining or other underground work. By the time we arrived, women had begun to protest about this type of legislation, which clearly had closed job opportunities to them.

Very new legislation in England included the Equal Pay Act of 1970, enacted under the Conservative government; in 1975, as Labour returned to power, the enactment of the Sex Discrimination Act indicated broad support for labor market equality.[9] As Val started his research there, the Equal Pay Act had just come into full effect (employers had been allowed a five-year period in which to make adjustments). The Act's implementation was assigned to a uniquely established Equal Opportunities Commission, and it was not clear whether trade unions supported it more as a safeguard for the position of their male members or to gain parity for women. In selecting unions for study, our attention was directed to the National Union for Public Employees (NUPE) because a majority of its members were women and its recently installed progressive leadership had instituted a program for drawing women into active participation. We decided that Roberta should spend considerable time with NUPE. Val would concentrate on a general union,[10] a craft union, and a white-collar union in the private sector, as well as attending the annual trade union conference, in a year when it was chaired by a woman.

We arrived in Germany to find that Maria Weber had retired as first vice president of the Federation of German Trade Unions (DGB) and had been succeeded as director of the Women's Division by her assistant, Irmgard Blaettel. I decided to direct my attention to the Metal Workers Union, the world's largest union, where women constituted about 15 percent of the membership. Despite this small proportion, it appeared that women were often leaders in introducing program reform. By contrast, several other unions contained a strong majority of women members, although men dominated their staffs and elected officers: among these were the Textile Union, the private white-collar unions, especially in banks and insurance companies, and the Food Workers, who were in the process of introducing a wage reform in their bargaining. In addition, I decided that I would look at the unaffiliated white-collar union.

Under the direction of the Socialist minister of labor, a study had been developed by two compensation specialists, Walter Rohmert and Josef Rutenfranz, using job analysis to achieve equal pay for work of equal value (the "Ru-Ro" Report).[11] I saw this study as a model for establishing the newly adopted ILO policy number 100, defining equal pay as compensation for work of equal value with that of men doing comparable but not necessarily the same work. In addition, in the late 1960s West Germany had adopted a series of legal reforms on family, pensions, maternity leave, and child care that provided a new basis for much of its social policy. My central question once I got to Germany would be: to what extent had these changes been reflected in union policy and program?

In Austria Maria Metzger was the head of the Women's Division of the Federation of Unions, as she had been during my 1973 study there. The White-Collar Union was clearly most progressive in terms of women's influence on leadership. The Textile Workers were endeavoring to train more women in leadership skills by providing training through local weekend programs, rather than in two weeks or more of residential classes away from home. Edith Krebs was still the head of the Women's Division in the Chamber of Labor (AK) and the initiator of social legislation in collaboration with Metzger in the unions. Austria continued to use German social legislation as a model, and unions operated in each plant under a Works Council law that required the election of representatives from among both blue- and white-collar workers. In Austria, as in Germany, the degree to which the unions were able to control Council leadership varied. In both countries, however, the Council administered the union contract at the workplace. And in both countries women elected to the Council tended to be assigned to household matters such as the cafeteria and to the implementation of women's benefits under the existing protective laws. The Austrian unions strongly endorsed these laws and to some degree saw equality legislation as a threat to them.

ADVISORY COMMITTEES

Once we were located in our separate countries, we realized that we needed to bring together from time to time representatives of these differing countries and their unions, as advisers to us. By late 1976 it was possible to have a first meeting of such people, together with a few academics. We met at Bad Homburg, outside Frankfurt, where a German foundation made meeting rooms available to us.

The object of this meeting was to acquaint our advisers with the programs we were reviewing and to receive their criticisms of our evaluation of those programs. We wanted to call attention to programs that seemed to us to be moving in the direction of genuine equality for parents as partners in the home as well as in the workplace. Thus we discussed Swedish social policy on dual-career families, German studies of comparable worth, reserved seats for women in British union executive bodies, and Austrian location of women's educational programs close to their homes. We held two such meetings during the two years we worked on this project. We also set up a similar committee in Washington with the help of a group there that had met regularly under the auspices of the Women's Bureau. We enlarged this group with Labor Department staff, some members of nearby Women's State Advisory Committees, and a few academics. Our hope was that, by reporting on structural and programmatic reforms from the unions of these four countries, we would interest American trade union women in taking up comparable issues.

REPORT IN TWO VOLUMES

We decided that we would write two books. Val would be responsible for the book that would compare union programs in the four countries to the status of trade union women in the United States and both implicitly and explicitly note social programs that might be adapted to conditions here. The other book, which would deal with issues of significance for working women, would be my responsibility. As we worked on these projects, I went twice to Eugene, where Val taught in the history department of the University of Oregon and where he arranged that I should work with Joan Acker in the Sociology Department. Joan shortly became deeply involved in the adoption of a law on comparable worth for employees of the state of Oregon; by accompanying her to meetings of the commission on this subject, I learned a great deal about the political process of adopting such a law, as well as of the internal political process within the unions that supported it in whole or in part.

My connection with other departments and administrative programs at Oregon flourished as well. I renewed acquaintance with my old friend from Stuttgart, Ed Beal, who was now a professor in the Business School at Oregon. Another very helpful informant was the woman who headed the Office of Equal Employment Opportunity at the university. After my ombudsmanship, it was she who had directed my attention once again to problems of women's equality in academe.

The book on trade unions in specific countries was early expanded from our reports on the four countries we had studied into a publication called *Women and Trade Unions in Eleven Industrialized Countries* (Philadelphia: Temple University Press, 1984). Some of this expansion resulted from my attendance at an international conference at Uppsala in Sweden,[12] where I met women from all the Scandinavian countries, whose papers and personal conversations allowed me to see that in other Scandinavian countries legislation had surpassed even the Swedish accomplishments. Thus, we added Norway, Denmark, and Finland to those countries we had ourselves studied.

Then in 1976 Edna Ryan invited me to return to Australia as the keynote speaker at the first national conference of trade union women. There I came to know trade union women and to hear about their problems as they had evolved since my visit in 1973. I wanted very much to include Australia in my volume and recruited Bill Ford's wife to write a chapter. Once we decided to expand beyond our own investigations, Val added his special field of European labor history, the French-speaking countries, and arranged for Margaret Maruani to contribute a chapter on France.

A recent student of mine, Debbie King, had married an Irishman, lived in Ireland, and been active in the Irish labor movement, about which little had been written. We asked her to write the chapter on Ireland. Then, my long association with Japanese unions compelled me to include a chapter on Japan. I asked my old friend Tadashi Hanami from the Japan Institute of Labor, who was now a professor of labor law at Sophia University, to write it.

Finally, a chapter on Italy suggested itself when I was a Mellon Fellow at Wellesley's Center for Research on Women in 1979. I was working there on my contributions to our volume and used the neighborly opportunity to visit Harvard's Center on European Studies, where I met Bianca Beccali of the University of Milan. Bianca's section of her university was devoted to studies of working women and trade unions. We became not only colleagues but also close friends in a relationship that continues today and has resulted in more than one trip for her to Cornell and in my several trips to Italy to work on equality in the workplace with Italian women trade unionists. Bianca was also helpful in arranging for my *Working Mother* to be translated into Italian.

With twelve chapters in view, we also asked Barbara Wertheimer to write a chapter on women's experience in U.S. trade unions. Barbara had written a popular women's labor history of the United States,[13] was a founder with Joyce Miller of the Coalition of Labor Union Women (CLUW), and headed the Institute on Women and Work at ILR's New York Office.

We needed at this point to have a meeting of this whole group to lay out an acceptable outline as a guide to each writer, around the theme of the status and goal of women's equality in each country. Val succeeded in getting a grant from the Rockefeller Foundation to enable us to hold a meeting of all our participants at their center at Bellagio.

I am sure other editors have experienced exactly what we now faced—many delays in our contributors' submission of manuscripts. Indeed, our Australian contributor was offered a job she could not refuse to accept and simply dropped out of the project. Then, most tragic of all, Val became ill with cancer, so that publication of this book fell to me. He had introduced me to one of his long-standing friends, Arlene Daniels, whom I had first met and enjoyed at Toronto, and she became coeditor of the book with me. She, too, has remained a close friend and coworker from that time forward, introducing me to many of her wide circle of friends and suggesting my appearance at many conferences. She also invited me back to my own alma mater, Northwestern University, where she was professor of sociology and women's studies for many years, and set in motion the process that culminated in 1987 with Northwestern's award to me of an honorary Doctor of Science.

MY SEVENTY-FIFTH BIRTHDAY

In 1978, as my seventy-fifth birthday approached, Fran Herman decided to make an occasion of it and took over all plans, some of which in fact came as a surprise—but for the most part I knew a party was impending. I was asked for a list of friends and relatives who should be invited, and I knew that I would arrive at the Big Red Barn on campus in a 1934 Rolls-Royce—the oldest luxurious automobile available that evening—and granddaughter Anya was chosen to accompany me.

I recently found a letter Jennie Farley sent me, containing her careful notes on what transpired. Because they were recorded at the time, I have attached them as an appendix to this book since they convey the range of greeting and the spirit of the evening. I was overwhelmed and perhaps for the first time compelled to reminisce, in the sense of looking for a consistent thread or two to explain and make a whole of my variegated life.

MY CHINA VISIT

In early 1979 I accepted an invitation to join a group of professional and academic women traveling to China, where we would meet our counterparts in several cities. I was happy to be included and looked up my notebooks on China accumulated in the Hong Kong summer of 1973. I first met my sixteen cotravelers in May in Los Angeles and found them to include a judge and other women well into their careers in journalism, accounting, and medicine. There were also several academics, a member of a board of education in Texas, and two women in civil service positions in Washington. Our leader was a young woman from the China-U.S. Friendship Society. We were accompanied by two interpreters. Our route took us over Tokyo, where we were able to rest a day in an airport hotel and I could phone a few of my friends to say that I would stop to see them in Japan on my way home in three weeks.

We landed in Beijing, visited Shanghai and Guilin, and had the opportunity to see a collective farm, visit an editorial office of a newspaper, and meet with two newly appointed women judges.[14] We visited clinics and hospitals, including a mental hospital. We had an afternoon with the revolutionary Soong sister who had received her education in the United States at a Georgia university. She spoke with pleasure about the "fellow Georgian" who was now president of the United States. Madame Soong was established in a villa with a beautiful garden and had a caretaker, who more than once suggested that she needed rest, but to no avail. At some point I mentioned a former YWCA worker, Talitha Gerlach, about whom I had repeatedly heard a great deal in my Y days and knew to be a close friend of Madame Soong's. She immediately promised to arrange a meeting with Talitha, now a very old woman.

To a former YWCAer like me, Talitha's story was fascinating. She had been in the Y's Chinese service for years going back before the Revolution and had not returned to the States during all that time. The Y had at times been unable to pay her, and when it came to her retirement had kept the money due her against the time when she would return to the States. Her loyalty to China was predicated on the Revolution and the freedom it gave the Chinese from the feudal system that had preceded Mao. She complained that from the thirties onward she had had no support from the Y. In nearly every respect she had become a Chinese, and they in turn had treated her as one of their own. They cared for her in her old age, as one of their own loyal supporters. I was and am still disappointed that the organization that I respected and that had taught me a great deal, had, for whatever reason, neglected a lifetime employee in its foreign service.

In each of the four cities we visited, we were entertained by the academic and professional women in the local branch of the All-China Women's Organization at a delicious dinner and a meeting that followed. I felt that these discussions were quite open. In each city these women brought interpreters with them, so that personal contact with one's counterpart was possible

Among our hostesses we found a number of older women who had visited the United States many years earlier as part of their professional training. Several of them told us of the years they had spent later in distant provinces doing farm work or other manual labor as part of their "reeducation." Indeed, one of the interpreters who traveled with us had been a member of the Red Guard as a teenager; she had no hesitation about telling us of some of her experiences of tearing down old temples, or teaching elementary classes in schools where teachers had been taken away.

On our last evening we were in an erstwhile summer resort as a relief from the extreme heat of summer near Canton, to which we were to travel the next day. Our hostesses for the first time asked for someone from our group to talk about the women's movement in the United States. I was selected to do it but given only ten minutes, during which I had also to be translated. I had hardly started before the ten minutes were gone, so that they learned very little. However, I had been able to say that we were challenging the legal concept of equality as written into our law, and that because of the fairly rigid gender division of labor between men and women, we had found little help from the law on equal pay for equal work. I doubt that anyone in the group remembers that evening; my recollection rests entirely on my sense of frustration, which lasts to this day, with my inability to deal with my book-length subject in the very limited time allotted me.[15]

Two members of the group took long walks whenever there was free time and came back to report to us of life in the narrow alleys of the cities. The in-group tension showed itself in a variety of small ways. Subgroups formed and sought the better hotel rooms or the air-conditioned ones, refusing to rotate with others in less comfortable circumstances. On the whole, however, diverse as the group was, we had the opportunity to indulge our special paths of inquiry, to meet our counterparts, and to see a good deal of the country, both as tourists and as visitors with a variety of special interests. We climbed the Great Wall, traveled through the strangely beautiful country near the Vietnamese border, strolled in Tiananmen Square and had the news bulletins there translated for us, spent several hours in the Forbidden City, and ate delicious Chinese food. I came away with new friends with whom I remained in contact for many succeeding years.

INVITATION TO OREGON

Because of a generous grant, Arlene and I were jointly invited by the University of Oregon's Sociology Department to spend a semester there, where we shared an office and pursued our work on Book II. During this period we went to the university's archivist to see whether Val's papers contained materials for the book on trade union programs that I had been delayed in writing as contributors changed and manuscripts came in only slowly. We found only scraps of paragraphs, references to clippings, and the like. It was clear that, in spite of considerable nudging from the Marshall Fund for Book I, Val had for some time been unable to get much writing done beyond his part in the Swedish and British chapters.

THE WELLESLEY EXPERIENCE

By the time Book I was finally ready for publication, I had become acquainted with Ronnie Ratner (later Ronnie Steinberg) at Wellesley. Like other dynamic women I met in this period, she has continued to be a close friend and stimulating coworker. She phoned me in the late seventies for advice on planning an international conference at Wellesley in the early spring of 1978 on "Equal Opportunity and Equal Pay for Women." The Wellesley Center for Research on Women (CROW) had set up a committee a year or so earlier to plan such a conference. Ronnie now asked me to suggest people she might contact in a forthcoming European trip to identify participants, institutions, and areas of interest and activity there. This process is recounted in the introduction to the book recording the conference, *Equal Employment Policy for Women*.[16] I was deeply surprised and happy when I discovered that the book was dedicated to me. Since many of the people whom Ronnie and her planning committee selected for the program were old friends and acquaintances, I did have a sense of parenting this memorable meeting.

I contributed two papers to the conference[17] and participated in the discussions occurring in and out of the sessions. My interest in the equal pay discussion was heightened and took on a United States focus through Helen Remick's contribution from the state of Washington, where attention to this issue first began in 1972. Helen made it clear that job segregation by gender accounted for the weakness of the long-advocated and legally compelled institution of "equal pay for equal work." Gender-mixed staffs rarely existed in factories, offices, or service businesses, however—a situation equally true whether in public or private employment. Helen also made it clear that firms such as the one employed by the state of Washington were prepared to meet this problem by applying job evaluation techniques to differing jobs in order to ascertain whether they were of equal value to an employer and therefore deserved equal compensation. Now that the German "Ru-Ro" recommendations had disappeared into history without having been used, I found this U.S. experience extremely heartening. As matters turned out, I devoted much of my time in the next ten years to this issue.

The next year I was awarded a Mellon Fellowship for a semester at the Center for Research on Women at Wellesley, where I continued with my writing and participated in the luncheon seminars in which each of the Fellows gave a paper. I met a number of the Wellesley professors and, as I have earlier noted, visited seminars from time to time at Harvard's Center on European Studies. For the purposes of this autobiography, however, the most important circumstance turned out to be the casual fact that Florence Howe and I had adjoining offices and apartments and often talked in the evenings of our separate and similar interests. After one of these evenings, she urged me to think of writing an autobiography.

I could not take her suggestion very seriously, for I saw so much of my life—because of its many career shifts and the variety of my interests—over the many years as fortunate though separate sets of happenstance. But for Florence the idea of my autobiography became something of an idée fixe. As she wrote to me each year about the work of The Feminist Press, thanking me for support or announcing new publications, she often included a handwritten message that amounted to "How is it going with the autobiography?" I began slowly to think in her terms. My problem was, as it had been at the birthday party, finding the threads that held it all together. I thought a good deal about them, but over the next years I continued to be engulfed with the comparable worth issue, both as researcher and as advocate, and was also frequently called for committee service at Cornell. Writing an autobiography would take time, and time was what I never had, in the face of these other demanding interests.

COMPARABLE WORTH

My interest in comparable worth, moreover, became immediate when New York State decided to undertake a comparable worth study, which the Center for Women in Government (associated with SUNY/Albany) would carry out. Together with her assistant, Lois Haignere, Ronnie Steinberg designed the research procedure for the state study.[18] In conformity with all the other states, cities, counties, school districts, and public agencies involved in similar studies, Ronnie's study ascertained a gender shortfall in wages of working women in public service in New York.

In 1979 several important women's groups jointly sponsored a conference on comparable worth in Washington, which I attended. The U.S. Equal Employment Opportunity Commission cosponsored the meeting under the leadership of Eleanor Holmes Norton, its director, who was also the keynote speaker. She predicted that comparable worth would become the touchstone issue of equality in the 1980s. It was at that conference that I realized how broad the range of interest and action on this issue had already become. An important case in Colorado was before the federal court. A National Committee on Pay Equity (NCPE), which a few unions had sponsored, was in the early stages of organization. Several labor lawyers, notably Winn Newman, were prepared to take cases to the courts. Minnesota had set up a committee to implement a study already made by the popular Hay firm on compensation equity. I met Donald Treiman, who had already written a book on job evaluation that analyzed the Hay approach, and dealt with other companies doing work in the field. He was confident that anything like Germany's Ru-Ro Report would not apply in a country as varied in its labor markets as the United States. He also questioned whether it would have satisfactorily covered all situations in Germany.

I also became acquainted with Heidi Hartmann, who shortly founded the Institute for Women's Policy Research (IWPR). Heidi's Ph.D. thesis appeared as a book that provided the theoretical basis for much of the thinking on comparable worth in the early days of its application.[19] Since then, with colleagues at IWPR, she has published on many other issues affecting women's status in the labor force; testified many times before congressional committees; and organized a biennial conference in Washington on one or another of these issues, which has drawn together specialists in those fields for mutual information, criticism, and discussion. In 1994 she received a five-year grant from the MacArthur Foundation. This recognition resulted in articles in major newspapers evaluating her twenty-five years of work on behalf of the status of women in the United States. In recent years IWPR has provided several valuable services; one on which I especially depend is a set of reprints of colleagues' articles; another is reprints of clippings from three major newspapers on working women's status and problems.

HAWAII

Soon after my return from the Ford study, Eleanor Emerson and I had begun to talk about getting away from Ithaca during the worst of the winter weather. I wrote my brother Ted in Honolulu to inquire whether we could make an arrangement to come there—his wife had died suddenly in 1972, and while his daughter, Sue, had come to live with him, I knew she was a busy professor of physical education at the University of Hawaii. I suggested we might take over some of the housekeeping. The reply was a cordial invitation, and in 1977 we went to Hawaii for the first time.

My first Ph.D. student, John Ferguson, had been director for several years at the Industrial Relations Center of the University of Hawaii. Professor Roberts of the Business School, who had died in 1970, had founded the Center. John invited me to bring any work I might be engaged in with me to the Center, where he would provide a desk and any assistance I might want from his staff. Joel Seidman of the University of Chicago came out every year in the winter semester to teach a labor relations course at the Business School. I saw this as an ideal opportunity to work on the issues book (Book II) several hours a day.

Both Ted and Sue took us into their family circle and invited us to return the following year. By that time I had been invited to join John's staff in a piece of research they were doing on the addition of the federal equality issues to legislated state government regulations. Our task was to discover and report on the law's implementation in every state department and unit. In 1979 the State Personnel Department published our report, *Equal Employment Opportunity, Collective Bargaining and the Merit Principle in Hawaii*. This report was sent to every departmental and state agency director, as part of the preparation for a conference for these officers on this subject. Its wording was a reminder that the state's original merit system's criteria had already been modified when unions for state employees were legalized and that the system now took into account the further equal opportunity legislation. Speakers at that conference were the director of the Western states' EEOC office in San Francisco, the director of personnel in the state of Pennsylvania, and myself.[20]

LONGHOUSE

When Rose Goldsen returned to Ithaca from Latin America in the early seventies, she renewed her relationship with the religious center at the university, Cornell United Religious Work (CURW), located in Anabel Taylor Hall under the leadership of Jack Lewis, a Baptist minister. Anabel Taylor Hall was the gift of an alumnus in memory of his wife and filled a historic lack of institutional affiliation with a church group that so many major universities have had. As well as providing space for ministers of all religions, including Jews and Muslims, CURW housed different organizations, including the one that probably brought Rose there, CUSLAR, the Cornell Latin-American circle.

Among other activities, the Center for Religion, Ethics, and Social Policy (CRESP) provided a sheltering home and sponsorship for new community organizations that needed a place to meet. In the newsletter that carried information about such embryonic groups, Rose read of a group seeking members for a housing community that would offer, in addition to separate homes for families, many joint community activities. Rose went to a meeting, after which she phoned me to say, "Alice, this is something for you." I attended the next meeting and got to know Steve and Liz Brouwer and their toddler; Sally Wessels and Scott Heyman, who soon adopted their Nina; and Ann Pitkin, a recently divorced mother of two preschool boys. None of us had much money, but the idea was that we would form a cooperative, buy shares in it to the extent that we could, look for some acreage near Ithaca, acquire a mortgage on our land investment, and begin to build a few homes while we recruited others to the project. Sarah and Peter Hess, with their baby, Emily, soon joined. With the six of us we had occupants for two houses, each of which would include three apartments.

I was drawn to the plan because of my fruitful experience in two previous community living arrangements, Commonwealth and the Soviet House, but chiefly because both boys were now gone for good and were married and setting up their own families. The house on Turkey Hill Road was too big simply for Eleanor and me, and I had had enough of finding upstairs tenants for my apartment. I was not sure that Eleanor would want to move with me, or could even plan to do so, given her frail health, but I decided to join the group anyway. When the new house was ready for occupancy, I would rent it out until I could move into it.

Scott and Steve quickly found farmland, two miles above the west end of Ithaca's "Octopus" (a messy traffic pattern with eight legs), where we could buy nineteen acres for about fifteen thousand dollars. Construction began on "House One" in 1975, under Steve's direction, with the cooperative crew that he had organized as Sawtooth Builders. We had no architect, and Steve took over the design of each dwelling in consultation with its future inhabitants. Everybody wanted as inexpensive a shelter as possible, and everyone except Rose and me wanted to finish the interior themselves as they gathered together the money and the time to do it. A good many mistakes were made. Steve built his own house without any closets, for example. Each apartment turned out to be very different, designed to its future owner's wishes. We would all heat with wood stoves, since we were beyond the end of the oil pipeline, and in any case, oil at this point was very scarce and very expensive. We used propane gas for our stoves and water heaters. Some of us had supplementary electric baseboard heat, which we quickly found hideously expensive. I thought Rose's one-story house with one bedroom, living room, and kitchen with an uncovered platform off her study at the end of her living room, quite ideal. I decided to use it as the basis for mine, which would also be one story high, between two-story houses on each side with common walls separating us.

Then, one day, as the main posts for my living room were up and I saw the view I would have from my living room windows—much wider and deeper than Rose's since my house was essentially a second story over the one basement in the project—I realized I wanted this house as soon as I could get it—no renters, no empty house. I went home to Eleanor to ask her whether she felt well enough to move. Her answer, which made me ecstatic, was, "I've been waiting for you to ask me." This answer, however, involved some quick replanning before the rapidly growing structure was beyond revision.

I returned the same day to talk to Steve. The result was a half second floor over the front of the house with a large bedroom, a bath and, mirabile dictu, a big walk-in closet. To give the room a crosscurrent of air, however, we had to build a gallery to the south, with a stairway leading to it from the downstairs living room. The gallery contained a pull-out sofa that could become a single bed, a chair and table, and a small bookcase. It could be my study or a child's guest room. Over the stairway was a platform that allowed grandchildren, of whom there were now three girls, to bring their sleeping bags for the night. I had increased my space to include guests, though with a squeeze, but certainly its main quarters were large enough to contain Eleanor and me, each with our own bedroom and bath. We also had a long view, a lordly stairway, and a fine open space leading to a summer-useful platform porch, in front of which a young oak tree was beginning to throw a branch or two of shade. It is still the loveliest house in the community.

Within a year or so, a third house of three apartments was built and occupied and a fourth planned. But at that point people who wanted to come were prevented by high mortgage rates, as interest rose to 18 percent or more. In the end, Bill Norman built a single house—mostly with his youngest daughter in a bag on his back—so designed that other houses might be added on either side of it. These have never materialized. After twenty years we have nine units, since two in "House Three" have been combined into a single apartment.

There have been many changes—indeed only Sally, Ann, and I remain as "founders." Now, as I am planning to leave for my last home at Kendal at Ithaca, there is no lack of would-be buyers of my house. If it takes a certain kind of person to seek community living in some one of its many forms, Ithaca supplies them.

ELEANOR'S DEATH

Eleanor's health continued to decline. Her hands were often icy and visibly blue in color. She had once wakened me in the middle of the night when she could hardly move, even in bed. Her abdominal muscles were stiff and her extremities blue. When the ambulance delivered her to the emergency room, the nurses themselves were shocked at her condition. She recovered from several hospital stays, but ate less and often nodded and slept during the day. She gave up driving and employed an elderly man to be her driver for shopping, the hairdresser, church, and visits to her doctor. We continued to assume somehow, more based on hope than reality, that we would travel to Hawaii again in the winter of 1979–1980. She enjoyed Thanksgiving dinner that year, which we shared with friends, and wrote her sisters in Buffalo that she had enjoyed it more than many recent meals. But then a few days later she was again in the hospital.

I was completely puzzled as to what to do about air reservations and arrangements with Sue and Ted about our usual visit to Hawaii, so I sought advice from her doctor, who said quietly, "Her end is very near; she has refused her medicine for several days. She will not live to go anywhere on this earth." I notified her sisters, and they planned to come as soon as they could to make arrangements. Fran and I visited her each evening at the hospital. In a day or two, we felt she was very weak. Fran tried to arrange for a nurse to be with her during the night, but the hospital desk had other instructions, presumably from the doctor, who was available at any hour. I brushed her hair and rubbed lotion into her dry, cold skin. We left reluctantly when the visitors' bell rang. I was not surprised when in the early morning I had a call from the hospital that Eleanor had died in the night. Her sisters were on the way to Ithaca but did not arrive for several hours. I arranged immediate steps with the funeral director, got her belongings from the hospital, met Mary Louise and Marjorie on their arrival, and conveyed the sad news. We revisited the funeral director to arrange for cremation, talked with her church pastor about a funeral, and found help in talking out our grief with each other. My relationship with these women, which had always been friendly, became much closer from this moment onward.

A few weeks later I returned to Hawaii and have been going every year since. I still suffer from a recurring sense of guilt in that I fear Eleanor may have chosen to die when she did in order not to interfere with my return to Hawaii. She loved the weeks there and enjoyed the relatively good health that its warmth and color gave her. At the same time I am sure she could not again have endured the long trip in crowded planes.

I made many friends in Hawaii during those years, among the women in the unions, the nurses' association, the government, and the university, and have come to look upon the state as a second home. As will become clear in the next chapter, I concentrated there during the eighties on the issue of comparable worth.

14

THE DECADE OF COMPARABLE WORTH: 1980–1989

WHAT IT WAS ALL ABOUT

The eighties was a very busy decade, centered for the most part on my engulfing interest on comparable worth. But Book I—on women in trade unions—hung over a good part of it, until Cornell University Press finally published it in 1992, ironically, at a price too high for the trade union women to whom it was primarily addressed. Its reviews were few and slow in appearing. Although they were on the whole highly favorable, the Press decided against a second edition. The book was, however, available for a time in the remainder of the paperback printing.[1]

By the middle of the eighties I was consumed with work on comparable worth and its spread throughout states and local governments. I did much of my writing on this subject at and for the Industrial Relations Center (IRC) at the University of Hawaii, where I participated in an advocacy group of women's organizations established by Hawaii's Commission on the Status of Women to lobby for state legislation. By the end of the decade my task had become keeping track of comparable worth's rise throughout the country. When the movement accelerated so rapidly that the follow-up required in telephone calls, letters, and visits became overwhelming, I decided to turn my records over to the National Committee on Pay Equity.

A third major enterprise in this decade took place at Cornell. There, Jennie Farley had set up a support committee for a group of women who were challenging the university in court on two issues: one was their rejection for promotion to tenure and the other was the matter of equal pay with men at their rank and qualifications. I was asked to cochair this support group with historian Mary Beth Norton.

I continued to travel to conferences abroad and at home, meeting old friends and making new ones. Fran Herman often accompanied me, and we tried to combine these trips abroad with sightseeing in countries we had long wanted to visit. All of these conferences, together with several meetings in the United States, called for papers. A celebration honoring the career of Jack Barbash at the University of Wisconsin took me back to my labor education career. My paper reflecting some of my questions about new developments in that field was entitled: "Labor Education in the U.S.: Marriage of Convenience?" In it I expressed what I saw as a trend of permitting both teaching and research to follow the changing, and often superficial, concerns of donors. For example, unions were now offering credit cards and group travel as incentives to join.[2]

During these years Fran and I revisited Israel, vacationed in Spain, and went to a conference in Portugal, organized under NATO auspices by a woman who knew little about any of the women's movements in any country. She had, however, assembled an interesting and representative group of women leaders from the NATO countries, together with a few male scholars from quite conservative research centers. This mixture resulted in several sessions where the conflict between the two types of views was both amusing and at times maddening. A male member of a Munich research center who was very pro-family—in the sense that women should marry to have many children and not leave the home for paid work—protested that a childless woman on the program had no right to present a contrary view since she had no children herself. She drew the applause of the group when she replied, "If we are to discuss these issues on those terms, I shall have to ask our chair not to recognize you!"

At this meeting I gave a paper that caught the attention of a British woman who was just launching a new journal, *Equal Opportunities International*. She asked me for a paper for an early issue of the journal. Since our host's promise to publish conference papers never materialized, I sent her a version of *The Most Difficult Revolution: Women and Trade Unions* for her second issue.

On intermittent trips to ILO headquarters in Geneva, I talked with people at the Institute for Labor Studies about women's role in unions. As a result I was asked to do an article for their journal *Women and Industrial Relations*. It appeared under the title of "The Representation of Women and Their Interests in Industrial Relations Institutions: Women in Trade Unions."

On two occasions Hiroko Hayashi asked me to prepare amicus briefs for her submission to Japanese courts hearing cases in which she was participating. Both were designed to provide the Japanese judges with information on what was going on in other industrialized countries on (1) the issue of gender equality in aging and (2) on the equal rights of male and female workers to child allowances as part of their wages. Both were based on information gathered in the course of international research, and were designed to instruct the Japanese judges on what other industrialized countries provided to protect older workers in the first case, and to single female parents in the second case.[3]

I turn now to discuss more fully my major fields of interest during the eighties, and the contributions I tried to make to them.

Hawaii and Comparable Worth

Among the many Hawaii state organizations that I had come to know more or less closely, as I did the study for the State Personnel Office, was the Commission on the Status of Women. It had been established in the late sixties or early seventies at the instigation of the U.S. Women's Bureau and the National Commission on the Status of Women, both under the leadership of Esther Peterson, my old friend from Bryn Mawr Summer School days. In Hawaii, this Commission was made up of women from each of the five main islands and included women in politics, the unions, and various women's voluntary groups.

As I pursued the issue of comparable worth in Hawaii, I met the director of the Commission and was invited to attend its meetings, as well as its committee on comparable worth. Members whom I came to know particularly included Rochelle Gregson, then a staff member of Local 5, Hotel Employees and Restaurant Employees (HERE), and Nancy McGuckin-Smith, in charge of collective bargaining for the Hawaii Nurses Association. Mike Miller of the staff of the state employees organization (HGEA-AFSCME) also attended many of these sessions.[4] By 1981 both houses of the Hawaii legislature had adopted resolutions requesting all employers to recognize the concept of equal pay for work of comparable value in public employment.

In Resolution 208 the following year, the House requested the Industrial Relations Center at the University of Hawaii, where I had by now worked each winter for four or five years, to undertake a review of preparation for or actual adoption of this issue in other states, including in both the private and public sectors. The Center thus asked me to undertake this survey of other states' activities to help with their own statewide study. Consequently, I spent that summer in the Northeast, visiting eight states (Connecticut, Maine, Maryland, Massachusetts, Michigan, New Jersey, New York, and Pennsylvania), in all of which I had information from friends and correspondents that some positive action was underway. At the same time I began a correspondence with persons in nine other states in an attempt to get information from them. The result was a report to the Hawaii Legislature, the IRC, and the Commission on the Status of Women.[5]

Year by year the work in Hawaii continued. Bills were introduced in both houses of the 1983 legislature calling on the Hawaii Conference of Personnel Directors, the Board of Regents of the State University, the statewide Department of Education (DOE), and the judiciary department to reevaluate job classification and wages, establish standards, revise compensation rates, and establish a schedule of implementation for civil service, university, DOE, and judiciary employees. Both bills died in committee. For the first time, the steady push for comparable worth at least in public employment came to a standstill.

But in 1984 a senate bill (SB 2119-84), called for the establishment of

> a temporary commission on comparable worth to conduct a review and study of existing classification and compensation systems in state and local government in Hawaii, determine the extent of job segregation and wage differentials, recommending a job evaluation system or alternate means of achieving comparable worth, examine the compatibility of the recommended job evaluation system with existing civil service compensation and collective bargaining laws, and make an interim report prior to the 1985 session with a final report to the regular 1986 session of the legislation.

This bill passed both houses and was signed by the governor. The legislative auditor was appointed chair of the Commission, which was then made up of the head of state personnel, each county's head of civil service, representatives of the DOE and the university, the chair of the Public Employees Compensation Appeals Board, the administrative director of the courts, the state affirmative action director, the director of the IRC, and the representatives of each of the unions dealing with the state and counties. In 1986 the Commission issued a report that said it had been impossible to carry out its task because the attorney general had advised the Personnel Office not to release any information, so long as an HGEA suit against the state was before the courts.

To get things going the backers of this concept in the senate wanted to set up a task force in charge of a job evaluation study and to authorize an appropriation of $150,000 to pay for an outside consultant. In the Ways and Means Committee the state agreed to accept the bill if HGEA would withdraw its suit against the state, and to this the union agreed. When the bill finally reached both houses, the $150,000 was officially sanctioned with the proviso that a nationally prominent individual would conduct the study. The bill passed, and the governor signed it. The ensuing study found women earning 93.7 percent as much as men, although wider differentials existed in several bargaining units, notably in HGEA's white-collar and professional units.[6]

The Hawaii experience is unique in that its total achievement was limited to one unit of HGEA, but many states suffered severe limits to the bills or collective agreements that finally empowered their programs.[7] On the other hand, Minnesota's eventual solution of the issue must be deemed a success. The state adopted comparable worth in all government employment by extension in the mid-eighties to include every local government in the state, a total of about sixteen hundred, including school boards and local independent agencies such as water authorities, cities, counties, towns, and villages.[8]

I saw the need for a tabulation of what was going on across the country in all its variety of legislation and collective bargaining, of coverage of public and private employment, and of large and small institutions and firms. In 1985 the IRC Press at the University of Hawaii brought out *Comparable Worth: A Case Book of Experiences in States and Localities,* recording my work up to that date. But in the following year the updated *Comparable Worth: A Case Book* (1986 Supplement) was even thicker than its predecessor. With these two publications, it became clear to me that the job of recording all the activity on this issue in the country, without assistance in staff and money, was too much for one person to carry on further. I began discussions with Claudia Wright, then the head of the National Committee on Pay Equity, with the result that somewhat later I turned over all my files on the subject to that committee. I then ceased to try to keep track of developments in the whole field—although as major changes are reported in the daily press, I still add these clippings to my ever-growing files.

The Cornell Eleven

When I returned to Ithaca in the spring of 1981, Jennie Farley told me about a support group she had organized on behalf of five women whose names were attached to a legal complaint against Cornell University charging sex discrimination in matters of promotion and salary. They badly needed help in raising money, procuring one or more attorneys, and the preparation of their cases. The five complainants included four professors, one in sociology, one in anthropology, one a photographer in fine arts, and one in Russian literature, while the fifth was in Extension in the College of Human Ecology.

Jennie told me that many more women had filed complaints on these issues, of whom eleven (hence the name of the group, "The Cornell Eleven") had talked with her over the years when she was head of Women's Studies. She saw the need for a support committee, particularly for the women who were willing to have their names used and who were ready to appear in court against the university. A group had formed, with Mary Beth Norton, a professor in the History Department, as temporary chair. Would I be cochair with Mary Beth? I wanted first to meet the group and to talk with Mary Beth. I found they were meeting every Saturday morning and had been doing so for several weeks. My meeting in that April was the first of more than a hundred that followed, in which I came to know Jennie intimately. In addition to the many skills she had used for Women's Studies, she showed herself in this endeavor as an indefatigable and talented organizer. Several women who joined us in the claim that eventually reached the federal court had exhausted the grievance procedure then available at Cornell and had gone elsewhere to look for work.

We quickly saw that the gifts of money that women professors could afford in support of this case would never add up to the amounts we needed to pay court expenses and finance an attorney. We sent out appeals in many directions. Jennie, who was president that year of the local chapter of the American Association of University Women (AAUW), proposed that that group lend its assistance both monetarily and in supplying volunteers to our support group. This request resulted in the national AAUW setting up its defense fund for academic women bringing cases against their universities. Over the years that passed till our case was settled, the AAUW made several contributions critical to our pursuit of the case to a conclusion.

When we were at last docketed in the federal court in Syracuse, the judge agreed with our attorney's request to make this a class action case. He also divided it into two parts, promotion to tenure and unequal pay, and then proceeded to hear the promotion argument. On this issue the judge decided against all five named complainants, and for the university.

However, when the unequal pay case was docketed, the university immediately wanted to negotiate the amount to be paid to the complainants and asked us to appoint a negotiator. When the university's offer reached $250,000, our representative felt he had done his best and urged our committee to accept that amount. We realized we had reached something like our limit in money raising—altogether we had received about $110,000 over several years. Our attorney could not wait longer for reimbursement, and the complainants had long since exhausted their claims to unemployment insurance and had had to find other work. Among the five who were named in the case, one had found employment at Syracuse University (where she later became tenured), and the Russian scholar received and accepted repeated requests of the Russian literary academy to present papers on nineteenth-century Russian writers. The three remaining women had left the academy: one became self-employed, producing calendars; one took a management job with the student paper; and one moved with her husband to another university, adopted two children, and devoted herself to her family.

We had then to consider all the other women on campus who had complained against the university, of whom there were almost fifty, and to figure out how to divide the money among them. The named complainants received what at the time was somewhat less than a year's income, and the others, small sums for which they had all waited several years. We had, however, gained a procedure, even if it has favorably supported only a few complainants.

Although we lost in court, the university administration decided that an internal appeals system within the university was needed. It is a step procedure of peer judgment, aimed to precede and even circumvent the delays and expense of court action, though of course still allowing for it, should its result be negative. I am not aware that any complainant, once embarked on the procedure, has challenged its finding. And no wonder. A negative vote at any step would certainly influence a court. I do not believe, on the other hand, that any provost has rejected a third-step recommendation.

The university's system requires complainants of errors in the promotion process first to go through its three-step procedure: in case of rejection for promotion to tenure, the complainant must ask for the establishment of a committee within the university made up of four persons nominated by the complainant and the dean of the college. The two parties can then cancel out two of their opponent's nominees, and the remaining four then select a chair. This committee's judgment is returned to the department head. If it is favorable to the complainant, the department must vote again, either to accept or reject. If this recommendation is rejected, the complainant may ask for the establishment of an outside committee of three who recommend their finding to the provost. The provost has a limited time in which to accept or reject this finding, and his decision is final and binding. My information is that only two of the complainants who have used this procedure have been retained and promoted.

HEALTH PROBLEMS

In the spring of 1983 I was preparing to leave Hawaii with Joyce Najita, the director of the Industrial Relations Center, when I got a series of telephone calls about Philip. He had suffered a massive heart attack and was not yet out of danger. At the Easter season it was difficult to get a seat to the mainland on a plane. On the eleventh day after his attack, I finally departed for Albany, where I had a room in a motel where Philip's relatives and friends had gathered. Among them were my ex-husband, Wes, and his wife, Rita, as well as Philip's ex-wife, Marjorie, with her husband, Peter, and their baby, Sara, and of course, Debra, Philip's own daughter.

On one evening when only Wesley, Rita, and I were in the motel at dinnertime, I invited them to join me for dinner. In the course of our conversation, Rita turned to me and said, "Alice, you ought to be grateful that I took Wesley off your hands. You would never have had your brilliant career if you had stayed with him!" I was somewhat embarrassed by this remark, and am still not sure what lay behind it. I have often wondered since then, however, whether her observation did, after all, hold a kernel of truth.

Philip made rapid improvement, and before we left, he was out of the hospital under directions to lose weight, carefully observe a prescribed diet, and above all, change his employment so as to lessen the demands and stress upon him. The result was that he shortly moved back to Buffalo, took on a job with the city as its treasurer, and later accepted another political appointment as head of the Water Authority of Erie County, the area surrounding Buffalo—a job in which he became something of a specialist. Although he radically reduced his weight as long as he was recuperating from the heart attack and has done so once or twice since, as a kind of model to his men in the Authority, he loves to eat and eat well. But after each weight reduction, he has returned to the overweight state against which his cardiologist repeatedly warns him. His response has been to carry a heavy life insurance policy, payable to his wife.

Philip has in fact created a situation in which he holds two jobs: the one with the Water Authority, and the other a polling business of his own, which he set up and continues to run. His second wife, Hope, manages the office, while Philip recruits a great deal of the business, especially that outside the city of Buffalo. As well as conducting polling on campaign issues in various locations, they manage candidates' election campaigns. Hope has become something of a specialist in advising would-be judges, with the result that, at least within the office, most of the successful candidates are known as "Hope's judges."

I continued to suffer from time to time from heart fibrillation, and in the following year during a visit from my granddaughter Maia, I had a persistent attack. My method of treating such recurring episodes was, if possible, to go to bed, try to relax, and eventually to get back to normal. But on this Sunday afternoon, hour followed hour without improvement. I had planned to drive to Syracuse to put Maia on her plane for New Haven and realized I could not do it. I called the good Jennie Farley, who immediately agreed to take over that responsibility, and I went to the hospital emergency room for help.

Under that treatment, I was better within the hour, when the doctor told me he preferred I spend the night in the hospital where the staff could monitor me. When my own doctor arrived in the morning, he told me my heart had stopped for several seconds within the night and he had decided I should have a pacemaker. I would be prepared for an operation in case my cardiologist agreed with my doctor. He did, sitting in silence for some time after the examination while he decided what kind of pacemaker should be implanted.

The operation was under local anesthetic, and the surgeon instructed me to talk to him during the entire procedure. When I failed, he would rather peremptorily remind me to keep up the chatter. I could hear the cardiologist, who was following the procedure on a transmitted picture nearby, advising the surgeon where to place the wires from the pacemaker battery into my heart. When it was all over, the cardiologist told me the pacemaker might not need any change for as much as fourteen years, a time that is now rapidly approaching. He pointed out also that it was a demand pacemaker and would take charge of the heart, should it fail, but otherwise would perhaps not be in use at all. He provided me with a machine through which he could monitor the pacemaker monthly by telephone and arranged for me to have an annual personal examination. With that arrangement I have lived ever since. When I had to change cardiologists, as this man decided to leave Ithaca for a research appointment, the new man thought the telephonic machine need be used only every three months. This meant that I was able to go to Hawaii each year without it.

This episode was the first of a number of treatments that have made me what Fran Herman calls "the bionic woman." The next operation was in 1982 on my left knee, which had been deteriorating ever since a hiking accident at Lake O'Hara in 1972. An orthopedist had told me then, after he had done his best to remove damaged tissue, that this would at best relieve me of some pain for a period, but that eventually I would probably want to have a knee replacement. He was correct.

MY EIGHTIETH BIRTHDAY

Jennie and Fran decided on a celebration of my eightieth birthday in the fall of 1983. Fran gave a party for family, friends, and colleagues at her house on a Friday evening. Of the many gifts I received (I still have the long list of people to whom I sent thanks), two particular memories remain with me. The first is that of Gerd Korman, orthodox Jew and Holocaust survivor who with two of his children on a Friday night had walked all the way to Fran's house in order not to dishonor the Sabbath, to present me with their token. The second was a weighty reproduction of my name in eighty Susan B. Anthony dollars, created by my brother Fred and still hanging in my home office.

Jennie's part was to organize a weekend conference at the university, which she called Women Workers in Fifteen Countries.[9] Friends came to present papers from most of the countries in which I had worked. My thanks at the end acknowledged that all the travels since my retirement had only confirmed my commitment to improving the lot of working women, and that since the Ford Foundation trip in 1972 there had been varying degrees of progress in the industrialized countries for women in the labor force:

> The women's world of 1983 is different from the world into which I plunged in 1972. But we still have a long way to go. Nowhere is child care adequate to meet the need for it. Paternity leave, while more and more recognized as a desirable contribution to infant care and care of sick children, is largely unused, even where it has been made available. Women's needs for job training have been forgotten in the face of worldwide unemployment, indeed in most countries, women's unemployment rates and even numbers exceed those of men. Women's job opportunities are severely limited by the constraints of job segregation, and women's work continues to be paid substantially less than men's, even when their contributions to the employer are virtually equal. Sex harassment on the job as well as on the street, and in the home, testifies to the expression of the worst aspects of patriarchy in the male-female relationship on and off the job. Protective legislation continues to be applied only to women, with resulting restrictive effects on their opportunities for work, while men, free of these protective restrictions, continue to be exposed to killing stress and lethal toxic exposures.
>
> Progress takes place piecemeal for the most part. . . . While I will not live to see the realization of the goals we have set, the joy and the rewards I have experienced from this tribute encourage me to say, "Let's go on! Women's equality deserves our every effort."

Ongoing Travel

Preceding the birthday parties, I had been in France, England, Germany, and Italy that year. The trip to Germany came at the turn of the year and began on Christmas Day, 1982, with the celebration of Tasso Tröscher's eightieth birthday. This turned out to be a celebration in an official European model, with visits and tributes from the many agricultural groups in the province of Hesse that he had served as its minister of agriculture. Telegrams on special birthday forms, supplied by the public telecommunications corporation, came from leading Social Democrats, including former Chancellor Helmut Schmidt. There followed spoken tributes from old friends, of whom I was happy to be counted one. It ended with a fanfare from the forest rangers on their tiny trumpets. They knew Tasso as a highly successful huntsman and blew the traditional calls for deer, boar, and other animals. All this was followed by a family dinner at a forest inn, to which we were transported from our Wiesbaden hotels on a bus. There grandchildren performed their music, a local group provided dance music with grandfather dancing with granddaughters, while old friends and the one remaining sibling, a sister, reminisced about their childhood on a family holding on Lake Constanz. Tasso promised to come to my eightieth birthday party, but instead sent Adi.

In the early morning after this celebration Adi and I departed for a holiday in the Black Forest, where we expected snow for her cross-country skiing but found none. I satisfied my need for exercise by swimming in the hotel pool.

The trip to France was a by-product of Fran's appointment to teach in the Hotel Program at École Superieure des Sciences Économiques (ESSEC), a graduate-professional school at Cergy-Pontoise, reached by commuter train from Paris. Since the students were an international group, I was asked to give some lectures on international labor relations with emphasis on Germany and Japan. Our friend, Bea MacLeod, Ithaca drama critic and theater specialist, joined us at Cergy as the course ended, and we three left for a week of theater in London. There I was able to see my old friends, Mitzi Bales, a self-employed editor, and Harry Pollak, then the labor attaché in our London embassy. Spring in France was by no means pleasant that year. We were visited by many days of heavy rain, and strolls about Paris were impossible. I did see some old friends, among them Andrée Michel, and got to know Margaret Maruani, who had contributed the chapter on France to our book, *Women and Trade Unions in Eleven Industrialized Countries.* Fran and I took a long train ride for a weekend in Carcassonne, the ancient and picturesque walled town on the Spanish border. We also went to Turin for a conference I had agreed to attend, "Women: Production and Reproduction," called by trade union women, where I gave a paper on the comparable worth campaign in the United States.

The year 1983 ended with a twenty-fifth-year celebration of my efforts in opening the faculty club's lunch hour to women. It was sponsored by the Women's Studies Program and was a very happy moment. In the view of the younger women who had followed us, the story was already an incredible one—they were able to assume that this sort of discrimination had never existed within current human memory. That celebration was one of the first times I had the sense that I was indeed old in the minds of women I saw as contemporaries. Nevertheless, I persisted in feeling that I still had work to do, work I should keep doing.

This pattern of travel and work continued in 1984, though somewhat slowed down by my breaking my wrist in a fall on the ice in front on the house on the evening before I was to leave for Hawaii. I was allowed to leave a week later with a note to a doctor at the Straub Clinic in Honolulu. When I met him I was a bit frantic since I could not use the typewriter; I asked him for any suggestion he was able to make that would allow me to go back to writing before the projected six weeks of healing would end. I remember well the calm tone in which he said, "You can't rush nature, and she needs six weeks."

I spent a lot of time on the telephone in those six weeks, tracing down localities where some attempt was being made to introduce comparable worth. The accumulated material in about 130 such colleges, cities, and states formed the basis for my original casebook (*Comparable Worth: A Casebook of Experiences in States and Localities,* Honolulu: Industrial Relations Center, University of Hawaii, 1985). I kept on with this job after I returned to Ithaca, and on my return to Hawaii in January, 1985, I turned over a final draft to Joyce, who published it that year. At that time, Helen Remick, the affirmative action officer at the University of Washington, and my chief source of contacts and information on the history of the efforts of that first state to introduce comparable worth, was editing a book on comparable worth. She asked me to contribute a chapter that would summarize my record keeping on the subject in the United States.[10]

In June Ronnie and I with Brigid O'Farrell made a hurried trip to Milan for another conference under Bianca Beccali's leadership, again with trade union women. An equal opportunity law had recently been adopted in Italy and was the topic of the conference. We were to deal with the U.S. experience, while a colleague of Bianca's who was a member of the national committee for implementation dealt with the problems in Italy.

The meeting was held in a mountain trade union resort. On the night we arrived, the head of the Italian Communist Party died and we found an empty kitchen; all of the staff from the building had taken off for the funeral in Rome. We had to go out for meals that took hours we did not have on our calendar, though they were very pleasant in terms of informal contacts and talk with colleagues from Canada, Germany, France, and Britain. As a result, I felt there was no summary, no conclusion to the meeting. We ran out of time and parted, knowing that a great deal of work lay ahead but with no plan for attacking even the Milan trade union side of it. I got no hint from the Italians—either participants or leaders—of frustration on this score, and I sensed that time is not a demanding factor in discussions in Italy.

In the fall of 1985 I attended a round of conferences to speak on the U.S. experience with introducing comparable worth studies and carrying them into various stages and scopes of implementation. Among the meetings were those at the Ontario Institute for the Study of Education (OISE), a Toronto research center, the University of Minnesota, the University of Michigan's Labor Extension Program under Joyce Kornbluh's organization, and the summer school for eastern trade union women, which met this year at the University of Connecticut. It was there that I first met Maria Luz Sampere of the Connecticut Labor Extension program. I also caught up with my former student, Debbie King, who was head of the Hospital and Health Care Employees Union, Local 1199's activity in organizing and pushing forward the comparable worth movement in Connecticut.[11] I used all of these visits to educate myself further on developments in the comparable worth field and published this information in the 1986 Supplement to the case book, *Comparable Worth: A Case Book* (Honolulu: Industrial Relations Center, University of Hawaii, 1986.)

THE LOSS OF FRIENDS

My friend from the twenties, the late forties, and the early fifties, Nels Anderson, professor of sociology at the University of New Brunswick, died in

1983. One of his colleagues, Noel Iverson, wrote me the sad news as he invited me to join other friends in contributing to a memorial book celebrating Nels's long and varied life—from his thesis on the hobo in the twenties to his influence in Germany on postwar sociological research through the UNESCO Institute in Cologne, followed by his many years at the Canadian university, where Eleanor and I had visited him as part of our extensive trip to the Canadian Maritimes. For the memorial volume, I wrote on "Women and Work in Industrial Societies."[12]

In 1985, as I returned from Hawaii, I had a call from one of Rose Goldsen's friends in Washington, D.C., where Rose was teaching in the Cornell program for undergraduate student interns in government offices. His message was that Rose was ill and needed me. He and other of her recent friends in Washington had done what they could, but the situation was beyond their knowing what to do. She had asked for me. I went at once.

I found her suffering from a very painful middle back, which she thought had been brought on by carrying heavy baggage during a recent South American trip. She had been to a doctor and a therapist but the pain persisted. She was treating it with frequent hot baths that helped only momentarily. She had been to George Washington Hospital for tests and was to return in a few days for a diagnosis. I went with her to the hospital as she heard the ugly word "cancer." It was cancer of the spleen. An operation was out of the question. In a few days she returned with me to Longhouse.

We all rallied to her care. I took on the responsibility of recruiting and scheduling caretakers from among her friends. I also handled her bank account. We consulted her doctor for a cancer specialist and found a woman who began prescribing a series of treatments. From time to time, she seemed to improve, but never enough and never for long. Her old Puerto Rican friend, Monserrat Zayas ("Monsie") came to live with her to ensure that she had company day and night. We called on Hospicare. Its remarkable head helped us all and supplied volunteers to augment our efforts. None of this sufficed. After a few weeks of what appeared to be remission, she learned on a routine checkup with the doctor that the chemical treatment was no longer effective. The only remaining possibility was a treatment in the hospital with experimental drugs. She was immediately admitted, but after two or three days asked to have the treatment stopped. She died two days later on August 2.

In managing her checkbook, I had realized that Rose was living on a very low income, the result of her putting maximum deductions into her retirement fund. I think she herself had no idea of how much her holdings there were. In her will, however, she had directed that her estate, after some gifts to individuals and institutions, should be given to Cornell as a lecture fund or to be used otherwise in behalf of her interests in education in various areas. She designated Professor Linda Waugh, with whom she had been coteaching in semiotics, as the chair of a committee to administer the fund. Altogether the available amount added up to almost $500,000, most of which still exists ten years later, and which we on the committee have decided to dispose of along with its income within the next few years. We have invited a few lecturers to the university but chiefly we have used it to give supplementary funds to Latin-American projects, to student research in a variety of departments, and to Women's Studies conferences and the like. In addition we have assisted the organization of Rose's papers in the Cornell archives.

THE MOST DIFFICULT REVOLUTION

In the later years of the decade, I spent a lot of time in Europe at conferences, and in individual interviews and attendance at union meetings to update my material on women in trade unions. I had completed a first draft of our Book II on our trade union research by the winter of 1986, but Arlene Kaplan Daniels was not happy with it, and as I said at the time, "If Arlene is not happy, I am not happy." Since I had begun to work on the book several years had gone by, and more current data were essential.

In 1986 I attended the IIRA meeting in Germany in 1986 as part of the Equal Pay working group headed by Harish Jain of McMaster University. At this meeting I lived only a few blocks away at the Cornell-in-Germany apartments that were now located on the same street as the house where Wes and I began our first German stay in June 1929. When I realized this, I had a real sense of déjà vu, recalling vividly our happiness at the breakfasts in a sunny garden outside our room.

After the conference I interviewed women in the DGB offices in Düsseldorf, as well as the head of the Women's Division of the Labor Market Board in Nuremberg. Then in 1987 I attended the European regional meeting of IRRA in Tel Aviv, where I remet several German professors in labor relations with whom I had first had contact in Hamburg and where I gave a paper on "Conflicts Between the Demands of Work and Family." It was there, while staying with Dafna Izraeli and her family, that I met Helen Hootsmans of the Netherlands, who invited me to join a group of three women working on a book on dual-career families.[13]

During this period I worked with Ronnie Steinberg on a chapter for a book edited by Ann Helton Stromberg and Shirley Harkess,[14] which we titled "Policies Affecting Women's Employment in Industrial Countries." I had met Shirley at the University of Kansas in 1986 when I was already at work on this article and where I was invited to be the keynote speaker at a conference sponsored by the departments of women's studies, law, gerontology, sociology, and business, in all of which I held colloquia.[15]

A RENEWED FOCUS ON ELEMENTS OF THE "DOUBLE BURDEN"

After sending my comparable worth materials to the National Committee for Pay Equity (NCPE), I focused my own research and reading once more on the elements of women's double burden and its consequences; in a word, on women's handicaps in the labor market and the adjustments the market might make to women as they flooded into it. The section of the women's movement concerned with working women sought solutions to the problems women faced in the "double burden" in "partnership" relationships in which both parents tried to share child care and housekeeping. These "solutions" proved very slow in their realization. The effort indeed has often resulted in what are in fact very traditional "solutions" in defining men's and women's roles within marriage or its more informal male-female ties.

I set up a new file, which has accumulated perhaps a thousand titles related to family and dual work. These include, among some twenty subtitles, Child Care, Child Caregivers, Child Support, Glass Ceiling, Health, Hours (including Part-Time Work), Marriage and Family Law, Men's Views, Promotion, Vocational Guidance and Training, and the Wage Gap. I was directing much of my research and speaking to many of these problems. As I wrote to my friends in my annual Christmas letter in 1988:

> I have come to see that support systems such as child care must be organized not only for working women, but for working parents of both genders. Moreover, I believe that the world of work, organized as it has been by and for men, has made demands upon the family to accommodate to its presumable needs and that these from the beginning have been rigid in respect to hours per day and week, weeks per year and years per lifetime of the worker. I look now for ways in which work can be reorganized to accommodate the family in its various stages and with both parents, or the single parent working. Altogether this past year I have written five papers on various aspects of this problem, read a great deal, part of it summed up in published book reviews, part of it still a buzzing set of questions in my head.

This set of questions continues both to buzz and to grow in scope. Two or three years later, the university set up a Work and Family Office under Marilee Bell. I happily joined her Advisory Committee on these problems because I saw her office as representing an employer of many women, many of them single parents or dual earners. The Committee identified such issues as flex-time, job sharing, the regularization of a part-time work program, the inclusion of unmarried partners in benefit programs, the development through community agency counseling of a consulting service for employees, and the development of workshops on such topics as parenting and career counseling.[16]

As a result of the information and insight I had gathered by 1989, I undertook the organization of a cross-college workshop of academics who were specialists in some aspect of work-family issues and succeeded in bringing together about twenty women under Women's Studies auspices. We met twice weekly for a semester to hear and discuss each other's work in this area. Through this workshop, I met women who had merely been names or who had been quite unknown to me before these meetings.

Changes in the Family

During these years, Philip married Hope Hoetzer, and Tom and Ellen divorced so that Tom could remarry. Philip's wedding was a beautiful affair held in a park outside Buffalo, combining both civil and Jewish elements, and with many friends and all of both families attending. Among the friends there was Margaret Rawson, one of Philip's preschool teachers, now in her nineties and highly honored for her work on dyslexia. Eleanor Emerson's sisters were also invited. Wesley and Rita, their daughter, Susan, and her lesbian partner were all there. Debra of course came, and Hope's father and stepmother. In the course of the afternoon when many friends spoke, her father told us of Hope's growing up on Long Island.

It was the last time I saw Wesley, grown very silent, almost uncommunicative. When I asked him how he spent his days, it was clear they were mainly filled with therapy for a bad accident he had suffered, falling on hot tarmac in a parking lot when they lived in Arizona. Now they lived at a home their son, David, had found for them in a Seattle retirement institution. Wes ended his report by saying, "And otherwise I listen to my wife talking."

Tom's second marriage, to Dorie Solinger, occurred two years later at Dorie's sister's home. Tom's sister Barbara, Philip and Hope, and I all went to the ceremony. It was a Jewish wedding, perhaps the first totally Jewish affair that Tom had ever participated in, half Jewish though he is, but rehearsal had served him well. His girls came, though they had both suffered considerably from the divorce, close as they are to both Tom and Ellen. In the preceding year they had each visited Dorie, a professor in China studies at the University of California at Irvine, and had come to like her. Nevertheless, the breakup of their Connecticut home and of the family remained a tough blow. Thus, our family, like hundreds of others, deals with current problems that marriage and divorce present, and copes in various ways, doing so fairly well to excellently.[17]

But Tom and his sister, Barbara, an artist living in Ithaca, have the additional responsibility of visiting their real mother, Johanna, as often as possible in Berlin. As a writer of poetry and novels, she suffers from decreasing peripheral vision and other severe ailments, including a longtime heart problem. She needs her children, and each of them tries to visit her at least once a year. She has few friends, no one now shares her apartment, and she is less and less able to shop for her needs. Tom's efforts to mobilize available help for her have all been briefly tried, only to be rejected. She wishes them both nearer by, but they are clearly settled in the United States as citizens here, where they live their own lives.

Philip and Hope are after all not far from me and visit me with some regularity. From time to time, they have come with Fran and me on our annual Ontario visit to the Stratford Festival. Tom phones regularly, as does Dorie, and they have come several times to the annual Thanksgiving dinner at Ithaca, which is as much as possible an annual family reunion as well as a celebration of my birthday. Philip takes charge, cooking the meal and leading off with the toasts. Barbara and Fran are permanent members of the table, and frequently Debra joins her father for an all too short visit with me.

THE WOWS

In 1988, at the instigation of our friend Rachel Siegel, a group of older women—of whom I was clearly the oldest—gathered to talk among ourselves at regular intervals about matters of concern to us. We soon called ourselves the WOWs—Wise Old Women—and decided to meet on alternate Fridays, bringing our own lunches to each other's houses in turn. The group, which we decided should not exceed twelve or thirteen friends, has met faithfully ever since. We have lost two members in death; several individuals, including Rachel, have lost their husbands—indeed, only two husbands remain. We have replaced members as old friends moved away, but we have remained an ever-closer group of friends with whom we can talk about anything, from the most personal to national, international, and political topics. We have agreed not to repeat discussions to outsiders. We have come to see WOW as a support group for each of us in trouble, in doubt, and in celebration.

MY HISTORY IN FILM

Late in the decade Sandy Pollak, one of my early students, and now a professor of Women's Studies and English at the Tompkins Courtland County Community College, told me that a group of friends wanted to make a film about my working life. They had recruited Marilyn Rivchin, a filmmaker in theater arts; Sandy would be my interviewer; and Diana MacPherson, Marilyn's friend and a professor at Ithaca College, would be the general dogsbody. The ILR School would make an initial contribution, and Sandy and Marilyn would try to raise additional money.

I had already made many autobiographical tapes in the early years at Longhouse, which Fran had recorded. In a way I was willing enough to push the effort ahead, in the hope it would get me started on the autobiography that Florence wanted. Moreover, I hoped that with Sandy's help I would find the central theme that held my varying work experiences together. We began in 1988, worked through the next two and a half years, and had a film ready for its premiere in 1991. Marilyn reduced the almost fifty hours of picture taking and interviews to fifty-five-minutes, under the title of *Never Done: The Working Life of Alice H. Cook, Part 1*. Because I felt that too little had focused on my life at Cornell, Marilyn suggested that we might sometime do Part 2.

This process was a help to me, particularly the concluding hour-and-a-half discussion between Ronnie and me, in which we talked about the theoretical research paths that we both had taken from the seventies to the early nineties. We captured not only our individual experiences but also the shifts and turns of theory about the impact of combining work and family on the lives of modern women.

REVOLUTION IN EASTERN EUROPE

The collapse of the Communist Eastern half of Europe occurred as the decade ended. For years I had subscribed to several German papers and periodicals that were suddenly filled with the reality of what for the most part had been the unforeseen—the collapse of one Communist state after another, including East Germany, and above all of the Soviet Union itself. These events affected various countries in various ways, but because I had visited some of these countries I turned my special attention to those I personally knew something about. I determined to go back to Germany as soon as possible and to do what I could to get into the East again, meet some women there, and learn firsthand how such a fundamental change was affecting them and what role they might have played in it. David Soskice, a British scholar of trade unions and labor market policy, was visiting ILR. He told me that he was on his way to the Wissenschaftszentrum (WZB) in Berlin, as codirector of its section in this field, and urged me to inquire whether I might go there the next summer as a base for work of this kind. I already knew Eileen Appelbaum of Temple University, whom I had met more than once at Ronnie's Philadelphia home and who was working that year at the WZB. A little correspondence achieved the invitation to come and to work with Friederike Maier.

Through the decade of the eighties, which coincided with my own eighties, I continued to be as busy as before. I had seen and participated in a variety of issues, all related to working women's problems. I had moved, moreover, from a sharp focus on comparable worth to the possible ways of ameliorating the "dual burden." These included proposals to relieve it through the legal regularization of part-time work; the assistance employers might be able to undertake with innovations such as flex-time, flex-location, and parental leave; and—probably most difficult—the creation of attitudinal changes of parental pairs themselves on the meaning of partnership in the conduct of family life. I had firmly linked study to advocacy and action.

However, as the next and final chapter will demonstrate, this shift came at a time in my own life when the many symptoms of aging were intensifying. The limited physical mobility that inevitably followed has forced me into a major change in the way I must live my own life, however long or short that still may be. My interest remains high, however. It controls what I read and informs the conversations by phone and face to face with the many friends still available for these encounters.

Alice in Hawaii in the early 1980s, with brother Ted Hanson, niece Sue Hanson, and friend Fran Herman.

Alice in Germany on Tasso Tröscher's 80th birthday in 1982. From left to right: Alice, Adelheid (Adi) Tröscher, Edith Tröscher, Tasso Tröscher.

Alice with staff at Industrial Relations Center, University of Hawaii at Manoa, in 1983. From left to right: Helene Tanimoto, Joyce Najita, Mariko Yamashita, Randy Matsunaga, Jonelle Oshiro, Debbie Wong.

Alice and Joyce Najita, Director of the Industrial Relations Center, University of Hawaii at Manoa, 1983.

Alice and brother Fred Hanson at Alice's 80th birthday celebration, Ithaca, November 1983. Fred's gift: eighty Susan B. Anthony silver dollars spelling Alice's name.

Alice at work typing on her computer at the Industrial Relations Center, University of Hawaii at Manoa, 1983.

Alice's 80th birthday celebration, with sons Philip Cook and Tom Bernstein sitting behind her. The tee-shirt, a (prescient) gift.

Alice with son Tom Bernstein and granddaughter
Anya Bernstein, at Anya's high school graduation,
1989.

Rose Goldsen, sociologist and Alice's close
friend.

Alice in Uruguay in 1988, as guest of Japanese ambassador
Ryoko Akamatsu, longtime friend.

Alice and Fran Herman, 1989.

Alice in 1989 with Ronnie Steinberg and Michael Ames at Letchworth State Park, New York, near Rochester.

Alice in 1990, at breakfast in Stratford, Ontario, with Antje Lemke, formerly of Germany, now at Syracuse University.

Alice with Jennie Farley, former director of Women's Studies at Cornell University, circa early 1990s.

Alice with young friend Katya Levitan-Reiner, at Longhouse. Photo: Lois Levitan.

Alice with Constance Cook, attorney, former New York State assemblywoman, former vice president of Cornell University, in 1993. Photo: Peter Morenus.

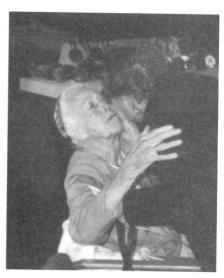

Alice with Esther Peterson: two old friends saying "Farewell," 1993.

Alice with son Philip Cook, his wife Hope Hoetzer-Cook, and their daughter Debra Cook, early 1990s.

Alice at home in Longhouse, 1996. Photo: Arlene Kaplan Daniels.

Alice with friends at As You Like It Motel on Romeo Street, in Stratford, Ontario, summer 1994. Left to right: Fran Herman, Alice, Joyce Najita, Helene Tanimoto, Antje Lemke.

Alice's favorite picture of herself, sometime in the 1990s.

Alice in 1993, at her 90th birthday celebration, with Adi Tröscher.

15

THE END OF THE LINE: 1990–1997

The nineties began much like the eighties, with a winter in Hawaii, to be followed by travel on the European continent, which included some study—neither deep nor broad enough in scope to be called research, but nevertheless motivated by a powerful concern. Its focus was the women in East Germany, about to be "unified" with their Western sisters. This was a transition already in progress, but not one the Easterners, the "Ossis," had yet grasped—although one they had begun to fear.

In Hawaii I met a new friend, Karen Mohr, an active member of the German Postal Workers Union studies program who had decided in her forties to take an undergraduate degree. She attended a university in Hamburg that admitted adults who originally had taken the vocational route in German education, leaving school at fourteen or fifteen for full-time vocational training. The program had been established after the war as a bridge for such people, to allow them to achieve higher education as mature students. In Hawaii, Karen wanted to begin her graduate studies by enrolling in the Women's Studies Program at the University of Hawaii, but because of her English—she was largely self-taught—she entered an extramural program for older students. Her support for these studies came from a German foundation, one of whose goals was to make graduate education available to nontraditional students.

She planned to continue her graduate studies in Germany that fall at the Free University of Berlin, after her round-the-world trip via Japan and China. Specifically, she wanted to contact working women and their organizations in several Pacific Rim countries. I expected to be in Berlin in August, when she would not yet have returned. We discussed my probable difficulties in finding a place to live, given the present fluid circumstances, and Karen offered me her room in her mother's apartment in the district known as Siemensstadt. I wrote her mother, Frau Alma Puhlman, and it was soon settled that I would live with her.

Fran and I had bought tickets for a cruise around the long Norwegian coast, which was to be our pleasure travel for the year. We set off in late June and went via Sweden so that I could meet women in the Arbeitslivcentrum, who were doing research on working women, and update myself on conditions in this promising country. The Center had recently reorganized and set up a women's section in each of its departments. In each of these sections I was the single student, with two or three teachers providing me with a seminar on the role of women in unions, in the political system, in education, and in the labor market. In return I gave a seminar in what we were doing in the States. I arranged also to see my old friend and exchange student from the Bryn Mawr Summer School days, Mai Larssen, who in 1950 had joined Mother, Philip, and me for my introductory trip to Norway.

Fran and I then moved from Stockholm to Bergen, Norway, where our own trip was to begin. On the advice of friends who had made this trip, we were on a mail boat that would make many stops, allowing us to see many towns along the way to the Arctic and back. We found ourselves assigned to a table for six, and during the two-week voyage we became friends with the Barkers of Maidenhead in England, and Jan and Ian Fleming of Scotland. In both cases the friendship has been sustained by correspondence, and Jan came to visit me in Ithaca three years later.

Although I felt very well, I had several experiences with vertigo on waking up in the morning both during this trip and later in Munich. I consulted doctors in both countries without much success, but I continued the travel and came home in what seemed good shape. Indeed, we both came out of Norway only wishing to repeat the trip.

MUNICH

Our advance itinerary took us next to Dresden, deep within East Germany, but once we arrived in Hamburg from Oslo, it was late evening. We abandoned the trip to Dresden and exchanged our tickets for the overnight train directly to Munich, from where Fran would fly home, while I would move on to Berlin. In Munich we met another old friend, Erika von Arnim, whom I had first known as the assistant to the United States director of adult education in Bavaria when its statewide organization was being reorganized at the end of the war. Now retired, she spent an afternoon with us to give us the first West German impressions of the recent upheaval in the East. We heard of the influx of East German skilled workers who, as the wall fell, had flooded into the West to earn the high salaries there. Only disappointment followed. Western employers found that these workers were incapable of the efficiency demanded of their Western counterparts. Many of them had not worked a full eight-hour day in years and could not maintain the pace or the quality set by their new fellow workers. They were still hand-workers by training, unskilled in dealing with the computer or the most modern tools. It was a story I would hear again and again in the following weeks in the West.

BERLIN

To my surprise, Karen met me at the airport in Berlin. She had lost her tickets and travelers checks when they fell out of her pocket into the ocean on a trip between Macao and Hong Kong. The German consul had helped her to get home, but her trip around the world had, with this accident, ended precipitately. She was in her mother's apartment as a visitor until the opening of the fall term at the university. Karen's mother, Frau Puhlman, seemed neither upset or worried about being overcrowded. Her immediate concern was the loss of her car through a collision that had occurred while it had been parked on the street. Her worry was that, while she waited for her insurance payment, she would be dependent on Karen for getting about.

AT THE WZB

Karen was my daily companion and insisted on taking me to work each morning at the research center, Wissenschaftszentrum (WZB). When my filmmakers arrived in Berlin to get pictures of me at work there, Karen joined the crew and made herself irreplaceably useful by helping with their gear as we all moved around Berlin.

This research center was located very near the old Potsdamer Platz, which had been cut off from the West by the wall, now gone almost without a trace. Nevertheless, it turned out to be a lively spot. Space just east of our building had become a huge parking lot, filled each day with Polish traders, ready to buy out West Berlin—specifically at a discount house down the street from us. Every half-hour or so a limited group was allowed to enter the store. The buyers would emerge loaded with TV sets and other desirable goods, which were taken to the buses that took off eastward, heavily laden for a round of eastern markets where the Berlin goods were sold or traded.[1]

David Soskice had arranged with Dr. Günther Schmid, his codirector of the Labor Market Division of WZB, for me to have Friederike Maier of the departmental staff as my mentor. On my first morning, Friederike introduced herself to Karen and me as a feminist sociologist, knowledgeable about and friendly with trade union women, and in touch with several sociologists in the East German universities. Her companion, Karl Röhrig, worked for the large and prestigious Metal Workers Union in its drive to organize East German metal workers.

In mid-1990 the unions in West Germany were still not of one mind about their policies with respect to the East German workers. Some sought to take over the Communist unions directly from the Freir Deutsche Gewerkschaftsbund (FDGB), the Free German Trade Union Federation. Others saw the task as one of organizing individual workers into a new union and then beginning to bargain with the new owner or manager of the industry. Organizing in this way was, however, hampered in several respects. Major industries and their branch firms were state-owned. A Treuhandgesellschaft or Trusteeship was in process of formation, to be staffed by West Germans who would sell and thus privatize these state owned properties, many of which were still being managed by their longtime Communist heads. Could the workers, who had enjoyed many protections under Communism, including lifetime job security, housing, and child care, assume that they would continue to enjoy comparable benefits? In short, what would a non-Communist worker gain from a

West German privatized (capitalist) takeover? With what assumptions would they face the future? Certainly, no one anticipated the reality, which arrived a few months later, in terms of lower pay for a considerable number of years to come, together with the withdrawal of housing and food subsidies. What lay immediately ahead, many hoped, was an independent, new East German Republic, which could organize itself around the most desirable elements of both economies.

Karl knew a teacher in the WZB who lived in its vicinity, and invited him to be our guide. The center's history during the forty years of DDR administration consisted of buying or otherwise acquiring various pieces of private as well as public property to provide space for its enlargement. The main building was intact. Our guide, displaced from his job as a former Communist, had ideas about how the institution might be used under the new circumstances, but all development of this transitional sort was in limbo while previous landowners petitioned to reclaim their property. The entire matter of finding a new use for such an institution was apparently in no one's hands. Some of its space was now rented out to a private entrepreneur. Our guide hoped that more of it might be taken over by the new unions or some other union-related applicants as a vocational training institution for East German workers. Torn between his own problematic future and his attachment to the institution, whose future was equally unforeseeable, he hoped that both an institutional and a personal solution might be found.

A few days later I interviewed Professor Nickel of Humboldt University, who expressed similar uncertainty at the academic level. Already the question of how many universities the city of Berlin could sustain had arisen. Many of the professors in this and other Eastern universities had been seen as too political—"unreconstructed Communists"—or too inadequately prepared for lifetime positions in historic institutions. Professor Nickel's personal uncertainty may have rested on the fact that she had for some time researched and written on the status of women and the family in Communist East Germany. However, for this very reason she had been drawn in to discussions with researchers at WZB, where her work was appreciated. When I last heard, she had become a tenured professor at Humboldt under the university's reorganization.

The uncertainty about the future permeated all meetings, discussions, and considerations of all kinds. One of Friederike's colleagues offered to introduce me to a group that had for some time included East German oppositionists, who had been meeting regularly in anticipation of an improvement in East-West relations. Its membership also included experienced politicians and economic specialists from the West. The bookshop in the building where the meeting was to be held had formerly been a source for all official East German publications. On the day we planned to attend the meeting, shortly after the wall had come down, the bookstore already had only Western materials. Because events were outrunning past and future plans, the group was, as it were, forced to a new beginning. It adjourned after a nearly futile effort to formulate an agenda for its next meeting.

On another occasion I met with two members of a much less prestigious group to talk with two school librarians, one from the East, one from the West. These two women were aware that major changes awaited them, but they could not imagine what they might be.

The school system itself had important decisions to make. One read of the need for total changes in teaching personnel, textbooks, the schools' relationship to the apprentice system, terminal education at the secondary level, and preparation for university education. Newspapers reported that truckloads of textbooks were headed for Eastern destinations, training sessions for selected teachers were being set up, and Western-trained teachers were being recruited for positions in the East. Similarly, Western civil servants were being encouraged to move to the East to assist in reestablishing provincial government staffs, and even to be available for ministerial positions in cabinets. The West's assumption was that, with unification, Western law and national structure would become the model for the five new Eastern provinces.

As for the trade unions, the future inevitably meant the adoption of the system of Work Councils in every workplace, existing side by side with the unions' administration of collectively bargained contracts through union stewards. But the unions still differed among themselves on this issue. They were concerned with how they should proceed for the future during this short interval before unification. Since Work Councils were prescribed as to structure and power by federal law, they would necessarily have to be introduced.[2]

In this uncertain period the German Trade Union Federation (DGB) in Berlin was designated as responsible for the development of the unions in the Eastern province of Brandenburg, bordering on Berlin. Among other decisions, it appointed the head of the Berlin Women's Division to take on responsibility for women in the Brandenburg area, with Potsdam as its capital. She arranged for me to meet and interview four women in Potsdam one afternoon. The filmmakers went along. One of my interviewees was a woman in the broadcasting union, which had already affiliated with the Deutsche Angestellte Gewerkschaft (DAG), the independent white-collar union in the West.[3] Another was a member of the Postal Workers Union, which had so far taken no action on affiliation, nor, I inferred, had its members been approached by its Western counterpart, since government employees in the East were still not eligible for membership in the Western government workers union. Her situation was particularly problematical. She was still the supervisor of a department in the postal service, which had no counterpart in the West. In the East, the post office had received and processed all newspaper and journal subscriptions, probably as a means of controlling the circulation of acceptable information. She was aware that such a department did not exist in West Germany and that her job was possibly at stake when the two Germanys would join.

These women were all puzzled as to how they would manage under "democratic capitalism." "How can the state expect us to work if it does not provide child care? Don't they need women?" These were some of the questions they put to me. None of them spoke as close adherents of Communism. They saw the benefits they had received under the Communist state as an inevitable quid pro quo for the jobs they needed if they were to provide for their families. Both Eastern and Western informants were aware of the lives of the majority of women in the East: that they married young; usually bore two children; that they could expect to enjoy maternity plus parental leave as well as child care provided in preschool and after-school programs. They also knew that women could divorce if they wished—the divorce rate in the East was high; that women could get subsidized housing; that they could expect cheap commuter transportation and controlled prices for their basic food needs, as well as free medical care for themselves and their children. And abortions were available at their own request.

As I listened to women's experiences and tried to understand their attitudes during this period of transition, I reminded myself repeatedly that almost sixty years had passed since East Germans had lived under democratic circumstances—and then only for the few years between the overthrow of the monarchy and the election of Hitler. Only the grandparents of these Germans had ever had the experience of being democratic citizens. Their parents had known Nazism and had probably for a while been enthusiastic supporters of Hitler. But this generation had been born into Communism, with the Russian regime as its model, and their own country had become the most productive of all the Eastern Bloc nations. Dissatisfaction there had been. But the thought that the future could possibly bring a lowering of their standard of living was certainly not part of any scenario that DDR demonstrators in 1989 might have had in mind as they filled the streets of Leipzig or other major cities in protest against Communism.

FRANKFURT

During a visit to Adi and the senior Tröschers, I set up an appointment with Dr. Eva Brumlop at the Institut für Sozialforschung (Institute for Social Research). The Institute was still alive and producing important work after more than sixty years and was now under the leadership of a friend of Tasso's. I wanted now to check with Brumlop about any research that she or her coworkers were doing on women and work in Germany. I received an armful of reprints and Xeroxed studies, which I took away with me to read at home.

HAWAII

Joyce Najita and I had been invited to attend a conference in Japan on trade union women in 1990, but I could not attend because of my illness—the first of a series of attacks that effectively caused me to withdraw from outside activity. Joyce, at my insistence, had gone alone. She came back with the strong impression that the Japanese women wanted a follow-up on matters of wages and affirmative action in the United States. After we discussed the situation with the Japan Center at the University of Hawaii, the director promised us some financial support. We decided to consult two Japanese women on these issues and hold a three-day meeting with Hiroko Hayashi and Machiko Osawa, as well as with some University of Hawaii scholars.

We designated the conference as one on Women and Work: Japan and the United States. We postponed a decision on whether it should be held in Honolulu or Tokyo. I hoped we could supplement the University of Hawaii money with a grant from Cornell and perhaps get some help from some of the new ILR staff members who were interested in Japan. I wrote one of them, who obliged with a list of Japanese companies and funds. We were able then in 1993 to bring two trade union women leaders from the new Japanese federation, Rengo, together with several male representatives of Honolulu unions. Ryoko Akamatsu was available and came as the head of a new organization, Women Employed.[4] Gloria Johnson, the new head of the Coalition of Labor Union Women (CLUW) in the United States, and Nancy Riche, vice president of the Canadian Labour Council (CLC), also attended.

In the course of our discussions, two difficulties from Rengo became evident. The first was that a conference had already been held under the heading Women and Work. Now the Rengo women wished to have such a conference specifically for and about trade union women. As we moved toward this possibility, the Rengo women made clear that they had not come as official representatives of their federation. If there were to be a trade union conference, the invitation to Rengo must come from the U.S. and Canadian trade union federations and not from a university. We turned to Gloria and Nancy, who had their own problems with AFL-CIO and CLC respectively. Gloria had not yet taken Joyce Miller's place as a member of the AFL-CIO Executive Council and felt she could not promise that the Council would pay attention to such a question.[5] Nevertheless, both women promised a response within a few weeks.

Japan was in political turmoil during these very days. For the first time in years the Liberal—i.e., conservative—Party could not produce a majority in the Lower House, from whence came the prime minister. A coalition of new parties was ready to take over the government. The prime minister designate called Akamatsu-san to ask her to join his cabinet. After a sleepless night of consideration, she agreed to accept his invitation. After giving us all a dinner, she flew back a day early to Tokyo, where she became minister of education. Unfortunately nothing came of all these preparations. Neither Gloria nor Nancy produced the necessary invitations, with the result that Joyce and I have had to drop our plans and hopes for an international trade union women's conference.

NINETIETH BIRTHDAY

Early in 1993 I learned from Sally McConnell-Genet, head of Women's Studies, that plans were under way for a conference to honor my ninetieth birthday and the completion of my forty-one years at Cornell. In our discussion of a timely theme, I said that my keenest interests now had to do with the fate of women in Eastern Europe. Sally accepted this topic, and the meeting was scheduled for the end of October.

To my happy surprise, friends I had not seen in years turned up: Aliza Tamir and her husband Chaim from Israel;[6] Lee Lee had returned to Ithaca after two years in Hong Kong; Bianca Baccali came for the weekend from Italy; Hiroko Hayashi was in the States for a sabbatical year at Rutgers; Karen Mohr was doing a year's study as an ILR graduate student;[7] Adi Tröscher came for a two-week visit representing her father, as well as herself. Many old friends from U.S. cities turned up. It was a reunion to top all others. In addition to Hanna Beate Schöpp-Schilling of the German Ministry for Women and Youth, there were women on the program from Hungary, Yugoslavia, Romania, and Russia. These women brought reassuring information of women's activity in behalf of peace and in opposition to the horror of the existing Yugoslavian ethnic wars. I very much hoped that the tapes from this meeting could be transcribed for a book, but funds were never available.

A personal birthday celebration also took place at dinner one evening. Ellen, Tom's first wife, came by bus from Connecticut. As the good dinner ended, Adi led off, speaking of my long connection with her family. Ellen and many other friends followed. And on my real birthday, November 28, my dear Ithaca friends in the WOWs gave a party at Betty Kassman's lovely home overlooking our Lake Cayuga. She and Fran invited ninety guests, almost all of whom came. Philip and Hope, Tom and Dorie were there, as were all the WOWs with the two remaining husbands, together with many longtime colleagues at the university. On that day, many calls came in from friends in Germany, London, Scotland, and Italy, as well as from a few of the remaining Soviet House pals, all three granddaughters, and Ellen. Greetings came in on cards and letters, as though it were Christmas, and indeed it almost was.

CHANGE OF ADDRESS

Early in the 1990s, a former dean of faculty headed a committee of the Retired Professors' Association, looking for a location where retirees might build smaller homes in a community to accommodate couples or singles, now in the final stage of life. He died before any solution was found and the matter was shelved. Then, a year or so later, former Cornell University president Dale Corson and retired provost Keith Kennedy called a meeting to introduce the possibility of a full-care retirement home under Quaker auspices. Persons interested in such a development attended a series of meetings that, after some four years, made Kendal of Ithaca a reality.[8] Committees, formed from among future tenants, began to think of the facilities that ought to be incorporated: a self-government association, a library, a hospital for people unable to take care of themselves, craft and woodworking areas, and the possible addition of tennis courts. I was interested from the beginning, and as my health deteriorated I saw Kendal as the most sensible solution to my problems.

After talking with the director in detail about my financial status, my wishes, and my needs, and how to fit them to my income, I believed I could afford to live at Kendal, in a one-bedroom apartment. I also saw from my various earlier community experiences—from Commonwealth College through Soviet House and Longhouse—that I could quickly adjust to this one. I realized it would be a different way of sharing life, with many more people close by, and a somewhat more formal sharing of the details of tenant management. At the same time, the experience of living in other communities had fully prepared me for the principle of civility as well as the essential give-and-take that occurred when residents had to divide their attention between personal relationships and the economic and political well-being of the institution they had voluntarily turned to for the final stages of their lives.

I moved in on January 10, 1996. From the beginning, I felt at home here. As I write, I have been here many months and find it ideally suited to my wishes and needs. Now in late fall, more than two hundred people live here. Five WOWs are here, and many acquaintances and former colleagues. One of many pleasures is the growing friendships with persons I knew only slightly and with new persons from other communities than Ithaca. The variety is of course great. We wear name tags as we go to dinner, in order to introduce ourselves to people previously unknown.

Early in the summer the administrator, Bill DeWire,[9] called us to a meeting whose purpose was to begin to set up self-government for the residents. Now, late in the fall of the first year here, we have set up almost twenty committees, with many more to come. I have joined the human resources task force and the library committee and also volunteered to work on a newsletter.

Kendal has provided me with an extra hour in the day—the one between five and six o'clock when formerly I was busy preparing an evening meal. Now in that hour I read the daily paper, open my mail and sort out the next day's calendar and, soon after six, walk down to choose my main meal of the day. It offers me my choice of least three main dishes, usually meat, fish, or a vegetarian dish, a salad bar, fruit, pudding, or pastry, drinks of choice, ice cream of choice, and seconds, should firsts not be adequate. Usually, an interesting dinner conversation accompanies the food. Now we are beginning to have concerts or other entertainment one night or so a week; transportation is available to all the many musical events on the two campuses or at one or two of the churches. Kendal provides full medical care in case of illness or to prevent illness, and the promise of full care if one becomes incapacitated. It has a beautiful swimming pool and a well-equipped fitness center. I take advantage of all its offerings, though I can no longer swim. As a result of all my illnesses I have lost twenty-five to thirty pounds in weight and seem unable to float! I walk in the pool instead.

Of course I discussed the move with both Philip and Tom and went over my reasons for moving. With the granddaughters, I tried to be clear about the possibility that the move meant they would have less to count on as my beneficiaries. But on the other hand it meant that they would not be called on to be my caretakers.

ANYA BECOMES OUR CENTER OF ATTENTION

Anya graduated cum laude from Barnard in the spring of 1993, in a ceremony that I attended with great pleasure. Anya had long ago said that while she hoped to do well in college, she was not going to sacrifice other experiences in New York, at work, or elsewhere for grades alone. She made many friends and developed close relationships with many of her professors. She gained experience as a dormitory counselor, as a volunteer with Planned Parenthood, and in summer jobs with the New York Museum of History. She developed a serious love affair with the man she would marry in the summer of 1994, Jonathan Bassett. On this day, she was very happy. Perhaps the only shadow was in the fact of her parents' divorce, but both were present for this celebration.

I found the graduation program itself inspiring. Not only was the college president's speech spoken in the words of a feminist educator but the speaker of the day was the retiring woman governor of Vermont, Madeleine Kunin. Moreover, the senior class speaker was already an assured young woman, grateful to be a product of this women's college. The impression I had first gained at Wellesley that women's colleges produced women ready for leadership in the large world was reconfirmed; I could see this, not only in Anya's views and in her participation but that it was the model for the graduating class.

Anya already knew that she would go to Harvard for her graduate degree and that she would probably choose government as her major. Her first semester in Cambridge was discouraging, however. She wrote and phoned me frequently in growing unhappiness. Her friend Jonathan was in New York and she in Cambridge, and by November Anya wanted to give it all up, or at best go for an M.S. in the shortest time possible and think, as Jonathan was doing, of high school teaching thereafter. Jonathan was a Columbia graduate with a Harvard M.S. in education, the son of a Unitarian minister in a Boston suburb. He was teaching in a private Catholic girls' school in the Bronx, where the majority of his students were Latinas. He was planning to start work in the near future for a Ph.D. in education and hoped for the next year to find a job in or near Boston. In the meantime, however, he was quite uncertain about whether he could find employment there. Anya very much wanted to marry Jonathan but did not see when and how that could happen.

I urged her as a first-year graduate student to make no decisions in this dark first semester. I had no evidence that this sound advice was in any way comforting or helpful to her, but in the end, she did finish the first graduate year. Conceivably Jonathan in his own way was sharing her unhappiness at the separation. He proposed marriage, and for Anya the clouds divided and began to disappear. She found her adviser who, she thought, had had little time for her in her first year, ready now to work with her. She set up a graduate committee with Sydney Verba and Theda Skocpol. "Lucky woman!" I said to her.

In her third semester Anya won a fellowship that made her the teacher of freshmen in a course on the Constitution. Things were going well, and in the fall I received word that Anya and Jonathan were going to have a wedding in June 1994. It was soon clear that this wedding was to include every traditional feature: bridesmaids and groomsmen, a wedding dress, "something old, something new, something borrowed, something blue." The vows would be traditional before two clergymen in a Congregational Church that Anya and Jon had searched out and joined. There would be lots of guests and a reception with food and dancing; Tom would dance first with Anya, and then with Ellen, and then with Dorie. A honeymoon would follow. Ellen joined happily in the planning, down to the last detail. I was somewhat uneasy, however, and talked with Tom. What, after all, was the meaning of setting up a wedding like a travel plan? Was Anya harking back to a romantic history of which she had been somehow deprived? I thought he shared my doubts at least to some degree, but when he concluded with "It's what Anya wants and it's her wedding," I saw that he was quite right and sent off my check to help make it all come true, just as she wanted it.

Planning paid off. The wedding went exactly as planned. Anya was radiant. Jonathan was immensely happy. The evening before the wedding, guests were invited to a dinner at Jonathan's parents' home. Because the weather was inclement, however, Jonathan's father opened the parlors of the Unitarian Church for the meal that was to have been in the Bassett garden. There it became evident that Anya was marrying into a widespread New England family. Almost a hundred people were present, nearly all of them Jon's relatives. On Tom's side were Philip, Hope, Ellen, Dorie, Dorie's sister, who had hosted Tom's own wedding the year before, and myself. The reception after the wedding rang with good music and happiness. Tom had taken dancing lessons in anticipation of his lead role in that department, and looked paternally happy with his own contribution and with his beautiful daughter's execution of her plans.

DEBRA'S GRADUATION

For Debra, school has never been easy. She has had to fight dyslexia all the way. Her first two college years were spent in a Virginia community college, where a professor had interested her in archeology as he conducted a dig in the garden of Virginia's first governor. She looked for a university that would allow her to continue in this field and decided on Southern Illinois. This decision rested partly on the fact that her stepfather, Peter, had moved from Baltimore to Champagne, Illinois, thus making Debra a citizen of that state. In addition, Southern Illinois had a guidance program for dyslexics. Philip drove Hope and me from Buffalo to the graduation ceremonies. As he said more than once, he could hardly believe she would get a degree and would not really believe it until he saw her switch the tassel on her cap, or saw her full name in print on the program. We saw both unmistakably. There followed a fine dinner, offered us jointly by Peter and Philip, and then the long trip home.

Debra has remained an archeologist, working for short periods with one or another organization that does searches on land that may contain historic relics to be rescued before builders are allowed to bring in the bulldozers. These jobs last a few months, so that she is constantly on the move, carrying a tent and a sleeping bag in her car, and frequently living on or very near the dig site. She hopes that when she applies for graduate work, these years of experience will enhance her mediocre undergraduate grades. Determination is her outstanding quality and will perhaps make her a winner in the end.

PHILIP'S BAD NEWS

In July 1996 Philip called to say he had lost his job as manager of the Erie County Water Authority. His board members had quarreled with the incumbent county executive, who won, and then summarily dismissed the board and fired Philip. Philip had turned fifty-seven in June, not a favorable age for reemployment. He faced the task before him with his usual sound sense of organization, by building a group of more than one hundred fifty persons who knew him and who agreed to help him in his job search. Like many others in this situation Philip turned to consulting. One of his clients, a Buffalo-based engineering firm, hired him as the management specialist on its World Bank–funded water, wastewater, and solid waste infrastructure project in Yunan Province of the People's Republic of China. He develops viable, financially and institutionally independent utilities in three project cities.

To add to the pain of rejection and uncertainty, Hope failed to be reelected to her leadership position within the Democratic Party, though both she and Philip retained their committee seats. The local Democratic Party had turned away, as has the national party, from a liberal to a more centrist agenda.

ILLNESS AND RECOVERY

These years were marked by continuing deterioration in the use of my legs. I could walk only an ever-shorter distance before my legs would become too painful to continue. The left leg was becoming deformed at the knee. However, periodic checks of my blood pressure by the spring of 1992 showed that it was down to almost normal levels, My doctor finally said that if I wanted to have the knee in my left leg replaced, it would probably be safe to do so. I visited two orthopedists and decided to go to the Guthrie Clinic at the Packer Hospital across the Pennsylvania line in Sayre. Dr. Allen, the chief of that department, agreed to take me, and in late September 1992 I had the operation. I was hospitalized for ten days and then spent weeks of rehabilitation at home, during which I drew on the help of several city agencies, my Longhouse friends, and the WOWs. Fran organized some of this and was always available for shopping, food preparation, trips to the hospital for checkups, and friendly chat.

In December, when I had an appointment for one of these checkups, I was, as usual, building a morning fire in my wood stove, when apparently I blacked out and fell against its iron body. When Fran came a few hours later to pick me up for the trip, I was still unconscious on the floor. I recovered a degree of consciousness in the ambulance on the way to the local hospital. Again, I was in professional care for several days, with a mild concussion.

Other problems followed—attacks of vertigo, and Bell's palsy, for which I have physical therapy to thank for a relatively rapid recovery. Bell's palsy was an ailment of which I had never heard. When I went into the hospital, I was totally puzzled as to what had happened to me overnight. I had no pain, but my face was twisted on the right side, in such a way that the emergency room doctor thought I might have had a stroke and treated me accordingly. After several hours he concluded that it was Bell's palsy. I had to cancel an elaborate program laid out for me in Washington. Once I was home, I began to hear from friends about their experiences. Among others, Leon Shull of Philadelphia days, from whom I had not heard personally in over twenty years, called to say that he had had it and it took him almost six months to recover. A local physiotherapist gave me facial exercises, which helped me to recover within six weeks.

The worst occurred in the fall of 1993, when I became very ill. I could not eat. When I pushed down a little food, it came back up. I was dizzy, totally without energy. I happened to read a newspaper description of carbon monoxide poisoning that exactly fitted my malaise, and I decided that its cause was my wood stove. When I called for an inspection, the men who came found multiple sources of lead fumes caused by worn-out parts. They recommended a new stove, and I inquired about propane gas. I found a stove as aesthetically satisfactory as my old one and had it installed as soon as it could be delivered. My immediate recovery sustained the correctness of the newspaper diagnosis. But I also noticed that my hearing and sight were both in some trouble. My legs and arms showed dermatological problems, and I was experiencing arthritis pain in both knees. While the operation seemed to have been quite successful, poor circulation in both legs still affected my ability to walk. I added a cane to my equipment.

There followed a series of ulcer attacks in 1994 and 1995. The first was treated with an operation, the second with transfusions. There followed a long period of weakness from which I believed I had recovered enough to attend a meeting called by the Sloan Foundation in Georgia. A year earlier I had been invited to join a group called together by this foundation to explore the work in progress on work and family. It was the subject to which I had turned my interest, and

I was happy to join. The meeting in Georgia to which I went in the early fall of 1995 was my third. By this time I was convinced that the direction this group was taking was not mine, and in a talk with the organizer I discussed my differences with the group. They were mainly that Sloan wanted the group to work on the problems of professional and managerial women, whereas my interest and research had centered mainly on blue- and pink-collar women. Especially after meeting with the group over the past year, I believed the class differences between these two types of working women raised fundamentally different problems and called for quite different approaches to remedies.

At the Sloan meeting I again fell ill with the ulcer symptoms. I did not want to go to a strange doctor and hospital, and waited twenty-four hours to start on the journey home. I arrived very weak, went at once to the doctor, and began a new kind of treatment. This was based on a new approach, which now treated the disease not as caused by food or stress but as of bacterial origin. My recovery was slow, and once more I was quickly and repeatedly exhausted, this time from the work of moving to Kendal. Again friends came to my aid. Ronnie and Michael came and helped me pack for the move; Adi, in Ithaca for a visit, stayed extra days to help out. Arlene came for a week and stayed two.

For some time my eyes had been deteriorating. The ophthalmologist I had used for decades had retired, and his successor on examination found no reason to change the prescription for glasses. A small cataract existed, but "at your age," as he put it, he did not wish to risk an operation on my one good eye. I checked with a second man, who supported this diagnosis and judgment. In a driving test, which the Motor Vehicle Office insisted on, I lost my driver's license shortly before I was slated to move into Kendal. I sold my car before I moved. So far as getting about is concerned, I find that getting to appointments, to lectures, to plays, and in response to social invitations is a new problem that I must learn to meet. I have been dependent on the reliable service of a local agency, Gadabout, for help in getting to appointments, but it does not function on weekends and evenings. Kendal provides a bus for attendance at concerts, but there is no service to theaters. Many friends have assured me of help, and I have had to learn to call them and to resign myself to not going to plays when their help is unavailable.

Calling for help is a matter in itself that I am still learning to do and to accept. A recent call from Women's Studies told me that I was "the winner in travel sweepstakes." It was a gift of some fifty rides by a new service to and from the university. I have used it frequently already and with pleasure. I, who had always been at the wheel of my own car, have had to realize that I am well on the way to becoming an invalid.

I am grateful for my health insurance, for in the course of this year I have seen six or seven doctors. Nothing, I decided, contributes more to invalidism than many medical consultations, together with having to swallow six or eight medications in the course of various times of the day and in varying amounts. The most cheerful remark from the doctors is prefaced with "at your age" or a conversational use of "senility." My achievement of living into my nineties has become the cross on which all incapacity seems to hang.

It became clear to me some months ago that grantors and foundations would of course much prefer to assist younger scholars who had their lives ahead of them and were conversant with modern methods of preparation for their work. I was therefore at best a marginal case for continuing scholarly activity. Moreover, given my various ailments and incapacities, I needed to rethink what I could best do with the rest of my life.

Approaching the End

The knowledge that I do not have many years ahead, now that I am nearly ninety-three, was sharpened by the news that another old friend of Soviet House days had died. Newman Jeffrey had fought many battles for his health, but now in his eighties had to admit defeat. He and his wife, Fannie, had left Washington shortly before, to live in an Episcopal home in the Maryland suburbs.

About this time, I had also begun a correspondence with John Daniel, the son of Franz and Zillah Daniel of Soviet House days. John, a poet and writer, lives in Oregon. His mother had recently died, after living her last years with John and his wife. Now John was trying to learn more about both his father and his mother. In this undertaking he turned to me and the Van Gelders for any insights helpful to him. I knew that Franz had left his papers to the Reuther Labor Library at Wayne State University and wondered if Newman Jeffrey might have done the same, in which case he would have the most intimate knowledge of Franz's life. I phoned Fannie to find out whether this was a sound supposition, and learned that a few things of Newman's were also there.

I decided to attend the annual labor conference in the fall of 1994 at Wayne State University, which houses the library. While there, I could talk with Newman's former wife, Mildred Jeffrey, about this whole web of events. Mildred is only a few years younger than I but puts my work history to shame. She founded the Women's Division of the Auto Workers Union and represented the union in a great deal of its political activity under Reuther's leadership and for years after his death. She was a powerful political force in Michigan and one of the state's two representatives to the National Democratic Committee. She had also been on the board of Wayne State University for years and served as its chair for a long period. In her eighties her days were filled with political activity anticipating the 1994 state elections. We had been intimate friends when we shared the Cheyney House during our children's infancies. She has been honored often by political and union-associated organizations.

Mildred introduced me to the new director of the library, and I spent an afternoon there going through the Daniel papers and the much thinner collection from Newman. It was evident that Newman and Franz had indeed been close friends, but the notes they wrote each other carried no news beyond their momentary locations and their hopes or endeavors to meet, as their routes crossed. It was clear that if one should wish to leave a paper trail, it was useless without eventful content.

In late 1996 and quite unannounced, I received a book from John Daniel, entitled *Looking After: A Son's Memoir*.[10] In it, he recounts with love and pain his close relationship with his mother in the years at the end of her life, when she lived with him and his wife, Marylin, and fell deeper and deeper into the forgetfulness that Alzheimer's produces. The search for his mother's life forces him to look at his own life and his efforts to acquaint himself with the personae of them both. He acknowledges my very slight contribution of telling him about Franz and Zillah, when they were young radicals dedicated to the changing labor movement of the thirties, and about our Soviet House days. I had lost touch with Zillah soon thereafter and had never understood the all-too-short and inexplicable reports that reached me from time to time of her years in Scotland and in India, as she searched for knowledge of her own "self." In his book John sought to find and to understand that self in terms of her search then and his now.

THIS AUTOBIOGRAPHY

With this chapter, I am concluding my life history, which is deliberately, though surely, running down. As I approach the end of writing my story, I see the unity connecting all change much more clearly than I did a few years ago when I started chapter 1. For instance, I have always been a radical, though not always of the same persuasion. This stance began in college, where I became an antiwar pacifist. From there, I moved with many of my friends and colleagues in the labor schools and the YWCA Industrial Department to Socialism of the Norman Thomas variety. I felt at home in the new labor movement that the CIO represented. This identification with organized labor is firmly set within me, steering my course in making judgments about the movement and urging my alignment with its national and international organizations. I believe firmly in the power of such groups, particularly when they are committed to the welfare not only of their members but of the whole society. I have allied myself with many of them. Their power, I believe, derives not only from the growth in the numbers of their members but also from the immediacy of their advocacy programs, exerted in union with other elements of political, social, and economic life of the country. I regret and have often criticized unions when they have failed to establish such cooperative relationships. I happily applaud and support those unions that include unskilled and semiskilled fellow workers—women, African Americans, Latinas and Latinos, Asians, lesbians and gays—who work for the same employers, and who are included in the setting and achieving of social as well as wage goals.

Achievement of equality within such unions frequently rests first on recognizing a history of prejudiced gender and racial practices. If these are to be corrected, a first step may well be to establish a structure encouraging women to discuss and present their special needs, both as workers and mothers.

In my own case, I have come to see that, although I have indeed had five different careers, each has flowed from its predecessor, and each has been by no means simply a lucky accident, though I often thought so at the time. I can now readily accept that the daughter of my suffragist mother and grandmother sought her own best place in a complicated society, guided by convictions based on observation and experience during critical years. The accidents that led me into each occupational change were, after all, built on what I had already learned to deal with. Thus the old woman that I am at ninety-three is a considerably different person from the untrained girl produced by a protective family, itself a product of the nineteenth century. My growth has flowed from advocacy and participation in programs of action and less from the kinds of formal education and training demanded today.

This chronicle bridges almost all of the twentieth century, an era of economic change from a social order dominated by individual efforts in agriculture to a global undertaking that now demands from individuals constant adjustment to the needs of large organizations and a great deal of learning on the job, after achieving a command of sophisticated technological tools at the highest levels of formal education.

My life has been lived within this century, beginning with the Progressive period, and now nearing its end as we approach the year 2000. As I moved into the world of work in 1924, children of lower-middle-class families were often the first to go to college, though girls still faced a choice between work and marriage. While many women worked all through their adult lives, these women tended to be African Americans and immigrants, and not the college trained. The exceptions were women who planned to become teachers, administrative assistants, nurses, and, by my time, social workers. Marriage was frequently an alternative to any of these; the career of missionary, for many women, was more tempting than other alternatives. Children's achievement of a college education meant that in families like mine their incomes and social status would rise above their parents.

Beginning with World War I, however, the century became one of horror that continued through World War II and endless civil wars, in most of which the United States participated not only with troops but with the production and use of death-dealing weapons devised to destroy civil societies as well as military forces. The attempts to construct worldwide civil government through the United Nations and such of its various arms as the International Labor Organization (ILO), UNICEF, and the World Health Organization (WHO), came to be based on the military power of NATO. In my childhood, the United States had a standing army of 35,000 men located entirely in the United States, but in my lifetime, we became militarily the most powerful nation in the world, with its forces located in hundreds of bases in dozens of countries. Much of the economic wealth of the United States has been converted into the power over needy nations that loans to them represent. Financial aid has repeatedly been used as the major tool of peacemaking, namely the effort to acquire and control various countries as allies, regardless of their political organization or the quality of their leadership. Overall, the political result has usually been ugly.

New political power-masters in the United States in 1994 presented an ultra-conservative program, falsely named a "Contract with America," which contained a set of radically conservative reforms, never discussed, much less contracted, with the American people. In the name of achieving a healthy economy, the program abandoned the helpless by equating poverty with laziness. It demanded that single parents, mainly women, find work after receiving no more than two years of welfare support, during which they must have no more children. Presumably this work would make them self-supporting. Experience has demonstrated that many women as well as many men need extensive training in work discipline as well as in techniques, if they are to succeed at remunerative work of any kind. This new legislation gave to the states the responsibility for formulating plans, to be paid for by block grants from the Congress, generally sums smaller than they had received under the former welfare programs. Not surprisingly, many programs that had assisted welfare families to care for children disappeared. Indeed, aid to children in many categories was cut off for tens of thousands. Almost a million children have become the victims of these rebudgeted programs. A recent program would abandon disabled children. In addition, the adoption of an upgraded minimum wage, restricted to employers of more than fifty workers, is still too low to allow many families to become self-supporting.

More and more social experts are seeing such requirements as making children the main victims rather than the beneficiaries of our social policy. This body of lawmakers that purports to insist that government should not interfere with personal lives is, at the same time, advocating control over the most personal elements of individual lives.

We have likewise moved into a whole new era in communication in which the meaning of words has been twisted to mean exactly what they did not mean a few years ago. A new vocabulary has been created in the labor market and in the discussion of social policy, one that is not understood by most employees, who are vitally affected by what these words purport to tell them. The new vocabulary is abstract. It prettifies the central elements of work and wages. It "downsizes" rather than fires workers. It overlooks the effect of the practice on the family. It results in the denigration of the liberal philosophy that justified long-standing welfare practice. Instead of people's needs as a measure for developing a social welfare program, the test has become cost-effectiveness, and not in terms of the needy but of the taxpayer. The result has been layoffs in tens of thousands of workers and a growing gap between the multiplying numbers of low-paid workers, most of them women and male members of minority groups, and those with the highest incomes.

Many of the jobs for which tens of thousands of women and men have been trained have disappeared in favor of highly technical skills now only possible with the sophisticated help of a computer. In fact, many male employees in the lower levels of supervision have monopolized the office computer, and in effect used their secretaries as gatherers of data, which they feed into their machines. E-mail and faxes have replaced letters and memos. The concept of adapting work to family has largely been limited to women's work, when firms have paid attention to it at all. These considerations have mainly provided access to off-worksite social workers familiar with local agencies programs. A very few firms have introduced job sharing, flexible work hours, and work at home to meet women's overload. Most of them have avoided dealing with family problems, even at this level.

THE NATURE OF OUR CONCEPT OF EQUALITY

Recently, I have come to see that, although in 1964 we adopted a rule of equality, meant mainly to correct the underemployment and underpayment of white women and members of minority groups of both sexes, in fact we did something quite different. We made the white male worker the norm that these under-privileged groups were to measure up to.[11] The result has been to exempt white male workers from changing their customs and attitudes, especially with regard to the interconnections between work and family. Their female partners who become paid workers must conform to time and custom as men have established them. They must work eight hours a day, five days a week, and fifty weeks a year. When they take time off to bear and rear children, most employers see them as less dependable than men. The demands on working women require them as mothers to become supermoms. Many African-American and immigrant workers of both genders must take on the care of younger siblings, or of grandparents, parents, nieces, nephews, and cousins in the extended family. Employers look at such solutions of family problems not in terms of family needs, but in terms of cost-effectiveness to themselves. Inevitably, the least vocal, least organized workers—women and minority men—and all their children suffer.

AN AGENDA FOR CHANGE

If I could set an agenda for change, I would put a new definition of equality at the top of the agenda, and make clear that it includes men as well as women as parents and workers. The definition of equality would thus recognize that our first need is to provide children with a guarantee of a healthy life with related adults.

Second, I would endeavor to allow for labor market adjustments, based on finding jobs for a maximum number of job seekers. This would involve attention not only to training for new occupations, but to shortening the working week and possibly the working day. These reforms have all been introduced in other countries. Their experience could provide us with guidelines to improving employment strategies.

Third, I would seek to develop child care in a number of regards. I would see that it is readily available, organized with a sliding scale of costs related to parents' income and the number of children in the family of school age. I would seek also to develop comprehensive after-school care for children up to twelve years of age. I would establish training programs for the male and female workers in these child care and after-school programs, and seek decent wages for them. I would also insist that, in cases of divorce, both parents must remain responsible for the support of children, with a monetary value placed on the parent maintaining the home care of the children. The non-resident parent's contribution should be made to a recognized public or private agency, so that the caretaker parent may be assured of receiving it regularly from the agency responsible for its reception and administration.

Once these essentials were established, I believe that human needs of other kinds would become apparent and would follow. The cost of caring for most ordinary human needs would have assumed its proper place in the system, and then the most essential needs of the helpless could also be seen to, those especially of the aged, the disabled, and the terminally ill.

Change is the continuing fact in our lives. Changing times demand that we change our social and economic and labor problems. We change more slowly, as do our political decisions. We must constantly insist upon seeing the sources of change, as well as its nature and scope, and adapt our programs accordingly. We do this most effectively in our advocacy organizations where scholars aid citizens to conceptualize problems and approaches to their solution. The twenty-first century thus may arrive carrying an enormous social burden made up largely of correctable mistakes, but containing as well the new problems raised by further growth and structural change in both the labor market and the family. As a born optimist, I believe we cannot spend time bemoaning the past. Rather, we must recognize that we have handled it badly, and should not repeat those errors.

APPENDIX

SEVENTY-FIFTH BIRTHDAY CELEBRATION

November, 1978

Dear Alice,

When Fran Herman was planning your seventy-fifth birthday party—your gift to all of us on Saturday, November 11, 1978—we decided it was in some ways like a wedding. That is, a seventy-fifth can be seen as a turning point in life; in this case, it was an occasion when many, many old friends and family were brought together; it was a time when it was earnestly wished by all that everything would be perfect. There were many arrangements on Francine's mind: the Hotel School graduate who was flying back to Ithaca from Washington, bringing the food with him; the accommodations for out-of-towners; the seating, flowers, wine, stocking of the bar, and especially the arrangements for the delivery of you to the Big Red Barn on Saturday night in a luxurious 1934 Rolls Royce. Many arrangements, some anxieties beforehand.

You should know that all of us who came to Fran's lovely open house on Friday night thought carefully about what we would bring you, what we would wear, and most of all, what we would say. It was hard to think how to express our affection for you, Alice. You opened your gifts of books and pictures and wine and other treats with delight but you didn't gush or wince at any of the sentiments on the cards, so we were all relieved. In fact, I thought we had said it all Friday night. But I was wrong.

On Saturday night, each of the nineteen people was invited to share his or her sentiments on your seventy-fifth birthday. The idea was an inspiration. Many of us are hams; there is nothing we like better than the sound of our own voices. Somebody could have spoken for all of us, I suppose. But this was so much better.

As each one spoke, I was seized with a hunger to remember it all, to capture the memories, the humor, the affection on paper. So I have written down what I heard.

First, the setting:
The weather:

The most beautiful, balmy fall in Ithaca, New York, in years. The evening was warm with only a touch of frost in the air; the heavens, clear and bright with stars and a harvest moon.

The place:

The Big Red Barn, clumsily named carriage house on the property of the mansion of the first President of Cornell University, Andrew Dickson White. The fire was warm; the room, comfortable and capacious.

The time:

A little after six p.m. when you rolled up amid applause in that noble car. The group sailed into the Big Red Barn amid greetings and kisses and singing of Happy Birthday and much, much laughter.

Preliminaries:

We all enjoyed the delicious canapes—none of your bowls of peanuts scattered about but each plate a masterpiece of design and deliciousness. There were tiny potatoes with caviar, plump mushrooms stuffed with I forget what, and 12-year-old Black Label Scotch, which was appreciated.

Dinner:

We lined up to fill our plates, choosing between sole stuffed with crab and delicate chicken with paté and made our way to the tables where name tags were provided, avoiding the awkwardness of any of us naughtily jockeying for positions close to you as opposed to Below the Salt. For my part, I was delighted to find myself in what I chose to think of as the Best Place; if furthest from you, right next to the hostess, across from the granddaughter of Ken Douty, the youngest dinner guest, whose observations on the evening were delightful to hear, and next to a very interesting aristocratic-looking young woman who proved to be your son Phil's companion. My Life's Companion was across from me and a little to windward, which was exactly right.

Then the talks began:

Fred Hanson spoke first, reminding us in bankerly fashion that nobody should be giving you credit for something really due your mother: your good genes. Your mother lived to be 93, he said. He remembered parts of your life together over the years that apparently had stuck out in his mind: a Christmas card whose sentiment was "Repeal Capitalism"; what he termed your love affair with Norman Thomas; and he ended with a limerick, which drew applause, and yet another limerick authored by his wife, Lucy. He presented you with a gift from his daughter and then his present: seventy-five of Washington's Best in a Marshall Field box. There were chuckles at my end of the table when somebody said it was just too bad he hadn't chosen a stable currency like the Deutsche Mark.

Next came **Lucien Koch,** who spoke with affection of the days when you taught at Commonwealth College.

Tasso Tröscher drew on fifty-one years of friendship in his talk. You had come to his seventy-fifth, he said, so it was fitting that he should come to yours. He said he remembered happy days with the Cooks and that his first CARE parcel from the United States had come from you. "A person had to have five children to know what that meant," he said, and it was clear that it meant a lot. The special things about you that he mentioned were your love for human beings, your truthfulness, your immense capacity for work. You are the best ambassador our country has, he said. And, he said, he looked forward to the next birthday either of you will celebrate and he hoped you would be together five years from now, and ten.

Millie Jeffrey said that, while she was honored to be there, there was one thing we should remember: It's hard to live with Alice. She reminisced about the days when you were YWCA secretary, telling us that her child had been born in your house. She had always thought of you, she said, as the person Joe McCarthy missed. Soviet House was a center of radical activity for both women and men, she told us, and said that Fred would have been shocked, really. "You were the glue which held us all together," said Millie.

Ken Douty agreed that Alice accumulates people. You had provided a home for his two boys, he said, and then added reflectively that people who visited you got assignments, which made everybody laugh delightedly. It seemed to be the springtime of the world, he said, and then gave a historical sketch beginning back in 1848 of radical activity. What he really appreciates about you, he said, is that you respond. Alice believes and Alice keeps on. "She knows people are innately good and not evil, and, in times of trouble, this is a great comfort," he said.

Betsy Knapp spoke as a member of the Cornell Woodchoppers and told about organizing unions in Syracuse.

Antje Lemke told of the work at Syracuse and added simply that you are and have always been an example to her because you truly realize your ideals in practical life.

Tom Bernstein said the time limit made it hard for him to say what he wanted to say, but he wanted all present to know that it was because of you that he had come to the United States. He might, he said, have come some other way, but he would never forget that you made it possible then. Because of you, he said, he learned to speak English and write it well. He said that most important to him was your tough-minded optimism and your high standards. And, he added, "My mother is a role model to my children."

Maurice Neufeld, in professorial fashion, sought to summarize what had been said by others, alluding at first to your purported retirement, to your work in local unions in New York, to dual governments in unions, and to the women's Y as unique in caring about working people. Alluding to socialism as transforming civilization, he went on to read a beautiful passage from Tennyson's "Ulysses," which included these passages: "I cannot rest from travel. . . I am a part of all whom I have met. Life piled on life . . . a bringer of new things. . . . He works his work; I, mine . . . death closes all . . . the long day wanes . . . 'tis not too late to seek a new world. That which we are, we are. . . ."

Lois Gray spoke admiringly of your extraordinary outreach to people, and said that what she really appreciated was that, with you, nothing is impossible. "Try to get time with Alice now," she said. What do you answer? Maybe in 1980. Or 1985.

Rose Goldsen said that, for you two, it had been love at first sight. You had always been a model to her, she said, and now were to everybody at Longhouse. You are a guiding star there as well as unofficial ombudsman. " You are sharing your reminiscences with the others at Longhouse, and," she remarked, "now we are to 1937. But let me say," she concluded, "how much it strikes me that the same themes appear and reappear in Alice's life."

Fran Herman said that the best definition of friendship she knows is that your friend is your needs answered. So as not to be too sentimental, she said, she would not dwell on that and instead would focus on an extraordinary unearned advantage: your hair. Her perfect poem concluded, "People like you have more time to spare/Because you're blessed with a lifetime of curly hair."

Ed Gray said it was hard to summarize in two minutes. It's been said of labor leaders like himself, he said, "Them sons of bitches can't clear their throats in two minutes." But Ed used his two minutes neatly to say that you are truly a legend. Your early days together were harder than the present, he feels, because there were exhausting struggles some of which go on even today. What he admires about you is the fact that you are interested in what goes on today and tomorrow.

Ellen Bernstein said her comments would seem perhaps surprising from a daughter-in-law, especially one whose mother-in-law was not infinitely available as a grandmother baby-sitter. "But the children love you," she said. It was clear that she does, too.

Barbara Wertheimer said she thought outreach to people was all very well but that we should not forget that Alice has a very effective outreach to money too. People at foundations say to her, "How much do you want, Alice?" Her research goes swimmingly in many countries; she chops down forests of verbiage.

Laura Holmberg said the real essence of you is that you are a secret clean liver and that your high integrity was something we all respect. "It is trying, however," Laura concluded, that "When we go swimming together, I can't catch up."

Jennie Farley said that you had been a prime mover in the founding of the Women's Studies Program at a difficult time when there was blood on the floor. Then I said that there are five things I really like about you:

—When you have a good idea, you call up even if it's ten on Sunday morning.

—When I have what seems like a good idea but which might be a little dopey, you say, with refreshing candor, "That's a dopey idea."

—When I have a problem, you don't fill the air with dumb counselingspeak, repeating my own words back to me with meaningless reassurances. You tell me what seem to be sensible options.

—You are the only one who chooses to identify yourself in the Staff Directory not only as Professor Emerita but also as a member of the Executive Board of the Women's Studies Program.

—And best of all, you make us laugh. One day you brought in a new researcher, a new protégé, to lunch at the Statler. We looked at her with our noses just a little out of joint because she was so young, so pretty, with such perfect white teeth, such a long elegant raincoat, and, you assured us, she was a really good scholar. One of us, I fear it was I, growled that she probably had big bosoms, too. You considered that question and then answered mildly, "Pretty big." And you laughed and laughed and so did I.

Ted Hanson said he had had little contact with you for some years but that you became markedly more friendly when he moved to Hawaii. "We think you like it here? No way. You really love Hawaii," he assured us. You'll be with him, he told us, in January, swimming 100 laps and going back for more. We shouldn't forget, he said, that you went to Northwestern and never lost a debate in four years. He could believe that, he said. You'd be with him on the third of January, he said, and you'd be working hard on the fourth.

Philip Cook was last, and he began by clearing his throat professorially and saying, "Now when I met Alice Cook." In a serious vein, he said he had some uncomfortable memories. Even though he has the genes (which his uncle had already mentioned), he said that there would be times when you would want to teach him things, but he would resist. You two would find yourselves in a witless struggle, each fighting yourself. Alluding to other problems in his life, he said that, although he lacked your facility with words, he did write things. One time, he was warned that, if he published something, he wouldn't have a job anymore. And he didn't. Another time, when he spoke out about a purchasing director on the take, he soon found himself without a job. The clear implication was that your kind of integrity doesn't make life easier but it makes a person proud to be your son.

And you responded, Alice. You mentioned dear friends you wished were there—Franz, Ada, Marie Algor, Eleanor. Taking a breath, you mentioned your husband Wes who had, you said, "accompanied me the first half of my adult life." Then came, you said, the advent of independence and liberation. Reflecting on your many careers in unions and as a researcher and activist in many parts of the world, you said you saw the many careers being combined in your latest work with Val Lorwin on women in trade unions in Europe. You thought back, you said, to your grandmother and mother marching as suffragists to Washington in 1916 and said proudly that you had picketed the White House for votes for women. Looking forward, you told of your second book to be planned in Bellagio, Italy, with fourteen coauthors from fourteen countries. You mentioned your plan for a brochure on affirmative action in public employment in Hawaii and told of your projected visit to Wellesley next fall. You said how much you enjoy your morning swim, how grateful you are to Barbara Wertheimer for her help in finding funds to support your work, how fondly you remember Tasso with ribbons on his manly bosom, honored with a troupe of trumpeters. And you ended on a simple note. "Thank you all," you said. "Thank you."

And I join with everyone who was thinking of you that day and wishing you Happy Birthday, dear Alice Hanson Cook,

Jennie Farley

NOTES

1. Although this village has the same name, it is not to be confused with the southern city of Kalmar. Mother and I, on our first trip to Sweden in 1950, found this village and even a farm that could have been the one on which Grandma Hanson grew up. It was on a small lake with an island in the middle where the cows were grazed in the summer and where she rowed out morning and evening to milk them. All this and the little more that we knew about her life in Sweden she told my mother, who became the daughter she never had.

2. Out of this period I have a few pages of my Aunt Lucretia's diary, which recorded on August 2, 1898, that she was seventeen and on August 21 that Flora was about to get married:

> Oh, God forbid . . . She is no more fit for marriage than anything. She would be buried in Milton with no chance for improvement of mind or health; she has no health and the first child would ruin her health. Then she don't care for any one person to have it last as long as the marriage vows call for . . . But the worst is to think the brilliant future I have planned and all her relatives believe is possible, and it is, will fade away forever. Oh, I can't stand it. She will leave me to fight alone and I can't. Yes, I can and will but she could help so much by staying with me. How can I go away off to begin life alone?
>
> Sep. 14. Wed. Evanston Township High School opened yesterday and Flora and I duly attended and were recorded as Seniors, she having 35 credits and I, 41 1/2 . . . Yesterday PM Flora started out to do some errands and when she returned had been to see Prof. Cumnock who will give her $12 per term for playing for the Physical Culture Classes. After due consideration and planning, Mamma decided that she can go the School of Oratory this year. Whoopee. She will try to get the scholarship for next year. I am glad for she wants to go so much and it will get her mind off some things I don't like. Of course I will have to go to School alone . . . but what's that compared to Flora going into the School of Oratory???

3. Many years later she joined me and some friends from Ithaca, for a trip to the Shakespeare Festival at Stratford, Ontario, where she rediscovered the very stage in the Avon Theater from which she had "declaimed" before my birth.

4. For a considerable period the Prohibition Party also existed as the direct political arm of the Prohibition movement. Although it never became a genuinely competitive political party in the sense of electing candidates to office, it was in some areas a potent political force in state and local elections. Somewhat comparable to the abortion issue today, anti-alcoholism became the single telling issue for its supporters, both men and women. On the male side, the supporting organization was the Anti-Saloon League.

5. Frozen food first became available after World War II. The basement, where it was cold but above freezing, was the storeroom for home-canned products and vegetables that could be stored for a few months. These conditions restricted menus considerably, but had always to be kept in mind.

CHAPTER 2

1. Later Lillian Herstein had among her students the future Supreme Court Justice Arthur Goldberg. She represented the Teachers Union in the District Council of the AFL, whose president, the great labor liberal in a conservative period of labor history, John Fitzpatrick, was her close friend. Lillian later appeared in my life when we were both board members of the summer schools for women workers. She served for years on the board of the Chicago branch of the American Civil Liberties Union (ACLU), as well as in the national leadership of the American Federation of Teachers (AFT) when I was an office holder in its Philadelphia local union. She remained to her death a liberal light in the Chicago political darkness and a spokesperson there for labor and its goals.

CHAPTER 3

1. Mary was a New Hampshire resident, who had gone to the University of Wisconsin and then trained in early childhood education at a progressive school in Alabama. Her mother, Margaret, had left her husband and taken Mary and her brother, Herman, to live with Hartley Dennett, an architect, in East Alstead, New Hampshire.

2. He embarrassed me by seeking my reaction to the top news of the day. In the course of moving, I had not read the newspapers since leaving Indianapolis and knew nothing of the fact that Henry Ford, the great and presumably liberal industrialist, had just declared he would pay five dollars for the basic eight-hour day. Nothing like it existed in the country, though the Progressive League had long included a minimum wage among its legislative goals.

3. The father, many years dead, had lost his sight early and had trained Brownie when he was only four or five to read to him not only in English but eventually in several other languages. When Brownie was not available, the story went, Father had lifted his chair up on the dining room table to bring him as close as possible to the one light source, probably at that time a gas jet, which enabled him to squint his way through some pages. While Brownie never appeared to mind his lack of formal education, Frances wanted to be a doctor. At the University of Wisconsin she found the support she needed among some independent alumnae. She went there for her undergraduate, medical, and psychiatric studies, and practiced in California for a few years before her untimely death in her

early forties. "Sweetie" seemed content to work as a librarian, supporting the family and, not least important, keeping her husband in books.

4. Ruth was the daughter of a radical miner from Coeur d'Alene, Idaho. He had been blacklisted for his union work and had moved his family to what he hoped would be the security of the Llano community.

5. The school was founded in a period when Brookwood and the Bryn Mawr Summer School, as well as many municipal labor colleges, existed both as residential and evening schools for working people.

6. Having finished paying for my college education, the family gave up the rooming house on Sherman Avenue and moved back to the Simpson Street apartment—a happy change, particularly for Mother, whose close friendship with "Knappy" remained a pleasure for both of them throughout the rest of their lives.

7. They consisted of Covington Hall, an IWW poet, who wrote under the name Covami and was a native Louisianian; F. M. Goodhue, a New Englander, who had for a while taught mathematics at the University of Cincinnati; Alice Chown, a Canadian radical educator; W. T. Benton, a lawyer; Harold Coy, a journalist, and his frail, arthritic mother, a retired English teacher. Brownie was school secretary and secretary to the founder and president, William Zeuch.

8. Kate O'Hare had been a well-known Socialist with a gift of persuasive oratory. She was a close associate of Eugene V. Debs and like him had been imprisoned during the First World War because of her antiwar activities. She had been considered as a vice-presidential candidate to run with Debs on the Socialist Party ticket in 1920, but the Party needed at least one candidate who could take to the campaign road. When President Coolidge commuted her penalty in 1920, Kate and her husband, Frank Sr., went to the Llano colony. Later in the summer, she campaigned steadily for her old friend, Debs, who was still in prison. Her husband, whom she divorced a few years later to marry an oil executive, had been in their active Socialist days her manager, advance agent, editor, and all-purpose aide and front man. Together, they had put out the *Socialist Vanguard*. They had four children: The youngest were twin boys, named Eugene and Victor for Debs. Next came Kathleen, the only girl, and then the oldest, Frank Jr., who was most loyal to Kate, visiting her often during her imprisonment. For a time he was a Commonwealth student. He and I shared a birthday and were closely in touch for many years. On her release from prison, Kate took a job with the conservative United Garment Workers to campaign against the sale of prison-made garments in the private market. She taught labor history intermittently when she was at Commonwealth and organized its faculty into a local of the Teachers Union, which enabled her to lead a small delegation (including me) to a meeting of the Arkansas State Federation of Labor.

For further information on Kate, see Richard J. Altenbaugh, *Education for Struggle: The American Labor Colleges of the 1920s and 30s* (Philadelphia: Temple University Press, 1990), pp. 81–85. This book includes a good deal of Commonwealth's history, particularly post-1931.

9. Coy's mother was, despite her age, closely associated with the younger group through her alliance to her son's views. She was a gentle, arthritic woman, almost an invalid, though not yet sixty. Nevertheless, she was a much-loved tutor to new, inadequately prepared students.

10. Coy had considerable experience as a working journalist, having worked on the *St. Louis Post-Dispatch,* as well as on a California paper or two. Among other jobs he had held on the West Coast was that of speechwriter for "a pompous old labor skate" (an enduring "labor leader" who liked to enrich his public utterances with multisyllabic expressions). He knew the most wild-eyed of the Wobblies (the IWW) and had written speeches for them as well as for the stuffiest of local AFL leaders. He had also ridden the rails with hoboes and shared their "jungles" with them. When years later he married a friend of mine, she wanted nothing so much as to repeat at least one of these routes across the country with him. He took her all the way on freight cars, and when, between rides, they came across a fellow passenger in the jungle, he introduced her as "queen of the jungle."

11. He confessed to me later that, when I was baby-sitting, he had come by the house to find Wes's car there and no lights on. "I feared that one day you would have to tell us that you were pregnant!"

12. We young organized ourselves into a scholarly group, calling ourselves "the Parnassians." We wrote papers on our ideas and read them at regular meetings for amused discussion. One of mine was entitled "The Names of Small Towns in the United States, with Special Reference to Arkansas." It was based on a scrutiny of the Postal Directory in search for the mildly pornographic.

13. For these quotes and much of the detailed information on this episode, I have relied on Ray and Charlotte Koch, two former students at the school, who stayed on for years as staff and whom I thank for *Workers' Education: The Story of Commonwealth College* (New York: Schocken Books, 1972).

14. When the school was in the process of being founded, Zeuch had named himself, Benton, and Kate O'Hare as the board of directors. These three now were fully persuaded that no further change was needed; indeed it was their view that it might even be dangerous to include people in decision making who, instead of adhering to Zeuch's elitist, intellectual, and rational leadership, proceeded from a Marxist or other radical point of view.

15. Around this time, the Y changed its bylaws to accept Catholics and established an International Institute as a center for working with foreign women. Before I had begun working there, the organization had included African-American women—albeit in special centers in their own communities where African-American staff were available—and African-American women community leaders made up their boards of directors. Citywide staff members could encourage interracial activities among all members through social affairs, business meetings, and conferences such as the one we were attending in 1927.

16. I lost touch with these women for a while, but later in the fifties when I had moved to New York State, they were still together, working in the Y Industrial Department in Buffalo, where manufacturers and small-business men again sought to abolish the department's work with working women by persuading the United Way to drop the Y from its list of supported organizations. This time, however, the Central YWCA agreed to assist its Industrial Department in raising its own budget. After proving its ability to provide successful self-support, the Y was accepted back into the United Way within a few years.

17. She left us to join a department of group work in the School of Social Work at Western Reserve University in Cleveland, headed by a former national industrial secretary. The creation of this department in a recognized professional school of social work was a breakthrough to a new, more inclusive concept of social work.

18. On the occasion of Niebuhr's 100th birthday, Arthur Schlesinger Jr. wrote an insightful and memorable tribute to this man who was a strong influence on his life. A few excerpts may convey the mixed flavors of a man whom I, too, found endlessly informative and stimulating:

> What gave his activities unity and power was his passionate sense of the tragedy of life, irony of history, and fallibility of humans—and his deep conviction of the duty, even in face of these intractable realities, to be firm in the right, as God gave us to see the right.
>
> His emphasis on sin startled my generation, brought up on optimistic convictions of human innocence and perfectibility. . . . Human nature was evidently as capable of depravity as of virtue.
>
> Of all his thoughts, I treasure this the most: "Man's capacity for justice makes democracy possible, but man's inclination to injustice makes democracy necessary."
> *The New York Times,* June 22, 1992, p. A17.

19. Since nepotism rules in this, as in most universities at the time, forbade the employment of two members of the same family in the same department, she maintained her status as a professor by serving as an adjunct at two other institutions in the Chicago area. However, in this capacity she would not become eligible for tenure.

20. The Bryn Mawr Summer School had been founded in 1921 by the president of the college, M. Carey Thomas, and friends of hers in the WTUL. These women then added representatives from six of the other "Seven Sisters" women's colleges. Indeed it was the original idea, though one never realized, that the school might move from summer to summer among the seven campuses. Faculty were recruited, however, from all these colleges.

21. By 1928 Jane's assistant was Eleanor Coit, a Smith graduate who had earlier been a Y industrial secretary. When Jane decided to go to Washington in the New Deal, Eleanor moved easily into the school's second decade of leadership. These two women, similar in age and family backgrounds, were very different temperamentally. Jane was a poet, warmly concerned about the people she worked with, many of whom became subjects of her poetry. She was straightforward, uncomplicated, deeply committed to and loved by her students. She was a good friend and neighbor of Eleanor Roosevelt at Val-kill, across the Hudson River from Jane's family home at West Park. When the Bryn Mawr Summer School closed in the mid-thirties, Jane offered her family home, together with a neighboring mansion, as quarters for the Hudson Shore Labor School, directed first by Jane's friend Ernestine Friedman and later by Marie Algor. Barbara Wertheimer published a booklet of Jane's poems under the imprint of the Cornell University Labor Education Program in New York. Eleanor Coit was, by contrast with Jane, preeminently an organizer and administrator, sometimes blunt and impatient with coworkers but tirelessly innovative in finding support for, and extending the scope of, labor education. With Tess Wolfson, Eleanor set up a summer school for white-collar workers, and when the United Nations (UN) was founded she organized programs that acquainted labor leaders with its functions. She won the cooperation of the Farmers Union in the Dakotas and Minnesota with the Adult Education Association (AEA), and established special projects with local labor organizations in St. Louis and Philadelphia and with the New Jersey CIO. She made the Washday Conference, founded at Brookwood in the twenties, an annual event for labor educators of all stripes, particularly a place where both AFL and CIO educators could meet during the bitterest warfare between the two federations. She was deeply concerned with adopting and adapting teaching methods designed to reach adults. Eleanor's most important written contribution was in generating a book edited by Theodore Brameld, *Workers' Education in the United States: Fifth Yearbook of the John Dewey Society* (New York: Harper and Brothers, 1941). Her personal papers are at Smith College.

22. In a sense the Bryn Mawr school was part of the adult education movement that included evening schools, high school equivalency programs, and the settlements' cultural programs, especially in music. Bryn Mawr offered both general and labor education. This combination meant that the program included courses from theory to advocacy, offering both tools and practice.

It encouraged students belonging to organizations—unions, Ys, and settlements—to work there effectively when they returned home, by using public libraries, evening schools, and union labor education programs where they existed.

23. The most successful of these was Kitty Pollak's economics text, *Your Job and Your Pay* (New York: The Vanguard Press, 1931).

24. I was deeply attached to the modern women poets, among them Edna St.Vincent Millay, H. D., and Sara Teasdale. Just before I finished college and for some years thereafter, I tried writing poetry myself. Another aim we teachers of English had was to produce an annual book of student writing. Much of it was autobiographical. A few years later a collection of excerpts from these annuals was published by the Affiliated School of Workers. My contribution in 1928 was to spend many hours interviewing an African-American woman from Chicago. We produced a detailed story of her family's migration from the South to Chicago, their settlement in and accommodation to the city, her education, and her subsequent work life in a factory.

25. The summer faculty included men as well as women. For many years, Colston Warne, Amherst economist and later the organizer of the group that began publishing *Consumer Reports,* came each summer. Corwin Edwards, economist at Princeton, and Ewan Clague, later head of the Bureau of Labor Statistics in the federal Department of Labor, were among other men who taught in the school.

26. Undergraduate assistants, from other colleges as well as Bryn Mawr, worked as tutors to students and aides to faculty. They organized trips and evening entertainment, picnics and folk dances, games and swim periods.

27. There were no closets in the rooms; instead, two wall hooks were available, one for everyday dress and one for Sunday garb. Bookshelves and desks were part of the furnishings. At a reunion more than fifty years later, many women climbed the dormitory steps to revisit a room they had seen as spacious—even gracious—still warm with the memories of a very special summer, with its view into the trees and out to the slope of the campus.

28. A vast number of these graduates of the American women's colleges and some from the Midwestern state universities never married. Among the women important to my development in labor education were Hilda Smith, Eleanor Coit, Ernestine Friedman, Brownie Lee Jones, Eleanor Emerson, Jane Addams, Lucy Carner, Annetta Dieckmann, Gladys Palmer, Alice Hamilton, Sophanisba Breckinridge, and Anne Guthrie.

29. I learned that the history of current workers' education began at Ruskin College at Oxford University in Britain. Other important influences came from the People's High Schools in Scandinavia. I became especially inter-

ested in a relatively new school, the International People's College in Denmark. My interest also centered on the Academy of Labor in Frankfurt, Germany. There were also so-called labor colleges, offering evening programs in the twenties in many American cities, whose leaders included Israel Mufson in Philadelphia. The AFL and many unions in the AFL had their own educational departments, the most famous of which were in the International Ladies Garment Workers Union under Fannia Cohn (and later Mark Starr); in the Amalgamated Clothing Workers with J. B. S. Hardman; and in the Textile Union under Elizabeth Nord. In the AFL, Spencer Miller was the director of the Workers Education Bureau. The first residence school in the U.S. was probably Brookwood Labor College under the direction of A. J. Muste. In the history of labor education in America, the twenties was the seed decade.

CHAPTER 4

1. All references to Frankfurt that follow through this volume are to Frankfurt am Main.

2. We visited Berea College, Kentucky; the University of Wisconsin to meet with the Commons-Perlman group named informally after John R. Commons (1862–1945), a leading historian of labor, and Selig Perlman (1888–1959), an economist who also wrote on labor history and there met two people we would later see in Germany. We also visited Clara Kaiser in her new position at the Western Reserve School of Social Work; two of Wes's maternal aunts in Franklin, Massachusets, where his mother was born; and finally, Mary Chase at her home in East Alstead, New Hampshire, where we met Mary's mother, Margaret, and her companion, Hartley Dennett. (After our time in Europe, we often returned to East Alstead for summer vacations.)

3. German universities at that time began the fall semester about November 1, though professors had some leeway in beginning the term, which lasted through February. The summer semester began about July 1 and ended about the middle of August. Students often attended more than one university in order to hear the best men in their field. The summer semester was a favorite time for moving about to another campus.

4. Etta was the daughter of an English mother and a German father who had been a dealer in British coal for Germany. The family was bilingual and very British middle-class. Despite her friendship and help during the summer in Hamburg, Etta found us, as she wrote my mother, "very unorthodox in their ideas and ways of life."

5. I immediately enlisted Father to take care of her American itinerary, for she would have to cross the continent by train to get to Palo Alto. Moreover, she wanted to see some cities, and certainly Washington, D.C. For that part of the trip I enlisted my godparents, the Prestons, in Alexandria. I was sure

that Dr. Stöppel, to whom we felt very indebted, would be received without question by all these people—even the Prestons, with whom my ties had by now grown rather weak.

6. Until 1948, German currency was called Reichsmark, abbreviated as RM.

7. Not much later, as the depression deepened in the United States, most of our states passed similar laws.

8. On its pages I read my first Hemingway, the German translation of *The Sun Also Rises.*

9. I still have my Belegbuch, my registration for all those courses, which one took to the professor for his signature at his first lecture. Among the professors I met in those early days were several with whom I had contact in the late thirties at the University in Exile, located at the New School in New York, to which many of them fled from Hitler's Germany. Among these were Professor Pribram, with whom I took World Economic Programs, and Professor Wertheimer, whose son and daughter-in-law, Val and Barbara, began to work in the Amalgamated Clothing Workers Union, with which I was also associated. I was also attracted to a seminar on Party programs taught by Ludwig Bergstruässer, a former Socialist deputy in the German Reichstag (the national parliament), and to one taught by Arthur Feiler, an editor of the *Frankfurter Zeitung,* on reparations that, under the Versailles Treaty, had to be paid by Germany to the victorious Allies. Since Germany was still making these payments eleven years after the end of the war, it was a touchy subject.

10. Immediately after Hitler came into power in 1933, Dr. Hellinger returned from a skiing trip to find that her office in City Hall literally no longer existed. Her response was to enroll herself as part of the Jewish community, with which she had previously had no ties, and to plan to come to the United States. She came first to me and lived for a short while in the Soviet House group with which I was then affiliated in Philadelphia. She married a German physicist, also in exile, and lived most of her life as an instructor at Purdue University, where her husband was a professor and where she joined the Quaker Meeting.

11. In her manuscript, beginning here and throughout the following chapters, Alice refers to the SPD as the Socialist Party. After Alice's death, fact-checking, led in Germany by Hanna Beate Schöpp-Schilling, advised that, though SPD was inspiringly Socialist from Alice's point of view, it was called the Sozialdemokratische Partei Deutschlands, which translates as the Social Democratic Party. What complicates the issue, Schöpp-Schilling writes, is that members of this party were called Socialists by members of the bourgeois parties at the time (and today). [Ed.]

12. Hans Stroh, who became a pastor in Baden, offered me not only personal friendship but religious comfort many years later in 1950, when divorce faced me and I had returned to Germany. Eberhardt Schultz, who had probably never been comfortable in a theological seminary, became a journalist who followed the army for the *Süddeutsche Zeitung* during the Second World War. After the war Eberhardt gave me many of his articles to read for a clearer picture of the effect of war on German civilian life.

13. Apartment schools were an invention of Gertrud Hermes, one of the few women then active in the field. Her concept was to reach unemployed young workers, bringing eight or ten of them together in an apartment supplied by the city from among the vacant ones it administered. She would organize these workers into a self-supporting living unit to which they each contributed a major portion of their unemployment insurance, or wages, if they got a job. They all shared the maintenance work. The live-in leader and teacher taught classes in the afternoons and evenings.

14. I began with Professor Karl Mannheim, newly arrived as head of the Sociology Department, whom the *Frankfurter Zeitung* described as the professor of the newly recognized social science, sociology, in Germany. I summed up my impression of him by writing, "He is comparatively young, and if he remains at Frankfurt, as he probably will for years, this university must then be considered seriously as the place to study sociology in Germany." I was also taking a course or two in the Institut für Sozialforschung (Institute for Social Research) under the headship of Professor Horkheimer and his assistant, Theodor Adorno. (Both these men became widely known in the United States, after they fled there when Hitler came to power.) Important as the Institute was then and later, its status was that of an experimental center at the university before sociology was yet recognized as a department of the Faculty of Philosophy (roughly corresponding to a Faculty of Arts and Sciences).

15. Zetkin had been the spokeswoman for Socialist women, in the trade unions, nationally and internationally since the late nineteenth century. She had early joined the Communist Party after its formation, and in her old age was permanently resident in Russia. With dual citizenship in Germany and Russia, she had appeared on the German Communist ticket honorifically near the top of that list and for her old district. As voters in this 1930 election moved to the extreme right or left, the Communist Party had received enough votes to entitle it to representation in the Reichstag.

CHAPTER 5

1. I still have in my files pieces of printed articles that I wrote for him between 1932 and 1935, mainly on the situation in Germany.

2. This submission of labor disputes to impartial, quasi-judicial third parties was introduced by the Amalgamated Clothing Workers, under the presidency of Sidney Hillman, early in its life in Chicago. The process was not yet widely accepted in the union movement and certainly had no recognition in law. Wharton School economist George Taylor was the third party selected by many Philadelphia unions; his students, rapidly spreading throughout industrial centers in the course of the thirties, became in demand as the move toward unionism strengthened.

3. They were both linotype operators for a leading Philadelphia paper and worked at night. Vinita was one of the few women in the trade and, for a considerable period, the only woman in the Philadelphia local union.

4. The son of a British anarchist family, John had grown up in the United States. Through his writing and reporting, he gave the union and its members a decidedly liberal cast, one the union president, Emil Rieve, an erstwhile Socialist immigrant, clearly supported. A few years later John Edelman was largely responsible for the union's construction of a union housing development, the Carl Mackley Houses, named as a tribute to the union martyr. Still later, in Washington, John had a long career as lobbyist and publicist for the Textile Workers Union and the CIO, and as a networker promoting New Deal programs with liberal organizations.

5. When the Public Employment Relations Board (PERB) was created in New York State many years later, the law carried George Taylor's name. See Ronald Donovan's study of PERB, *Administering the Taylor Law: Public Employee Relations in New York State* (Ithaca, N.Y.: ILR Press, 1990).

6. In 1928, Al Smith's running as the Democratic candidate against the Republican Herbert Hoover raised, for the first time, whether a Catholic could or should become president of the United States. Hoover won largely because of his humanitarian record in feeding the starving in the victimized countries at the end of World War I, and because he was seen as a man above politics in his long career as an engineer both in this country and abroad.

7. One such attempt was aimed at taking over the antiwar movement. This ended in bitter disillusionment in 1939, when the Russian Communist Party under Stalin signed the Hitler-Soviet Pact and the American Communist Party decided it must follow the Soviet lead.

8. A few years later he had turned 180 political degrees and, as a friend and valued staff member of Senator Joseph McCarthy, was engaged in burrowing out alleged Communists in the movie industry, in government, and in schools and universities.

9. Fifty years later, I rediscovered Mary in Philadelphia, where she told me of her continuing antiwar work, her association with Bishop Tutu of South Africa, and her ongoing activity in community affairs.

10. This "Washday Conference," held on Washington's birthday each year, had begun at Brookwood Labor College in the early twenties, under the auspices of its Teachers Union Local 189. After Brookwood closed, for lack of sufficient financial support in the depression, Eleanor Coit took over the organization of these meetings, thus providing a place where labor educators could meet and exchange their experiences. This opportunity became especially important after the creation of the CIO and the mutual hostility between it and the AFL unions.

11. At this time I first met Ewan Clague, who was teaching statistics in the Philadelphia School of Social Work. I took a course from him in which I made a study of women's weekly wages in the silk district upstate. The pay envelopes I collected showed base rates as low as ten to fifteen cents per hour, from which deductions for broken needles and other mishaps further reduced wages to as little as a dollar fifty to two dollars per week.

12. MacArthur was later the hero of the Pacific War and the conqueror of Japan.

13. The campus was moved then to Mt. Ivy, a Y camp in New York State for a year or so, before finding its permanent home on the family property of Hilda Smith at West Park on the Hudson.

14. There, Wes met staff member Barent Landstreet, a native Philadelphian, newly married, and a huge, blustery man with whose family we quickly became enduring friends. After World War II we were both in Europe at the same time. Barent's namesake son, known as Pete, spent several years at Cornell, where he took his degree in sociology, and where his parents often visited.

15. Paul came to Philadelphia from the YMCA at the University of Kansas, to become the first paid Socialist Party secretary for the Philadelphia Local; Newman Jeffrey, just graduated from the University of Kansas, and a long-time admirer of Paul, came with him. His wife was only sporadically in Philadelphia. Through Paul we quickly came to know a wide circle of Socialist Party members, including Franz Daniel, one of the few genuinely charismatic labor organizers I have known. Philip Van Gelder, a recent graduate of Brown, also moved into what became an intimate group that shortly established what today might be called a commune and within the year had become Soviet House.

16. Among those who came through my sponsorship were Hans Staudinger, Prussian minister of energy, who became dean of the University in Exile at the New School in New York; two officers of the Carpenters Union, whom I had

met briefly in our Hamburg days in 1929 and who found refuge for a time at the Highlander Folk School in Tennessee; and Hedwig Wachenheim, a member of the Prussian legislature and author of much of its pre-Hitler social legislation. Her career later overlapped with mine, when we both worked at the same time in Germany in the late forties, under the occupation.

17. Werner von Siemens opened his first factory in 1847, a small shop to manufacture the world's most advanced telegraph. Werner himself designed a fundamentally improved pointer telegraph, which maintained an automatic electrically controlled synchronism between transmitter and receiver. From 1927 onward, Siemans was critical to the German war effort, with its advances in heavy electrical engineering, e.g., water-based circuit-breakers, X-ray rotary anode tubes, teleprinters, autopilot aircraft control systems, the world's first electric locomotive, a TV intercom between Berlin and Leipzig (extended to Munich in 1938), among others. Development work at Siemens was interrupted by the war and was not resumed until 1950. Today Siemens is a world leader in communications and information systems. While the company's headquarters remain in Germany, eighty Siemens manufacturing and assembly plants are located in the U.S. Excerpted from Siemen's Web site: www.siemens.com.

18. Paul soon learned that he had tuberculosis and had to leave for a sanatorium in northern New York State.

19. Fran Herman reminds us that Alice was skilled in shorthand and often took full notes. [Ed.]

20. At Soviet House we often amused ourselves as we sat over coffee in the living room by creating rhymes about current events as we viewed them. We took on George Meany's handling of the depression:

Eeny, Meany, meiny mo,
American capital, go, stop, go!
You can stuff all your planning
Of investment and manning
If profits continue to grow.

21. I designate Michael as "ours" because he often spent weekends at Soviet House and was close to our group there. He went to Spain in the thirties, and after World War II, under the Marshall Plan, he became labor attaché to Sweden and then the State Department's labor attaché at Bonn in Germany, where our paths crossed again and again.

22. Either Gorman's weakened union was no longer a desirable base unit for TWOC, or the AFL persuaded him that they would be of more assistance to him than the CIO could be. Gorman remained in the AFL, and under his leadership the union became largely dependent for its continued existence

on its holding of the union label on work clothing. It could thus guarantee the manufacturers with whom it had contracts that they were assured of the market for clothing worn by skilled union manual workers.

23. Larry came from Brookwood Labor College. There he had come to the attention of Jim Maurer, a member of its board and the widely known and admired president of the Pennsylvania Federation of Labor. When Brookwood had to close in the mid-thirties for lack of sufficient support, Maurer took Larry to Reading, Pennsylvania, as head of the Labor College there. Larry was an early member of the CIO journalists' union, the Newspaper Guild. For more details on his career, see my memorial article, "Larry Rogin: Socialist, Unionist, Labor Educator," *Labor Studies Journal* 16:1 (spring 1995).

24. Millie and Jeff joined the Amalgamated's campaign among shirt workers in upstate Pennsylvania, under the direction of Bessie Hillman, the wife of the union president, Sidney Hillman. Franz was active there for a time but was soon sent south with TWOC. When Miriam became pregnant, she and Phil decided to leave Philadelphia for Camden, which was nearer his work with the Shipyard Union.

25. Payne was a close associate of Emil Rieve, president of the Hosiery Workers. With the founding of TWOC, he became director of the new Rayon Division.

26. Ken was one of our recruits for a staff job. He was born and brought up in Baltimore where he had taught school and was an active member of the Teachers Union and a member of the Socialist Party. I first became acquainted with him on my visit to Lewistown, where he was then located, and immediately became friends with him, his wife, Mary, and his young son, Michael. Our close relationship endured during his tragic life. At this period, his family and Wes and I rejoiced in our instant compatibility.

27. Pat later joined the staff of TWOC. Still later, in Marshall Plan days, she was stationed in Paris while we were in Vienna. This friendship still exists as I write.

28. Early in her career Dr. Hamilton had lived and worked at Hull House, where she had revealed the effects of lead poisoning among immigrants working in a Chicago plant, enameling bathtubs. She had studied, traveled, and worked abroad and knew the rayon industry in several countries there. She told me that all rayon plants in America at that time were foreign-owned, by Italian, Dutch, French, German, and British corporations. In all these countries laws existed prohibiting workers' exposure to the chemicals that so severely damaged the Marcus Hook workers. Dr. Hamilton visited the plants in our circuit that used the Marcus Hook method, and in Lewistown, where the company closed the doors to her, she called in the federal marshal to gain access.

29. The report was written by Val Lorwin, then in the Labor Department. Later, when he was in the State Department, Val was of immeasurable assistance to me in preparing me for my first postwar trip to Germany. Still later, he was my colleague in a major study of women in trade unions.

30. Within a few months a draft law was adopted, in the interests of labor peace in wartime. It exempted labor officials from army service. Wes was never called up.

CHAPTER 6

1. We had decided on names before the birth, and this boy became Philip Jeffrey, after two of our Soviet Housemates, Philip Van Gelder and Newman Jeffrey. The announcement to friends and relatives of the baby's arrival was made on a printed three-by-five-inch card entitled *LABOR NEWS,* Vol. 1, No. 1, and dated June, 1939. The text consists of six brief paragraphs, as follows:

> The first branch of the Hanson-Cook Union was chartered on Tue., June 13, at Women's Homeopathic Hospital, 20th & Dauphin Sts., Philadelphia. Alice and Wesley announced today with considerable pride in the success of their first organizing venture of this type.
>
> The new branch will be known as Philip Jeffrey. He weighed in for his bout with life and the capitalist system at 7 pounds, 4 oz.
>
> A closed shop agreement was immediately drawn up to govern living and working conditions for the new membership, with the parent organization acting as guarantor for fulfillment of the terms of the contract.
>
> This contract, worked out in more detail than the usual document of its type, covers hours not only of work but of play and sleep; intake and outgo of nourishment; indoor and outdoor life; type of work and play clothing; provisions for protection of health and safety. In a word it seeks to cover the entire life of the new organization.
>
> Although Alice and Wesley point with pardonable pride to the success of their own efforts in this organization job, they acknowledge with considerable gratitude the good services as rendered in assisting them by Dr. Samuel Myers.
>
> The headquarters of the new branch temporarily at least will be with the parent organization at Moylan, Penna., where interested parties are urged at all times to check up on the care with which the terms of the new contract are being carried out.

2. In its relatively long history the house had been remodeled a time or two. What in the original house had been two small rooms on the first floor, each with a fireplace, had been made into a single living room. A clapboard wing had been added to the original stone rectangle and then become the kitchen and dining room. At some less felicitous time a front porch had been built across the house. The second floor consisted of two large bedrooms, a third room with a fireplace that we decided to call the study, and the single bathroom. The third

floor had one large room across the front and a somewhat smaller room at the back. All the windows on that floor were small, but with sills deep enough to be window seats.

3. After leaving the Kensington Y, Marie had worked for a time in an evening program of labor education developed under the Philadelphia Board of Education's evening school for adults. I believe it was a unique undertaking. There she met and married a musician with two teenage children whose mother she remained, long after the marriage had ended. After Hudson Shore, in her mid-forties, she joined Eleanor Coit's new organization, the Affiliated Schools. Under its program she went to New Jersey at the request of Carl Holderman, who had become CIO director there, to direct the education program for new unionists.

4. She was a member of a close-knit group of women that included Charlie's wife as well as Gertrude Rosenberg, an organizer for the International Ladies Garment Workers, AFL, a kind of outside-inside group of its own.

5. Claire was the daughter of the first conqueror of Mt. Everest, while Glen was the son of a Nobel Laureate scientist. Glen later died in a mountain-climbing accident.

6. I am still in touch with Margaret, now in her nineties, an honored founder of and contributor to this field. The senior Rawsons were among the founders of the school, and Margaret was the daughter-in-law of "Mister," who still taught shop there and was loved by all the students from nursery school to sixth grade. All the third-generation Rawsons were enrolled in Rose Valley.

7. Annetta Dieckmann was employed in St. Louis; Marie Algor was first active in New Jersey and later in Philadelphia; and Brownie Lee Jones, under the auspices of the Southern Summer School, worked in several locations in the South with central labor bodies or other groups of local unions.

8. In addition, Eleanor Coit developed new programs, as I have noted in chapter 3, among them the alliance with the Farmers Union in the West and the introduction of union leaders to the work of the United Nations.

9. Clinton Golden, a machinist by trade, who had been at Brookwood for several years, had become assistant to Phil Murray, head of SWOC, and was later made president of the United Steelworkers of America. Clint had gone to Penn State University with a request that they provide extension training for union leaders, of the extent and quality they had been providing for many years to management. He succeeded, with the result that local steel unions have heavily used Penn State since the late thirties.

10. Ada would shortly leave the department to go to Library School on her GI Bill to train for a new career. Her new degree took her to the University

of Iowa, where she was very happily engaged with interesting people for several years until her untimely death.

11. Franz came from the chemical workers, CIO. Herb at that time had little background in the labor movement and a great deal to learn. He spent his whole career as a labor attaché in the State Department's Foreign Service, and I would meet him in Israel and Brazil in the years to come. But in 1947 Franz and Abe treated him like a young apprentice who had the good luck to work for beneficently strict masters. Franz remained abroad for many years. I next met him in 1966 as the International Chemical Workers representative in Singapore and Malaysia.

12. In many places in the American Zone, Communists were active in the trade union youth groups with the clear intention of influencing young people who, they hoped, might be future union leaders. From American provincial labor officers I heard of an American workshop that had been held at Bushey Park in England before the Armistice to discuss occupation strategies for Americans assigned to remain in Germany. American Communists in the army who knew about these plans asked for assignment to the workshop. Enrollment, however, had included anti-Communist Americans as well, often civilians nominated by the State Department. One such man with whom I talked made it his business to get to know local union officers within his area. He showed me pictures he had taken of men he believed to be Communists. Obviously the Cold War had begun in earnest by the spring of 1947.

13. In the course of a few years he was called to Hesse as the chief civil servant in the Ministry of Agriculture, a move that inaugurated his lifetime of devotion to and reform of Hessian agriculture. Eventually, he became minister of agriculture there.

14. His lunch, which consisted entirely of potatoes, was brought in while I was there; he hospitably offered to share it with me, but when I declined, he happily consumed it all.

15. I had visited her training school for leaders in my study of labor schools, although it was outside the then traditional labor movement, and had been very impressed both with its teaching methods and the people drawn to her philosophy, which had been originated by Leonard Nelson. I continued to meet some of her former students during the final weeks of my stay in Germany. She was now the director of a progressive secondary school not far from Frankfurt, the Odenwaldschule, where I later sent Philip.

16. The full story did not come out until after I was back in the States, when George Silver sent me a copy of an intelligence report on me that had reached him. He asked me for corrections of it, if any. It was full of errors. I had been confused with a Chicago Communist with a name close to, or like

mine. I was described as a graduate of Bryn Mawr College. My pacifist career was taken to be evidence of Communist or IWW affiliation, and so on. Although George and others had asked for a continuation of my stay in Germany, it had been denied.

17. See "Workers' Education in the U. S. Zone of Germany," Visiting Expert Series No. 1 (Berlin: Office of Military Government [OMGUS], 1947).

18. "Andy" was a Ph.D. candidate at the University of Chicago when I was an undergraduate at Northwestern. We were both then active in the pacifist movement. He was the son of Danish immigrants and had left home as a boy to make room for younger siblings. He had worked at casual labor all over the United States and shared the hoboes' life as a young adult. He had come to the attention of a sociologist at Chicago, who in a sense founded the field of occupational sociology and who persuaded Andy that despite his lack of formal education he could get an academic degree. He had written his thesis on "The American Hobo." He had landed in the Manpower Division in Germany, after living in Southeast Asia and the Near East for several years. (He never returned to the States because of difficulties with a wife who would not divorce him.) At the end of the occupation he stayed on in Germany as the director of a UNESCO Research Institute in Cologne, and then moved to the University of New Brunswick, where he taught sociology into his nineties. After his death, his colleagues issued a memorial volume to which I contributed. (See "Women and Work in Industrial Societies: Where We Are and Where We Are Going," in *Urbanism and Urbanization,* Noel Iverson, ed., Leiden: E. J. Brill, 1984.)

19. A number of her classmates had remained in Germany during the Hitler period, under assumed names. Some, still using those names, were now local leaders in the Social Democratic Party in Lower Saxony and North Rhine-Westphalia. On my next visit to Germany I worked closely with one of these people, then a leader in the provincial trade unions, on the creation of a new labor education organization that joined the evening schools with the trade union schools under the name of Arbeit und Leben (Work and Life).

20. This meeting with Karl Stadler began a lifetime relationship that was reinforced when I arrived in Vienna a year and a half later. Karl had been head of the Youth Division of the Vienna Socialist Youth, until the "Green Fascists" had made that work impossible. He and his future wife, Regina, had then gone to England, where Karl had established himself at one of the British red-brick universities as head of the WEA program there. When Hitler was defeated and Austria restored as a self-governing, democratic country, Karl had been elected head of the Austrian Adult Education Association (AEA). He spent his summers after 1949 near Salzburg in an AEA Summer School, where I visited and lectured from time to time during the fifties. Later, he was named a professor and director of a labor history institute at the University of Linz, at

which time he moved back to Austria and became a prolific author of books on Austrian labor history.

21. He had been on both Eastern and Western fronts, and once in a plane bound for a reconnaissance of New York City, as preparation for possible bombing of that city. The plane, however, had had to turn around for lack of fuel before reaching its goal.

CHAPTER 7

1. German fact-checking by Hanna Beate Schöpp-Schilling found no reference to "Green Fascists" in the literature for prewar Austria. She suggested that we change the term (which appears twice) to Austrofascists. Since Alice used the term twice in quotation marks to refer to the late nineteen-twenties, when she and Wes had been in Germany as students, we have left it as she had it in her manuscript. [Ed.]

2. Several years later she and her husband moved to Montreal, where they have since lived. We have remained in touch through one visit and then by correspondence.

3. When in the early seventies I returned to Vienna on quite another project, I met people who again and again wanted me to convey thanks to Wesley for his helpfulness during this immediate postwar period of rebuilding.

4. This project resulted in the publication of the report prepared for the High Commission on "Bavarian Trade Union Youth."

5. Hanna Beate Schöpp-Schilling reports that in February 1998, the two unions agreed to join forces by 2004. [Ed.]

6. After Alice Cook's death, Ellen Bernstein shared a letter that Alice had written to her when Ellen and Tom were in the midst of their divorce. This is a paragraph from Alice's letter, dated December 7, 1987, almost forty years after Alice's own divorce. "I am distressed and think of you a great deal, for I see the situation as close to the one I faced when Wes and I finally parted at his request and not mine. I had been doing a lot of independent talking for months and perhaps years before the parting, but then it was his initiative and not mine that brought the final break. Perhaps you are feeling too the sense of abandonment and rejection which I found so painful and difficult to deal with and indeed did not get over it and really recover my own feeling of independence and adequacy for a long time." [Ed.]

7. On my return trip in 1990 I was older than my mother had been on our 1935 visit. It was suddenly very important for me to visit the park containing the statues of people of all ages again—this time from the vantage point of my own old age.

8. I recounted this effort to a 1988 meeting of a group within the German-Austrian Adult Education Associations devoted to researching the origins of the postwar adult education movements. My account was published by Das Forum, VHS (*Zeitschrift der Volkshochschulen,* March 1992).

9. After Eleanor left the Y, her work was all related to labor relations and labor education. For a time she was with the Women's Bureau of the Department of Labor. During the war she worked as personnel officer on the management side in a Pittsburgh firm. She then went on to the new School of Industrial and Labor Relations at Cornell University, as head of the Extension Division's work with trade unions.

10. Eight universities with labor extension programs had formed a consortium, the Inter-University Labor Education Committee (IULEC), chaired by Ralph Campbell, the chief of Cornell's Labor Relations School's Extension Division. The project, financed by the Ford Foundation, via the Adult Education Association, was to be carried out in two years, as an experiment in introducing new methods and subjects for trade unions. Cornell's project was entitled "Integrating Labor Education into the Community."

CHAPTER 8

1. For an enumeration and evaluation of the work in each university, see Jack Barbash, *Universities and Unions in Workers' Education* (New York: Harper, 1955).

2. After Alice Cook died, the family found a letter from Jack Flagler among Alice's papers. A small portion is quoted here:

> Because of your encouragement, I became the first member of a very poor family to complete a graduate degree . . . I may never have told you but the three women who have shaped my ideas about and commitment to women's rights were my mother, who served as Secretary-Treasurer of USW Local 1823, my wife, whom I met when she directed the Women's Institute for Social Change here in Minnesota, and Alice Cook. . . . Bless you for all you have given and for all you continue to give to women and to us men. (Letter from Jack Flagler to Alice Cook, 26 October 1992.) Jack Flagler is an arbitrator living in Minneapolis. [Ed.]

3. Floyd Hunter, *Community Power Structure* (Chapel Hill: University of North Carolina Press) 1953.

4. As vice president her job entailed being responsible for the four statutory colleges to the State University of New York (SUNY), the legislature, and the various executive offices dealing with state educational finances.

5. "Draft of a Policy on the Role of the New York State School of Industrial and Labor Relations in Its Conduct of the Project on Increasing Labor

Participation in Community Affairs." Carried on under a grant from the Inter-University Labor Education Committee. Mimeographed 1954.

6. Barbash, *Universities and Unions,* pp. 94–96.

7. "Education for Community Activity" in *Labor's Role in Community Affairs: A Handbook for Union Committees* (Ithaca: ILR Press, 1955), pp. 21–32.

8. I became an assistant professor in 1955 and was tenured at the associate level in 1957. I was promoted in 1963 to full professor.

9. These negotiations were finally realized two years later, in 1957.

CHAPTER 9

1. This student was John Ferguson, who soon became director of the Industrial Relations Center at the University of Hawaii. When I decided to go out to Hawaii with Eleanor Emerson many years later, after we had both retired, John invited me to spend time at the Center and offered me space that is mine to this day. His remark on first introducing me to colleagues there was that I was distinguished by being perhaps the only person who had read his Ph.D. thesis. This evaluation was a product of his modesty, but it served to justify his invitation, for which I have always been grateful.

2. Foster Rhea Dulles, *Labor in America: A History* (New York: T. Y. Crowell Co., 1955) and Harry A. Millis, ed., *How Collective Bargaining Works,* (New York: Twentieth Century Fund, 1942).

3. Jean, who taught the courses in arbitration, had a powerful influence on her students, many of whom—both men and women—became arbitrators and are at the top of that field today. Recently, at an alumni reunion, an alumnus of the period identified himself to me. I had little recollection of him or even his name, but as we parted he said, "As you may know, I am an arbitrator and all I know I trace to you!" I had to say that he had confused me with Jean—perhaps after forty years all women look alike.

4. A constitutional amendment forbidding child labor had been adopted by Congress and sent to the forty-eight states for approval in 1924, after two attempts by Congress to legislate regulatory measures, both of which were declared unconstitutional. This amendment is indeed still pending, though long forgotten, at the end of the twentieth century. "There can be little question that the failure of the amendment to secure ratification within a comparative few years after its submission to the states was in large part due to the wide grant of powers to Congress" (Harry A. Millis and Royal E. Montgomery, *Labor's Progress and Problems* [New York: McGraw Hill, 1938], p. 450). However, many states and some cities had established laws against child labor, but many states

had not attempted any regulation; even among those that had, variations both in goals and enforcement were very wide (*ibid.,* pp. 416–62).

5. See Millis and Montgomery, pp. 301–375. The first attempts to regulate wages for adult males through the setting of minima occurred under the code system of the National Industrial Recovery Act (NIRA), 1933. Previous attempts to adopt federal or even state legislation had been declared unconstitutional. The NIRA, however, set no single hourly minimum. It called for a wage within each coded industry, of which there were well over two hundred. Each industry was to set up an employee-management committee that would determine a minimum within certain time and market limits. This varied from a low of 12.5 cents in Puerto Rico to a high for certain highly skilled occupations of 75 cents an hour. A presidential executive order covering all workers otherwise not reached set the minimum at 40 cents. When NIRA was declared unconstitutional in 1937 on an issue unrelated to wages, Millis and Montgomery believed that "the material position of the average person attached to industry during the life of the NIRA improved" (p. 370).

6. An inclusive health insurance program was never submitted to Congress in the days before the New Deal, and although such a program has been repeatedly discussed since then by both executive and legislative branches of federal government, it has not yet, as I write, become law. The closest legislation is embodied in Medicare for persons over sixty-five, and Medicaid for the impoverished—both of which are currently threatened by the Republican-dominated Congress. Miss Perkins authorized two committees to study and report on the British and Swedish systems, then already in operation. They reported that the experiences in those countries could not be replicated in the United States because of its much larger size and the constitutional limits on federal powers.

For unemployment insurance and social security for older workers, see Millis and Montgomery, pp. 221–85, and pp. 353–420. Before the New Deal a few craft unions and fewer companies had experimented with unemployment insurance. Governor Roosevelt had called a meeting of the states bordering New York, as a preliminary to the possible introduction of a bill in his state. He had some hope that if the border states would join the movement, New York would not become a dumping ground for the unemployed. Nothing came of this effort, however. Ohio and Minnesota had worked out plans but had not adopted them. Problems of unemployment during the first Roosevelt term were instead addressed through work programs, under the Works Progress Administration, the Civilian Conservation Corps, and the Federal Emergency Relief Administration.

7. For the history of the issues and enactments of protective legislation, see Ulla Wikander, Alice Kessler-Harris, and Jane Lewis, eds., *Protecting Women: Labor Legislation in Europe, the United States, and Australia, 1880–1920* (Urbana and Chicago: University of Illinois Press, 1995).

8. In these years Saturday, at least until noon, was considered a workday for students, faculty, and staff.

9. "Labor Relations in New York City," *Industrial Relations* 5, no. 3 (1966): 86–104.

10. The result was the publication two years later of a book, *Union Democracy: Practice and Ideal* (Ithaca: ILR Press, 1963).

11. Not much later she returned to the Y under its national reorganization, as head of its public affairs department. She lived in Washington and represented the Y on legislation affecting working women. In this capacity she set goals for a great enlargement of the Y's activities with working women in offices and factories, as well as in their families.

CHAPTER 10

1. Chie was a graduate of Kobe Women's College, an institution, like many others in Japan, founded by American women missionaries, many of whom were graduates of American women's colleges. Her name came up because JIL friends told me she had worked successfully with other visiting Americans. She had been one of the early exchangees from Japan to the United States and was proficient in English.

2. He was a young man who had grown up as the son of a Japanese soldier who had settled in China, after the Japanese had conquered territory there. He had learned English by listening at the door of language classes given to Japanese, who were possibly being trained for the eventual conquest of the United States. We traveled together both in Tokyo and in the provinces. After I left Japan he was employed by an American greeting card company for the rest of his working life.

3. Ted lived with his Japanese wife and two children in Azabu in a house both Japanese and American, not far from International House. He and his wife were active in the Tokyo Jewish Center, which often hosted concerts given by visiting American and Israeli musicians invited to perform with one of the Japanese orchestras. Ted often took me to these concerts.

4. I came to know them both well, since we took a trip together during which they came to be known as Setsuko I and Setsuko II. They have remained so over the years. We met for the last time when they both came to visit me in Hawaii in the summer of 1993.

5. Eleanor's knowledge of Japan began when she was an exchange student from Mills College in the thirties. After the war, she was an officer with the antitrust division in the occupation under MacArthur.

6. Among these were Arthur Ross of the University of California at Berkeley; Virgil Davis from the Railroad Firemen and Enginemen, for whom I had earlier written some educational programs; Tess Wolfson of Brooklyn College, an active labor educator, who had joined with Eleanor Coit in establishing the White-Collar Workers Summer School at Sarah Lawrence College, where she taught for several sessions; and Lillian Herstein of the Chicago Teachers Union and my friend since my pacifist days at Northwestern University.

7. Later, Mitzi worked in the headquarters of the Local Government Workers International Secretariat in London, where she remained (in other employment) for the rest of her working life.

8. Hiroko-san's first period of study and residence in the United States followed shortly. After her graduation in law from Kyushu she went to Tulane University in New Orleans, where she earned a master's degree. Later she spent a year at Cornell with our specialist in workers' compensation, John Burton, and has herself become Japan's expert in that field. She taught first at Kumamoto University of Commerce, where her father, a building contractor, built her a large house. When I visited her there several years later, we both worked on the book we wrote jointly on discrimination against Japanese working women and methods used to correct it (*Working Women in Japan: Discrimination, Resistance and Reform* [Ithaca: Cornell University, New York State School of Industrial and Labor Relations, 1980]). During that visit her house was filled with visiting colleagues and students, one of whom was assigned to me to help my reading of a book by Ryoko Akamatsu, head of the Women's Bureau in the Ministry of Labor, on case histories of gender discrimination. Akamatsu-san was the author of the original equality legislation. On this subject, Hiroko-san drafted the brief in the first case to be successful in the Japanese courts.

9. Professor Lois Gray, who teaches required graduate-level credit courses in programs at New York City's Extension Office, reports that she still uses this text in discussion of union structure and functioning.

10. Tony had directed the Labor Education program at Penn State since shortly after Clint Golden had been able to establish it. I had worked with him there and through IULEC.

11. My interpreter was a mainland Chinese woman who had come to Taiwan with her husband and children soon after the mainland revolution, fifteen years before. She said that she still felt an "outsider." This was true even in relations with her children, who were products of the Taiwan schools. She saw no prospect of ever getting back to her mainland home.

12. These were the first of several persons outside the labor movement, but close to it, who shared their information and evaluations with me. To the extent that their position and affiliation or the length of their own study of the unions

gave me confidence, I valued their views as guides to my own observations. On a trip during which I moved pretty rapidly from country to country, I may have given them undue weight. But to the extent that my own observations corroborated their conclusions, I certainly felt they had not misled me.

13. Jennie later wrote me that she had married a young doctor who was being sent to the United States for further study. They came to Chicago, and her husband eventually set up a private practice in a Chicago suburb where they have raised their children and become an American family and where I visited them all.

14. Sunny spoke some English and a few years later had the opportunity to come to Cornell's ILR library for several months to acquaint herself with its methods of accession and circulation. Still later in a period of especial tension in South Korea, her husband, Nick, decided to bring the family to the West, and they settled in Toronto with their three children. After several very hard years maintaining themselves by running a corner grocery store, Nick Sung was able to establish himself as a travel agent, mainly for Korea-Canada transportation. The children have all completed college and professional school and married, and two of them have had children of their own. I have remained closely in touch with the family throughout the forty years of our acquaintance.

15. This ingenious legislation was based on the hope of building universities in every state that would train future farmers and encourage scientists to come there to engage in agricultural research. Through a system of extension education, that research was to be made immediately available to practicing farmers. This scheme was financed through gifts of nationally owned land throughout the boundaries of the United States, which the universities could sell to homesteaders and retain the earnings to finance their own establishment. For the history of one such agricultural college and its unsteady beginnings, see Gould Colman, *Education and Agriculture: A History of the New York State College of Agriculture at Cornell University* (Ithaca: Cornell University Press, 1963).

16. Almost the only U.S. exception to this generalization was Eleanor Coit's successful inclusion of the Farmers Union in the northern Midwest during the early postwar period. Her representative succeeded in bringing standard labor education to these unions. Eleanor did this, I believe, by employing a committed educator whose origins were in farm life and who had labor education experience in both arenas.

17. She was appointed to be the first adviser to the prime minister on women's affairs. She next became minister to the United Nations, a position she held for three years in New York City. I was then a Mellon Fellow at Wellesley's Center

for Research on Women, where she came at least twice to visit. Earlier, when her husband, Professor Tadashi Hanami, was a resident Fellow at Cornell's ILR School, she had visited him in Ithaca. As such, she succeeded in negotiating with at least three other ministries in addition to labor to bring about changes in their laws in order to be able to sign the UN Equality Resolution for Japan, at the second Women's World Conference in Copenhagen. After her term at the UN ended, she became ambassador to Uruguay, where she invited me to visit her, which I happily did. At the age of sixty-five, she retired to Japan to see where she might still be useful to Japanese women. She founded Women Employed, an organization supported by the Labor Ministry. In the summer of 1993, when I was working with the director of the University of Hawaii's Industrial Relations Center on plans for a conference of Japanese, Canadian, and U.S. women trade unionists, she came to a planning session, representing her organization. While there, she received an invitation from the new prime minister to join his cabinet as minister of education.

18. "Political Action and Trade Unions: A Case Study of the Coal Miners of Japan," *Monumenta Nipponica* 22, No. 5 (1967), and "Labor and Politics," *Issues in Industrial Society* 1, no. 2 (1969).

Chapter 11

1. Named for the George Taylor whom I first knew at the Kensington YWCA, when he was the permanent arbitrator for the hosiery industry. He was an authority on industrial relations and appointed chair of the committee to make legislative proposals, hence the attachment of his name to the New York law. Although he had never practiced in that state, his influence and the weight of his experience were strongly felt in the granting of organization and collective bargaining rights to public employees.

2. A few years later, after my retirement, I was associated with the Industrial Relations Center in Honolulu and visited there every year. Among other activities, I was involved with its attempt to set up a conference for Japanese, American, and Canadian women trade unionists, in the course of which I frequently consulted Glenda Roberts. See *Staying on the Line* (Honolulu: University of Hawaii Press, 1993).

3. Mediation is assistance in direct negotiation and is acceptable only by mutual agreement. It differs from arbitration in that the arbitrator through agreement of the disputing parties is asked to settle the dispute, using his or her best judgment after a hearing in which both parties argue their positions. The arbitrator's judgment then becomes part of the collective agreement between the parties.

4. "The International Labor Organization and Japanese Politics," *Industrial and Labor Relations Review* (October 1965); *An Introduction to Japanese Trade Unionism* (Ithaca: Cornell University Press/ILR Press, 1966); "The International Posture

of the American Labor Movement: The Relevance of American Experience to World Problems," in *The Labor Movement, a Re-Examination: A Conference in Honor of David J. Saposs* (Madison: Industrial Relations Research Institute and the State Historical Society of Wisconsin, 1967); "The ILO and Japanese Politics, II: Gain or Loss for Labor?" *Industrial and Labor Relations Review,* April 1969.

5. *Working Women in Japan: Discrimination, Resistance, and Reform.* (Ithaca: Cornell University, New York State School of Industrial and Labor Relations, 1980).

6. Cornell was founded in the period of rationalism, without any religious tie. Anabel Taylor Hall was given to the university as a home and educational center for all kinds of religious groups, including Buddhist, Muslim, Jewish, Catholic, and Protestant Christianity. It provided offices for all resident designated heads of such groups, as well as rooms for their gatherings, chapels for their weddings and funerals, and space and support for secular organizations engaged in the support of nonprofit, newly founded social agencies not yet eligible for inclusion in United Way. These included the Learning Web, Displaced Homemakers, the Support Committee for the Advocates of the Cornell Eleven—in this case, against the university—and the Task Force for Battered Women.

7. In that year, the only African-American professor on campus was a professor of wines in the Hotel School.

8. For a very critical evaluation of the university's handling of this chain of events, see the book by Allan Bloom, *The Closing of the American Mind* (New York: Simon & Schuster, 1987).

9. These events have been published many times from varying points of view. For an autobiographical account, see William Foote Whyte, *Participant Observer* (ILR Press: Ithaca: 1994).

10. *Report of the Ombudsman* (Ithaca: Cornell University Press, 1970 and 1971).

CHAPTER 12

1. Barbara M. Wertheimer and Ann H. Nelson, *Trade Union Women: A Study of Their Participation in New York City Locals* (New York: Praeger, 1975). Barbara was the daughter-in-law of a professor I had studied with at the University of Frankfurt, in the last days of the Weimar Republic, who had come to the University in Exile at the New School after Hitler's rise. His son, Barbara's husband Val, was an organizer for the ACWA in the South.

2. Alva Myrdal was then the minister for peace in the Socialist cabinet. Her report, "Towards Equality," had already appeared: *Report to the Swedish Social Democratic Party,* (Stockholm: Prisma, 1971). I went to see her, however, mainly to discuss the book she had written in the fifties with Viola Klein, *Women's*

Two Roles: Home and Work (London: Routledge & Regan Paul, 1956). She now regretted its title, which she said the publisher had chosen. It was in fact a misunderstanding of what she and Klein had meant as their main theme. With an "It is now quite out of date," she dismissed further discussion of the book.

3. The Labor Market Board received advance notice, as did the affected workers, of projected layoffs and aided them personally to find new employment. If this involved moving to a new location, it could help with sale of local property, travel of the worker and his or her spouse for interviews and house seeking in the new community. If layoffs or dismissals affected employment of a whole community, it could assist in calling on the municipality for its statement of needs in public services, and then assist in putting them into effect.

4. The municipalities and the towns were assigned to measure and plan for child care needs, although the counties supplied the funds for buildings.

5. Mai Larssen, my former Swedish exchange student at Hudson Shore School, now retired from work, took me to the old age home in her small city, where all the inhabitants were well into their eighties and had come there only after living many postretirement years in their own apartments.

6. After the work in Sweden, with friends old and new, I took a series of short breaks from the heavy schedules of interviewing after Sweden and between work in Israel and East Germany. With Bila (Billy) Zamir, I visited Arad, a new city in Israel experimenting with settling immigrant families into a mixed pattern with Israelis of established residence. Then Billy and I went to Masada, the high plateau city above the Dead Sea, where in Roman times, Jews had held out for years against attempts by the Romans to conquer them. Here, the Israeli army still brought its recruits for the swearing-in ceremony. Later, Fran joined me in Israel to travel to Caesarea with its layers of various civilizations clear enough still to appreciate and marvel over. Then we went to Sharm-el-Sheik, just beginning its life as a tourist area. The highlight of this trip was a long and dusty, unforgettable ride through the desert to Santa Catarina, which still served in its surviving state as a livelihood for monks of the original order.

Much later on, after work in Israel, Fran and I spent a few days in Natayna, and then went on to Marseilles and a holiday in Corsica, where my dear Adi Tröscher joined us for ten days. There we hiked and toured in a rented car. Although Corsica is a Mediterranean island, we were unable to cross its mountains because of snow accumulations at high elevations. We were the only guests in our hotel, where we talked for extended periods, often about aspects of my ongoing study. I shared my early impressions with them as well as the directions I thought I was going to take in the countries coming up.

7. Frau Klewe was assistant to the National Federation's director of Women's Affairs. She had risen through the ranks in a chemical factory from

shop steward to chief shop steward and then had been sent to a Party school for a year's political training, and thereafter into a Ph.D. program in chemistry. She credited this opportunity to her commitment to trade union work and to the Party.

8. I found her very eager to talk with me about library resources for research, but unaware of how barren the National Library seemed to be in this regard. Shortly after the Wall fell, I endeavored to bring Dr. Kuhrig to the United States for a conference on women in East Germany. She was not allowed a visa. Quite accidentally, as I attended a women's meeting on my last visit to Germany in the summer of 1990, she recognized me, reintroduced herself, and told me she was just at retirement age and very uncertain about what life held for her as a lifelong Communist official of the DDR.

9. In rural areas, I was told that older workers were also organized to take on the day care of children where child care centers did not yet exist, or to take on such family services as mending and laundry. When I asked about retired women, I found that they were often employed in museums, theaters, and such. When approached, they were frequently crotchety, suspicious, even resentful about being asked for information or other assistance. This was particularly noticeable on my trip to the Goethe Museum in Weimar, after the director failed to arrive as scheduled on a Sunday afternoon. When an assistant finally arrived, she would not admit us until precisely four o'clock, and then she ushered us through the museum with minimally brief explanations of exhibits and dour responses to questions. She ended the tour abruptly without taking us as scheduled to the Schiller half of the museum.

10. For a full description of work in a Japanese factory mainly staffed by older women, most of whom were married, see Glenda Roberts, *Staying on the Line* (Honolulu: University of Hawaii Press, 1993).

11. See footnote 17 in Chapter 10 for a sketch of Ryoko Akamatsu's career.

12. I was asked on two occasions somewhat later to write amicus briefs on the handling of female retirement benefits and eligibility for pensions in the United States and other countries. Japan finally adopted a uniform retirement age for men and women at sixty-five, a limit that is quite rigidly enforced, although public and private agencies frequently find new employment for former high-ranking officers, beyond their retirement.

13. The most definitive of these studies was one commissioned by the American Association of University Women and completed under the direction of Susan Bailey at the Center for Research on Women (CROW), Wellesley College. Its publication and the discussion of its findings among teachers, school administrators, and those who teach teachers, has been a primary focus of the AAUW's

action agenda. See *How Schools Shortchange Girls* (Washington, D.C.: AAUW Educational Foundation, 1992).

14. For a full description of these aspects of training, see Sharon L. Harlan and Ronnie J. Steinberg, *Job Training for Women: The Promise and Limits of Public Policies* (Philadelphia: Temple University Press, 1989).

15. The extent of this constantly expanding movement is nowhere better demonstrated than in the United Nations meetings on women that began in Mexico City in 1975 and that were continued in Copenhagen in 1980, Nairobi in 1985, and Beijing in 1995. More than 180 countries now participate, with official as well as non-governmental delegations (NGOs). In addition, under the auspices of the UN's Commission on the Status of Women, which also meets annually, the Committee on the Elimination of All Forms of Discrimination Against Women (CEDAW) now meets twice a year to hear and discuss reports from designated countries that have ratified the Convention to End All Forms of Discrimination Against Women, and are therefore obliged to report at fixed times on steps they have taken under the articles of the Convention to improve women's situation.

16. Historically, these journeymen actually went on a journey through Germany and neighboring countries that had gradually adopted the German system. Thus, they acquired experience and acquaintances throughout their area, to whom they could turn when jobs disappeared at home. Alternatively, they might receive men from other locations who might also need jobs. Before the First World War, each tradesman had his own recognizable form of dress and carried his own toolbox on these foot journeys.

17. Books explaining such systems began to appear and to be used in the states of Minnesota and Washington, followed shortly by other states and localities.

18. When I asked Donald Treiman, the author of a study in the United States, whether the Ru-Ro Report might not serve as a guide for an American study, he replied that he believed that U.S. size and diversity better suggested individual regions. He apparently considered regionalism of some sort a determining factor for this country's policies.

19. Chief among these were Helen Remick, affirmative action officer at the University of Washington, and editor-author of *Comparable Worth and Wage Discrimination: Technical Possibilities and Political Realities* (Philadelphia: Temple University Press, 1984); Ronnie Steinberg and Lois Haignere, who did a study for the state of New York, and wrote, spoke, and consulted with public agencies on their various studies both in the United States and abroad; and Nina Rothschild, who was responsible for the introduction of comparable worth as the basis for compensation in every public agency in the state of Minnesota, a total of about sixteen hundred departments, towns, counties, and governmental agencies.

20. My secretary during this period had two children in their teens. She worked in the expectation that her income would contribute significantly to their higher education. She rose at four every morning to do household chores: laundry, food preparation, organization of household affairs. She accepted this not only because she saw no way not to but also because, as she put it, "The work has to be done," and because, "It is for me the only quiet time of the day, when I can think or dream or plan for the girls."

21. See Arlie Hochschild, *Second Shift: Working Parents and the Revolution at Home* (New York: Viking, 1989).

22. Hungary, a country I had not yet visited, was the first to offer three years' paid maternity leave to mothers (but not parental leave). The information I received led me to believe that it was only when the need for women as additional workers had decreased that women could thus drop out of the workforce for many consecutive years with each new birth. This leave may also have been motivated to some degree by a natalist policy.

23. Studies shown me in several countries concluded that unions were often opposed to part-time work because these workers could produce in a few hours better work results than could regular full-time workers whose efficiency declined as the day wore on. Consequently, unions often saw part-timers as putative wage-busters.

24. In British unions the office of president is largely representational, while the secretary is the full-time officer who carries the main administrative work of the union.

25. A number of recent descriptive and historical books on trade unions and women have appeared since my travels of 1972–1973. Among them are: Alice H. Cook, Val R. Lorwin, and Arlene Kaplan Daniels, eds., *Women and Trade Unions in Eleven Industrialized Countries* (Philadelphia: Temple University Press, 1984); Karen Shallcross Koziara, Michael H. Moskow, and Lucretia Dewey Tanner, eds., *Working Women: Past, Present, and Future* (Washington, D.C.: Bureau of National Affairs, 1987); Jennie Farley, ed., *Women Workers in Fifteen Countries* (Ithaca: ILR Press, Report No. 11, 1983); Dorothy Sue Cobble, ed., *Women and Unions: Forging a Partnership* (Ithaca: ILR Press, 1993); Brigid O'Farrell and Joyce L. Kornbluh, eds., *Rocking the Boat: Women's Voices, 1915–1975* (New Brunswick, N.J.: Rutgers University Press, 1993).

26. See for the complete text, *Beijing and Beyond: Toward the Twenty-first Century of Women,* an issue of *Women's Studies Quarterly,* Vol. 24, Nos. 1, 2, spring/summer 1996.

CHAPTER 13

1. Each day in the field I recorded on tape the visits I had made that day. These tapes went off to Danilee at frequent intervals to be typed up. In the

end they constituted two thick volumes, plus documents of all kinds given me as I went along. The file begun by Mary McGinnis now contains several thousand references in eleven file drawers, organized by country (a few quite sparse, but others filling full file drawers). These are in turn organized by fifteen or more similar topics, covering various aspects of women's work lives, organizations, labor market circumstances, and feminist theory.

2. These were by no means the first courses offered by Women's Studies. The first was probably one taught by Harold Feldman, a founding board member.

3. *The Working Mother: A Survey of Problems and Programs in Nine Countries,* Ithaca: Cornell University, New York State School of Industrial and Labor Relations, 1975; 2d ed., 1978.

4. Among the papers I wrote in 1974 and 1975 were: "Maternity Benefits in Nine Countries," for a joint committee of the New York State Legislature, 1974; "Mothers at Work Abroad," in the Winter 1975 issue of *Industrial and Labor Relations Report;* "Maternity Benefits" for *International Society for Labor Law and Social Legislation,* U.S. National Committee, in Bulletin 8, no. 3, October 1975; and "Public Policy and Support Systems for Working Mothers: An International Comparison," paper prepared for the Groves Society Conference: Conference on Changing Sex Roles in Family and Society, Dubrovnik, July 1975.

5. Governments of countries affiliated with the United Nations send official delegations to these meetings, which occur every five to ten years. In addition, nongovernmental organizations (NGOs) send representatives to an NGO series of simultaneous meetings. As the years have gone by, the NGO groups have drawn literally tens of thousands of women.

6. The German Marshall Fund had been established in 1972. As Harvard's commencement speaker that year, Chancellor Schmidt of Germany announced a substantial gift to the United States—a twenty-fifth commemoration of the United States's 1947 institution of the Marshall Fund to aid the economic restitution of the countries of Western Europe. The new Fund's purpose was to explore areas of common social and economic interest between any of these countries and the United States.

7. This is the only federation of unions—some national, some regional or even local—in Great Britain. By comparison with Sweden, the TUC was much less centralized, and many unions were not affiliated with it. Contracts were usually with local employers, rather than with national or regional employers' organizations. Many unions traced their origins, structures, and purposes back well into the nineteenth century. A considerable number were also affiliated with the British Labour Party, which was an early twentieth-century product of trade union initiative. (In most Western countries cause and effect were reversed: unions owed their origins to the Labor parties.)

8. Over the years this number has slowly increased, and today six places are reserved for women, in addition to any women sent to the executive by their national unions.

9. A Race Relations Equity Act had been adopted in the mid-1960s.

10. A general union is one that recruits both skilled and unskilled workers across industries and working for many different employers. Chief among these in Britain are the Amalgamated Engineering Workers Union (AEWU) and the General and Municipal Workers Union (G&MWU).

11. Walter Rohmert and Josef Rutenfranz, *Arbeitswissenschaftliche Beurteilung der Belastung und Beanspruchung an unterschiedliche Arbeitsplätzen* (Bonn, 1975).

12. For this conference, my Japanese friend and coworker Hiroko Hayashi and I prepared a paper we had been working on during my several visits to Japan in the sixties and seventies on discrimination against Japanese women workers. We reported on movements in Japan to remedy the many cases that had come to official attention either as cases before the courts or to the office of the adviser on women's affairs on the prime minister's staff. Much of this material had been assembled by my friend Ryoko Akamatsu, when she was head of women's affairs in the labor ministry and later when she was an adviser to the Prime Minister. Hiroko had assigned one of her students to translate this compilation for me. We called the paper "Resistance and Reform in Japan," and later expanded it as a book published in 1980, *Working Women in Japan: Discrimination, Resistance, and Reform.*

13. *We Were There: The Story of Working Women in America* was published in 1977. At her untimely death in 1983 Barbara was at work on a second volume, which would have brought the history up to date.

14. Up to this time, we were told, judgments had usually been made by consensual votes of persons who had been victimized by the accused. To introduce arguments of prosecution and defense before a judge operating under law was of course a major change, and these judges were only very recently appointed.

15. In some respects, the dynamic within our own group was as compelling as anything that could occur between American visitors and Chinese hostesses. One of our group, a well-known academic then at the Wilson Institute in Washington, was dying of cancer but had insisted on using this opportunity to come to China. Her interest was in planning under Communism. One evening when two women city planners came to speak to us in Shanghai, our group leader asked me to chair the meeting and urged me not to let this academic take over the meeting. I had no idea why this restriction was put on me, but I was not curious enough to obtain more information or to protest. She, however, in a note that followed, accused me of interfering with her work. Before the trip ended,

the leader had to send for the woman's husband, a high civil servant in Washington, to take her home–she was too ill to travel further with us.

16. Philadelphia: Temple University Press, 1980.

17. "Collective Bargaining as a Strategy for Achieving Equal Opportunity and Equal Pay: Sweden and West Germany" and "Vocational Training, the Labor Market, and Unions." These two very different themes were both on my ongoing agenda of issues of major concern to working women if they were to achieve equality in their national labor markets.

18. Ronnie's personal history accounts to some extent for her moves from Wellesley to Albany to Philadelphia. She divorced her first husband and reverted to her own name of Steinberg. She accepted a job as head of research at SUNY/Albany's Center for Women in Government and there met Michael Ames of the Temple University Press when he visited. Michael brought her to the attention of the press's chief, and she was asked to become the editor of a series of books on women in the political economy, which the press had only begun to publish, an activity she carried out with distinction. In a few years she moved to a professorial appointment at Temple University and in 1997 moved to Vanderbilt University.

19. The unpublished dissertation was completed at Yale University in December 1974: *Capitalism and Women's Work in the Home, 1900–1930.* It is available from university microfilms. With Don Treiman, Heidi then wrote *Women, Work, and Wages: Equal Pay for Jobs of Equal Value* (Washington, D.C.: National Academy Press, 1981).

20. Because the ethnic makeup of the population of Hawaii differed from that of any other state or part of the country, the database on which diversity in employment rested differed from the national categories adopted by the EEOC. Rumor has it that an understanding on this matter was reached at an early visit from the San Francisco office, when that representative heard of Hawaii's unique population distribution among Asians, Caucasians, and African Americans. The agreement was said to have been first recorded on a hotel cocktail napkin. The status of the white male as norm hardly existed in many occupations, including fruit packing, hotel service, food processing and serving, maintenance and operations, all of which were major occupations in Hawaii. Black workers were so few as to be statistically unimportant. In the state governmental departments Japanese far exceeded any other ethnic group, among both women and men.

CHAPTER 14

1. Alice H. Cook, Val Lorwin, and Arlene Kaplan Daniels, *The Most Difficult Revolution: Women and Trade Unions* (Ithaca: Cornell University Press, 1992).

2. A second request in the same field came from my colleague Barbara Wertheimer, who was editing a book on *Labor Education for Women Workers* (Philadelphia: Temple University Press, 1981). I asked Roberta Till-Retz to work with me in reporting on the work she had done with Val in England and with me in Austria, and I added what I had learned over the years from the women's division of the German DGB.

3. These were "On the Treatment of Equality in Aging in the United States and Japan, and by a Number of International Governmental Agencies," in the case of Asako Kuramitsu and Tsuyohi Makashima, Karasu Red Cross Hospital, Fukuoka, Japan, in 1982; and in the case of *Four Plaintiffs v. the Nissan Automobile Company,* in pleadings for the equal right of men and women workers to child allowances, before a district court.

4. The Hawaii Government Employees Association (HGEA), a civil service organization including all local and state government employees, joined the American Federation of State, County, and Municipal Employees (AFSCME) soon after state law permitted collective bargaining of these associations with representatives of the public employer in 1972. Under the agreement between the two employee organizations, HGEA retained its name and a good deal of initiative. AFSCME, however, was already deeply involved in the comparable worth issue in the state of Washington, where the first step toward adoption of a comparable worth study and program had begun in 1974.

5. The report was issued by IRC in 1983 under the title, *Comparable Worth: The Problem and States' Approaches to Wage Equity.* I presented a paper at the spring meeting of the Industrial Relations Research Association (IRRA), held in Honolulu that year entitled "Comparable Worth: Recent Development in Selected States." It appeared in the IRRA publication that resulted from that meeting. Still later, it was published by the Albany, N.Y., Center for Women in Government, as its *Working Paper* No. 14.

6. I later wrote up the full history as a chapter in a book on the history of implementation of comparable worth in many states that Ronnie Steinberg was putting together. I discussed the conflicts and nonparticipation on the part of several unions in the public sphere, and described the formation of a Pay Equity Task Force made up of twenty women's organizations in the state that strongly supported the proposed legislation and its studies. That book is now scheduled for publication in 1999 as Ronnie Steinberg and Deb Figard, eds., *The Politics and Practice of Pay Equity* (Philadelphia: Temple University Press).

7. For one very complete report on the state of Oregon, see Joan Acker's book, *Doing Comparable Worth: Gender, Class, and Pay Equity* (Philadelphia: Temple University Press, 1989).

8. For the Minnesota legislation (1984) and its history of implementation, see Sara M. Evans and Barbara J. Nelson, *Wage Justice: Comparable Worth and the Paradox of Technocratic Reform* (Chicago: University of Chicago Press, 1989). Chapter 6, "Paradoxes and Unintended Consequences: Implementation of Comparable Worth in Local Jurisdictions," also deals with the traps placed in the way of inexperienced feet.

9. Jennie then edited these contributions and added to them. They were published as *Essays in Honor of Alice Hanson Cook* (Ithaca: ILR Press, 1985).

10. *Comparable Worth and Wage Discrimination: Technical Possibilities and Political Realities* (Philadelphia: Temple University Press, 1984). My chapter was entitled "Developments in Selected States."

11. Soon thereafter Debbie went to New York as adviser to the president of the Health and Hospital Workers Local 1199, and only recently left that union to become a member of the Extension staff in Cornell's New York City office.

12. Noel Iverson, ed., *Urbanism and Urbanization: Views, Aspects, and Dimensions* (Leiden: E. J. Brill, 1984).

13. A colleague at Cornell, Peter Katzenstein of the Government Department, talked with me about a book he was going to edit on Germany and invited me to sit in on meetings of contributors and advisers. The first meeting was held in 1986 in Ithaca and the second two years later in Berlin at the Wissenschaftszentrum. I played no part in the book, but attendance at these two meetings introduced me to experts on Germany whom I had not previously met. It also provided me with a broader view of both past and future in that country, particularly in respect to the relationship between industry and politics that now served as a background to my concern with employment. The book was published as *Industry and Politics in West Germany: Toward the Third Republic* (Ithaca: Cornell University Press, 1989).

See *Dual-Earner Families: International Perspectives,* Suzan Lewis, Dafna Izraeli, and Helen Hootsmans, eds. (London: Sage, 1992). My chapter was called "Can Work Requirements Accommodate to the Needs of Dual-Earner Families?" As work progressed on this book, its international participants met as often as we could. Our best meeting came at a late stage when the International Interdisciplinary Conference on Women and Work met at Hunter College in New York in 1990. For this, Helen Hootsmans organized a panel in which I participated with a version of my chapter. A final version of this chapter had appeared as "Public Policies To Help Dual-Earner Families Meet the Demands of the Work World" in the *Industrial and Labor Relations Review* 42, No. 2 (1989): 201–215, and was issued as Reprint No. 605 by the ILR School.

14. Ann Helton Stromberg and Shirley Harkess, eds., *Working Women: Theories and Facts in Perspectives* (Mountain View, Ca: Mayfield Publishing, 1978; 2nd ed., 1988)

15. The session with the gerontologists was an early attempt to get help on an approach to writing this autobiography—the search for a unifying theme in a wildly and widely varying history. It was not the center of their interest, however, and I came away feeling that neither they nor I had been of much assistance to the other. Ann Schofield of sociology was my hostess during the week I spent there, and we have renewed acquaintance on several occasions since then, including a trip she took to Ithaca when she stayed with me.

16. Later, when the Cornell University's Personnel Department was reorganized under a new director and was renamed Human Resources, this Bell program became a section of that department. Its various advisory committees continue to function, though progress in gaining acceptance for it from supervisors in many of the nonacademic departments of the university is very slow.

17. Ellen, Tom's first wife, continued her job in a New Haven child care center, and continued teaching Lamaze classes on weekends, while she earned her M.A. at the Yale Theological School. She kept her time fully occupied by working with a psychiatrist on a book they had decided to write jointly. She decided as well to go on with courses at Yale on a schedule by which she would get her Ph.D. in counseling late into the nineties. Ellen has always worked by strict budgeting of time and money. Concerned with winning the optimal effect—even to the low decimal point, it seemed to me—she decided to get up at 4:30 each morning to write for two hours before she commutes to New Haven to begin her day at the center. Filling every minute, day and night, has undoubtedly enabled her to deal with the divorce in positive ways. As for the girls, it is still a problem. For Tom and Dorie, themselves, the problem is the continental distance between their workplaces—she in California and he at Columbia. They have managed this commute by adjusting her quarter sessions to his semesters, together with her taking a quarter's leave every fall, which she spends in New York.

Chapter 15

1. The results of this buyout of West Berlin are well illustrated by Frau Pühlmann's search for a secondhand automobile. None was available for months. The explanation was that the Easterners, who for years could only buy their own product, a notoriously smelly and inefficient machine, now used hoarded money to buy the highly desirable Western cars. For these few months before formal unification, West Berlin was a unique source of supply for all kinds of Western goods. No citizen of the former Communist countries needed a visa

to get into East Germany. Once there, the new, totally opened Berlin was accessible to anyone from the East.

2. Trade unions had historically had something of the status of voluntary organizations, although over time and to some degree they had been retrained and redefined by law. Works Councils had been introduced under the social-democratic initiative in the Weimar period to allow for participation by all workers in every plant, including both union members and unorganized white-collar workers and lower levels of supervision. Unions sought to dominate the administration of the Works Councils. Unions in coal and steel had acquired importance in political opinion building, not only through affiliation with the SDP but also because, depending on the issues before the lawmakers, union leaders were often included in consultation with other significant organizations, such as the Catholic and Protestant Churches and their social agencies, manufacturers' associations, and veterans.

3. DAG membership had been fairly static for several years. As early as 1989 the union had seized the opportunity to move aggressively into the East, attempting to persuade almost any white-collar affiliate of the FDGB to join a local unit of the DAG. At the same time, DAG engaged in negotiations with the HBV, the insurance and banking affiliate of the DGB, over possible amalgamation and thus eventual return to the DGB after fifty years of independence.

4. Shortly thereafter, this name was changed to something like Employment in Japan in order not to leave out men, under the equality law that Akamatsu-san had originally drafted when she was head of the Women's Bureau.

5. Gloria had just been elected to the chair of CLUW, after Joyce Miller had resigned to become executuve director of the new Glass Ceiling Commission chaired by the secretary of Labor. Although during the conference she heard that she had been appointed to this post and saw it as a positive recognition of CLUW's place in the federation, yet she apparently did not want to make international recognition her first request in that capacity. Altogether the episode was an indication that women's recognition within the U.S. unions was still not to be taken for granted. Rather, they were under an admonition to "wait your turn, and in the meantime, take the men's needs into consideration and vote the right way."

6. Chaim, who was seriously wounded in the 1966 war with Egypt, had come to the United States for treatment of his leg. A few months later after their return to Israel, he died.

7. Karen had come to the United States for a visit in 1992, just as the ILR School was instituting a one-year graduate program leading to an M.S. for foreign students. She was interested enough to interview a number of professors who might be engaged in some of the teaching, and enrolled for the academic year of

1993–1994. At the conference, she was two months into the program and was already a leader among her fellow students. When she celebrated her fiftieth birthday in Ithaca in the spring of 1994, her apartment was crowded with students of many nationalities. She brought her mother, Frau Pühlmann, to Ithaca for her graduation. When she returned to Germany, she enrolled in a doctoral program at the Free University of Berlin and often taught in one or another of the DGB schools near Frankfurt. She called me later to tell me that she had been offered a very good job at a high salary. She believed that her work at Cornell has made her eligible for this work, which consisted of being an adviser to the participants in collective bargaining as to the legality (and advisability) of proposals on the table. (This law and its position exist in only this one German state.)

8. Kendal's history began many years ago, and I had lived close to its first institutions in southeastern Pennsylvania. Kendal at Ithaca was home number six, after the recent opening of homes in New Hampshire and Ohio. I had known two people who had lived out their lives in the Pennsylvania homes.

9. Bill's father was a professor and ombudsman at Cornell, while his mother was a volunteer expert on health care in the community and central New York region. Bill himself went to Ithaca High School and of course knows well the community from which 80 percent of Kendal residents come.

10. Washington, D.C.: Counterpoint Press, 1996.

11. This law has been amended and expanded to include public workers, the disabled, persons over forty, and veterans. Executive orders of various presidents have further defined beneficiaries and procedures that affected persons may use in the courts, both state and federal. Its administrative agency is the Equal Employment Opportunity Commission (EEOC).

SELECT BIBLIOGRAPHY

1999

"From Sex Equity to Pay Equity? Hawaii's Devious Course." In *The Politics and Practice of Pay Equity*, edited by Deb Feigart and Ronnie J. Steinberg. Philadelphia: Temple University Press.

1998

With Lamont E. Stallworth. "Challenges in Managing the New Diverse Labor Force." In *Industrial Relations at the Dawn of the New Millennium*, edited by Maurice F. Neufeld and Jean T. McKelvey. Ithaca, N.Y.: Cornell University, New York State School of Industrial and Labor Relations.

1993

"Comments," on "Meeting Family Needs." In *Women and Unions: Forging Partnerships*, edited by Dorothy Sue Cobble. Ithaca, N.Y.: Cornell University Press/ILR Press.
Never Done: The Working Life of Alice H. Cook. Produced by Marilyn Rivchin, Sandra Pollack, and Diane McPherson. Over Forty Productions/Community Animation, Inc.

1992

"Can Work Requirements Accommodate to Needs of Dual-Earner Families?" In *Dual-Earner Families: International Perspectives*, edited by Suzan Lewis, Dafna N. Izraeli, and Helen Hootsmans. London: Sage Publications.
With Val R. Lorwin and Arlene Kaplan Daniels. *The Most Difficult Revolution: Women and Trade Unions.* Ithaca, N.Y.: Cornell University Press.
Review of *Working Parents: Transformation in Gender Roles and Public Policies*, by Phyllis Moen. *Industrial and Labor Relations Review* 45, no. 2 (January).

1991

"Larry Rogin: Socialist, Unionist, Labor Educator." *Labor Studies Journal* 16, no.1 (spring).
"Pay Equity: Theory and Implementation." In *Public Personnel Management: Current Concerns, Future Challenges*, edited by Carolyn Ban and Norma M. Riccucci. New York: Longman.
"Rose Goldsen: Recollections and Reminders." Presented at the Communications and Technology Conference, Cornell University, Ithaca, N.Y., September.
"Women and Minorities." In *The State of the Unions*, edited by George Strauss, Daniel G. Gallagher, and Jack Fiorito. Madison, Wisc.: Industrial Relations Research Association.

1990

"Can Work Requirements Accommodate to Needs of Dual-Earner Families?" Paper presented at the World Interdisciplinary Conference on Women, Hunter College, N.Y., 5 June.
"Public Policies to Aid Dual-Earner Families." In *Risks and Challenges: Women, Work and the Future.* Washington, D.C.: Wider Opportunities for Women.

1989

"Employer Responsibility: Current Issues and Concerns." Paper presented at the Netter
Seminar, School for Industrial and Labor Relations, Cornell University, Ithaca, N.Y.,
24 September.

"Die Entwicklung der Erwachsenenbildung in der amerikanischen Besatzungszone."
Paper presented at the Arbeitskreis zur Aufarbeitung historischer Quellen der
Erwachsenenbildung, Buchenried, Bavaria (Germany), 5 October. In *Bericht der achten
Konferenz Buchenried bei München, Oktober 4–8, 1989.* Frankfurt am Main.

"Public Policies to Help Dual-Earner Families Meet the Demands of the Work World."
Industrial and Labor Relations Review 42, no. 2 (January).

"Work and Family." Presented before the Hawaii Commission on the Status of Women,
Working Women of Hawaii, and the YWCA, Industrial Relations Center, University of
Hawaii, Honolulu, 2 March.

"Work, Family, and Collective Bargaining." Report prepared for the Panel on Employer
Policies and Working Families, National Academy of Sciences, Washington, D.C.

1988

"Family and Work: Challenges to Labor, Management and Government. *Proceedings,
1987.* Quebec: Canadian Industrial Relations Association.

With Ronnie J. Steinberg. "Policies Affecting Women's Employment in Industrial
Countries." In *Working Women, Theories and Facts in Perspective,* edited by Ann Helton
Stromberg and Shirley Harkess. 2d ed. Mountain View, Calif.: Mayfield Publishing.

1987

"Incomparable Worth." Paper presented at Villanova University, Villanova, Penn., 23
September.

"International Comparisons: Problems and Research in the Industrialized World." In
Working Women: Past, Present, Future, edited by Karen Shallcross Koziara et al. IRRA
Research Volume. Washington, D.C.: Bureau of National Affairs.

"Resolving Conflicts Between Work and Family: Changes at Home for Dick and Jane—
Changes at Work for Mom and Dad." Paper presented at the meeting of the Society
for the Study of Social Problems, Chicago, 15 August.

1986

Comparable Worth: A Case Book (1986 Supplement). Honolulu: Industrial Relations
Center, University of Hawaii.

"The Politics of Compensation." Paper presented at the National Convention of the
American Nurses Association, Anaheim, Calif., 14 June.

Japan. District Court in Tokyo. Amicus brief prepared for hearings of *The Case of Four
Plaintiffs v. Nissan Automobile Company* for the equal rights of male and female workers
to child allowances.

1985

Comparable Worth: A Case Book of Experiences in States and Localities. Honolulu: Industrial
Relations Center, University of Hawaii/Manoa.

1984

"Developments in Selected States." In *Comparable Worth and Wage Discrimination:
Technical Possibilities and Political Realities,* edited by Helen Remick. Philadelphia:
Temple University Press.

"Experience with Equity Opportunity Administration in the United States." Paper presented at the Conference on Sex Equality, University of Milan, Italy, 9–14 June.

"Introduction" and "Federal Republic of Germany." In *Women and Trade Unions in Eleven Industrialized Countries*, edited by Alice Cook, Val R. Lorwin, and Arlene Kaplan Daniels. Philadelphia: Temple University Press.

"The States Approach Comparable Worth." Paper presented at traveling seminar, Industrial Relations Center, University of Hawaii/Manoa and University of Hawaii/Hilo, Hawaii, 27 February and 1 March.

"Women and Work in Industrial Societies: Where We Are and Where We Are Going." In *Urbanism and Urbanization: Views, Aspects and Dimensions*, edited by Noel Iverson. Leiden, Netherlands: E. J. Brill.

Hawaii Legislature. Committee on Human Resources. Testimony on "Comparable Worth." Honolulu, 24 February.

1983

"Comparable Worth: An Approach to Pay Equity in the U.S." Paper presented at the international meeting on Women and Work: Production and Reproduction, Turin, Italy, 27 April.

Comparable Worth: The Problem and States' Approaches to Wage Equity. Honolulu: Industrial Relations Center, University of Hawaii/Manoa.

"Comparable Worth: Recent Developments in Selected States." *Proceedings of the 1983 Spring Meeting, IRRA*, edited by Barbara Dennis. Madison, Wisc.: Industrial Relations Research Association. Also published as *Working Paper No. 14* (Albany: Center for Women in Government, State University of New York).

"Equality in the Workplace: The Role of Trade Unions in Market Economies." Paper presented at the Conference on Women and Structural Transformation: The Crisis of Work and Family Life, Rutgers University, New Brunswick, N.J., 18–19 November.

1982

"Comparable Worth: Background and Current Issues." Honolulu: Industrial Relations Center Report, University of Hawaii/Manoa.

Japan. Fukuoka High Court. Amicus curiae on "The Treatment of Equality in Aging in the United States and Japan and by a Number of International Governmental Agencies," prepared for hearings in *Asako Kuramitsu and Tsuyoshi Makashima v. Karasu Red Cross Hospital, Fukuoka, Japan.*

1981

"Labor Education in the U.S.: Marriage of Convenience?" In *Trade Unionism in the United States: A Symposium in Honor of Jack Barbash*, edited by James L. Stern and Barbara D. Dennis. Madison, Wisc.: Industrial Relations Research Institute, University of Wisconsin.

With Ronnie S. Ratner. *Women, Unions and Equal Employment Opportunity.* Paper prepared under grants from the National Commission on Employment Policy, U.S. Department of Labor, Employment and Training Adm. Albany: Center for Women in Government, State University of New York.

With Roberta Till-Retz. "Labor Education and Women Workers: An International Comparison." In *Labor Education for Women Workers*, edited by Barbara M. Wertheimer. Philadelphia: Temple University Press.

1980

"Collective Bargaining as a Strategy for Achieving Equal Opportunity and Equal Pay: Sweden and Germany" and "Vocational Training, the Labor Market, and Unions." In *Equal Employment Policy for Women: Strategies for Implementation in the United States,*

Canada, and Western Europe, edited by Ronnie S. Ratner. Philadelphia: Temple University Press.
"The Most Difficult Revolution: Women and Trade Unions." *Equal Opportunities International,* London, 1, no. 2.
"The Most Difficult Revolution: Women and Trade Unions in Four Countries." Paper presented at the NATO Conference on Women and Work, Lisbon, Portugal, 4–9 August.
"The Representation of Women and Their Interests in Industrial Relations Institutions: Women in Trade Unions." In *Women and Industrial Relations: Working Papers of an International Symposium.* Geneva: International Institute for Labour Studies.
"Women and Unions: Cause for Celebration?" Convocation address at New York State School for Industrial and Labor Relations, Cornell University, Ithaca, N.Y., 1 September.
"Working Women in Japan." Paper presented at the New York Conference on Asian Studies, Hartwick College, Oneonta, N.Y., 9–10 October.
With Hiroko Hayashi. *Working Women in Japan: Discrimination, Resistance, and Reform.* Ithaca, N.Y.: Cornell University, New York State School of Industrial and Labor Relations.

1979

"The Effects on the Structure of Society of the Growing Number of Women in the Work Force." Paper presented at the College Board National Forum, 30 October.
"Working Women: European Experience and American Need." In *Women in the U.S. Labor Force,* edited by Ann Foote Cahn. New York: Praeger. Originally published in *American Women Workers in a Full Employment Economy,* a report to the Joint Economic Committee of Congress, Washington, D.C.: GPO, 1977.
With Joyce M. Najita. *Equal Employment Opportunity, Collective Bargaining and the Merit Principle in Hawaii.* Honolulu: Hawaii, Department of Personnel Services.

1978

"The Trade Union Movement and Working Women." Paper presented at the International Sociological Association, Uppsala, Sweden, August.
The Working Mother: A Survey of Problems and Programs in Nine Countries. 2d ed. Ithaca, N.Y.: Cornell University, New York State School of Industrial and Labor Relations.
With Hiroko Hayashi. "Resistance and Reform in Japan." Paper presented at the International Sociological Association, Uppsala, Sweden, August.

1977

"Mothers Working." *Cornell Alumni News,* Cornell University, Ithaca, N.Y.

1976

"Zwei Jahre deutsch-amerikanische Zusammenarbeit." *Das Forum* [Journal of the Bavarian Adult Education Association] (Munich, Germany) 4.
Contributor. "Women in Blue Collar Jobs," a Ford Foundation Conference Report, New York.

1975

"Maternity Benefits." *International Society for Labor Law and Social Legislation.* U.S. National Committee, Bulletin 8, no. 3.
"Mothers at Work Abroad." *Industrial and Labor Relations Report* XI, no. 2 (winter).
"Public Policy and Support Systems for Working Mothers: An International Comparison." Paper presented at the Conference on Changing Sex Roles in Family and Society, Groves Society, Dubrovnik, Yugoslavia, July.

1974

New York State Legislature. Testimony on "Maternity Benefits in Nine Countries," October.

1972

"Sex Discrimination at Universities: An Ombudsman's View." *AAUP Bulletin* 58, no. 3 (September).

1971

Report of the Ombudsman. Ithaca, N.Y.: Cornell University.

With Solomon B. Levine and Tadashi Mitsufuji. *Public Employee Labor Relations in Japan: Three Aspects.* Ann Arbor, Mich.: Institute of Labor and Industrial Relations, University of Michigan/Wayne State University.

1970

Report of the Ombudsman. Ithaca, N.Y.: Cornell University.

"Public Employee Bargaining in New York City." *Industrial Relations* 9, no. 3 (May).

1969

"The ILO and Japanese Politics, II: Gain or Loss for Labor?" *Industrial and Labor Relations Review* 22, no. 3 (April).

"Labor and Politics." *Issues in Industrial Society* 1, no. 2.

"Labor Relations in the Public Service: A Unique Branch of Labor Relations Practice: The Japanese Case in Local Government." In *The Changing Patterns of Industrial Relations in Asian Countries,* 1969 Asian Regional Conference Proceedings on Industrial Relations. Tokyo: Japan Institute of Labor.

1968

"The Status of Working Women." *American Labor Review,* Tokyo (January).

"Women and American Trade Unions." *Annals of the American Academy of Political and Social Science* 375 (January).

1967

"The International Posture of the American Labor Movement: The Relevance of American Experience to World Labor Problems." In *The Labor Movement: A Re-examination,* edited by Jack Barbash. Madison: University of Wisconsin, Industrial Relations Research Institute and the State Historical Society of Wisconsin.

"Political Action and Trade Unions: A Case Study of Coal Miners in Japan." *Monumenta Nipponica* 22, no. 5 (January).

1966

"Adaptations of Union Structure for Municipal Collective Bargaining." *Collective Bargaining in the Public Service, Proceedings of the 1996 Spring Meeting, IRRA,* edited by Gerald G. Somers. Madison, Wisc.: Industrial Relations Research Association. Also published as "Union Structure in Municipal Collective Bargaining," *Monthly Labor Review* 89, no. 6 (June).

An Introduction to Japanese Trade Unionism. Ithaca, N.Y.: Cornell University, New York State School of Industrial and Labor Relations.

"Organization Among Local Government Employees in the United States." *American Labor Review,* Tokyo (August).

With Lois Gray. "Labor Relations in New York City." *Industrial Relations* 5, no. 3 (May).

1965

"The International Labor Organization and Japanese Politics." *Industrial and Labor Relations Review* 19, no. 1 (October).

1963

Union Democracy: Practice and Ideal. Ithaca, N.Y.: Cornell University Press.

1962

"Dual Government in Unions: A Tool for Analysis." *Industrial and Labor Relations Review* 15, no. 3 (April).

1960

"Education of Workers for Public Responsibility in Community and Political Affairs." In *Labor's Public Responsibility.* Madison, Wisc.: National Institute of Labor Education.

1958

With Agnes M. Douty. *Labor Education Outside the Unions.* Ithaca, N.Y.: Cornell University, New York State School of Industrial and Labor Relations.

1957

"New Goals for Labor Education." *Adult Leadership*, 6 (October).

1956

Labor's Role in Community Affairs. Rev. ed. Ithaca, N.Y.: Cornell University, New York State School of Industrial and Labor Relations..
"Labor's Search for Its Place in the Community." *The Journal of Educational Sociology* 29, no. 4.

1955

"Labor Participation in Community Affairs: An Experiment in Adult Education." *ILR Research* (March).

1954

Adult Education in Citizenship in Postwar Germany. Occasional Papers, no. 3. Pasadena: Fund for Adult Education.

1951

"Arbeiterbildung in den USA: II. Die Methodik der Arbeiterbildung." *Bildungsarbeit* (Austria) 22, nos. 1–4.

1950

"Arbeiterbildung in den USA: Die Organisation." *Bildungsarbeit* (Austria) 21, no. 5.
"Bavarian Trade Union Youth" ["Bayerische Gewerkschaftsjugend"]. Visiting Expert Series, no. 17. Frankfurt: High Commission of Germany (HICOG) for the United States.

1947

"Workers' Education in the U.S. Zone of Germany." Visiting Expert Series, no.1. Berlin: Office of Military Government, United States (OMGUS).

1941

Contributor. *Workers' Education in the United States*, edited by Theodore Brameld. New York: Harper.

1939

"Workers' Education on the March." *American Teacher* (April).

INDEX

Entries concerning Alice Hanson Cook are grouped and listed under her name as follows: personal life, publications, and working life.